Reading and Deafness

Reading and Deafness

Cynthia M. King, PhD
University of North Carolina at Greensboro

Stephen P. Quigley, PhD
University of Illinois at Urbana-Champaign

 COLLEGE-HILL PRESS, San Diego, California

001447

College-Hill Press, Inc.
4284 41st Street
San Diego, California 92105

Library of Congress Cataloging in Publication Data
Main entry under title:

King, Cynthia M.
    Reading and deafness.

    Includes bibliographies and index.
    1. Deaf Education–Reading. 2. Reading (Elementary). 3. Reading–Aids and
devices. 4. Deaf–Education–Reading–Bibliography. I. Quigley, Stephen Patrick,
1927–   . II. Title.
HV2469.R4K56 1985   371.91′24   85-5694

ISBN 0-88744-107-6

Printed in the United States of America

DEDICATION

For Ken and Bette King, in loving appreciation

and

For Jim and Dorothy McCarr, in recognition and appreciation of
their significant contributions to the language and reading
development of deaf children

CONTENTS

PREFACE

Reading and written language generally have been considered common denominators in the education of deaf children. Educators, regardless of the primary communication forms they espouse for deaf people, have usually agreed that deaf persons need to learn to read and write the general language of society. And lay persons, when confronted with the enormous problems of teaching spoken language to deaf children, often point to reading and written language as obvious solutions to the problem of developing language in some form. But centuries of diligent effort by teachers have not yet resulted in the typical deaf child's being able to read as well as the typical hearing child. In fact, as described in detail in Chapter 3, reading seems to present just as great difficulties for deaf children as does spoken language. By the school-leaving age of 18 years, the typical deaf student scores at only about the fourth or fifth grade level on standard reading achievement tests, or about the same level as a typical 9 or 10 year old hearing student; and the written language of that deaf student will vary greatly from the written language of the typical hearing student. (See samples in Table 1.) Some possible reasons for this great retardation in reading development are discussed in Chapter 1, and a few of the reasons deserve emphasis here since they are recurring themes in the book.

The great difficulty deaf children have in learning to read seems to lie in the auditory-based nature of reading. Prereading hearing children, through fluent aural-oral communication with their parents, readily symbolize and internalize in auditory form the experiences of infancy and early childhood. This provides a base of real-world knowledge for use in "top-down" reading processes. It also aids the development of cognitive and linguistic abilities needed for success in reading. Deaf children lack this auditory language and its associated experiential, cognitive, and linguistic skills. Thus, for them, learning to read becomes also a process of experience building, cognitive development, and language learning. It should not be surprising, therefore, that most deaf children do not learn to read well.

Reading is a secondary language form which is imposed on the primary auditory form by a recoding process. In one view (a narrow one), reading can simply be considered as decoding from the written form into the auditory form in which words can then be understood. In this view, it can be argued that the only skills unique to reading are the skills involved in decoding writing or print. It is more commonly accepted, however, that reading is much broader than simply decoding print. Reading is now viewed as part of the general language-comprehension process and as such involves higher order cognitive, metacognitive, and linguistic skills, such as inferencing, syntax, and semantics, as well as lower order decoding skills and

Table 1. Written Language Samples Elicited from Deaf Students

The girl said give the dog into the bread.
The Father he go to the far.
Father and Mother Wait for you the dog.
We go to the park the famils show she is paly with the dog.
The boy said help please.
The grandpa he hepl is little boy he afraid show.
The grandpa is can hepl.
The little boy he cry.

   10 year old male, Better Ear Average 100+ dB (ASA),
   deaf prior to two years of age

   Mother and family went to pinic today. Mother fixed bag food. We so exicted to go. Family said ready to go to pinic how. The Kids took something game.
   Then father took Key for car ride and forget left dog at home. The boy out of the car and hug the dog on sidewalk and The dog was wild and excited to him.
   It took the dog to the pinic and played with dog on playfeild.
   Mother cooked food for everybody and have good time good luck.

   14 year old male, Better Ear Average 100+ dB (ASA),
   deaf prior to two years of age.

   The girl gave the dog a bread in the kitchen. The dog wanted go in a car. The boy opened the door a car and the dog jumped the boy. The family drove to the park. The woman maded hamburger's and the girl open a glass on the talbe. The boy played ball and the dog caught the ball in the park. The dog was very happy, because he played a ball.

   18 year old female, Better Ear Average 110+ dB (ASA),
   deaf prior to two years of age

letter and word recognition. Whereas the typical prereading hearing child brings to the reading task through auditory language experience substantial development in these higher order skills, the prereading deaf child typically lacks substantial development of any of them. By applying these higher order mental skills to reading in "top-down" processes, the hearing child can concentrate on learning the new decoding or "bottom-up" skills that are unique to reading. The deaf child must struggle with both "top-down" and "bottom-up" processes. The task for this child becomes one of acquiring a real-world knowledge base and basic cognitive and linguistic skills as well as decoding skills. The task is further complicated by the use of reading techniques that assume the existence of an auditory language which the deaf child does not have and reading materials that assume a level of real-world knowledge and basic linguistic skills which the deaf child has not acquired.

From this brief exposition, it can be reasoned that improved reading for deaf children requires the following: (1) prereading development of real-world knowledge, cognitive abilities, and linguistic skills comparable to those of prereading hearing children; (2) development of techniques for teaching reading that are related to the communication mode of the deaf child, which is usually visual rather than auditory; and (3) development of reading materials that match the real-world knowledge and linguistic skills of deaf children more closely than do most of the materials developed for hearing children. Research and development in all three areas are required; progress in any one alone will not suffice. These three areas are treated throughout the text in relation to both research and instruction.

Every experienced teacher of deaf children is aware of the importance of the first of these prerequisites that a basic and primary internalized language must be established before reading can be taught successfully. But the development of English (or any auditory-based language) is slow and difficult for deaf children, and reading usually is begun long before even rudimentary language development has been attained. It is unlikely that any typical deaf child ever acquires the necessary language base for reading before reading instruction begins.

Teachers and others involved in the education of deaf children might not be as aware of the problems of the second area of concern as they are of the first. Whether stated explicitly or not, techniques for teaching reading to hearing children assume the existence of an aural-oral language and build reading on that language. But any language the deaf child has internalized is likely to be visual-motor and not to have an internalized auditory representation. The problems this poses for the development of reading for deaf children are discussed in detail in Chapters 1 and 3. In particular, the possible importance of speech coding to the reading of connected discourse is stressed.

The third concern is dealt with in detail in Chapters 5 and 6. At present, there is considerable interest in the development of special reading materials for deaf and other children with special education requirements and research support for the value of such materials. As with any new enthusiasm, however, there are the accompanying tendencies to regard the development as original and to overstate its role in the reading process. Special materials for deaf children are not new. As shown in Chapter 6, they have a very long history. And such materials should be only part of a total experience-based language and reading program. They concern only one of the three problem areas listed previously and not the most important one. If the first area described above could be dealt with satisfactorily (which would involve the second area also) then special materials would not be needed. The prereading deaf child would have the necessary real-world knowledge, cognitive abilities, and linguistic skills to become a successful reader with the reading materials used by hearing children. As every teacher of deaf children probably knows, this ideal situation is rarely, if ever, realized and so special materials have an important place in language and reading programs.

The material in the book can be grouped into four categories. Chapters 1, 2, and 3 provide a theoretical and knowledge base for reading in hearing and in deaf children. These chapters can be considered as dealing with basic processes and problems of reading. Chapters 4, 5, 6, and 7 deal with specific issues and techniques of developing reading and reading materials for deaf children. They can be considered as dealing with reading instruction. Chapter 8 is a chapter on reading and other language-variant populations written by Peter V. Paul. Its purpose is to show similarities in the reading and language problems of deaf and other special populations. The appendices contain resources and procedures that have direct, practical application for teachers and future teachers. Appendix A provides an outline of steps and a list of resources for developing skills in preparing special materials for deaf children. Appendices B, C, D, and E contain selected bibliographies that provide readers with references to consult concerning suggested methods and materials for teaching reading.

Much of the material in Chapters 1 and 3 and a small part of the material in Chapter 2 is contained also in a companion book, *Language and Deafness* (Quigley & Paul, 1984a). The overlap was deliberate. As stated in this Preface, reading comprehension is considered part of language comprehension and similar basic cognitive processes underlie both. By having the books published by the same publisher, it was possible have the books overlap in common areas without engaging in the frustrating task of writing two differently worded versions of the same material so as not to violate copyrights of different publishers. Another commonality of the two books is that they are concerned primarily with children who are prelingually deaf. As described in detail in *Language and Deafness*, these are children who have sensorineural hearing impairments of 90 dB or greater hearing threshold level (HTL) and in whom the hearing impairment was present by two years of age.

Chapter 1 presents basic information and supporting research on the development of the real-world knowledge, cognitive abilities, and linguistic skills that are requisites to successful reading. Emphasis is given to the cognitive abilities that seem to be related directly to deaf children's basic reading problems—in particular, the storage of linguistically codable materials in short-term (working) memory and the significance of speech coding in that process. A case is made for the position that reading instruction techniques might have to vary according to the primary internalized language of a deaf child. If the prereading deaf child is successfully oral, the techniques used with hearing children might be appropriate. If the child's primary language is American Sign Language (ASL), then these techniques (which assume the existence of an auditory-based language) might not be appropriate. Moreover, children who are exposed primarily to manually-coded English (MCE) might require still another set of instructional techniques.

Chapter 2 deals with the reading process in hearing children. Considerable discussion is devoted to the "top-down" and "bottom-up" theories of reading and to detailing the strengths and limitations of each. The "interactive" theories are presented as better representations of the research-documented reading process than "top-down" or "bottom-up" theories. A large amount of research documentation is provided in presenting the most recent views of the reader, text, and context variables that are important in the reading process.

Chapter 3 presents basic data on the reading achievement levels and the reading process and problems of deaf children. The same format as in Chapter 2 is followed in the presentation and interpretation of information and an attempt is made to relate the processes and problems to those of hearing children. The importance of speech coding as perhaps the most efficient means of storing information in short-term memory is stressed, and its possible significance in the reading problems of deaf children is discussed. Emphasis is also given to the possible need to relate reading instruction techniques to the primary language of each deaf child: oral English (OE), manually-coded English (MCE), and American Sign Language (ASL).

Chapter 4 presents an in-depth review of current practices in reading instruction with deaf children. Of particular note in this chapter is the lack of experimental research efforts toward developing better instructional strategies and materials. Specific research needs are identified and exemplary studies from the research literature on hearing children are described as potential models for future research efforts. The final section of Chapter 4 outlines 20 instructional issues that are debated within the field of deafness.

Chapter 5 presents a synthesis of available research on instructional reading materials. Three major factors are identified that influence how difficult particular material is for a particular individual: text-based variables, reader-based variables, and task-based variables. The chapter addresses studies with both hearing and deaf children. A major conclusion is that the use of adapted materials appears to have a positive effect on comprehension of young readers and those with lower ability. With an average reading ability of less than the fifth grade level on leaving pre-college programs, obviously many deaf children fit within the group for whom adaptations or simplified materials can be helpful. A second major conclusion is that, although research has identified a large number of variables which influence how a reader and text interact, little is known about what the difficulty level of materials *should be* to provide the optimal development of reading.

Chapter 6 provides a description of reading materials used in teaching reading to deaf children. A major purpose is to identify materials that have been developed specifically for deaf students. Evaluation procedures and guidelines for materials preparation are also discussed.

Chapter 7 provides an extensive review of reading assessment. Both basic information regarding assessment and detailed information concerning the performance of hearing-impaired students on reading tests are covered. Advantages and limitations of specific assessment tools are discussed. The process of assessment is also traced from determining what to assess through utilization of the assessment results. Of particular note in this chapter is the discussion of test-taking strategies used by deaf students. Knowledge of these strategies can help the classroom teacher both in assessing his or her students and in providing effective instruction.

Chapter 8 presents information on the reading and language problems of other special populations. The purpose of the chapter is to demonstrate similarities (and differences) in language difficulties experienced by learning disabled (LD) individuals, mentally retarded individuals, individuals learning English as a second language (ESL), and deaf individuals. From this, it is argued that reading difficulty can be attributed in part to inadequate language development causing a breakdown in the interactive process between reader and text.

ACKNOWLEDGMENTS

The authors are indebted to many people for assistance in the preparation of this book. A major debt is acknowledged to those who provided much of the material on which the book is based. That includes the many authors whose works are cited in the text and the many teachers and students with whom we have interacted. Grateful acknowledgment is extended to the graduate students who assisted in library research, typing, and other activities in preparing the manuscript: Janet Blank, Michelle Blevins, and Kathy Hildebran. The contributions of the computers on which this text was prepared are also acknowledged. Finally, we wish to thank our families, our supportive colleagues, and our many friends who were forced to learn the true meanings of the words patience and no. To each of you, we express our heartfelt appreciation.

Chapter 1

Cognition, Language, and Reading

The typical prereading, normally hearing child brings to the reading task a rich background of experiential, cognitive, and linguistic skills. These prereading skills and knowledge provide the base for the development of reading. The typical deaf child lacks this base. It follows from this alone that the deaf child will have great difficulty learning to read and that the reading process will be entangled with the basic primary language-learning process and with the cognitive and experiential deficits of the deaf child. In the companion volume for this book, Quigley and Paul (1984a) have discussed the problems of lack of prereading skills in deaf children and much of this chapter is from that book. There is a somewhat different emphasis, however, in that most of the cognitive and experiential deficits are treated in general fashion to emphasize those cognitive abilities, particularly the storage of linguistically codable materials in working (short-term) memory, that seem to be directly related to the problems deaf children have with the reading process itself. This chapter describes some basic cognitive differences found in deaf and hearing children, such as in Piagetian tasks; discusses specific differences in various short-term memory tasks, such as temporal-sequential memory; explores the internal coding and language processes of deaf and hearing children; and attempts to relate all of these factors to some of the reading problems of deaf children.

RELATIONSHIP OF COGNITION AND LANGUAGE

Two questions have engaged the interest of researchers in the areas of cognition (thinking) and language, and resolution of these questions has practical significance for teachers, clinicians, and other persons working with deaf children and adults. First, there is theoretical and practical significance to knowing whether quantitative or qualitative differences exist between deaf and hearing people on various aspects of cognitive functioning, such as memory, perception, creativity, and so forth. If certain differences do

1

exist, they might indicate limitations in the abilities of deaf persons to acquire particular cognitively based skills that are acquired readily by hearing people (such as reading), or they might dictate that to acquire those skills different developmental and teaching approaches need to be used with deaf children than are used with hearing children. Second, study of the cognitive and language functioning of deaf individuals might shed light on the persistent philosophic and scientific question of whether there is a relation between language and thought and if there is, what is its nature. Is language dependent on thought; is thought dependent on language; are the two mutually dependent; or are they mutually independent? This question, too, has practical significance. For example, if language is dependent on thought (cognition), then any differences or deficits in cognitive development will likely affect language acquisition, including reading.

Pintner and a group of colleagues, starting in the 1910s, were among the first to study these questions (and the psychology of deafness) in a systematic way with deaf people, and their research conclusions led to the first of three positions that have been taken with respect to the first question. Their conclusion was that deaf people were intellectually inferior to hearing people and showed definite deficits in various aspects of cognitive functioning (Pintner, Eisenson, & Stanton, 1941; Pintner & Reamer, 1920). It is important to note that most of the tests used by these investigators were paper-and-pencil tests, which often required verbal manipulation and verbal responses in the English language. Much of the historical development in the study of cognitive functioning of deaf people is a history of increasingly successful attempts by investigators to devise truly nonverbal tests of cognition. The goal is to assess the deaf person's performance on cognitive tasks, such as sequential memory, without the involvement of language. This is extremely difficult because of the pervasive influence of language in most of human behavior, but as attempts to accomplish it have been increasingly successful, differences between deaf and hearing persons in various cognitive abilities have tended to decrease and often to disappear.

The theoretical position of Pintner and his colleagues was dominant until the 1940s when it was challenged by the formulations proposed by Myklebust (1960). Myklebust interpreted a series of studies he and a number of his students performed as showing that there are quantitative similarities but qualitative differences between deaf and hearing individuals when verbal factors in cognitive and intellectual tasks are controlled. The types of differences found by Myklebust and his students led him to conclude that on global measures (e.g., total score on IQ tests such as the Wechsler Intelligence Scale for Children [WISC]) deaf individuals equalled hearing individuals, but that the profiles of deaf and hearing individuals on specific abilities differed. That is, deaf and hearing persons performed differently on the various subtests of such tests as the WISC. Similar findings were revealed on tests of a variety of cognitive functions, such as memory and creativity. The findings led Myklebust to conclude that deaf individuals were more concrete and less abstract cognitively than hearing individuals. He further concluded that the basic experiences of deaf people are altered as a direct consequence of hearing impairment and that all subsequently developed behaviors are also altered, thus making the deaf person inherently different from the hearing person in many ways. Myklebust proposed the "organismic shift hypothesis" to explain these alleged inherent differences of deaf people.

The third stage of this historical perspective is the one that seems to prevail today—that deaf and hearing people are intellectually and cognitively similar in all important abilities. Rosenstein (1961), Furth (1966b), and Vernon (1967) have taken the position that few if any differences exist between deaf and hearing individuals in cognitive functioning. This position is based on a substantial body of research conducted by numerous individuals (mostly in the 1960s and 1970s), some of which is discussed in this chapter. It is now generally accepted by researchers that any differences that do exist between deaf and hearing individuals on cognitive abilities are the result of environmental or task influences rather than being inherent in deafness. Quigley and Kretschmer (1982) categorized these task influences as: "1) the inability of the researcher to properly convey the task demands because of language differences or deficits on the part of the subjects, 2) implicit bias within the solution of the task, or 3) general experiential deficits (including verbal language and communication in general) on the part of the subjects" (p. 51).

The second question posed, concerning the relationship between cognition and language, has also had various answers at different historical stages. The early position (known as the language-dominant position) was that language was primary and that thinking (beyond early and primitive stages) took place in language. This position is exemplified by the linguist Sapir (1958) who states that

> It is quite an illusion to imagine that one adjusts to reality without the use of language and that language is merely an incidental means of solving specific problems of communication or reflection...we see and hear and otherwise experience as we do because the language habits of our community predispose certain choices of interpretation. (p. 162)

In this view, the child's linguistic development is determined largely by experience with language, and language accounts for the acquisition of concepts that are expressed within it (Quigley & Kretschmer, 1982). The opposing (and the presently prevailing) view is the cognitive-dominant hypothesis, which proposes that basic perceptual and cognitive development precedes language and provides the basis or underpinning for linguistic development. Language, in this view, is a natural extension or subset of the previously developed cognitive processes (Slobin, 1979).

The present evidence does not appear to support the language-dominant hypothesis (also known as the Whorfian hypothesis). Studies of hearing children by numerous investigators (notably Piaget and his followers) and of deaf children (notably Furth and his colleagues) have shown that much perceptual and cognitive development takes place prior to language development and also concurrently but independently of early language development. In Piaget's view,

A symbolic function exists which is broader than language and encompasses both the system of verbal signs and that of symbols in the strict sense. . . . [I]t is permissible to conclude that thought precedes language. . . language is not enough to explain thought, because the structures that characterize thought have their roots in action and in sensorimotor mechanisms that are deeper than linguistics. (1967, pp. 91–92)

Although the present weight of empirical evidence does not seem to support the language-dominant hypothesis, a number of investigators have presented a weaker version of this hypothesis (Cromer, 1976; McNeill, 1978; I. Schlesinger, 1977). This weak form of the Whorfian hypothesis suggests that although language does not dictate thought, it can and does influence thought. The evidence for this position comes primarily from linguistic intuitions rather than from direct studies of cognitive and linguistic development. It has been pointed out, for example, that certain distinctions are made in languages, such as gender and verb transitivity, that are language specific and do not have real-world correlates or referents.

It is not the purpose of this chapter to analyze in depth the enduring question of the relationship between thought (cognition) and language. The present weight of evidence in favor of the cognitive-dominant hypothesis is accepted. Interest in the issue and in the comparative cognitive functioning of deaf and of hearing individuals is concerned with how this hypothesis, and more importantly the data collected in pursuing it, can illuminate the problem of language development in deaf individuals. This interest centers on two questions. First, how does the cognitive development of deaf individuals compare with the cognitive development of hearing individuals? Second, what are the internal symbolic mediators of thought in deaf people?

Both questions have direct implications for educational practice with deaf children and youth. As stated earlier, it follows from the cognitive-dominant hypothesis that problems (differences or deficits) in cognitive development will be reflected in problems in language development. In relation to the second question, hearing people are known to use their initial phonologically based language as an internal mediator (internal speech) in various thinking tasks and to a certain extent in reading. It is important to developing language and reading in deaf children to know what internal codes they use (visual imagery, internal speech, signs, manual alphabet, and so forth) as symbolic mediators. In pursuing answers to these questions, some definitions and background information are presented. Research in three areas is then examined: (1) how deaf persons perform on certain cognitive tasks in comparison to hearing people; (2) the coding and mediating processes that deaf people use to perform certain cognitive tasks as compared with those used by hearing people; and (3) the language systems deaf persons use as mediators of thought. Finally, some conclusions are presented to show the implications for the development of reading and language practices with deaf children.

DEFINITIONS AND BACKGROUND INFORMATION

Slobin (1979) has defined *cognition* as the processes and structures of knowing and as the branch of psychology that deals with knowing, including the study of perception, attention, memory, problem solving, thinking, and language. It can be seen that this is a cognitive-dominant point of view that includes language as an extension or subset of cognition. *Language* has been defined as "a code whereby ideas about the world are represented through a conventional system of signals for communication" (Bloom & Lahey, 1978, p. 4). This definition is broad enough to include any conventionalized symbol system, such as American Sign Language (ASL), and the more typical spoken languages.

Much of the cognitive research with deaf individuals has been influenced by the work of the Swiss psychologist Jean Piaget. Piaget (1955) portrays the child as progressing through four stages in the development of mature thinking. The first stage is the period of *sensorimotor* intelligence and typically occupies the first two years of life. During this period, the child perceives and reacts to sensory data as related to basic needs and begins to organize and integrate these data into schemata. He or she goes through a process of establishing an equilibrium between adapting to the environment (accommodation) and acting on the environment (assimilation). Interactions between accommodation and assimilation further develop schemas as the child's representations of experience. According to Yussen and Santrock (1978) these schemas are the units necessary for an organized pattern of sensorimotor functioning. The child, for example, will organize the schema for face as an integrated pattern of eyes, nose, and mouth in a spatial relationship to each other. Schema theory has become a highly developed area of cognitive psychology and has been incorporated into modern theories of reading, as discussed in Chapter 2.

Piaget's second stage is known as the *preoperational* stage of cognitive development and extends from about two to about seven years of age. This represents a period of establishing relationships between experience and action. The child's symbol system is expanding during this period, and language use and perceptual abilities continue to develop well beyond the child's capabilities at the end of stage one (Yussen & Santrock, 1978). In this stage, egocentrism prevents the child from separating his or her perspective from that of others, and this is manifested in the child's social interactions. In this stage, also, the child is limited in cognitive processes by inability to understand such basic Piagetian concepts as conservation and reversibility. The classic Piagetian example of conservation and reversibility is the ball of clay, which when changed into another shape, still retains the same mass and can be restored to its original shape. Another example is the volume of water, which remains the same when poured from a short, wide glass into a tall, narrow one. Again the process can be reversed. Such concepts are difficult for children to grasp until they reach what Piaget calls the concrete operations stage.

The *concrete operations* stage is the third of Piaget's four stages of cognitive development and extends from about 7 to about 11 years of age. The child is now capable of distinguishing himself or herself from others (egocentrism to relativism), and begins to understand such concepts as conservation and reversibility (Yussen & Santrock, 1978).

The final stage is *formal operational thought*, which begins at about 11 years of age. This stage is characterized primarily by abstract thinking and a shift from the need for concrete objects and experiences.

Various psychological investigators have used deaf children and adults as controls in examining the existence of these Piagetian stages of development. The assumption has been that deaf children lack formal symbolic language and thus cognitive development can be examined in the absence of language influence, something which is difficult to do with hearing children, in whom language is so pervasive that it is difficult to devise cognitive tasks that are symbol free. One of the foremost investigators was Furth (1966b) whose book presents much of the early Piagetian research with deaf children.

Several cautions should be observed in interpreting the work of Furth and others in this area, who have assumed that deaf children used as subjects in these investigations have been truly nonverbal. First, as is unfortunately true with much other research using deaf individuals, hearing threshold levels are not given in some cases, and in other cases subjects had thresholds as low as 60 dB (probably ASA standards). At least some of those subjects must have had internal auditory based language which could have contaminated experimental results. Also, Conrad (1973) has shown that even some deaf children (90+ dB, ISO) use internal speech as a mediating code. Finally, it cannot be assumed that because deaf children are deficient in standard oral English skills they are deficient in language abilities in general. As will be shown in this chapter, many deaf individuals might be using internal language-mediating coding systems other than speech codes.

PERFORMANCE ON COGNITIVE TASKS

Furth (1966b) perceived his research as confirming that cognitive operations exist largely independently of language and that language is of minor concern in investigating cognition. His research can also be interpreted, however, as being supportive of the view that language and its acquisition are natural outgrowths and a direct result of basic cognitive processes and operations. According to this orientation, it is the dominance (but not independence) of cognition over language that explains why deaf individuals are able to function adequately in most situations even though they have not acquired fluent command of the core culture's language. Furth's investigations were characterized by the construction of ingenious tasks for assessing various thinking processes and by their comprehensive coverage of the various stages in Piaget's theory of cognitive development.

Piagetian Tasks

As stated earlier, one of the greatest difficulties in assessing nonverbal cognitive development is to devise tasks that are truly nonverbal or symbol free. This includes performance of the task itself and the directions given to the subject. Numerous studies have been designed specifically for studying nonverbal cognitive development in deaf persons, and Quigley and Kretschmer (1982) have categorized them as follows: "studies into 1) the abilities of deaf children to learn or discover various predetermined concepts or principles (rules), 2) the ability to transfer knowledge of a concept or principle (rule) to novel exemplars, 3) the ability to associate stimuli, 4) the ability to multiply, sort, or categorize objects requiring flexibility, 5) the ability to solve Piagetian and practical problems, and 6) the ability to demonstrate complex logical thinking and symbol manipulation" (p. 57). Extensive summaries of these studies are provided by Furth (1970) and Ottem (1980).

In spite of a large amount of research during the 1960s and 1970s, it is not yet clear to what extent deaf children can successfully perform various Piagetian tasks. Deaf children have been observed to progress normally through the sensorimotor stage (Best & Roberts, 1976). Delays have been noted, however, in some aspects of the preoperational and concrete operational stages. Although essentially normal functioning has been demonstrated in seriation (the ability to rank order items), significant delays have been noted in the ability to conserve items (liquid and matter) and to engage in transitive thinking (Furth, 1964; Rittenhouse, 1977; Youniss & Furth, 1966). The ability to conserve involves recognizing that objects do not change weight or volume when they change shape, and transitive thinking involves understanding the following type of logical operation: $A > B$, $B > C$, therefore $A > C$.

There is even less certainty about comparable performance of deaf and hearing subjects at the formal operations stage of Piagetian theory. Furth and Youniss (1965) have shown that deaf adolescents and adults can be taught to use very complex logical operation principles, but they also found that their subjects had impaired ability to discover these principles spontaneously. Thus, it must be concluded that the performance of deaf individuals on Piagetian tasks shows normal order of progression through the stages of development but delay in actual level of performance, particularly in the later stages of concrete operations and formal operational thought. The effects this delayed performance might have on language acquisition is a practical consideration for educational practitioners.

Memory Tasks

Memory is a basic function that exerts an influence on all other cognitive abilities. It is usually considered as having three levels. The first of these is the sensory register, which is rapid and relates to memories that last for one second or less. The second level, short-term memory, is the working memory which lasts for a few seconds to a minute and provides temporary storage of approximately five to seven unrelated items. Presumably there is a sensory information (register) storage system for each sensory modality that feeds directly into short-term (or working) memory. Long-term memory, which lasts from a minute to weeks or years, is the third level.

Certain processes of memory allow information to be transferred from short-term (or working) memory to long-term memory. One such process is *rehearsal*, which is simply the repeating of a response. A second process is *elaboration*, in which new information is associated with already familiar information to facilitate retention. A third is *organization*, whereby new information is incorporated into meaningful units with already familiar information to improve retention. Chunking information is one form of organization that has found application in the development of special reading materials (Quigley & King, 1981, 1982, 1983, 1984).

A distinction in type of memory that is important in studies with deaf individuals is that between spatial (or simultaneous) and sequential memory. This distinction is also related to the way in which different senses process information. Hearing processes input in a temporal-sequential manner, whereas vision can process spatially (simultaneously) as well as sequentially, although vision might be a less efficient sequential processor than hearing. The spatial-sequential distinction might be important for the processing of speech as compared to the processing of signs and print. The several studies reported here are concerned largely with this spatial-sequential distinction.

Blair (1957) examined deaf and hearing children on three simultaneous (or spatial) memory tests (Knox Cube, Memory-for-Design, and Object Location) and four sequential memory span tests (Digit Span Forward, Digit Span Reversed, Picture Span, and Domino Span). The results showed that the deaf children were equal or superior on the simultaneous (or spatial) memory tests, whereas the hearing children were able to retain spans of greater length in the sequential memory tests.

Withrow (1968) tested 14 hearing children, 14 orally educated deaf children, 14 fluent manual deaf children, and 14 special deaf children (probably learning disabled). Familiar silhouettes, familiar geometric forms, and random geometric forms were presented first simultaneously, then sequentially. It was found that the deaf groups performed the same as the normally hearing group for immediate recall when stimuli were presented simultaneously, but the normally hearing group was significantly superior in its recall of all levels of meaningfulness of stimuli presented sequentially. An interesting analogue to this is the study by Stuckless and Pollard (1977) in which 19 deaf students were tested on their ability to process words in print as compared to words fingerspelled. It was found that the printed letters were processed more readily than those that were fingerspelled. The difficulty of fingerspelling was attributed to its temporal-sequential characteristics. White and Stevenson (1975) have reported similar findings favoring print over signs.

Belmont, Karchmer, and Pilkonis (1976) tested seven college-bound deaf students and seven normally hearing young adults on a short-term memory sequential recall task. Each subject paced himself or herself through a list of consonant letters and then was asked to specify where in the list a particular letter had appeared. Left to their own strategies, the deaf subjects performed more poorly than hearing subjects. When the deaf subjects were instructed in fingerspelling mnemonics involving primary and secondary memory components, two things happened: (1) the mnemonic strategy brought the performance of the deaf subjects up to the level of that of the hearing subjects for the number of correct responses, and (2) the response time for sequences with strategies directed toward primary (echo) memory was the same for both groups; however, the response time of sequences directed toward secondary (rehearsed) memory was significantly slower for the deaf subjects. Even when the deaf subjects were well rehearsed and recalled accurately, their secondary memory retrieval functions revealed slower access to the stored contents. The authors state that

> The instruction strategy led the deaf subjects to such striking immediate increases in recall accuracy...that their original gross deficiencies in these measures must in large part be reflecting a simple ignorance of or disinclination to use effective information-processing strategies. (p. 46)

However, Belmont et al. declined to support a suggestion by Conrad and Rush (1965) that "the intellectual deficiencies of the deaf result because 'they lack practice in the exercise of those communication modes that are most efficient for them' " (p. 342).

It can be seen from these studies that deaf individuals seem to perform more poorly than hearing individuals in memory abilities primarily on tests involving sequential memory. Since auditory language is processed sequentially, and since some visual language inputs (such as print, signs, and fingerspelling) can be considered to have sequential components also, this difference has implications for both primary and secondary (reading and writing) language acquisition. Recent research with hearing individuals indicates that this form of memory and information processing might be particularly important in the reading of connected prose.

Summary: Relationship of Cognition and Language

Only a limited number of areas of cognition have been considered here and within each of these areas only a small number of studies have been presented, but they are representative of the body of findings on the cognitive abilities of deaf individuals. Several major conclusions can be drawn from the literature presented.

First, there are enough inconsistencies in the findings in the literature on the cognitive development of deaf individuals to warrant caution in reaching any definitive conclusions. Although better understanding of the various factors influencing cognitive studies and increasing experimental control over those factors has led to findings of smaller and smaller differences between deaf and hearing individuals in cognitive performance, certain differences still exist in various areas. Even when extreme care has been taken to control possible sources of error, differences still have been found in favor of hearing individuals in various Piagetian tasks, memory performance, abstract thinking, creativity, and other cognitive areas.

Second, even though some differences are still found, there is disagreement as to how they should be interpreted. It can be concluded that the differences are real and represent a true cognitive penalty of deafness. This would be supportive of the Myklebust "organismic shift hypothesis" that deafness imposes a different view of the world through the remaining senses, resulting in qualitative differences between deaf and hearing people. This could be reflected in similarity on overall quantitative cognitive performance but differences on specific aspects of cognition, with deaf people being superior in some areas and hearing people being superior in others.

It can also be concluded, however, that the differences in cognitive performance are due to a remaining lack of experimental control over verbal and other factors that influence performance on tasks that are believed to be nonverbal. It is extremely difficult to construct nonverbal tasks, because hearing individuals can usually verbalize almost any task internally, which would aid in performing the task. In addition to the pervasiveness of language, it can also be argued that lack of the language of the core society deprives the deaf individual of the interaction with his or her environment, including people in it, that is necessary for exposure to certain experiences that contribute to cognitive growth. The important point about blaming language and experiential differences for the differences in cognitive performance is that they are remediable. From this point of view, it should be possible to provide an early environment in which the deaf child can be exposed to appropriate experiences through some appropriate language and communication forms that will permit appropriate cognitive development.

The third conclusion that can be drawn from the studies of cognition is that cognitive development is not critically dependent on language in many instances. But although language might not be enough to explain thought, as Piaget claims, some of the studies cited indicate that it becomes so intertwined with cognition after language has developed that the differential effects of language and cognition are almost inseparable for practical purposes. What is perhaps most important from all this for the teacher, the clinician, and other practitioners is summarized by Quigley and Kretschmer (1982):

Most researchers and most educators of deaf children presently accept that any differences that do exist in intellectual and cognitive functioning between deaf and hearing persons are not significant for adequate functioning in society, and that educational, occupational, and other deficiencies in deaf people are the result of our present inability to fully help deaf people develop and use their abilities rather than the result of any inherent deficiencies in those abilities. (p. 63)

SYMBOLIC MEDIATION

The second question of major interest in this chapter concerns what internal symbolic mediators of thought deaf people use. This question is of particular interest and importance in studying the development of primary language and of reading with deaf children. Since most people learn to listen and speak before they learn to read and write, it is assumed that a person's lexicon must be coded internally for speech; that is, initially an individual needs a speech-like representation of a word to access its meaning. This has led to the formulation of the speech-recoding hypothesis that readers must convert a printed word to its speech (phonological) equivalent in some internal way to understand its meaning. As shown in Chapter 2, evidence now indicates that words in reading can be accessed directly through internal visual representation as well as indirectly through phonological mediation. But phonological (speech) mediation retains importance in reading, and a question of interest is what do deaf people use as symbolic mediators if they do not have phonological representations of words. Do they use visual imagery, partial or full, of the direct referents of words? Or do they use visual representation in the form of signs, manual alphabet letters, or some other system? A considerable number of studies have addressed these questions. A limited number of studies are discussed here to illustrate the importance of this issue and some present thinking concerning it.

Sign Coding

At about the same period that Furth and his colleagues were studying cognitive processes in deaf people, a number of investigators were considering the internal coding and mediation processes of language in deaf persons. Odom, Blanton, and McIntyre (1970) tested deaf students and hearing students on their ability to remember words with or without sign equivalents. The groups were matched on reading ability. It was found that deaf students had little difficulty memorizing words for which there are corresponding signs but greater difficulty memorizing words that did not have sign equivalents. Other studies by these investigators found that deaf subjects could understand connected prose better when the syntax of printed messages had been changed to the syntactic order of American Sign Language. Bellugi,

Klima, and Siple (1974) reported that deaf children could remember in signs without recoding into printed or acoustic words.

Moulton and Beasley (1975) tested hearing-impaired students who were fluent signers with a paired-associate verbal learning task to determine perceptual coding strategies. Four lists of word pairs were devised in which the word pairs in each list were characterized as follows:

Similar sign	similar meaning	(e.g., mad-angry)
Dissimilar sign	similar meaning	(e.g., cold-freeze)
Similar sign	dissimilar meaning	(e.g., black-summer)
Dissimilar sign	dissimilar meaning	(e.g., doctor-green)

Hearing-impaired subjects were required to replace a word missing from the word pairs. The results showed that, although the subjects were able to code the verbal material on both a sign basis and a semantic basis, the semantic coding strategy appeared to be more efficient than the sign coding strategy for long-term memory. The study indicates that at least two coding strategies might be used by hearing-impaired individuals, and it is possible that they are capable of switching codes depending on the communication situation.

To determine whether signs could be stored in memory in terms of their semantic characteristics, Siple, Fischer, and Bellugi (1977) conducted a long-term memory experiment using hearing-impaired and normally hearing college students. Specially prepared lists of items were presented to the subject—printed and signed to the hearing-impaired subjects and printed and spoken to the normally hearing subjects. One significant result was that subjects in the printed-signed condition group did not falsely recognize items on the basis of their physical sign similarity. In a second experiment, subjects ignorant of sign language were given lists of signed and printed words. Signs were meant to be meaningless visual stimuli in this second test. This resulted in formationally similar signs being falsely recognized 38% of the time. The authors concluded that if the hearing-impaired subjects had experienced intrusion errors of a visual nature, as the normally hearing group did in the second experiment, they would have been encoding items according to their visual characteristics; however, since this was not the case, it was concluded that signs were stored in long-term memory on the basis of semantic organization in the same way that spoken or written language is stored for normally hearing people.

Tweeney, Hoeman, and C. Andrews (1975) sought to learn how words were organized semantically in deaf adolescents. A list of concrete nouns, a list of pictures, and a list of words representing sounds—for example, meow, toot, hiss, crash—were presented to hearing-impaired persons with severe or profound hearing losses and to hearing persons. Subjects were asked to sort each set into categories of similar meanings. It was found that deaf and hearing subjects differed only in minor ways with the nouns and the pictures but differed greatly for the words representing sounds. The sound words were apparently unfamiliar to the deaf subjects, and they grouped them in ways not always based on semantic relations. Some, for example, were based on visual similarity (whine, whack). The authors suggest that the deaf subjects resorted to such criteria for clustering only when they lacked adequate semantic grounds for classification.

In general, these studies indicate that deaf people store information in long-term memory in terms of semantic characteristics just as hearing people do. But important differences seem to exist in short-term memory coding and storage such that many deaf people seem to code in terms of the visual characteristics of signs and manual alphabet letters whereas hearing people code phonologically. These differences are not clear-cut, however. Hearing people who are skilled readers can access meaning in long-term storage both directly by visual access and indirectly by phonological mediation (Vellutino, 1982). And, as the next group of studies will show, some deaf people also use phonological, as well as visual, coding and mediation in accessing meanings in long-term memory.

Speech Coding

Probably the first clear evidence that many deaf persons code, store, and retrieve verbal information in short-term memory differently from the ways in which hearing persons do came from experiments by Conrad and his collaborators (Conrad, 1964, 1970, 1971a, 1979; Conrad, Freeman, & Hull, 1965; Conrad & Rush, 1965). Conrad changed Furth's question ("What do deaf people think in?") to "What do deaf people memorize in?" His substantive question became "Regardless of the sensory nature of the input, . . . when the moment for recall comes, what form, state, code, image, etc., is the memory of the material stored or retained or held in?" Conrad presented clear evidence that many of his deaf subjects coded material according to visual characteristics, but that some even profoundly hearing-impaired (deaf) persons use phonological (speech) coding.

Speech coding of information in short-term memory is important because of the major role it has played in some theories of reading development and methods for teaching reading. These theories and methods have assumed that the internalized auditory language of the hearing child, besides providing a major cognitive tool for thinking, is the base on which reading and writing are developed. The lack of internalization of spoken language has been blamed as a cause of the deaf child's major problems with reading and writing. A number of studies have been interpreted as showing that speech mediation is important to reading.

Conrad et al. (1965) tested 45 hearing subjects on their immediate recall of sequences of six consonants, for which the main factor in ease of recall was acoustic confusability. Items that are acoustically similar (e.g., d-t, hat-cat) are more likely to be confused in recall than are acoustically dissimilar items. Factors of acoustic familiarity and frequency of occurrence in the language were compared. It was found that the acoustic property of the letter was the dominant factor for short-term encoding.

Locke and Fehr (1970) tested 11 hearing adults in a sequential recall task using visually presented disyllabic words characterized by the presence or absence of letters representing labial phonemes. Analysis of electromyographic activity at a chin-lip site showed greater peak amplitudes for labial than for non-labial words during presentation and rehearsal periods. The authors inferred from this that covert oral activity occurring during verbal learning and reading is most likely speech.

Conrad (1971b) tested hearing children age 3 to 11 years in a sequential recalling task using matched pictures of common objects. Up to the age of five years it made no difference to the recall whether the objects memorized had acoustically similar names or not. Beyond five years, there was a systematic progressive advantage when the pictures had unlike sounding names. This change was taken to represent the onset of the use of verbal code as an aid to memorizing.

In another study, Liberman, Shankweiler, Liberman, Fowler, and Fischer (1977) tested 46 eight year old hearing children from three reading-skill groups—poor, marginal, and superior—on phonetic-recall skills to assess the effect of phonological coding on reading skills. They found that the superior readers were sharply distinguished from the inferior groups in their better recalling of nonconfusable items but were nearly identical to the others in their recalling of confusable strings. The implication is that the superior readers felt greater effects of the phonetic confusability. One interpretation was that the superior readers relied on speech coding during reading.

These studies and others with hearing subjects (Hardyck & Petrinovich, 1970; Kavanagh & Mattingly, 1972) were supplemented by studies of deaf subjects on the assumption that lack of hearing would force the use of internal coding other than speech. To probe the nature of the imagery used by deaf children when memorizing verbal material, Conrad (1970) fashioned and presented a list of nine alphabet letters in sequences of five and six letters one second apart. Deaf subjects read the sequences aloud and silently before transcribing, whereas hearing subjects read aloud only. Errors seemed to be based on articulatory confusions and possibly shape confusions. The hearing group and part of the deaf group made primarily articulatory errors, whereas the rest of the deaf subjects made primarily what seemed to be errors based on shape confusion.

Hearing subjects	Articulatory errors	Significant
	Shape errors	Not significant
21 Deaf subjects	Articulatory errors	Significant
	Shape errors	Not significant
15 Deaf subjects	Articulatory errors	Not significant
	Shape errors	Significant

From these results it was proposed that 21 of the deaf subjects were probably relying on speech cues (articulatory group) and the other 15 were not (nonarticulatory group). Speech ratings were obtained from the deaf students and these correlated significantly with the type of coding cues attributed to the subjects such that most members of the articulatory group had speech ratings of above average; those of the nonarticulatory group were rated below average. It was also found that the nonarticulatory group experienced an increase in errors when members were requested to read aloud whereas members of the articulatory group experienced no change after reading aloud. This is interesting, for hearing people usually experience fewer errors after reading aloud. Conrad suggested that forcing a nonarticulatory child to vocalize during an educational setting possibly imposes a hindrance on recall.

In another study, Conrad (1972) tested three groups for coding in short-term memory with six acoustically similar letters and six visually similar letters. Test subjects were 32 hearing subjects aged 10 to 11; 40 high functioning deaf oral students aged 11 to 16; and 56 normally functioning, deaf oral students aged 9 to 16. An articulatory index (AI) was computed as the proportion of acoustical-articulatory errors to the total number of errors. A subject with a high AI would be one who found the acoustically similar letters difficult to recall. A high AI person is inferred to be using a speech (acoustic-articulatory) short-term memory code. The results of the experiment were that the hearing subjects had very high AI, the high functioning deaf subjects had a middle range AI, and the normally functioning deaf children had a low range AI.

Conrad (1973) tested short-term memory coding of normally hearing women and hearing-impaired college students with hearing impairments ranging from 47 to 115 dB, speech quality ratings from 2 to 5 (on a 5 point scale), and speech hearing rating from 1 to 5 (on a 5 point scale). Stimuli were a series of letters with high phonological similarity and a series of letters with low phonological similarity. Recall was measured against a speech coding index (SCI). SCI is the proportion of all errors that are phonologically based (it is the same as AI in the preceding experiment, except that it is meant to imply the lack of focus on an acoustic component). SCI of hearing subjects ranged from 50 to 100, indicating a high level of speech coding; SCI of hearing-impaired subjects ranged from 0 to 96, with a median of 50. It was further found that there was no association between IQ and SCI; however, there was a significant association between greater hearing loss and lower SCI, and between poor speech quality and lower SCI. Hearing-impaired subjects who had SCIs in the same range of values as the hearing subjects used the same short-term memory code, namely one based on speech.

Additional studies by other investigators have confirmed the findings of Conrad that some deaf persons use speech as well as various forms of visual coding in storing and retrieving information in short-term memory. Chen (1976) tested 40 college students on acoustic factors in a visual detection task. Subjects were asked to cancel every letter "e" in a passage from *Treasure Island*. Individuals in group A were congenitally deaf (hearing threshold level [HTL]: 80+ dB); those in group B were adventitiously deaf (HTL: 80+ dB); those in group C were hard of hearing (HTL: less than 80 dB); and those in group D were subjects with normal hearing. Results showed that the hearing and the partially hearing subjects were more likely to miss a silent "e" than a pronounced "e" whereas there was no significant difference in type of "e" missed by the profoundly deaf subjects. The tentative conclusions drawn from the results were that for hearing and partially hearing individuals, an acoustic image of a word is scanned with the written word, so that when an acoustic factor is lacking, the letter is more likely to be missed; for deaf individuals, whether the deafness is congenital or adventitious, an acoustic image of a word is not easily available, and they rely on mainly visual information.

Locke (1978) conducted a test similar to that of Chen's using three target letters: c, g, and h. Students were asked to cancel the target letters. Results were that hearing subjects were almost three times as likely to miss a nonphonemic use of the letters than they were to miss a phonemic use, whereas the deaf subjects showed no differences, suggesting that deaf children, as a group, do not effectively mediate print with speech.

Locke and Locke (1971) tested three groups of teen-agers on a grapheme recall test: 26 normally hearing subjects, 28 hearing-impaired subjects whose speech was intelligible, and 28 hearing-impaired subjects whose speech was unintelligible. Stimuli were three lists of letters paired either by (1) phonetic similarity (e.g., B-V); (2) visual similarity (e.g., P-F); or (3) dactylic similarity (e.g., K-P). Analysis showed that the three groups recalled at essentially the same level, but confusion errors differentiated the groups (Table 2). Overt coding was also observed. The researchers concluded that deaf children's communication capabilities and their apparent coding strategies in short-term memories seemed to agree closely.

Some of the studies discussed in this section indicate that many deaf people seem to store information in long-term memory in terms of semantic characteristics of signs just as hearing people do with spoken language. Other studies indicate that coding in short-term (working) memory is in different form for many deaf people than it is for hearing people. Although some deaf people seem to use speech coding as do hearing people, many others seem to code in short-term memory on the basis of visual characteristics of signs and manual alphabet letters.

Multiple Coding

Probably the most extensive studies of the internal coding and recoding systems of deaf people have been conducted by Lichtenstein (1983). His research confirmed the findings of Conrad (1979) and Hanson (1982) that

Table 2.   Results of the Grapheme Recall Test

		Hearing	Deaf with Intelligible Speech	Deaf with Unintelligible Speech
	Phonetic errors	High	Moderate	Low
	Visual errors	Low	Moderate	High
	Dactylic errors	Low	Moderate	High
overt {	Phonetic coding	High	Moderate	Moderate
	Dactylic coding	None	Low	Moderate

working-memory capacity is related to the extent to which students can make efficient use of a speech-based recoding strategy in various language tasks and that this strategy is positively related to reading ability.

Lichtenstein reports extensively on the studies of working memory with hearing people to show that problems related to memory capacity and recoding processes are closely associated with difficulties hearing children have in learning to read (Bakker, 1972; Shankweiler, Liberman, Mark, Fowler, & Fischer, 1979), even though those children already know the language they are attempting to read. He also cites evidence that indicates that reading a second or less familiar language places increased demand on working-memory capacity (Sokolov, 1972). As Quigley and King (1982a) have reported, deaf children often confront the tasks of both learning a language (English) and learning to read at the same time, since few of them have adequate mastery of English in any form by the time reading instruction begins. Lichtenstein argues that this dual task must make large demands on the working-memory and recoding processes of deaf children. Yet the evidence indicates that deaf children have quantitative and qualitative limitations in these processes compared with hearing children.

Lichtenstein's extensive studies (1983) of the working-memory processes of deaf individuals and their relations to language skills, particularly reading comprehension, involved students at the National Technical Institute for the Deaf (NTID), all of whom had reading abilities considerably above the average for prelingually deaf students. His subjects exhibited a considerable range of competence in English skills and came from a variety of educational and communication backgrounds. Lichtenstein's goal was to study their working-memory processes with word and sentence memory tasks, obtain extensive self-reports through questionnaires of their conscious coding and recoding strategies, gather extensive descriptive and performance data on their auditory, intellectual, and linguistic abilities, and then analyze the relations among these data in the framework of a series of hypotheses connecting working memory to coding and recoding processes and to psycholinguistic functioning. His detailed investigations produced results and conclusions of critical importance to understanding the role of working memory in the development of primary and secondary (reading and writing) language in deaf children.

1. Lichtenstein found that individual deaf students usually used two or more codes rather than just one exclusively and that the various codes were used with varying degrees of effectiveness. The most commonly used codes were sign and speech.

2. There was clear evidence that the capacity of working memory is related to the extent to which students make use of a speech-based recoding strategy.

3. Lichtenstein used a model of working memory involving separate subsystems (Baddeley & Hitch, 1974). One subsystem, the Central Processor (CP), performs higher level or control functions but also has a limited amount of processing capacity that can be used for temporary storage of information. A second subsystem, the Articulatory Loop (AL), is a more peripheral system, which maintains coded information by subvocal speech rehearsal. This model proved useful to Lichtenstein's research in suggesting why deaf persons generally have shorter memory spans than hearing persons for linguistically codeable materials. Lichtenstein found that the more central cognitive components (CP) of working memory in deaf people appear to function as effectively as those of hearing individuals. He also found, as have other investigators (e.g., Belmont & Karchmer, 1978; Conrad, 1979; Hanson, 1982), that the more peripheral components of the deaf person's working-memory system are not as capable as those of the hearing person's in maintaining English linguistic information in working memory.

Lichtenstein was also able to relate his experimental findings on the limited efficiency of the coding strategies available to his deaf subjects to the manner in which the codes are used during reading to represent English linguistic structure. Some of his findings have direct implications for the development of primary language and of reading in deaf children.

1. Although most of the students used speech, sign, visual information, and to a small degree fingerspelling for recoding printed information during reading, the better readers relied very heavily on speech recoding. This confirms similar findings by Conrad (1979) and by Hirsh-Pasek and Treiman (1982).

2. Reliance on speech recoding was not confined to those deaf students who had intelligible speech. Just as Conrad (1979) had found for English and Welsh students, Lichtenstein found that many of his American students whose speech was not readily intelligible nonetheless were using internal speech of some form for recoding during reading.

3. Sign was rarely used consistently for recoding by the most highly skilled readers, although many of them used it selectively for specific memorial purposes.

4. The various codes used by students, particularly speech, sign, and visual, seemed to be selectively related to various aspects of English. Vocabulary test scores and semantic writing errors were not significantly related to working-memory capacity or to recoding processes, especially when syntactic

abilities were statistically removed from the relationships (partialled out). Research with hearing subjects has demonstrated that visual access to meaning is typical in reading without the need for recoding. This seems to be true also for deaf persons.

5. The primary relationships of working-memory capacity and recoding processes seem to be with syntactic skills. Speech recoders tend to be better readers, apparently because speech recoding can better represent the grammatical structure of English than sign or visual coding. This allows the short term retention of enough information to decode grammatical structures, which often are not linear (e.g., medial relative clauses, passive voice). This finding of Lichtenstein's confirms similar findings reported by Lake (1980).

6. Lichtenstein found that skill in the use of bound morphology was most highly related to the self-reports of dependence on speech to represent English information in working memory and to the ability to retain visual word-shape information in working memory.

From all of this, it would seem that speech recoding is important to reading development. Visual coding and sign coding might suffice for adequate vocabulary development, but faithful representation of English structure seems to be peculiarly sensitive to speech recoding. However, it does not necessarily follow from this that deaf children who do not develop speech recoding are doomed to be non-readers. It might simply mean that new methods must be developed to teach reading to such children. It might also signify that means other than reading should be sought for imparting information to some deaf children. After having learned to read, children in school read primarily to learn, and other means than the printed word can likely be found to impart information.

MEDIATING LANGUAGE SYSTEMS

In addition to using some means for storing information in long-term memory (apparently semantic) and for coding information in short-term memory (apparently visual as well as phonological), deaf people must use some system of connected language (or grammar) for the manipulation of verbal thinking. Again, there is a question as to what form this connected language takes. And again, as with coding in short-term memory, the answer seems to be various forms. Most hearing persons in the United States have spoken English as their primary language and printed and written English as their medium for reading and writing. The basic symbols (words) are connected in a common grammatical system, of which syntax is a primary component. Deaf people, however, may have any of several systems, and a number of studies have revealed some of these.

Some deaf persons acquire sufficient fluency in spoken language that English becomes their primary internalized language system. A study by Ogden (1979) of 637 former students of three private oral schools for deaf children found them to be highly successful educationally and occupationally. Measures of their reading abilities and samples of their written language attested to the fact that English in some coded form was their internalized language and their medium for verbal thought. The former students themselves attributed their academic and occupational success largely to their development of oral English.

The low reading levels and inappropriate written language (see samples in the Preface, page xii) of most deaf children attest, however, that this situation is not typical. Many specific studies of written and spoken language samples of deaf persons confirm this (Brannon, 1968; Monsen, 1979; Quigley, Power, & Steinkamp, 1977; Quigley, Smith, & Wilbur, 1974; Quigley, Wilbur, & Montanelli, 1974). If English structure is not the typical internalized language structure for deaf children, then what is? A number of studies indicate that the structure of American Sign Language (ASL) is the functional structure for some deaf persons whereas some hybrid of ASL and English is for others. These studies explore both the linguistic characteristics of ASL and the emergence of semantic and syntactic relationships in deaf children exposed naturally to ASL, systems of manually-coded English, and gestural systems. They demonstrate the adequacy of ASL and other manual systems as linguistic mediators of thought.

The following are a few of the studies that demonstrate and explicate the linguistic characteristics of sign language. Klima and Bellugi (1979) have shown how subtle modifications of movement of certain signs can impart a wide range of aspectual modifications to them (frequency, continuation, intensity, approximation, inception, result). Fischer and Gough (1978) showed how changing the spatial arrangement of a verb can incorporate both subject and object pronouns, location, reversibility, reciprocity, size, continuation, and manner into it. Bode (1974) videotaped 16 signers to study how communication of agent, object, and indirect object took place in signs. Ingram (1978) discusses how elements within a signing sequence are ordered to show different informational perspectives. Liddell (1975) discusses how facial expression is used as a syntactic marker to convey the equivalent of relative clauses in signs.

There also appear to be similarities between deaf children's acquisition of signing as their first linguistic medium and hearing children's acquisition of English. Newport and Ashbrook (1977) found the emergence of eight semantic relationships in the expressions of five deaf children learning sign language to be in the same order as they were for four hearing children in a study by Bloom, Lightbown, and Hood (1975). Other systems in sign language that do not have exact parallels in English nevertheless seem to evolve in a developmental way in deaf children. Hoffmeister (1978) traced the development of a pronominal referential system until it was completely learned by a six-year-old girl. Ellenberger and Steyaert (1978) report that a deaf child they studied learned the directional modification of verbs and the structuring of space by age five. Collins-Ahlgren (1975) found a facilitative and simultaneous effect of sign language with English. Two deaf girls she observed produced complex grammatical functions in simple signs first and then gradually moved into standard English form using function morphemes.

In an educational setting, Higgins (1973) found sign language effective for communicating factual information. Bellugi and Fischer (1972) found that although signs were communicated more slowly in their study, the rates for producing propositions were similar in both sign language and English. They agreed that signs could compact linguistic information in ways not available to English. Jordan (1975) compared the communicative speed and abilities of deaf signers with hearing speakers and found that both groups communicated with the same degree of accuracy, but that the deaf signers included more information per unit of time than the hearing people did. Dalgleish (1975) studied reports from educational institutions in the United States, Holland, and England and reported that sign language was the preferred mode of communication by deaf children.

Studies by Babb (1979) and Brasel and Quigley (1977) suggested that signs might be a valuable medium of early linguistic input contributing to later academic improvement. Max (1935) used a biofeedback approach to test whether deaf subjects might be dreaming in sign language. Electrodes were fastened to the fingers and hands of deaf and hearing subjects. Electromyelograms were obtained during undisturbed sleep and during dream sleep. The onset of dreams in the deaf subjects caused a current response in the arm and finger muscles of the deaf subjects but not in the hearing subjects. Other studies by Crittenden (1975), Hawes and Danhauer (1978), and Lane, Boyes-Braem, and Bellugi (1976) have supported the concept of distinctive perceptual features for the hand configurations and movements of sign language.

These studies demonstrate a growing belief among psychologists and linguists that a gestural form of language, such as ASL, is probably as efficient a thought-mediating system for deaf persons as English and other spoken languages are for hearing persons.

SUMMARY

Present resolution of the enduring question of the relationship between language and cognition (thought) seems to favor the primacy of basic cognitive processes, with language being dependent on them. Perception, attention, memory, and other abilities need to develop appropriately to ensure the adequate evolution of the abstract thinking processes and language, on which educational development is largely based. Deficits or problems in the development of basic cognitive processes will be reflected in problems of language development and ultimately in most academic educational areas. This is why the work of psychologists such as Piaget and others with hearing children and Furth and others with deaf children have major implications for teachers and clinicians.

While the "language first or cognition first" question seems at this stage to have been resolved in favor of the primacy of cognition, the question of how deaf individuals compare with hearing individuals on cognitive tasks seems to have been resolved in favor of equality of performance; however, this should be treated with caution. It has long been obvious from the successful social and occupational functioning of deaf individuals that the Pintner position of deficits in the general cognitive and intellectual functioning of deaf people is untenable. As greater control has been exerted over the variables that influence studies of cognitive abilities, especially verbal language, differences between deaf and hearing individuals have decreased, and in some cases disappeared. They have not disappeared in all areas, however. Some differences continue to be found on various Piagetian tasks and in areas such as sequential memory which are important to language and educational development. There is a tendency to assume that even greater experimental control will eventually eliminate those differences also. But the possibility that they are true differences should also be entertained. This is particularly true of linguistically codable materials, in which studies have consistently shown deaf people to have shorter memory spans than hearing people (Lichtenstein, 1983).

It does not follow that, if we accept the existence of true differences between deaf and hearing individuals in some cognitive areas, inferiority in cognitive, linguistic, and educational development will inevitably be found. Knowing the nature and effects of any true differences allows developmental and educational programs to be shaped to capitalize on the differences. For example, if deaf people perform as well as, or better than, hearing people on tests of spatial memory but less well on tests of sequential memory, and if these are true differences, there are several implications for educational practice. First, since hearing is an efficient processor of temporal-sequential input (such as auditory language), and vision is more efficient at processing spatial information, ASL might have some advantages over spoken language as the initial linguistic input for at least some deaf children. ASL makes use of motion and position in space to convey some concepts that depend on temporal-sequential transmission in spoken language. This might be particularly true in connected discourse in which certain syntactic constructions might be heavily dependent on temporal-sequential storage in short term memory. According to the work of Lichtenstein, this type of processing of information is important in comprehending embedded or interrupted syntactic constituents, such as sentences with medial relative clauses (e.g., "The boy who kissed the girl ran away"), which require integration of information from the beginning and end of a sentence for proper understanding. Deaf persons have great difficulty in understanding the spoken and written forms of such syntactic constructions (Quigley, Smith, & Wilbur, 1974), yet it is possible that the constructions can be readily understood through ASL, in which language they are conveyed in terms of space, movement, and facial expressions. ASL might be uniquely adapted to capitalize on the cognitive differences between deaf and hearing individuals by using space and motion where spoken language uses time for the same purpose.

A second implication in the same area is that manually coded English systems might have some advantage over spoken language in that, like ASL, they make the individual units of language (words) more visible than does speech, but they might have the same disadvantage as speech in connected discourse in that they rely on time rather than space as an important element in syntactic transmission. A third in this chain of implications derived from possible differences between deaf and hearing individuals in spatial and temporal-sequential memory is that teachers and clinicians, in order to teach deaf children the language of the core society, need to know some of the basic ideas of cognition and the comparative performances of deaf and hearing children in various cognitive abilities. They need also to know ASL and perhaps the various manually coded English systems as well, but particularly ASL.

At first glance, the findings on the importance of speech recoding in the reading process, particularly with regard to grammatical structure, appear to present a dilemma for the teaching of reading to deaf children. Most deaf children at present do not learn to read English well; and if this is due in any considerable part to the lack of a speech coding system, then those deaf children who are unable to acquire this coding system might simply be unable ever to learn to read well or even adequately. At second glance, the findings on speech recoding do not present as bleak a prospect. There are at least three potential solutions to the problem.

1. Speech could be developed far better with far more deaf children than is the case at present. Ling (1976), Ling and Ling (1978), and others have shown that this is possible. Moreover, there is no strong evidence that this requires the abandonment or prohibition of ASL or whatever other manual means of communication deaf children prefer.

2. Other means of teaching reading could perhaps be developed that do not depend on speech coding or recoding. If reading, as we presently conceive it, is not possible without a speech code, then using ASL as the first and basic language of young deaf children might preclude the learning of reading. This is a dilemma. Proponents of developing ASL as the first language of the deaf child with English being developed later as a second language seem to overlook that not only a new language must be learned but also a new code (speech versus sign) and a new modality (auditory-kinesthetic versus visual). This might be a much more difficult task than the learning of a second spoken language by a hearing person who already has a first spoken language and a well developed cognitive and experiential base. In this case the modalities (auditory) and the codes (speech) are the same for both languages. However, deaf children of deaf parents who are using ASL often read better than other deaf children, so perhaps a speech code is not indispensable. Conrad (1979) and Lichtenstein (1983) have shown, however,

that many of these deaf children might be using internal speech coding even though their speech is unintelligible or rarely used.

3. One basic purpose for reading is to acquire information. But it should be possible, however, to find other means than the printed word to accomplish this purpose. Talking books for blind people are one means by which this is done. Translation of the printed or written word to signed videotapes in ASL for deaf people is another possible means.

It should be emphasized again, though, that speech recoding seems to play a vital role in reading, particularly in providing efficient storage for syntactic units. This role of speech recoding in the short-term memory storage of linguistically codeable materials has been stated succinctly by Lichtenstein (1984).

> Considerable research has indicated that a primary function of working memory during the reading process is to provide temporary, short-term storage of text surface structure. Logically, some form of temporary storage is required for language comprehension. Information about the syntactic form of the sentence along with information about individual lexical items must be retained and used to determine the correct underlying semantic relationships between the words in a sentence (e.g., Kleiman, 1975; Norman, 1972).
>
> The short-term memory literature for hearing persons has shown that speech recoding processes play an important role in increasing WM [working memory] capacity. Research has also found that recoding processes play a similar role during the normal silent reading process, assisting in the storage of incoming information necessary for the comprehension of complex linguistic materials. Studies with hearing readers have suggested that speech recoding processes are especially important when comprehending difficult or unfamiliar material (Hardyck & Petrinovich, 1970), when retention of word-order information is crucial in order to correctly combine concepts into their correct semantic relationships (Baddeley, Eldridge & Lewis, 1981), and when information needs to be retained in WM to permit integration of information across clause or sentence boundaries (Slowiaczek & Clifton, 1980). Thus, speech recoding helps to provide the materials for temporary storage of sequential surface structure information during normal prose comprehension. (pp. 333–334)

Chapter 2

Reading in Hearing Children

Information on the reading process in hearing individuals presented in this chapter deals with (1) the three types of current reading theories ("bottom-up," "top-down," and "interactive"); (2) a selected sampling of research on various aspects and problems of the reading process organized under the categories of the reader, the text, and the context; and (3) a summary of what seems to be the present state of knowledge and in what directions research seems to be moving.

REQUISITES FOR READING

As R. Anderson (1981) has pointed out,

> Beginning readers are familiar with many components of the reading task. Through oral experiences, they already have acquired a substantial vocabulary and a basic syntactic competence. They are used to making sense of language and have a wealth of real world experience to draw on in this effort. . . . What the beginning reader is most obviously lacking are the lowest level skills in the hierarchy: the skills involved in recognizing printed words. (p. 51)

This is reflected in the fact that the prereading child can understand beginning readers when the books are read orally to the child, provided that the stories are related to previous experiences and are within the linguistic ability (semantic and syntactic) of the child.

Besides bringing to the reading task a rich background of experiential, cognitive, and linguistic experiences, the typical prereading hearing child also has the strategies to link textual information to these abilities. In particular, such a child has developed inferential and figurative language abilities that enable him or her to understand textual information by relating it to experience and information already acquired. Inferential processes are ubiquitous in reading comprehension. Although much of the special materials prepared for beginning readers is literal or text explicit in that all the information required for comprehension is stated explicitly in the text, most reading materials beyond the third grade rely heavily on inference for full comprehension. Inferencing is a process essential to reading text that seems to create major problems for deaf children (Wilson, 1979a) and it will be considered later in more detail.

Just as considerable use of inference has been demonstrated in prereading children by recent research (Gelman, 1978; Trabasso, 1980), so also has figurative language usage. Reynolds and Ortony (1980) and Winner, Engel, and Gardner (1980), among others, have shown that even very young children have some figurative language comprehension. Like inferencing, figurative language seems to present major obstacles in the reading of standard English for deaf students (Giorcelli, 1982; Payne, 1982). The importance of this is emphasized by the findings of a detailed examination by Dixon, Pearson, and Ortony (1980) of reading series (grades K through 6) published by Houghton-Mifflin, Ginn, and Scott, Foresman. The investigators found that, with the exception of the Scott, Foresman series, the materials use an abundance of figurative language (especially metaphors and similes) at all levels.

All of the abilities and mental processes that have been discussed briefly are important to the reading process and most of them, as part of the larger domain of cognitive development, have been developed to at least some extent prior to the usual age for beginning reading. The practical needs and developing interests of the child in early life shape the child's experiences and cognitive and linguistic development. These practical considerations are also reflected in written discourse in the developing area of pragmatics. This has led to the consideration of written discourse as a form of pragmatic speech acts—the view that speakers or writers (just as children and parents) use words to do things or to get a hearer or reader to believe or do something (Morgan & Sellner, 1980; Searle, 1969). In this view, larger units of text, or discourse, become the unit of study rather than words and sentences.

Of the various abilities and mental processes discussed thus far in connection with beginning reading—early experiences, cognitive development, linguistic development, the use of inferencing and figurative language, communication acts as pragmatic acts expressed in discourse units, and decoding—only decoding is unique to reading. This perhaps explains why difficulties at the level of letter and word processing have consistently been found to be the single best class of discriminators between good and poor readers (e.g., Biemiller, 1977–1978; Graesser, Hoffman, & Clark, 1980). These processes are the ones that are unique to the printed medium and uniquely foreign to the beginning reader.

READING THEORIES

The three classes of theories of the reading process to be discussed differ in how they incorporate these elements and in the emphasis given to individual elements. Bottom-up theories, such as proposed by Gough (1972) and LaBerge and Samuels (1974), place major emphasis on the text material as the major factor in reading and are also known as text-driven or data-driven theories. In these theories, elements of the text—letter features, letters, words, phrases, sentences—are integrated from smaller to larger units to arrive at meaning. Instruction based on these theories usually emphasizes decoding skills and the teaching of separate sub-skills in reading comprehension in some sequential hierarchical order.

Top-down theories, such as proposed by Smith (1978) and K. Goodman (1970), emphasize the importance of prior knowledge and its interaction with the processing of text in reading and view proficient reading as "constructing meaning [from text] with the least amount of time and effort, selectively using the fewest and most productive cues to construct meaning" (K. Goodman & Gollasch, 1980, p. 10). Smith (1971, 1973) argues that skilled readers rely as little as possible on the graphemic details of a text and use prior knowledge and textual context as the main elements in reading. These theories view reading as one part of a larger problem of language comprehension in general. Thus, instruction based on these theories tends to deemphasize decoding skills and specific comprehension skills.

Interactive theories indicate problems in both bottom-up and top-down theories that result from their very one-sidedness. The bottom-up theories fail to recognize that even very young children bring a considerable body of prior knowledge and higher order skills (e.g., inferencing) to the reading of text. And top-down theories fail to recognize the importance of lower level processes such as decoding. A considerable body of knowledge attests that skilled readers fixate virtually every content word in a text and use graphemic knowledge and skills extensively in the course of reading (Just & Carpenter, 1980; McConkie & Zola, 1981).

These three types of theories are examined here in some detail, and selected evidence is presented in support of each. Interactive theories are judged to provide better explanations for more of the established empirical data than do bottom-up or top-down theories. It is further concluded that the class of interactive theories known as schema theories seems most promising at present. Schema theories incorporate the idea of schemas (or plans) as organizing frameworks for knowledge based on recent research in memory and cognition (Bobrow & Norman, 1975; Chafe, 1976).

Bottom-up Theories

Bottom-up theories place initial emphasis in reading on word recognition, either as a whole unit (whole-word or look-say approach) or as strings of letters or letter clusters which are related to spoken equivalents (phonics approach). Reading at the phonics level seems to be seen as putting together small units (letters, letter clusters) to form words; words are then combined into the larger units of phrases and sentences to arrive at meaning. Beyond the level of decoding, reading comprehension also is seen as a hierarchy of subskills, such as locating details, recognizing main ideas, and so forth, which combine into larger units to provide the meaning of a text (Mason, Osborn, & Rosenshine, 1977).

The issue of the place and form of decoding in beginning reading in bottom-up theories has been at the heart of a long-standing controversy in reading instruction (Chall, 1967; Flesch, 1955) as to whether emphasis should be placed on the whole-word approach or spelling-sound correspondences (phonics). It has also been an issue in the psychological study of the unit of perception involved in word recognition as summed in the question posed by Vellutino (1982), "How does a skilled reader recognize a word?" Vellutino uses this question as the basis for an exhaustive analysis of an impressive body of literature on the topic, extending back to the work of Cattell in 1886. In the course of his analysis, Vellutino presents much of the significant research literature and the bottom-up reading theories related to the research.

Vellutino, on the basis of extensive analysis of almost a century of research data, concludes that the unit of perception in word recognition is relative, that it involves the basic perceptual recognition and interpretation of graphemic details, that it is heavily influenced by contextual clues in the text being read, and that it is also heavily influenced by prior knowledge and skills of the reader (in particular, the linguistic and nonlinguistic knowledge and information-processing strategies the reader brings to the task). This analysis indicates that elements of both bottom-up and top-down theories are involved in the reading process in some interactive fashion.

Top-down Theories

Top-down theories are best exemplified in the writings of K. Goodman (1970) and Smith (1978). Both reject what they term the emphasis on reading as a precise process that involves exact, detailed, sequential perception and identification of letters, words, spelling patterns, and larger units. According to K. Goodman (1970), "In phonic centered approaches to reading, the preoccupation is with precise letter identification. In word centered approaches, the focus is on word identification. Known words are sight words, precisely named in any setting." In place of this, K. Goodman sees reading as a "psycholinguistic guessing game" involving an interaction between thought and language. Skill in reading is seen as involving not greater precision but more accurate guesses at the unfolding meaning of a text based on better techniques for sampling the text, greater control over language structure, broadened experiences, and increased conceptual development. Increasing skill and speed in reading are accompanied by decreasing use of graphic cues.

Smith's views (1978) are similar to K. Goodman's despite some differences in terminology. Smith refers to the primary role of "prediction" in reading rather than "hypothesis testing" or "psychological guessing" (K. Goodman's terms). The concepts, however, are similar. As Smith (1978) states, "My aim is to demonstrate that prediction is essential for reading, that everyone who can comprehend spoken language is capable of prediction, and that prediction is routinely practiced in reading by beginners as well as by fluent readers." Smith presents four main arguments for the primary role of prior knowledge, context, and prediction in reading and against the precise sequential and hierarchical view of the reading process: (1) individual words are often polysemous (have multiple meanings) and their intended meanings can be obtained only from context aided by prior knowledge; (2) according to Venezky (1976), there are more than 300 spelling-to-sound correspondence rules of English and there is no precise way of knowing when any of the rules must apply or when an exception to the rules is being encountered; in brief, the rules of phonics are very complex; (3) the amount of visual information from print that the brain can process at any given moment in reading is limited–to four or five letters or other units according to a substantial body of research; (4) short-term memory (or working memory) is limited; only a small number of items can be stored at any time and increased input leads to displacement of items already in storage.

Referring to data from information theory, Smith (1978) points out that there are sequential dependencies in English among letters, words, and larger units, which aid in comprehension. A large body of research data attests to this: individual letters are recognized more readily when embedded in groups (Wheeler, 1970); even more readily when the letter groups form pseudowords, such as *gorp* (Adams, 1979a); and still more readily when they form real words (Adams, 1979b). The same situation applies to words in the context of meaningful phrases and sentences and phrases and other syntactic units in the context of sentences and larger units. Meaningfulness apparently allows the reader, or listener, to group the material in larger and larger chunks in working memory and aids in comprehension. As Smith (1975) states,

> The limited capacity of short-term memory is overcome by filling it always with units as large and as meaningful as possible. Instead of being crammed uselessly with half-a-dozen unrelated letters, short-term memory can contain the same number of words, or better still, the meaning of one or more sentences. In fact prediction works better at these broader levels; it is easier to predict meanings rather than specific words or letters, and very few words or letters need to be identified to test predictions about meanings. (p. 309)

Two basic conditions that Smith states must be met for children to use prediction for learning to read are the following: (1) the material that children are expected to learn to read must be potentially meaningful to them; and (2) the children must feel free to predict even though this will result initially in errors rather than in precise reading.

The importance of context and prior knowledge in reading is now generally accepted, but there is less general acceptance of the lack of importance of textual detail to the reading process. Top-down theories, such as espoused by K. Goodman and by Smith, assert that textual detail (letter and words) need only be sampled from the text. As quoted from Smith (1975), "very few words or letters need to be identified to test prediction about meanings" (p. 309). The remainder of the text presumably can be "guessed at" or "predicted." This concept of sampling of text is not supported by the data on skilled reading.

Recent developments in computer techniques make it possible to control the text displayed on a screen (a cathode-ray tube) contingent on eye movements and to make various changes in the text during the reading process. For example, it is possible to change a particular letter or word in the text from one eye fixation to the next. It then can be determined from the reader's reports of what he or she saw and from the analysis of eye movements whether the reader perceived the change. It is also possible to place errors in the text for a single eye fixation and to physically shift the text on the screen during a saccadic eye movement and thus change where the eyes come to rest.

Data from the use of these and other recently developed techniques (McConkie, 1982) to study mental processes involved in reading through analyzing eye movements contradict the top-down theorists' contention that skilled readers only sample words and letters from text. A substantial body of data now attests that the skilled reader responds to letters as units and that words are not identified strictly on the basis of more global stimulus patterns. Zola (1981) demonstrated that even replacing a single letter in the center of a highly constrained (predictable from context) word with its most visually similar letter resulted in some disruption of the reading process compared with a no-error control situation, thus indicating that even minimal visual distortion in a word was evident to skilled readers. These, and many other studies, show that, contradictory to top-down theorists' contentions, skilled readers fixate virtually every content word in a text and use individual letters and other graphemic knowledge and skills extensively in the course of reading (Just & Carpenter, 1980; McConkie & Zola 1981).

Interactive Theories

The interactive theories emerging in recent years are replacing the one-directional (bottom-up and top-down) theories of the reading process. According to R. Anderson (1981), interactive models emphasize that the reader is an *active* information processor whose goal it is to *construct* a model of what the text means. Two aspects of these models are of primary importance: (1) the central role of background knowledge in constructing meaning from text; and (2) a range of dynamic processing strategies from the specific aspects of decoding print to the metacognitive strategies of consciously monitoring the individual's processing of information. Comprehension proceeds from the top-down as well as from the bottom-up; that is, it is driven by preexisting concepts as well as by the data from the text. There are times when the information processor is largely data-driven or text-driven and is controlled by the visual data from the printed page. It seems then to be assuming a relatively passive role waiting for data from the text to activate and relate to preexisting concepts. At other times the processor seems to assume a more active role and seeks to predict the probable data ahead in the text. In contrast to this alternation of bottom-up and top-down roles, some models such as Rumelhart's interactive model (1977) suggest a constant and simultaneous generation of hypotheses about visual information and meaning, both from data-driven (bottom-up) and concept-driven (top-down) sources.

The schema theory form of interaction theory uses a model similar to Rumelhart's with the added concept of schemata as organizing frameworks for preexisting knowledge. R. Anderson (1981) defines a schema as "a hypothetical knowledge structure, an abstract mental entity to which human information processors bind their experiences with the real world" (p. 606). He states that the abstract character of schemata is important because they are prototypic rather than specific (i.e., a person can have a schema for chair but probably not for every particular chair he or she experiences). When applied to objects and simple ideas, schemata are identical to what are called concepts or categories. But schemata can be constructed for all levels of knowledge from something as specific as a letter of the alphabet to something as abstract as a philosophy of life and for such concepts as love, kindness, perseverance, and hope.

Thus, the schema concept provides a powerful tool for organizing knowledge into meaningful units, which aids in acquisition, storage, and retrieval. The effect of meaning on memory functioning is well documented; words are easier to recall than unrelated letters, sentences easier than unrelated words, and so forth. In fact any body of semantically related data is easier to retrieve from memory than any comparable body of semantically unrelated data. Schemata are the devices by which knowledge is organized into meaningful units and incoming data (such as from a text) are incorporated into the existing schemata, modify such schemata, or help form new schemata. And schemata, at various levels, are combined with related schemata into higher order, and usually more general, schemata.

TEXT VARIABLES

The material herein is presented under the categories of words, sentences, and discourse. Other units will be discussed within these categories, such as letters and syllables within words and phrases and clauses within sentences, but the three units are considered here as the basic ones in written communication. Concepts are considered basically synonymous with words, sentences as the vehicles for relating concepts into propositions by means of syntactic devices, and discourse units as the basic meaningful communication units, which can vary widely in size. Pragmatics is considered along with discourse in discussing the view that language should be viewed as action (Austin, 1962; Searle, 1969) undertaken for a purpose—to influence the listener or reader. Spoken and written language then are seen as special forms of this general concept of language as action.

Word Processing

As previously cited studies have indicated (McConkie & Rayner, 1976; McConkie & Zola, 1979; Rayner, McConkie, & Zola, 1980), the performance of skilled readers depends heavily upon their processing of individual words, even though this is largely an unconscious activity and conscious awareness in skilled reading is usually directed to high-level aspects of the text such as seeking the main points and monitoring one's comprehension of the text. Word processing, however, is not necessarily an unconscious and automatic process for beginning readers, less skilled readers, and persons with reading disorders. In fact, there is a substantial body of consistent findings that differences in abilities at the level of letter and word processing are the single best class of discriminators between good and poor readers (Biemiller, 1977–1978; Graesser et al., 1980).

Biemiller's research (1977–1978) is illustrative of the many studies in this area. He studied the relationships between oral-reading rates for unrelated letters, unrelated words, and simple text in the development of reading achievement. The subjects were children drawn from three schools, two in Canada and one in New York, and adult students and staff members of the Institute of Child Study at the University of Toronto. Two important findings for the issue of word processing were (1) the younger and poorer readers were slower than the older and abler readers in reading material without redundancy of structure (unrelated letters) and with orthographic structure (words), and the two areas were related; and (2) no evidence was found (contrary to top-down theories) that the poor readers used interword structure (context) less effectively than the more able readers. Biemiller raises the question from other findings of the study as to why his good readers identified words as fast as unrelated letters whereas the poor readers took longer to identify words. He believes the explanation is to be found in the failure of poor readers to extract the orthographic structure. He cites a number of studies that provide direct evidence that poor readers are deficient in using orthographic structure. In general, these studies consistently indicate that differences in abilities to process letters and words are the single best class of discriminators between good and poor readers. Along with the work cited earlier showing that skilled readers fixate virtually every content word when reading and that they process a great deal of graphemic detail, the evidence is very strong that detailed word processing is an essential part of the reading process.

A substantial body of evidence also indicates that heavy reliance on top-down rather than bottom-up processing is characteristic of younger and less able readers (Adams, 1980; Juel, 1980; Stanovich, 1980; Stanovich & West, 1979). Beginning readers, like skilled readers, tend to apply their relevant prior knowledge and higher order mental processes in top-down fashion as they read. Since they have not yet developed adequately the bottom-up processes (such as decoding) needed for processing print, their top-down processes substitute for bottom-up processes instead of complementing and interacting with them, as seems to be the case with skilled readers. The research literature indicates that this overreliance on context by beginning readers and less able readers is not good and is apparently due to lack of adequately developed word processing skills.

The study by Juel (1980) is representative of findings in this area. Juel studied the extent to which second and third grade students used a text-driven (bottom-up) or a concept-driven (top-down) process in reading. That is, she examined the conditions under which readers use context to identify words. Readers with high, average, and low ability read target words that varied in decodability, frequency, and number of syllables in isolation, poor context, and moderate context. Juel found that her good readers were predominantly text-driven (bottom-up) on her tasks, whereas her poor readers were concept-driven (top-down), and the average readers fluctuated between the two types of processing. Her conclusion was that as readers became more skilled, they read in a predominantly text-driven fashion. The other studies cited earlier present similar findings on the primarily top-down or concept-driven processing of poor readers.

R. Anderson (1981) points out that a critical question in word processing concerns the kinds of patterns or units skilled readers use in the recognition process. Do they use letters, whole words, or units of in-between size such as syllables or morphemes? This question is related, of course, to the controversial issue in reading of the respective roles played by phonics (spelling-sound correspondences) and whole word (look-say) approaches in reading instruction. As stated earlier, Vellutino (1982) devoted an extensive report to an exhaustive analysis of a century of research on the issue of the unit of perception in word recognition. He concluded that the perceptual unit is relative and is determined by three interacting factors: (1) the context in which the word is encountered (top-down processing), (2) the characteristics of the word itself (bottom-up processing); and (3) the skill of the reader. In other words, the reader can use whole word processing to access his or her lexicon for word recognition (Cattell, 1886; Johnson, 1977) but is also able to process words down to their individual letters (Adams, 1979a; Zola, 1981), depending on the nature of the reading task and the skill of the reader. Skilled readers have a thorough knowledge of orthographic redundancy and spelling-to-sound correspondence (phonics). Although they do not normally need to use this knowledge in recognizing words, they can use it when required, such as to facilitate letter recognition (Adams, 1979a) and letter order (Adams, 1979b) and probably to detect syllable boundaries.

The issue of the unit of perception in word recognition is related to the issue of speech recoding in reading. As has been stated, the beginning reader brings to the reading task many already developed skills and types of knowledge that are applicable to that task. The beginning reader has been exposed to a variety of infant and early childhood experiences and has formed a cognitive base for future learning activities; he or she has, on the basis of various needs, developed pragmatic use of oral language through physical and linguistic interaction with parents and other important early childhood figures; and he or she has at least partially developed higher order skills, such as inferencing and the use of figurative language, that are directly applicable to reading. Reading is, to some extent, only another means of accomplishing various goals by written rather than by spoken means. The cognitive, linguistic, and inferencing processes that the child uses to satisfy needs through physical and spoken actions can be applied also to the reading process. The internalized auditory vocabulary and syntax (basic semantic and syntactic competence) that the hearing child has acquired can be related to the same processes as reflected in written or printed language. The speech-recoding issue is related to this relationship between the auditory code of spoken language and the visual code of written or printed language. It can be argued that the only skills that are unique to reading are skills dealing with print and that what the beginning reader is most obviously lacking are the lowest level skills in the hierarchy of reading skills—the skills involved in recognizing and relating printed words.

Since most people learn to listen before they learn to read (with some notable exceptions, such as deaf children), a person's lexicon must initially be coded internally for speech; that is, initially a speech-like representation of a word is needed to access its meaning. This has led to the formulation of the speech-recoding hypothesis, which claims that even skilled readers must convert a printed word to its speech equivalent in some internal fashion before accessing the lexicon. An alternative hypothesis is that the lexicon of a skilled reader is coded visually, as well as for speech, and consequently speech recoding is not needed for reading.

As stated earlier, there is a considerable body of evidence that skilled comprehenders in reading have basic word skills that are superior to those of unskilled comprehenders. Experiments by Perfetti and Hogaboam (1975) and others have demonstrated that word decoding through speech recoding is a basic skill in reading. Kleiman (1975), however, has demonstrated that speech recoding is not necessary for lexical access (which can be made visually) but that speech recoding does occur after lexical access (after the word has been recognized visually) and facilitates the temporary storage of words for sentence comprehension. Kleiman (1975) conducted three experiments to explore whether recoding to speech occurs before lexical access, after lexical access, or not at all. The results of the first two experiments indicated that lexical access occurs without speech recoding (i.e., is visual). The third experiment showed that speech recoding does occur, but after lexical access, and facilitates the temporary storage of words necessary for sentence comprehension. There is now considerable evidence for this point that speech recoding is *not necessary* for obtaining access to *word meanings* (Baron, 1973; Kleiman, 1975), although speech recoding can be used for this purpose whenever required. There is also accumulating evidence, however, that speech recoding is an important process in the *comprehension of sentences and connected prose* (Baddeley, 1979; Hardyck & Petrinovich, 1970; Kleiman, 1975; Levy, 1977). This is an important point to be considered again later in connection with the reading problems of deaf children.

It has been possible to present here only a few studies on the issue of the role of speech recoding in word recognition and reading. A much fuller account can be found in the exhaustive analysis of research on the issue performed by Vellutino (1982). Vellutino concludes:

> Suffice it to point out. . .that all theories that advocate only one mechanism for identifying printed words can be questioned by research findings that suggest that: (1) there may be at least two lexical access routes for printed words, one involving direct visual access and the other involving direct phonological mediation; (2) there may be individual differences in the relative use of both routes; (3) those who tend to utilize one or the other exclusively may be significantly impaired in reading. (p. 177)

Vellutino cites extensive research evidence to support each of these conclusions and provides extensive documentation that phonological translation is useful (when required) for skilled as well as for less skilled readers.

One more study is of interest in the issue of speech recoding. It has long been assumed that ideographic languages such as Chinese map orthography (characters) directly onto meaning as contrasted to English where orthography may be related to meaning through phonological mediation (speech recoding). Tzeng, Hung, and Wang (1977) have presented evidence that disputes this assumption. They studied the role of phonemic (speech) recoding on the reading of isolated Chinese characters and of sentences printed in Chinese. The subjects were 20 Chinese students from Taiwan who were graduate students in the United States and who were fluent readers in Chinese. The results showed that phonemic recoding operated for the subjects in both the short-term retention task and the sentence-judgment task. These results indicate that even ideographic characters have phonological representation in the brain and that reading such characters does not by-pass this internal phonetic representation, as was formerly thought. Tzeng et al. (1977) conclude that the phonetic recoding of visually presented nonphonetic symbols such as Chinese characters "suggests that even if lexical readout may occur directly from visual input, speech recoding is still needed for the working memory stage. This view is reasonable if reading is regarded as one form of general linguistic ability" (p. 630). The concept raised here and earlier of working memory is another critical point for review.

Recent thinking in cognitive psychology and in reading has adopted from theories of human information processing the concept of the human mind as a central, limited-capacity processor (Norman & Bobrow, 1975). This concept of the mind as a limited-capacity processor equipped with limited-capacity working memory means limited time and attention are available for storing and processing the various types of information involved in reading. For the skilled reader, much of the processing (such as decoding) has become so automatic and unconscious that most of the reader's attention can be directed to the higher order processes of comprehension (LaBerge & Samuels, 1974). The less skilled reader, however, for whom many of the reading processes are not automatic and unconscious, must struggle with devoting limited time and attention capacity to word and sentence processing at various levels which interferes with higher level comprehension processes involved in text prediction and relation of text information to prior information.

The concept of limited capacity and time for processing information is particularly critical for deaf children. Whereas a hearing child from a typical middle class home is likely to approach beginning reading with well developed general language comprehension skills, the typical deaf child is likely to approach beginning reading with poorly developed general language comprehension skills resulting from experiential, cognitive, and linguistic deficits. These accumulated deficits apparently are not due to any lack of inherent ability in the deaf child (Quigley & Kretschmer, 1982), but result simply from an impoverished early background owing to lack of appropriate experiential and linguistic input. Since the concept of limited human capacity for information processing appears to be of primary importance in sentence processing, it will be considered with the latter topic.

A final study of significance in the area of word processing should be noted. R. Anderson and Freebody (1979) have presented an extensive discussion of the role of vocabulary knowledge in general language comprehension and particularly in reading. They state that measures of vocabulary knowledge are potent predictors of a variety of indices of linguistic ability and that the strong relationship between vocabulary and general intelligence is one of the most robust findings in the history of intelligence testing. A series of studies is presented to show correlations between vocabulary subtest scores and total test scores on a number of different IQ tests ranging from .71 to .98. Other studies are cited to show that an equally consistent finding is that word knowledge is strongly related to reading comprehension. The same is true for analyses of readability. Coleman (1971) is cited as showing that, while sentence complexity is a fairly important variable, "any measure of word complexity (number of letters, morphemes, or syllables; frequency of usage) will account for about 80% of the predicted variance" (p. 184) in readability. R. Anderson and Freebody (1979) conclude that word knowledge is an important (perhaps *the most* important) requisite for reading comprehension and that people who do not know the meanings of very many words are most probably poor readers.

Sentence Processing

In processing information at the sentence and intra-sentence (phrases, clauses) level, the key factor seems to be the ability to *integrate* information across linguistic units. As R. Anderson (1981) states,

> information from individual lexical items must be integrated with that from other lexical items according to syntactic rules to form semantic units corresponding to propositions, and propositions must be integrated with other propositions, both from within and across sentence boundaries, to form larger interrelated semantic structures. (p. 177)

Many theorists have suggested that working memory capacity plays a critical role in reading comprehension (Just & Carpenter, 1980; Kintsch & van Dijk, 1978) but that it is not simply a short-term memory capacity, which seems to work largely as a passive storage buffer. It seems instead to be an active working memory, which includes processing as well as storage functions and serves as the site for executing processes and for storing the products of these processes (Baddeley & Hitch, 1974; LaBerge & Samuels, 1974). As stated earlier, the processing and storage functions must compete for a shared limited capacity. If a task makes heavy processing demands on this limited capacity, storage of information must be reduced; conversely, if a task does not require heavy processing, storage of information can be increased. Daneman and Carpenter (1980) suggest that this trade-off between processing and storage in working memory is a possible source of individual differences in reading comprehension. The more skilled reader might be a more efficient processor of information and as a result have more capacity for storing and maintaining information. Working memory capacity and trade-offs between its storage and processing functions might also be a source of reading difficulty for deaf children.

Daneman and Carpenter (1980) devised a test with heavy processing and storage demands to measure the trade-off between the storage and processing functions of working memory. A group of college students read aloud a series of 60 unrelated sentences, 13 to 16 words in length. Each sentence ended in a different word and after having read sets of the sentences of two to six sentences in length, the subjects were asked to recall the final words of the sentences. Subjects also were given a reading comprehension test and a traditional word span test. Subjects' performances on the reading span test (the 60 unrelated sentences) were compared with performance on the other tests. The significant and high correlations were interpreted as showing that the reading span task was significantly related to working memory capacity. Similar results were found with a listening span test, thus showing the results were not unique to reading.

Analysis and interpretation of other findings showed that there were qualitative as well as quantitative differences between the more and the less skilled readers. Daneman and Carpenter (1980) suggest that less skilled readers may be doing fundamentally different things than skilled readers and their different processes also may be less efficient. They offer the chunking process as one example of how quantitative differences in capacity could result in qualitative differences in processing. The chunking process is seen as recoding concepts and relations into higher order units in reading (and in listening). The recoding of many concepts and relations into a single chunk has the economizing effect of reducing the load on working memory and increasing the functional working capacity for subsequent processing. The good reader has more functional working memory capacity available for chunking, and his or her chunks should be richer and more coherent than those of the less skilled reader.

In a study of the role of chunking in reading, Mason and Kendall (1979) found that separating the pausal units of complex sentences, or dividing complex sentences into several shorter sentences, resulted in better reading comprehension for less skilled readers. The same procedure did not affect the comprehension of skilled readers. This type of chunking of text into smaller units seemed to allow the less skilled readers to spend more of their time and working memory capacity on higher level integrative processing at text intervals by reducing the amount needed for storage of information. This finding indicates that encouraging less skilled readers to chunk text into phrasal units, thus attempting semantic integration more often, might significantly improve their reading comprehension.

The Daneman and Carpenter (1980) research was reported here in some detail as illustrative of a considerable number of studies (Perfetti & Lesgold, 1977, reviewed many of these) that demonstrate differences among individuals in the functional capacities of working memories for handling linguistic information (Baddeley, 1979; Jarvella, 1971, 1979; Levy, 1977; Sachs, 1974). These studies provide evidence that working memory is sensitive to linguistic structure as well as to the demands of linguistic processing. Clause and sentence boundaries seem to influence the chunking of information in working memory, and Jarvella (1971, 1979) and others have shown that verbatim memory for recently processed text declines sharply following a sentence boundary. The storage and processing functions of working memory capacity are probably important in the processing of particular syntactic constructions, such as embedded or interrupted constituents, which require integration of information from the beginning and the end of a sentence. An example is found in sentences with medial relative clauses (e.g., "The man who was sick went to the doctor").

The integrating of information into chunks and their temporary storage, which seem to be critical in sentence comprehension, seem also to require some form of speech recoding. The Kleiman study (1975) and others were cited earlier as demonstrating that speech recoding does not appear to be necessary for obtaining lexical access (access to word meanings) but that it is perhaps an important process in the comprehension of sentences and connected prose. Studies by Kleiman (1975), Levy (1977), and Baddeley (1979) have supported the theory that speech recoding plays a role in the storage of sequential information necessary for the comprehension of connected discourse. Thus, working memory (with its limited capacity for storage and processing of linguistic information) and speech recoding (as the form in which temporary storage of linguistic information is accomplished by readers who can hear) seem to be critical elements in integrating linguistic information in sentences and connected prose.

Discourse Analysis

As Freedle and Fine (1982) have stated, discourse theory is in its infancy. Many of the problems studied in this area of applied psycholinguistics (Rosenberg, 1982) are at the first stage of science—the categorization stage. Freedle and Fine introduce the reader to the variety of topics that are being studied under the rubric of discourse theory, but the chief concern here is with the general domain of prose composition and comprehension.

Early research on language development as reviewed by McCarthy (1954) dealt largely with straightforward descriptions of such matters as the first words a child uses, the growth of vocabulary, and descriptions of developing sentence structure. With the publication of Chomsky's *Syntactic Structures* (1957), there was a pronounced shift to characterizing and accounting for general aspects of the form and content of utterances (Rosenberg, 1982). The units of interest became the sentence and intra-sentence components. During the past decade there has been a sharp increase in research on the pragmatic aspects of utterances, that is, their *use* in communication (Rosenberg, 1982). The emphasis on pragmatics, on language in action, has focused attention on larger units of text than words and sentences.

Utterances (or texts) are not objects to be viewed in isolation but can be regarded as the results of speakers performing *speech actions* for the purpose of influencing a hearer. Writing can be regarded as a particular form of speech action in which a writer attempts to influence a reader. Reading is then seen as an active process in which a reader uses his or her linguistic skills, prior knowledge, and higher order reasoning processes to *construct* meaning from a text. Reading, in this light, is seen as a much more complex and more broadly based process than simply extracting information through decoding of print. Study of reading, then, includes not only decoding of words and sentences, but also other, larger aspects of text structure (discourse analysis) as well as the reader and the context.

The driving force in the meaning to be constructed from a text by a reader is the purpose of the writer. With a purpose (e.g., to inform, to entertain) in mind, the writer, depending on his or her level of skill, uses various devices (outlines, schema) to construct the general form of the text and proceeds to finer and finer units—including words and sentences—to complete the final form of the communication. The reader, in turn, uses the text, decoding skills, linguistic skills, and prior knowledge to construct meaning from the text. Discourse analysis, in recent years, has directed attention to the larger units of text organization, including the different genres (forms), such as stories, plays, fables, and expository texts, that the author may select to accomplish his or her purpose. Only narratives will be discussed in this chapter to illustrate discourse analysis. Other genres, and the many other aspects of discourse analysis besides genres, are presented in Freedle and Fine (1982) and Spiro, B. Bruce, and Brewer (1980). An interesting and brief history of linguistically oriented discourse analysis has been written by Morgan and Sellner (1980), who also present an excellent analysis of the theoretical issues and the research literature.

Brewer (1980) has proposed a classification of written discourse types in terms of the type of schema that underlies the discourse and in terms of the intended force of the discourse. Three basic types of schema are proposed—description, narration, and exposition; four basic discourse forces—to inform, to entertain, to persuade, and to allow for a literary-esthetic form. *Descriptive discourse* is discourse that attempts to embody in linguistic form a stationary perceptual scheme. Since vision is the most frequently involved sense, Brewer considers the underlying representation to be some form of visual-spatial schema. *Narrative discourse* attempts to portray in linguistic form a series of events that occur in time. The underlying representation is considered to be organized either in terms of plan schemata (Brewer & Lichtenstein, 1980), or in terms of causal event schemata. *Expository discourse* attempts to represent in linguistic form a series of logical arguments. The underlying organization is considered to reflect the schemata for logical processes such as induction, classification, and comparison.

R. Anderson (1981) clarifies the differences in these various underlying schemata by translating each type of discourse into another modality. He states that typical descriptive passages can be represented by a picture; typical narratives can be represented by a motion picture; and typical expository passages can be represented by some form of logical notation. One form of discourse analysis (and the only type considered here) is concerned with analyzing the surface structures and underlying schemata of texts and how they are used, consciously or unconsciously, by the reader in constructing meaning from test.

Blom, Waite, and Zimet (1970) analyzed children's primers for the period 1950–1960 and reported that more than half of the items in them were bland narratives of children carrying out everyday activities. In contrast, Dunn (1921) reported for the 1910–1920 period that more than half of the selections in children's primers consisted of poetry. Thus, there has been a major shift in the types of genres used in such primers over the past half century.

Mandler and N. Johnson (1977) conducted an influential study of the underlying structure of simple stories. They claimed that this type of underlying structure is used to form schemata that aid in reading comprehension. Their approach is analogous to transformational grammar theory in explaining syntax. They found that analysis of stories could be performed similarly to syntactic analysis, with a "deep structure" that represented the true or fixed order of story events in time and a surface

Table 3. Categories Included in a Simple Story

Setting	Introduction of the protagonist; can contain information about physical, social, or temporal context in which the remainder of the story occurs.
Initiating Event	An action, an internal event, or a natural occurrence which serves to *initiate* or to cause a response in the protagonist.
Internal Response	An emotion, cognition, or goal of the protagonist.
Attempt	An overt action to obtain the protagonist's goal.
Consequence	An event, action, or endstate which marks the attainment or non-attainment of the protagonist's goal.
Reaction	An emotion, cognition, action or endstate expressing the protagonist's feelings about his [or her] goal attainment or relating the broader consequential realm of the protagonist's goal attainment.

Example of a Well-formed Story

Setting	1. Once there was a big gray fish named Albert. 2. He lived in a big icy pond near the edge of a forest.
Initiating Event	3. One day, Albert was swimming around the pond. 4. Then he spotted a big juicy worm on top of the water.
Internal Response	5. Albert knew how delicious worms tasted. 6. He wanted to eat that one for his dinner.
Attempt	7. So he swam very close to the worm. 8. Then he bit into him.
Consequence	9. Suddenly, Albert was pulled through the water into a boat. 10. He had been caught by a fisherman.
Reaction	11. Albert felt sad. 12. He wished he had been more careful.

From Stein, N. (1978). *How children understand stories. A developmental analysis* (Tech. Rep. No. 69). Urbana, IL: University of Illinois, Center for the Study of Reading. (ERIC Document Reproduction Service No. ED 153 205) Reprinted with permission.

structure which, for various purposes of the writer, might differ from the order of events recounted in the deep structure. The deep structure or underlying schema can be described as linked to the surface structure of the text by means of a series of transformations; thus, the whole process of analysis has been termed "story grammars." The purpose of story grammar analysis is to develop a grammar that will relate the surface structure of stories to the underlying structures on which schemata are based. It is assumed that the knowledge and use of underlying schemata influence what readers will comprehend and remember from connected discourse. Story grammar theories attempt to give an account of why some arrangements of sentences are coherent stories whereas other arrangements of sentences are not. All of these theories, while differing in detail, postulate a set of categories that must be included in a story and provide rules that specify relations among categories.

An example of the story grammar proposed by Stein (1978) is provided in Table 3. This story grammar has been used by various researchers to determine how children develop an understanding of various aspects of stories (Applebee, 1978; Hansche & Gordon, 1983; Mandler & N. Johnson, 1977;

Stein, 1978). Stein and Trabasso (1981) provide a detailed review of work in this area. Briefly, the studies have yielded the following conclusions:

1. Children as young as six years old make few errors in recalling the correct temporal order of stories that correspond to the expected sequence (story grammar) (Stein, 1978).

2. When stories deviated from the expected story structure, recall corresponds to the order of the story grammar rather than to the order of presentation (Stein, 1978).

3. The following categories from the story grammar are recalled better than others: setting statements that introduced the protagonist, initiating events, and consequences (Stein & Glenn, 1979).

4. The following developmental trend for the appearance of the six categories of the story grammar in the children's own writing has been found: first graders included only setting, initiating event, and consequence; fourth graders added the response category; and for eighth and tenth graders recall protocols included all six categories (Hansche & Gordon, 1983).

5. Poor readers differ from good readers at some levels of development. For example, poor first grade readers consistently omitted the consequence element from their own written stories (Hansche & Gordon, 1983).

Story grammars have come under attack in recent years (Black & Bower, 1980; Brewer & Lichtenstein, 1980). Brewer and Lichtenstein (1980), for example, have argued that story grammars are not descriptively adequate because the rules of these grammars accept many nonstories as stories. Brewer and Lichtenstein (1980) provide support for a theory of story schema of which story grammars are only a subset concerned with goal directed narratives.

Previous theories of story structure (story-grammar approach) used measures of comprehension or memory for validation. However, Brewer and Lichtenstein have argued from their research that stories are not necessarily designed for ease of comprehension or recall (*Tristram Shandy* is a good example of this). They hypothesized and confirmed that there are three kinds of knowledge about stories that readers could have. *Structured knowledge* is information about discourse structure, such as contained in story grammars. In addition to this, the reader may have *direct affect knowledge*, which is knowledge about the types of affective responses that stories produce. *Metacognitive knowledge* is intellectual knowledge of the types of situations that could lead to particular affective states. Brewer and Lichtenstein (1980) conclude that a theory of stories must include a component that relates the organization of the discourse structure to the affective processes of readers.

Leaving aside differences in detail, all theories of text structure of various genres (stories, informative material, and so forth) attempt to provide an account of the underlying representation of events in the genre and a series of rules linking the underlying representation to the sequence of events in the surface structure of the text. This is seen as another form of prior knowledge that readers bring to the reading process and that aids their comprehension, appreciation, and enjoyment of a text. Readers are likely to recall much more information from text if they identify and use the author's structure while reading the text than if they use a different organizational scheme or no scheme at all. It is also likely that providing readers with information about the conceptual organization or superordinate structure of text can aid recall. Authors often supply such help by providing outlines of texts and summaries and abstracts. This is particularly true for informative text, which is text constructed to add to the reader's information base and the type used in content-area textbooks.

Knowledge of the underlying structure of various genres is probably inductively and continuously developed. Highly skilled readers probably have such knowledge to a much higher degree than less skilled readers. But even young children seem to reach the beginning-reading stage with at least the intuitive understanding that some stories are designed to inform and some to entertain. That this is a developing skill is obvious in that children can appreciate *Gulliver's Travels* as a humorous story long before appreciating its satiric force. Similarly, many books, such as *Alice in Wonderland* and *Tristram Shandy*, and much poetry can be read and reread at deepening levels of enjoyment, appreciation, and understanding.

Figurative Language

Although very young children seem to produce many metaphorical utterances (Bloom, 1973; Carlson & Anisfield, 1969), much of the experimental literature suggests that metaphorical ability is acquired late in development, after the acquisition of basic language skills (Inhelder & Piaget, 1958; Kogan, 1975). Recent research has apparently resolved this contradiction by suggesting that prior research methodology obscured much of what children actually know about figurative language—metaphor, simile, and idiom (Gentner, 1977, 1978; Reynolds & Ortony, 1980; Winner, Engel, & Gardner, 1980). The literature on the development of metaphorical understanding has been extensively reviewed by Reynolds and Ortony (1980). The report of a research conference edited by Ortony (1979) also provides exhaustive treatment of the topic. The treatment in this chapter is brief and general.

Emphasis is given here to figurative language chiefly for two reasons. First, once the beginning reader progresses beyond simple literal texts, inferencing ability and the ability to comprehend and use the various forms of figurative language assume major importance in the reading process. An analysis of reading series by Houghton-Mifflin, Ginn, and Scott, Foresman revealed an abundance of figurative uses of language (especially metaphors and similes) from books at the very beginning levels, and many of the uses were not easy to understand (Dixon, Pearson, & Ortony, 1980). Second, a series of studies will be cited in the chapter dealing with the reading abilities of deaf children to show the many problems of comprehension that deaf children have with various forms of figurative language in standard English texts.

For the student of English as a second language and for severely to profoundly hearing-impaired English-language learners, the difficulty of the language learning task is greatly increased by the profuse use of figurative language in standard English. Figurative language occurs at all levels of usage: at the informal level (e.g., conversational language); the semi-formal level (e.g., classroom language); and at the more formal level (e.g., textbook, legal, and religious language). The ability to comprehend and produce the various forms of figurative language is essential to communication in English (Giorcelli, 1982).

Although the essence of figurative language is its nonliteralness, figurative expression takes a variety of forms: metaphor, simile, and idiom are the most common. Other literary devices or non-literal forms include irony, oxymoron, proverbs, litotes, epithets, neologisms, allegory, catachresis, allusions, and zeugmas (Giorcelli, 1982). The most commonly recognized forms (metaphor, simile, and idiom) are popularly enough known not to need definition and are the only forms discussed here.

In attempting to comprehend figurative expressions, Petrie (1979) suggests that the reader operates within a four-stage paradigm wherein he or she (1) recognizes the analogy or literacy puzzles presented by the figurative expression, (2) compares the new, unknown material to old, known material, (3) interacts with the new material to create nonlinguistic similarities, and (4) corrects the initial interpretation and repeats the whole process to arrive at a correct interpretation of the figurative expression. This model assumes the reader's ability to employ his or her existing knowledge schemata, cognitive processing abilities, and current linguistic and nonlinguistic competencies to derive meaning from a figurative expression.

Research on the comprehension and explication of figurative language by hearing individuals has revealed that these abilities develop in an incremental manner. Children are able to recognize correct paraphrases of figurative language first (Pollio & Pollio, 1979), are then able to paraphrase figurative language independently (Cometa & Eson, 1978), and are subsequently capable of explicating their paraphrases (Billow, 1975). Arlin (1977) and Billow (1975) have shown that different metaphors are understood at different ages, with representational metaphors (e.g., "He is a rock") comprehended first; similarity metaphors (e.g., "Night was a blanket") next; and proportional metaphors (e.g., "Time was a thief, robbing her of life") comprehended last (Giorcelli, 1982). The frequency of exposure to metaphor has also been shown to affect comprehension at all ages. The common (or "frozen") metaphor (e.g., "time flies"), which enjoys general usage, is easier for children to understand than the less common (or "novel") metaphor (e.g., "a curtain of hate") (Cometa & Eson, 1978; Pollio & Pollio, 1979). Greater detail on figurative language and the acquisition of its various forms can be found in the literature (Ortony, Schallert, Reynolds, & Antos, 1978; Ortony, 1979; Reynolds & Ortony, 1980).

This brief presentation on figurative language, and the common experience of any native user of English, reveals the ubiquitous nature of figurative expressions in English. The difficulty of this form of language for nonnative learners of English is also readily apparent. In recent years, attention has been directed to the problems of deaf children in understanding and using the figurative language of English, and several studies of the matter will be presented and discussed in Chapter 3.

READER VARIABLES

The range of variables in the individual reader that could affect the reading process runs the gamut from genetic to social. This is not surprising since, to quote Huey (1910), "To completely analyze what we do when we read would almost be the acme of a psychologist's achievements, for it would be to describe very many of the most intricate workings of the human mind" (p. 6). Obviously, this range of endeavor is beyond the scope of the present chapter. This chapter accepts the modern concept of reading as a much broader human endeavor than converting a printed code to meaning, either directly or through phonemic mediation. Readers use prior knowledge, inferencing, and figurative-language processing, cognitive and linguistic abilities, and other skills as well as some form of decoding to construct meaning from a text. It should be borne in mind, however, that one can reasonably argue that of all of these skills and abilities only the decoding of print is unique to reading. All of the others are important in general language comprehension and other mental tasks in addition to being used in reading.

With this caveat, three reader variables will be discussed as important to the reading process and reading theory in general and to the reading of deaf children in particular. These are schemata, inferencing, and metacognitive strategies.

Schemata

It has been accepted that the recently developed interactive theories of reading (Rumelhart, 1977) offer at present the most adequate explanations of the existing empirical data on reading. These theories can account for data that support both bottom-up processes (such as decoding) and top-down processes (such as inferencing and prediction) and can explain how interaction of bottom-up and top-down processing produces skilled reading. With the aid of the concepts of automaticity of basic skills (LaBerge & Samuels, 1974; Stanovich & West, 1979), working memory as a storer and processor of information (Daneman & Carpenter, 1980; Perfetti & Lesgold,

1977), and of the human mind as a limited information processor with limited selectional attention capacity (Norman & Bobrow, 1975), interaction theories can adequately explain how reading can develop into a fast and efficient process in the skilled practitioner with conscious attention being directed to constructing meaning from a text while many of the important basic level skills, such as decoding, and higher order skills, such as inferencing, proceed automatically, without conscious effort or attention. These theories can also show how important basic processes, such as decoding and word processing, which are automatic and unconscious in the skilled reader, require conscious attention in the developing reader and in the low ability reader, which reduces the amount of attention that can be devoted to higher order processes; and thus reading problems can be produced.

Schema theory is a recently developed form of interaction theory and is accepted here as the most promising form at present. So, one reader variable of importance to reading is the schema and how it serves as an organizing concept in cognition and in reading. It should be noted again that, as is true for most mental abilities, schemata are not unique to reading. They have had a substantial history of development in cognition and have been commonly applied to reading theory only in the last decade. A detailed explanation of schemata, and their historical development in cognition, can be found in Rumelhart's review (1980). Rumelhart (1980) traces the term schema from Kant (1787/1963) in philosophy to Head (1920) in neurology to its early use in psychology by Bartlett (1932). For Rumelhart and predecessors, schemata are the building blocks of cognition or knowledge. As has been stated repeatedly in this chapter, recent research has led to the conclusion that reading is a constructive process that involves interaction of knowledge-based and text-based processes. A text provides input and the reader constructs the intended meaning of the text by interpreting the input in terms of his or her own knowledge about the subject of the text.

As Adams and B. Bruce (1980) put it, "Without prior knowledge, a complex object, such as a text, is not just difficult to interpret; strictly speaking, it is meaningless." In this view of reading, a central role is played by the preexisting knowledge the reader (or listener) brings to the task of comprehending. As a consequence of this view, much theoretical work and empirical research has been devoted to the context and organization of knowledge and much of this research is applicable to the reading process.

According to Rumelhart (1980), schema theories view all knowledge as being packaged into units. These units are the schemata, and they contain not only knowledge itself but also information about how the knowledge is to be used. Schemata, then, are structures for representing in memory the generic concepts of knowledge and knowledge use. And schemata can be embedded within schemata at various levels; for example, the schema for face would have subschemata for *eyes, nose,* and *mouth,* which in turn would have subschemata for their various parts such as *pupil, iris, eyebrow.*

The concept of schemata provides a structure for organizing meaningful concepts in memory and is an obvious aid to recall of information.

The influence of background experience (schemata) on reading can be seen in a study by R. Anderson, Reynolds, Schallert, and Goetz (1976). These authors compared the interpretations of ambiguous passages by a group of physical education majors and a group of music majors. One of these passages was the following:

> Every Saturday night, four good friends get together. When Jerry, Mike, and Pat arrived, Karen was sitting in her living room writing some notes. She quickly gathered the cards and stood up to greet her friends at the door. They followed her into the living room but as usual they couldn't agree on exactly what to play. Jerry eventually took a stand and set things up. Finally, they began to play. Karen's recorder filled the room with soft and pleasant music. Early in the evening, Mike noticed Pat's hand and the many diamonds. As the night progressed the tempo of play increased. Finally, a lull in the activities occurred. Taking advantage of this, Jerry pondered the arrangement in front of him. Mike interrupted Jerry's reverie and said, "Let's hear the score." They listened carefully and commented on their performance. When the comments were all heard, exhausted but happy, Karen's friends went home.

The interpretation of the passage was strongly related to the subject's background (i.e., the music majors gave a music interpretation of the passage as a rehearsal of a woodwind ensemble, while the physical education majors [and most other people] interpreted the passage as a story about an evening during which four friends played cards).

Rumelhart (1980), Rumelhart and Norman (1978), and Spiro (1977) describe how schemata function in remembering and learning and how new schemata are developed. A number of theorists have tried to characterize how schemata are acquired. K. Nelson (1974, 1977) presented a theory that adopted Piaget's (1964/1967) two equilibration processes of *assimilation* and *accommodation*. Incoming information is either shaped to fit existing schemata (assimilation) or existing schemata are changed to adapt to novel information (accommodation). Similarly, Rumelhart and Norman (1978) proposed three means of change within the context of schema theory: *accretion* (which is similar to assimilation); *tuning* (which is similar to accommodation); and *restructuring*. According to Rumelhart (1980), restructuring provides for the creation of new schemata through "patterned generation" or "schema induction." Patterned generation is the formation of a new schema based on the structure of an old schema. The second mechanism posits that an individual can inductively extract a pattern from previously incomprehensible stimuli, but the process is not yet well understood. The schema concept will be discussed a little further in the final summarizing and synthesizing section of the chapter where it is embodied in an interactive reading theory.

Inference

As stated at several points in this chapter, inferencing is ubiquitous in reading comprehension. The meanings of words, sentences, paragraphs, or entire passages are affected by the contexts in which they occur and by the prior knowledge of the reader about the material being read. The text input at any given instant is being interpreted by the reader in terms of prior knowledge, the schemata in his or her repertoire that have been activated by the subject of the text, by what has just been read, and by what the reader predicts is ahead in the text. Inferencing is vital to reading comprehension beyond the level of very literal texts, which means just about all material beyond a third grade level and probably much that is below that level.

R. Anderson (1981) discusses a new functional, four-level classification of inferences. (A similar, although slightly different, classification system is discussed by K. Wilson (1981) in guidelines produced for captioned television for hearing-impaired individuals.) The first level is lexically based and is a level in which inferences follow from the meanings of words. At this level, lexical inferences depend very much on an individual's knowledge of language, and they are relatively independent of the particular context in which the lexical items occur. At the second level, inferences are driven by the need to connect textual propositions. At this level of text connectedness, inference is involved when readers use their knowledge of the world, as well as the information contained in the text, to infer the semantic and logical connections between otherwise unconnected propositions (or sentences). The third level of inferencing is involved when the schemata, or knowledge structures, of the reader that have been activated by the text have unfilled slots (missing or unsupplied information, which makes the schemata incomplete and tentative). The fourth level of inferencing is seen as driven by the constant and repeated interaction of text and schemata (knowledge structures) to select and refine schemata to provide an interpretive framework for the text. These inferencing processes operate for the skilled reader, as do the lower order skills of decoding, at an automatic and probably unconscious level. As a result, inferencing becomes such an integral part of skilled reading that skilled readers often cannot distinguish, at recall, between what they read from a page and what they added by the use of inference (Brewer, 1975; Spiro, 1977).

Following Piaget's assertions that children's logic prior to the stage of formal operations is structurally adequate to deal with objects and their properties, most researchers had accepted that young children were incapable of drawing inferences from texts. More recent research on children's reasoning abilities, however, has demonstrated that young children can and do engage in inferential processing (Omanson, Warren, & Trabasso, 1978; Stein & Glenn, 1979). Omanson et al. (1978) have also shown that the amount of inferencing increases with age. It has also been demonstrated that no particular form of inferencing causes any special problems. What seems to develop with age and experience is the ability of the child to apply inferencing to an increasingly larger domain of tasks and contexts. This is likely due, at least in part, to an increasing store of background knowledge in a greater number of areas on the part of the child.

Paris and Lindauer (1976) noted that some of the perceived deficits in children's inferential abilities may reflect a child's inappropriate strategy utilization rather than inability to make inferences. They had third and fifth grade students recall sentences with or without an explicit instrument (e.g., "The truckdriver stirred the coffee in his cup [with a spoon]"). The younger children recalled fewer of the sentences that did not supply an explicit instrument. However, if these same children acted out the sentences, they recalled both types of sentences equally well. Thus, it may be that young children are capable of making inferences but do not do so spontaneously unless forced to do so by task demands. These findings have obvious and important implications for reading development and instruction. Insufficient prior knowledge keeps emerging from recent research as a powerful factor in reading comprehension. It is, of course, probably as important a factor in informed listening.

Guszak's observational studies (1967) of classroom questions indicated that only about 20% of teachers' questions require inferential reasoning. Guszak also found that students typically perform more poorly on inferential than on literal test items. Hansen and Pearson (1980) found that implicit attempts to improve inferential question answering behavior resulted in positive gains with no loss in literal comprehension. Pearson, Hansen, and Gordon (1979) attempted to improve inferential behavior by directly attempting to increase children's knowledge of a topic before the children read about it. Their results did not support the expectations for improved reading comprehension, whereas a study by Hayes and Tierney (1980) showed positive effects for short-term prereading knowledge instruction for advanced secondary students on both literal and inferential questions.

These studies offer some promise that short-term knowledge acquisition efforts might provide an improved knowledge base for text comprehension, especially when inferencing is involved. The results are mixed, however; and it is possible that short-term fix-up strategies (or the preteaching of concepts and vocabulary) might have only limited effects on reading comprehension. It is possible that a broad knowledge base to assist reading comprehension must be assimilated gradually over a considerable period of time and cannot be acquired suddenly and immediately prior to reading. This has important implications for reading instruction with deaf children. Because of lack of early experiences and cognitive and linguistic skills, deaf children are likely in many cases to reach beginning reading with very limited background knowledge on a variety of common subjects.

Metacognitive Abilities

Metacognitive skills in the reading process are largely consciously applied planning, monitoring, self-questioning, and summarizing skills used in critical reading and studying. Extensive information on research in metacognition can be found in Brown (1980) and Collins, Brown, Morgan, and Brewer (1977). Brown (1980) cites Vygotsky (1962) as describing two phases in the development of knowledge: first, its automatic unconscious acquisition, and second, gradually increasing conscious control over that knowledge. Brown considers this distinction between initial unconscious acquisition and later conscious control of knowledge to define essentially the separation between cognitive and metacognitive aspects of performance. "Metacognition refers to the deliberate conscious control of one's own cognitive actions" (Brown, 1980, p. 453).

Of the various forms of metacognition that have been studied, only those related to the self-regulatory mechanisms used by active readers are discussed here. These include (1) evaluating and planning the purposes of reading; (2) identifying the important aspects of a text; (3) directing attention to major content rather than unimportant details; (4) monitoring ongoing activities to determine whether comprehension is occurring; (5) engaging in summarizing and self-questioning to determine whether reading goals are being achieved; and (6) taking corrective actions when failures in comprehension are detected (Brown, 1980, p. 456).

Metacognitive skills of this type assume increasing importance in the later grades of school (fourth grade and beyond), where the emphasis in reading shifts from learning to read to reading to learn. This can be a difficult transition for younger and poorer readers, who have been shown in many studies to have little awareness that they must attempt to make sense of text; they focus on reading as a decoding process rather than as a comprehension activity. This trait has been found in children as late as sixth and seventh grades. One solution for this might be to stress from the very beginning of the reading process that the purpose is to read to learn rather than simply to learn to read and to develop early some of the metacognitive abilities associated with highly skilled reading. Sullivan (1978) has reported that poor readers even at the high school level lack the metacognitive awareness that text should be interpreted in relation to what the individual already knows about the subject of the text.

With the shift from learning to read to reading to learn there is also a shift from the concept of reading to the concept of studying, of which reading of text is an essential part. And at the center of effective studying is the ability to adequately summarize the material that has been read. Research has identified six basic rules that are essential to effective and efficient summarization and which are similar to the macrorules proposed by Kintsch and van Dijk (1978) as basic to comprehending and remembering prose. Two of the rules involve the *deletion* of unnecessary material—that is, unimportant or redundant information. A third rule involves the *substitution of a superordinate term* (such as furniture) for a list of items (such as table, chair, lamp, and so forth). This essentially involves activation of a higher order schema, which will incorporate the individual items as related units. A fourth effective summarization technique involves the *substitution of a superordinate action* for a list of subcomponents of that action. The other two rules involve the highest levels of metacognitive skills and concern providing a summary of the main constituent unit of a text, the paragraph. One rule is the *selection of a topic sentence*, if any, as the author's summary of the paragraph. The final rule is the *invention of a topic sentence*, if one is not supplied.

Brown and Day (1980) conducted an extensive study of the application of these rules of summarization by subjects who ranged from the fifth grade level to the college level, including graduate students who were instructors in rhetoric. Reading status ranged from a remedial level to a highly skilled level. The investigators found that even the fifth graders were able to use the two deletion rules with about 90% accuracy; they understood that the basic rule in summarizing was to eliminate unnecessary material. Developmental differences were apparent on the more complex rules, however. Students became increasingly skilled with age in applying the topic sentence rule, with college students performing extremely well. The most difficult rule, inventing a topic sentence, was rarely used by the fifth graders, used on only one third of appropriate occasions by tenth graders, and only on half of the appropriate occasions even by the college students.

The highly skilled readers (mostly college rhetoric instructors) were excellent at using the deletion and superordinate rules. The most noticeable developmental differences were on the most difficult rule, inventing a topic sentence, which the experts applied on 85% of appropriate occasions as compared to 49% for the college students. These highly skilled readers also used a paragraph combining strategy which was rarely used by any other of the subjects in the study. The general strategy of the expert readers was to select or invent a topic sentence first and then to write their summaries around the topic sentences. They also made routine use of the paragraph-combining strategy.

A final point on this matter of metacognitive skills in reading is that some research studies have shown that they can be taught (Brown, Campione, & Day, 1981; Day, 1980). Also, Schallert and Kleiman (1979) have presented a paper discussing some reasons why some teachers are easier to understand than textbooks. They listed four advantages of these teachers over textbooks. First, the teachers tailor the message to the child's understanding; second, they continually focus the student's attention on the main points; third, they force the student to monitor comprehension by asking them questions that probe their degree of understanding; and, fourth, they help the students to activate schemata; i.e., they help the students to see how the new information can be related to knowledge the students already have.

This last point is especially significant. The importance of background knowledge in comprehending text has been stressed throughout this chapter and the teacher can make the student aware of (1) the contribution of background knowledge to reading comprehension and (2) the importance of considering reading as an active process. The studies cited indicate that much can be accomplished in the area of metacognitive skills, even with less skilled and problem readers. The enlargement of background knowledge itself is a more difficult problem. As discussed previously, the task of enriching the reader's store of background information is a slow process and takes much time to accomplish. One way of alleviating the problem, especially for the beginning reader, would be to select texts that match as closely as possible the reader's store of knowledge on a topic and his or her cognitive and linguistic skills.

SOCIOECONOMIC AND CULTURAL VARIABLES

Sociocultural influences have been shown repeatedly to be a major factor in learning to read (Cummins, 1979; Labov, 1970; Troike, 1978). In the United States, the teachers who do the teaching and the materials used for teaching often reflect the values and background of the white middle class. This can result in a mismatch between the home backgrounds of children who do not belong to this social class and the materials and background they will encounter in school. Much effort has been devoted to resolving this problem in the past two decades through diversifying the types of teachers in schools, improving teachers' preparation in relation to the problem, and modifying teaching materials, including basal reading series. The problem, however, is still far from resolved. It is a matter of major interest here because few deaf children approach the reading process with the kind and extent of infant and early childhood experiences, cognitive competencies, and linguistic abilities that the typical hearing child has. As noted in Chapter 3, the young deaf child can be viewed as a member of a minority culture, and the background he or she brings to the beginning reading process will depend on the extent and type of experiential and communicative interaction that took place between child and parents in the preschool years.

R. Anderson (1981) noted two distinct themes in research on the question of low-income minority children's failure in school as related to the children's home backgrounds or to community-based differences in discourse style. One line of research emphasizes what R. Anderson terms the pathological factors of the child's family structure, of early socialization patterns, and of the linguistic environment to account for failure in school (Hess & Shipman, 1965). The other line of research emphasizes that the low-income or language minority child's home background is not deficient but merely different from the average middle class home, and it is this difference that creates cultural and linguistic problems in school (Baratz & Baratz, 1970; Labov, 1970).

Both viewpoints can be found in research with deaf children; however, the analogy between deaf children and children in socioeconomic and cultural minorities groups is imperfect. Deaf children come from homes with a variety of socioeconomic and cultural environments. It is their hearing impairment that makes the educational results resemble those of cultural and socioeconomic minority group children. Deafness restricts, or at least reshapes, the physical and communicative interaction between parents and child, which apparently is essential for development of cognitive and linguistic skills that are important for learning to read, although this interaction might be heavily dependent on the type and quality of communication (ASL, manually coded English, or oral English) used by parent and child.

Within one or the other of these two lines of research, numerous studies of mismatches between children's backgrounds and the demands and requirements of schools have been conducted. Hall and Tirre (1979) and Labov (1972), among many, have demonstrated effects of mismatches between the language and dialect of the teacher and the student. B. Bruce and Rubin (1984), B. Bruce, Rubin, and Starr (1981), and others have demonstrated mismatches between the backgrounds of socioeconomic and cultural minority children and curricula, tests, and textbooks. Mismatches in background and schema knowledge have been revealed by Adams and B. Bruce (1980) and LeVine (1970).

One other interesting area of reading research with children from socioeconomic and cultural minorities that has important implications for research on the reading abilities of deaf children is the study of children from such groups who have become skilled readers. R. Anderson (1981) reported that common factors found in studies of schools that succeeded with poor minority children were principals who were knowledgeable about reading and who had high expectations for what their faculties and students could accomplish (e.g., Venezky & Winfield, 1979; Weber, 1976).

Durkin (1966) conducted an extensive study of children who could read prior to attending school. Fewer than 2% of these early readers were black, but home interview data suggested that high socioeconomic level was not responsible for all the successes among the black children. In one case that was cited, the socioeconomic level was low and the home was meagerly furnished, but there was a highly literate environment with an abundant supply of library books. All seven of the children, including a preschool child, were good readers. This appeared to result from the influence and tutelage of the mother, who was an avid reader, and the oldest child, who read daily to the younger children. Thus, socioeconomic level seems to be more a related than a causative factor in reading development. The factors of literate and involved parents, plenty of reading materials, and parental expectations, encouragement, and assistance for the child to read are likely to be more contributing than socioeconomic level per se. Socioeconomic level relates so highly to reading level simply because the factors that promote good reading skills are more likely to be present in homes of people of high socioeconomic level. As Durkin's data show, however, these factors and reading success need not be mutually exclusive. Studies of successful deaf readers, similar to Durkin's study, would be of significant value.

SUMMARY

Although this chapter has covered only some of the factors encompassed by modern conceptions and theories of reading (e.g., see Spiro et al., 1980), it might seem to have included many factors that have not traditionally been considered part of the reading process. This is perhaps a matter of how reading is defined. As stated throughout the chapter, many of the factors now included as part of reading function prominently in other mental processes, most particularly in general language comprehension. It is probably defensible, therefore, for some purposes, to define reading as involving only those factors that are unique to print, which would be largely decoding skills. The argument would be that all other factors involved in reading are developed primarily for functions other than reading and are used only secondarily for that process.

It is most commonly accepted now, however, that reading is part of the general language comprehension process and cannot practically be considered apart from it. Thus, early childhood learning experiences, early schema development, cognitive and linguistic development, inferencing and figurative-language abilities, prior knowledge of content, decoding skills, and metacognitive skills are all seen as essential to the development of skilled reading, and all of these factors, in turn, are influenced by the socioeconomic and cultural background of the reader. The practical aspect of considering all of these factors is that, with the exception of the early socioeconomic and cultural environment (a highly significant exception), all of them can be developed and improved by instruction.

An Interactive Schema Theory of Reading

This quotation from Brown (1980) illustrates the condition of skilled reading.

> Consider skilled readers, who can be characterized as operating with lazy processors. All their top-down and bottom-up skills are so fluent that they can proceed merrily on automatic pilot, until a *triggering event* alerts them to a comprehension failure. While the process is flowing smoothly, their construction of meaning is very rapid, but when a comprehension failure is detected, they must slow down and allot extra processing time to the problem area. They must employ debugging devices and strategies, that take time and effort. The difference in time and effort between the normal *automatic pilot* state and the laborious activity in the *debugging state* is the difference between the subconscious and conscious levels. (p. 445)

The differences between highly skilled readers of this type and less skilled and problem readers are perhaps that top-down and bottom-up processes are not always as fluent and automatic for the latter groups. Such readers encounter more comprehension failures and consequently spend more time in the debugging state than in the automatic pilot state.

Comprehension failures, for any type of reader, can occur at any level of the reading process: word recognition and processing, syntactic processing, figurative language processing, inferencing, incorrect schema activation, no schema activation. Highly skilled readers will only rarely encounter comprehension failures. Perhaps they will encounter an unknown word that cannot be interpreted from context and will need to resort to a dictionary. Perhaps they will encounter unfamiliar subject matter and highly complex syntax, such as in legal documents, and must read very slowly, with frequent recourse to dictionaries, other reference works, or experts on the subject matter. But all of these are relatively minor failures of the knowledge base and are relatively easily remedied.

For less skilled and for problem readers, more serious deficiencies may be present in the knowledge base. This can create problems in schema activation, with either no cognitive schema or an inappropriate schema being activated, as well as problems in inferencing. Supplying material from prior knowledge through inferencing to make explicit material that is implicit in the text requires that the needed information be available in the knowledge base. The smaller the base, the less likely this will be, and reading comprehension will suffer. Problems can arise in the other processes also. As stated many times in this chapter, problems at the word processing level have been found repeatedly to be the best single class of discriminators between good and poor readers. It has also been demonstrated that poorer and beginning readers rely too heavily on context and do not have the fluent bottom-up skills that skilled readers have. Finally, on this topic, skilled readers have been shown to fixate almost every content word when they read and to be capable of detailed phonic and graphemic analysis when required.

It is apparent, from the research discussed in this chapter, that all of the levels of information processing presented are important to reading and that problems with any of them will lead to reading difficulties. As noted by Brown (1980), most of the processes become automatic and fluent in the skilled reader. LaBerge and Samuels (1974) and Stanovich and West (1979) have described how automaticity for these processes can occur. With most of the processes proceeding automatically, conscious attention can be devoted to comprehension of the text.

With all of the bottom-up and top-down processes having been demonstrated as important to reading, bottom-up and top-down theories separately can account for only part of the empirical data. This has led to the development of interactive theories that allow both types of processes to occur and to interact. And the concept of schema has been added to develop a particular form of interactive theory with activated schemata as central elements. In this theory, the cognitive or knowledge base for reading assumes critical importance. Units of related knowledge or action items, packaged as schemata, are activated by the text being read. These schemata then guide inferencing from the text and prediction to the text ahead. As more information is acquired from the text, a schema can be modified or replaced to fit the incoming information. All of this, of course, requires that the bottom-up, text-based, skills of lexical and syntactic processing are proceeding automatically and unconsciously. If they are, fluent and skilled reading should result.

Chapter 3

Reading in Deaf Children

The problem facing the teacher of reading to deaf children is that all or most of the multiple processes involved in reading, as described in the preceding chapter, are likely not to be developed to the same level by deaf as by hearing children by the beginning reading stage. Much of this may be a result of lack of appropriate environment and developmental procedures with deaf children in infancy and early childhood. Whatever the cause, however, deaf children are likely to arrive at beginning reading with a very limited knowledge base, inadequately developed cognitive and linguistic skills, and little or no comprehension of English figurative language. Any language they have internalized is likely to be in a form other than English and in a mode other than aural. These differences will result in problems of decoding, inferencing, and predicting in the reading process. In short, deaf children are likely to have problems with every aspect of the reading process. There might be significant exceptions to this, such as highly intelligent deaf children of well-educated deaf parents, but the situation described can be shown to be accurate for most deaf children.

READING ACHIEVEMENT LEVELS

Although educators of deaf children have probably always been perfectly aware that the achievement levels of deaf students in reading English text are far below the levels of hearing students of comparable chronological and mental ages, it was only during the first and second decades of the present century that systematically collected quantitative data first documented the extent and nature of the deficits. Pintner and Patterson (1916) reported that deaf children of 14 to 16 years of age had median reading scores on the *Woodworth and Wells Test* for following directions that were usually attained by seven year old hearing children. Studies over the next 60 or more years have consistently confirmed these findings (Fusfeld, 1955; Goetzinger & Rousey, 1959; Myklebust, 1960; Pugh, 1946). National norms for reading levels of deaf children were supplied by Wrightstone, Aronow, and Moskowitz (1963) who administered the elementary level battery of the

Metropolitan Achievement Test to 5,307 hearing-impaired students between the ages of 10½ and 16½ years. In a detailed analysis of the data from that study, Furth (1966a) showed that only 8% of the national sampling of hearing-impaired students read above the fourth grade level. Furthermore, reading grade levels for the sample increased from a mean of only 2.7 between the ages of 10 and 11 years of age, to only 3.5 between 15 and 16 years of age. This represented an increase of less than one grade level in five years.

The most comprehensive information on the reading achievement levels of deaf students has been supplied in a series of studies by the Office of Demographic Studies (ODS) at Gallaudet College. The ODS (now called the Center for Assessment and Demographic Studies [CADS]) regularly collects and reports a wide range of educational and other data on most deaf students in schools in the United States. These national studies have confirmed and expanded the findings of the earlier studies cited. In one such study, Di Francesca (1972) reported that, for approximately 17,000 students between the ages of 6 and 21 years, the average growth on the Paragraph Meaning subtest of the *Stanford Achievement Test* was only 0.2 grade level per year of schooling. This is almost identical to the figure reported earlier by Furth (1966a) for the data of Wrightstone et al. (1963) on the *Metropolitan Achievement Test*. In a more recent ODS study, Trybus and Karchmer (1977) reported reading scores for a stratified, random sample of 6,871 deaf students. They found that the median reading level at age 20 years was a grade equivalent of only 4.5 and that only 10% of the very best reading group (the 18 year olds) could read at or above the eighth grade level.

Other studies have documented that these low reading levels and the slow rate of progress in reading are not unique to students or to the United States population. Hammermeister (1971) reported a significant increase in scores on the Word Meaning subtest but not on the Paragraph Meaning subtest of the *Stanford Achievement Test* for 60 deaf adults 7 to 13 years after they had left school. She interpreted these findings as indicating that the subjects' vocabularies had increased since they left school but their abilities to read connected language had not. A number of studies cited in Conrad (1979) attest to the universality of the reading problems of deaf persons. Using the *Wide-Span Reading Test* with 468 deaf students in England and Wales between 15 and 16 years of age, Conrad found they had a reading age equivalent to 9 year old hearing children. He also cited a number of studies conducted in Sweden, Denmark, and New Zealand that reported performances of deaf students at about 16 years of age as being no higher than the level of typical 10 year old hearing children.

Quigley and Kretschmer (1982) have pointed out that national norms obscure the achievements of individual schools and that some schools might greatly exceed those norms. For example, Lane and Baker (1974) compared reading levels of 132 former students of Central Institute for the Deaf (a private oral school) aged 10 to 16 years with the reading levels of students of similar ages reported by Furth (1966a). The rate of progress in reading level was much higher for the CID students than for the national sample reported by Furth and also by the Di Francesca (1972) study cited previously. Both Furth and Di Francesca reported progress of about 0.2 grade level per year of schooling, whereas Lane and Baker reported 0.6 grade level for the CID students. Lane and Baker attributed the more rapid reading progress of the CID students to continuous education in the same school with the same educational philosophy at all levels, maximum use of residual hearing, and oral communication in the school and in the home. Ogden (1979), who conducted a large follow-up study of students from the same school, also reported that the student body and their families were a socioeconomically elite group.

Even though studies of reading achievement levels consistently show greatly depressed performance by deaf individuals, there is evidence that the performance might be even more depressed than those studies show. Moores (1967) compared the reading performance of 37 deaf students with the performance of 37 hearing students using the cloze procedure. The two groups were matched on reading scores on the *Stanford Achievement Test.* Subjects read passages of 250 words each, selected from fourth, sixth, and eighth grade reading texts, and were requested to replace words that had been deleted from the passages. Using measures constructed to indicate the subjects' abilities to use their vocabularies and syntax in replacing the missing words, Moores found substantial and statistically significant deficiencies in vocabulary and syntax for the deaf subjects compared with the hearing subjects. Since the two groups had been matched on reading levels, it was reasonable to expect that their vocabulary and syntax levels would have been comparable. O'Neill (1973) found deaf students performed significantly more poorly than hearing students on the ability to judge the grammaticality of pairs of grammatical and ungrammatical sentences. As in Moores's study, the deaf and hearing subjects of the O'Neill study had been matched on reading achievement levels. These two studies suggest that the reading levels of deaf students might be even lower than the low levels obtained on standard reading tests.

The studies cited are only part of a much larger literature indicating that deaf individuals do not perform well at any age level on tests of *general* ability to read standard English text. Some of the *specific* difficulties that deaf persons have in reading English text have been explored and are discussed here under the categories used to present the literature on the reading of hearing children–text variables, reader variables, and socioeconomic and cultural variables.

TEXT VARIABLES

Vocabulary

As stated in Chapter 2, many studies have indicated that vocabulary knowledge plays a primary role in reading skill. This would seem to be the situation with deaf children also. In studies of educational achievement using such tests as the *Stanford Achievement Test*, a typical profile of performance on the various subtests has been found consistently. Deaf students usually have their lowest performance on the vocabulary or word meaning subtest, with a typical pattern of better performance on the other subtests. Performance tends to be lower on any subtest involving meaningful language such as Word Meaning, Paragraph Meaning, and Arithmetic Reasoning and higher on subtests with lesser language involvement, such as Spelling, Arithmetic Computation, and Language. (The Language subtest is simply a test of language mechanics, such as capitalization and punctuation, and not a test of meaningful language.) The consistently lowest score for Word Meaning indicates the difficulties that understanding of English vocabulary poses for deaf students. The somewhat higher scores for Paragraph Meaning (and for Arithmetic Reasoning) probably reflect the well-documented facilitating effect of context on language comprehension.

Extensive studies of vocabulary development have been reported by numerous authors (e.g., Fusaro & Slike, 1979; Griswold & Cummings, 1974; Hatcher & Robbins, 1978; Kyle, 1980; Myklebust, 1960; Schulze, 1965; and various ODS surveys). All of them confirm that deaf students at all age levels typically comprehend from print substantially fewer words than hearing children and that the distribution of types of words, such as nouns and verbs, is different for deaf than for hearing children. Some of these studies have attempted to isolate various factors that influence vocabulary development in deaf children. Hatcher and Robbins (1978), for example, found that deaf children they studied had developed vocabulary and reading skills beyond the level expected from their knowledge of primary word analysis skills.

Walter (1978b) conducted a study of vocabulary in deaf children that has diagnostic value beyond simple reporting of deficits in vocabulary level. He selected lists of words sampled from the *American Heritage Dictionary* distribution of words (Carroll, Davies, & Richman, 1971) based on their frequency of occurrence in texts used widely in schools in the United States. These lists were administered to a national sample of deaf children, and scores were obtained. Theoretically, it should be possible to use a deaf child's score on one of these tests to estimate, from the *American Heritage* word frequency distribution, the approximate size and composition of the child's vocabulary. This has considerable educational value beyond simply knowing of the existence and extent of a vocabulary deficit.

Paul (1984) conducted a study on deaf and hearing subjects' comprehension of multimeaning words within the 10,000th frequency level (Carroll et al., 1971). He constructed a picture vocabulary test containing 60 five-option, multiple-choice items. Forty-five items required two correct responses and the remaining 15 items required only one correct response. The most common meanings of the words were taken from a study that used a national sample of hearing students (Dale & O'Rourke, 1976). As expected, Paul found that the hearing subjects performed better than the deaf students on selecting two meanings of the words. In addition, they outperformed the deaf subjects on selecting at least one meaning for the same words. For both groups, however, knowing two meanings was more difficult than knowing only a single meaning. Finally, the subjects chose the primary, or most common, meanings more often than the secondary ones. Paul concluded that (1) both deaf and hearing subjects have difficulty with the notion that a word may have several meanings, and (2) not being aware of the most common meanings of words appearing frequently in print may contribute to reading comprehension problems.

Syntax

Although the pattern of subtest performance on educational achievement tests and surveys of teachers' recommendations for special reading materials (Hasenstab & McKenzie, 1981) indicate that vocabulary is perhaps the area of primary concern in the reading development of deaf children, syntax has also always been a major concern to teachers and researchers. This has been true for the more than 200 year history of educational work with deaf students in France, the United States, and other countries (Moores, 1978). The reason for this interest is apparent from study of the variance from standard English syntax of the written samples in Table 1 (page xii in the Preface). Also, as discussed in Chapter 1, the relation of short-term (working) memory and speech recoding to syntax might mean that development of English syntax presents special problems for deaf persons.

The study of syntax in deaf children's use of English has usually been influenced by the prevailing linguistic theories. In recent times that has meant the transformational generative grammar of Chomsky (1957, 1965, 1968) and generative semantics (Chafe, 1970; Fillmore, 1968; McCawley, 1968). A substantial number of studies have detailed the syntactic variance in the use of English by deaf individuals with these theories as frameworks. A series of publications by Quigley and a group of associates (e.g., Quigley, Power, & Steinkamp, 1977; Quigley, Smith & Wilbur, 1974; Quigley, Wilbur, & Montanelli, 1974) detailed the performance of a national, stratified, random sample of deaf students between the ages of 10 and 19 years on tests of comprehension of various syntactic structures presented singly in sentences. Table 4 presents a summary of the findings, showing (1) the order of difficulty of various syntactic structures for deaf students between 10 and 19 years of age, (2) the order of difficulty for the same structures for hearing students between 8 and 10 years, and (3) the frequency of occurrence of each structure in a reading series from Houghton-Mifflin (McKee, Harrison, McCowen, Lehr, & Durr, 1966).

It can be seen from Table 4 that the average 8 year old hearing student scored higher on the various tasks than the average 18 year old deaf student. It can also be seen that there is a large gap between the age when deaf students comprehend various syntactic structures in single sentences and the typical

Table 4. Summary of Performance on Syntactic Structures and Their Frequency of Occurrence per 100 Sentences in the *Reading for Meaning* Series

Structure	Deaf Students				Hearing Students	Frequency of Occurrence	
	Average across ages	Age 10	Age 18	Increase	Average across ages	Level at which structure first appeared	Frequency in 6th grade text
Negation							
be	79%	60%	86%	26%	92%	1st Primer–13	9
do	71	53	82	28	92		
have	74	57	78	21	86		
Modals	78	58	87	29	90		
Means	76	57	83	26	90		
Conjunction							
Conjunction	72%	56%	86%	30%	92%	1st Primer–11	36
Deletion	74	59	86	27	94		
Means	73	57	86	29	92		
Question formation							
WH-questions:							
Comprehension	66%	44%	80%	36%	98%	2nd Primer–5	6
Yes/no questions:							
Comprehension	74	48	90	42	99	1st Primer–5	3
Tag questions	57	46	63	17	98		
Means	66	46	78	32	98		
Pronominalization							
Personal Pronouns	67%	51%	88%	37%	78%		
Backward Pronominalization	70	49	85	36	94	4th grade–1	0 (4 per 1000)
Possessive Adjectives	65	42	82	40	98	1st grade 4	27
Possessive Pronouns	48	34	64	30	99	3rd Primer–1	0 (3 per 1000)
Reflexivization	50	21	73	52	80	2nd grade–1	2
Means	60	39	78	39	90		
Verbs							
Verb Auxiliaries	54%	52%	71%	19%	81%	1st grade–1	18
Tense Sequencing	63	54	72	18	78		
Means	58	53	71	18	79		
Complementation							
Infinitives and gerunds	55%	50%	63%	13%	88%	2nd Primer–4	32
Relativization							
Processing	68%	59%	76%	17%	78%	3rd Primer–2	12
Embedding	53	51	59	8	84		
Relative Pronoun referents	42	27	56	29	82		
Means	54	46	63	18	82		
Disjunction & Alternation	36%	22%	59%	37%	84%	1st grade–1	7

Adapted from Quigley, S., Wilbur, R., Power, D., Montanelli, D., and Steinkamp, M. (1976). *Syntactic structure in the language of deaf children.* Urbana, IL: University of Illinois Institute for Child Behavior and Development. Reprinted with permission.

age level when the same structures appear in the reading series. This would indicate a serious reading problem based on syntax alone. When the typical vocabulary, conceptual, and experiential problems of deaf students are added, it would seem that commonly used reading materials might present serious reading difficulties for many deaf students.

Hatcher and Robbins (1978) concluded from an intensive study of the development of reading skills in six primary and six intermediate grade deaf children that the essential skills for learning to read seem to be those related to comprehension of standard English syntax. In another study of 36 deaf students, 9 to 12 years of age, Robbins and Hatcher (1981) reached the same conclusion. They found that controlling for word recognition and training in word meaning did not improve performance in reading single sentences containing various syntactic structures. Their analyses revealed that passive voice sentences were the most difficult to comprehend, followed by relative clauses, conjunctions, pronominalization, and indirect objects. Active sentences were the easiest to comprehend. This order of difficulty is similar to that shown in Table 4.

Some studies have shown that deaf students seem to comprehend syntactic structures more easily in connected discourse than in single sentences (Gormley & Franzen, 1978) and that in some instances comprehension of a particular structure is not necessary for comprehension of a larger unit of discourse (Ewoldt, 1981b). These topics are discussed in the section on Discourse. It seems reasonable to conclude at this time, however, that English syntax presents problems for deaf persons both in reading and in writing.

Figurative Language

As stated previously, the difficulties for deaf children in learning English are compounded by the profusion of figurative expressions in the language. This applies to the written as well as to the spoken form of English. As Dixon et al. (1980) have shown, the beginning reader will encounter many figurative uses of language even in the very first books of commonly used reading series. In recent years, a number of studies have investigated some of the problems that figurative language presents for deaf children in reading English.

Conley (1976) compared comprehension of idiomatic expressions by 643 hearing and 137 deaf students. No significant differences were found in the performance of deaf and hearing students matched on reading levels from grade 2.0 to 2.9; however, significant differences in favor of the hearing students were found for reading levels above 3.0. Scores on the test of idiomatic expressions were significantly and positively related to reading for both groups of subjects. The results of the study may be confounded with variables other than idiomatic expressions. Some of the idioms, for example, were phrased in complex syntactic structures, such as relative clauses, complements, and passive voice, which have been demonstrated to present comprehension difficulties for deaf readers.

Iran-Nejad, Ortony, and Rittenhouse (1981) constructed metaphorical expressions that were controlled for vocabulary and syntax in accordance with reported comprehension levels for deaf students at various ages (Quigley et al., 1976). In general, the deaf subjects at all age levels (9 to 17 years) scored high on literal comprehension and also at unexpectedly high levels on the metaphorical tasks. A related training study showed improvement in comprehension of metaphors with practice. The authors concluded that deaf children do not have any cognitive deficiency that prevents their comprehension of metaphorical English and that their subjects were able to interpret metaphorical language if their tendency to interpret literally was counteracted in practice sessions.

This study is important for two reasons. First, it attempted to control textual factors other than metaphorical expression (e.g., vocabulary and syntax) so that figurative language was the independent variable of study. Second, it is one of a very few studies to show relatively good comprehension of figurative language by deaf subjects. Problems are present in the design, particularly in how figurative language can really be expressed when vocabulary and syntax are controlled at very low levels, but it is important to note the conclusions that difficulties deaf children might have with figurative language are not due to cognitive deficits. This is in agreement with much of the presentation in Chapter 1.

A study by Wilbur, Fraser, and Fruchter (1981) also showed unexpectedly high levels of comprehension for figurative language by deaf subjects. In this case, the aspect of figurative language studied was idiomatic expressions. The authors speculated that at least some idioms might be memorized or learned as a whole so that vocabulary and syntax might not present confounding problems. Studies by Page (1981) and Houck (1982) concluded that deaf children are not impaired in their comprehension of idioms when there is sufficient contextual information in the written material and when "extraneous factors" are controlled.

It probably would be very difficult to convince experienced teachers of deaf children on the basis of any research study or group of studies that figurative language does not present major comprehension difficulties for deaf children in reading. Teachers seem to regard this as one of their major problems in language development, including reading. Some possible explanations for the contrary findings from some research studies are offered in the section on Discourse.

Two recent studies of figurative language produced findings which, along with those of Conley (1976) already cited, are probably close to teachers' perceptions of the matter. Giorcelli (1982) constructed a *Test of Figurative Language* consisting of 100 multiple-choice items. The test assesses 10 specific aspects of figurative language which include: analogical and syllogistical reasoning, associative fluency, linguistic problem solving, interpretation of anomaly, and discrimination between paraphrases of novel and idiomatic metaphors. Choices of idiomatic phrases, syntax, and vocabulary were carefully controlled. Isolated and short and long contextual conditions were used. High measures of reliability, validity, and usability were obtained for the test battery.

Three groups of 25 deaf subjects, each ranging in age from 9 years 9 months to 19 years 11 months and one group of 25 hearing subjects aged from 8 years to 9 years 4 months were tested. Results showed that the hearing subjects scored significantly higher than the deaf subjects on total test performance and on seven of the ten subtests. Performance for the deaf subjects improved with the addition of context but still remained well below the performance of the hearing subjects. The 18 year old deaf subjects did not perform as well as the 9 year old hearing subjects, which is similar to the findings for syntax by Quigley et al. (1976). There also was very little improvement in performance of deaf subjects beyond 13 to 14 years of age, which is similar to the plateaus in reading reported by Di Francesca (1972) and others.

Payne (1982) studied the extent to which deaf and hearing subjects could understand verb-particle combinations of English. This structure is one of the most common means by which English is expanded. Verb-particle combinations can be literal (e.g., "*run up* a hill") or idiomatic (e.g., "*run up* a bill"). Payne assessed his subjects' performance on verb-particle combinations at three levels of semantic difficulty (literal, semi-idiomatic, and idiomatic) and in five syntactic surface structures with a written test of 64 items with vocabulary controlled to the first and second grade levels. He found that the hearing subjects scored significantly higher than the deaf subjects on all levels of semantic difficulty and for all syntactic structures.

Although there are contrary findings, extensive studies of figurative language lend support to the contentions of teachers that figurative expressions present a major problem in reading for deaf students. When added to the problems presented by vocabulary and syntax, and the obvious interactions among all of these, it is apparent that many textual variables contribute to the low performance of deaf students on standard reading tests. Some of the contrary research findings on figurative language raise the question of whether the problem is with the deaf person's lack of the form in which the figurative concepts are expressed (i.e., the English language) or lack of the underlying concepts themselves. Some studies in discourse shed some light on this.

Discourse

Most of the research discussed in this category of textual variables has focused on single, controlled aspects of text–vocabulary, syntax, figurative language. The purpose has been to try to determine to what extent these various aspects of text contribute to the general low performance of deaf students on standard reading tests. Reading tests provide only a general measure of reading comprehension. Knowledge of the contributions of specific aspects of text, such as vocabulary and syntax, to the general measure and the general problem should provide more detailed understanding of the matter. It can be argued, however, that such an approach distorts the typical reading process. Studies by McGill-Franzen and Gormley (1980) and Ewoldt (1981b) have taken this position and have attempted to investigate larger units of discourse than words and sentences.

McGill-Franzen and Gormley (1980) studied deaf children's comprehension of truncated passive sentences (e.g., "The wolf was killed") presented in context and in isolation. Their results indicated that deaf children who could not comprehend a passive sentence presented in isolation could comprehend the same sentence when it was embedded in the context of a *familiar* fairy tale. The results were interpreted as demonstrating that deaf children could understand passives in context. The results of the study have been criticized by Robbins and Hatcher (1981) on the grounds that the use of highly familiar material (known fairy tales) meant that probably very little knowledge about the stories was text-dependent. In other words, given the topic of a passage, subjects probably could have responded appropriately to questions without even reading the passage. Furthermore, a study by Israelite (1981) found that the use of context did not aid in correct interpretation of passive sentences.

Ewoldt (1981b) also stresses the contextual analysis skills of deaf children and claims that deaf children can by-pass English syntax and move directly to meaning. Ewoldt conducted an intensive analysis of the reading of four prelingually deaf children aged 6 years 11 months to 16 years 11 months. The children read and interpreted 25 stories in sign language which were videotaped. Comprehension was assessed by K. Goodman's miscue analysis (1976), cloze procedures, and retellings of the stories by the children. Ewoldt concluded that the subjects were users of language and were able to read and retell stories written in English by interpreting them into their own sign language. She reported that the subjects made extensive use of the syntactic and semantic cueing systems but did not "overrely" on graphic information. This was interpreted as support for the top-down theory of reading and its use by deaf children. It will be recalled from the discussion of reading theories, however, that a top-down approach to reading is typical of beginning readers and poor readers who have not acquired automatic and unconscious control of bottom-up processing of text. This approach can enable the beginning reader and the poor reader to acquire a "general idea" of the meaning of a text without fully understanding it. It is difficult from Ewoldt's report to determine the extent to which context did allow her subjects to by-pass the syntax of the stories. Only two examples are given, and other interpretations of these can be made than that syntax was being by-passed.

A final study is of interest in the analysis of discourse. It will be recalled that Mandler and N. Johnson (1977) and others demonstrated that there is underlying intersentential structure to text that aids (and perhaps directs) reading comprehension. Gaines, Mandler, and Bryant (1981) have extended this type of discourse analysis to the reading of deaf children. They compared immediate and delayed recall of stories by hearing and deaf children. Three stories from Mandler (1978) were used: (1) the first story consisted of standard prose; (2) the second contained nonphonetic misspellings (e.g., "throgh" for "through"); and (3) the third contained confused anaphoric references. Six deaf and six hearing subjects were matched for reading age (*Gates Vocabulary Test*). Deaf subjects ranged from 14 years 3 months to 15 years 1 month of age (mean, 14 years 5 months); reading ages ranged from 11 years 6 months to 13 years 9 months (mean, 12 years 6 months). The deaf subjects were from an oral school. The very high reading ages and the high quality of the written English used by the deaf subjects on the recall tasks indicate that they were highly select individuals.

Results of the study revealed no significant differences between the deaf and hearing subjects in the amount of recall of story propositions on the normal prose story, but the deaf subjects had significantly higher amounts of recall for both of the confused stories. However, in accuracy of recall of story content deaf subjects made significantly more distortions than did the hearing subjects. Most of the deaf subjects' distortions were semantic confusions and there was no significant difference in the mean number of written syntactic errors between the deaf subjects (5.2) and the hearing subjects (3.5).

The investigators speculated that the deaf subjects used a "broad reconstructive 'top-down' schematic approach" to reading (p. 467). Thus, they were able to comprehend the overall meaning of the stories and recall an *amount* of story propositions similar to the hearing subjects; however, they did have significantly more semantic distortions than the hearing subjects. This is typically what would be expected from hearing students who were beginning or poor readers. As stated, such readers can often get the "general idea" of a passage by the use of top-down strategies but will have a lack of understanding or even misunderstanding of important details.

READER VARIABLES

A number of researchers have attempted to define the personal variables that account at least partially for the performance of deaf readers. Jensema (1975) found (as have many investigators) that vocabulary and comprehension performance are inversely related to degree of hearing impairment; the greater the impairment, the lower the performance. Similarly, and also well known, age at onset of hearing impairment was related to reading performance—prelinguistically impaired students read less well than those impaired at later ages. Rogers, Leslie, Clarke, Booth, and Horvath (1978) conducted an extensive study of the factors influencing vocabulary and comprehension scores for a large part of the hearing-impaired student population in British Columbia. In addition to the factors reported by Jensema (1975), these investigators found that students who used oral communication performed better on both vocabulary and reading comprehension than students who used simultaneous manual and oral (total) communication, and students who wore hearing aids scored higher in comprehension than those who did not.

The three reader variables discussed in Chapter 2 were development of schemata, inferencing, and metacognitive strategies. Research on schema development with deaf children is almost nonexistent, although the study by Gaines et al. (1981) reported that highly literate oral deaf readers were using "a broad reconstructive 'top-down' schematic approach" (p. 467) to the reading process. Also, T. Kluwin, Getson, and B. Kluwin (1980) found that deaf adolescents interpreted an ambiguous passage, which could have been interpreted as a story about a lost foreigner or about a person learning signs, differently from their hearing peers, thus confirming that deaf readers can bring their world knowledge (schemata) to bear on the reading process.

As Kretschmer (1982) has pointed out, research into metacognitive processes with deaf readers has been limited to studies of judgments of grammaticality (Kretschmer, 1976; Quigley et al., 1976). Kretschmer (1982) reports that research with deaf readers in metacognitive processes—ranging from what hearing-impaired children think reading is to study skills approaches—might result in better ways to teach productive study skills to deaf students.

In the area of inferencing, there has been at least one extensive study conducted with deaf students. K. Wilson (1979a) pointed out that many studies of reading achievement levels have shown that deaf students tend to plateau at about the third or fourth grade level, at 13 to 14 years of age, and their scores change very little from then through at least age 19. He speculated that this might be due to changes in the format and content of reading materials and tests at the fourth grade level. Up to the third grade, most reading materials emphasize word analysis skills and vocabulary, and reading tests assess these factors. Beyond the third grade, materials increasingly require the utilization of prior knowledge to infer meanings that are not explicitly stated in the text. As stated in Chapter 2, inferencing becomes ubiquitous in the reading process; its assessment becomes ubiquitous in reading tests as well. K. Wilson (1979a) reasoned that if deaf children had problems with inferencing, this might account at least partially for their plateauing in reading at the third or fourth grade level.

Wilson (1979a) constructed a series of short passages in which inferencing was studied in various syntactic environments and with vocabulary controlled. The purpose was to determine how well deaf students could understand material that required inferencing compared with material that could be understood literally. For example, given the sentences (Wilson, 1979a):

The shirt is dirty.
The shirt is under the bed.
The cat is on the shirt.
The cat is white.

it can be understood readily by most people that "The cat is under the bed" even though this is not stated explicitly in the text. Using these techniques, K. Wilson found that inferencing presented much greater difficulty for his deaf subjects than for his hearing subjects, and that inferencing was independent of type of syntactic structure. So, what this represents is another ability important to reading on which deaf students exhibit low performance.

Another finding of K. Wilson's is important to note. His stories were administered in speech, signs, and writing, and he found that the hearing subjects scored highest with the spoken presentations, whereas the deaf subjects scored highest with the written presentations. This supports findings of other studies of efficiency and effectiveness of communication. Quigley and Frisina (1961) reported that reading appeared to provide a more stable means of communication for deaf students than the reception of speech or fingerspelling. White and Stevenson (1975) similarly found reading print to be superior for receptive communication to reading speech or signs, and Stuckless and Pollard (1977) showed that children raised using fingerspelling could process the written form more readily than fingerspelling.

SOCIOECONOMIC AND CULTURAL VARIABLES

Just as socioeconomic and cultural influences have been shown repeatedly to influence the reading development of hearing children, so have they been shown to influence the reading development of deaf children. Brasel and Quigley (1977), Ogden (1979), and many others have shown that the standard measures of socioeconomic status (SES)—family income, occupations, and educational levels—are related to language and reading development for deaf children just as they are for hearing children. The unique factor in this area for deaf children is whether they are actually members (or destined to be members) of a separate culture of deaf people rather than members of the general culture. If it is accepted that at least some significant portion of deaf children are members of a separate culture, and that American Sign Language is the language of the culture, then the approach to the development of reading could be significantly affected.

For hearing people, reading can be regarded as a parasitic function that is founded on the primary auditory based language developed during the first few years of life. In spite of the current emphasis on top-down processes, reading in the narrow sense can be regarded as the decoding of print. This is all that is unique to reading. All of the other factors of prior knowledge and inferencing are the result of experience and of linguistic development, which occur as natural processes when an intact human organism raised in a reasonably responsive family interacts with its environment for the satisfaction of its needs and wants. Prior knowledge and inferencing develop as part of the total auditory based language process even if reading is never taught.

Probably all methods of reading instruction with deaf as well as with hearing children assume the existence of an auditory based language in the prereading child. If such an auditory based language is not present, then how should reading be developed? And, more importantly, is it worth the effort to develop it at all, given the meager results of 200 years of educational effort?

SUMMARY

National surveys, individual studies of reading achievement, and studies of specific aspects of the reading process all indicate that most deaf children have difficulty with reading the English language. Few of them become really skilled readers. This seems not to be due to any single factor (excepting, of course, deafness itself), but to problems with all of the factors involved in the reading process. Whereas the typical hearing child brings to the reading process a substantial knowledge base resulting from a wide variety of infant and early childhood experiences that have been internalized through the spoken language acquired by interaction with parents and significant others, the deaf child typically brings to the same process a very impoverished knowledge base. This is not always due to lack of exposure to early experiences; often it is due to the lack of a fluent language and communication system with which to signify and internalize those experiences in some manipulable code.

In addition to the lack of a substantial knowledge base, deaf children often are lacking in inferential skills and in figurative language and other linguistic skills that develop automatically in young hearing children. In short, they do not have the experiential, cognitive, and linguistic base needed to learn to read fluently. Because of this, learning to read becomes also a basic language learning process for deaf children.

In view of the many deficits the deaf child brings to the learning to read process, the wonder is that the child ever learns to read at all. Yet, some deaf children learn to read very well. There is a need to determine from studies of successful deaf readers just what factors account for their success. Studies by Conrad (1979), Lichtenstein (1983), and others have indicated that the ability to use speech coding and recoding is related to reading success. And Conrad (1979) has shown that even some deaf children who have unintelligible speech have acquired a speech code. This could be one factor accounting for success.

Speech recoding seems to be important for hearing readers not so much for access to word meaning as for temporary storage of words in working memory to comprehend clauses and sentences. This form of coding and storage involves temporal-sequential memory and, as discussed in Chapter 1, this is one aspect of memory for which deaf persons have consistently been found to have shorter spans than hearing persons. These two facts, shorter temporal-sequential memory spans and lack of a speech code, could account for some of the language acquisition and reading problems of deaf children. They might also help explain why acquiring the syntax of English (and perhaps of any spoken language) seems to present extreme difficulty for many deaf persons.

Given the deficits deaf children bring to the learning-to-read process, it seems that the methods and the materials used with hearing children might not be appropriate for many of them. Chapters 5 and 6 presents an extensive analysis of the research on the construction and use of special materials for deaf children. The conclusion reached is that special materials have value for less able and problem readers, including deaf children. There is a need with many deaf children to provide materials that will match their limited experience and limited knowledge of the vocabulary, syntax, figurative expressions, and other aspects of standard English and which will increase in difficulty at a limited pace. If language instruction is proceeding concurrently, such special materials could gradually be phased out until the deaf child eventually is using the regular materials of the general school system.

The methods of reading instruction used with deaf children generally are those used with hearing children with some concessions to the limited language base of deaf children (Clarke, Rogers, & Booth, 1982). These are methods based on spoken and auditory language, which many deaf children do not have. Such methods might work for those deaf children who, by whatever means, have acquired a speech code (Conrad, 1979), but many deaf children do not acquire this code. It would seem logical that teaching reading to those deaf children would require special methods based on visual language. The methods probably would have to take into account whatever form of visual language the child had internalized prior to beginning reading. This might be some form of manually coded English (MCE), some form of Pidgin Sign English (PSE), or a variety of American Sign Language (ASL). It would seem that in order to teach reading to these children, the teacher would need to be able to determine which language or communication form the child typically used and use it as the base for teaching reading. This, in turn, would require that the reading teacher be fluent in ASL and other forms of visual language. The similarity of this process to the teaching of English as a second language is obvious and is discussed in detail by Quigley and Paul (1984b).

The need for special methods might be most pronounced for some deaf children of well-educated deaf parents who have used ASL as the primary language with their children. These children might bring to the beginning reading process all the experiential, cognitive, and linguistic skills that hearing children typically do, but in a language (ASL) different from English and in a communication mode (manual-visual) different from oral-aural. This might be considered a special case of teaching English as a second language.

But it also has been argued that for some of these children—and for other deaf children also—the teaching of reading of print might simply deter their educational progress. Although reading has an almost revered status in the educational system, it basically is a means for transmitting and acquiring information, which can be accomplished by other means. For example, printed English material could be transformed to ASL on videotapes for use by deaf persons. This is analogous to "talking books" for blind people.

In spite of the problems deaf persons have with reading English, the studies by Quigley and Frisina (1961), White and Stevenson (1975), Stuckless and Pollard (1977), and K. Wilson (1979a) cited earlier indicate that many deaf children find it a more effective means of receiving *English* than speech, signs, or fingerspelling. In view of this, Stuckless and a number of associates at the National Technical Institute for the Deaf (e.g., Stuckless & Hurwitz, 1982; Stuckless & Matter, 1982) have used a computer and a stenotypist to produce on a screen and on paper printed versions of the spoken word while the word is being spoken. This is called real-time graphic display and has promise as an educational tool for deaf people. Although the equipment and the methods are not yet fully developed, they are far enough advanced to make feasibility virtually certain.

Even from the limited treatment in this chapter, the rapidly developing research interest in reading for deaf people should be obvious. This research will increase, and the next decade holds promise for greater understanding of the language and reading processes of deaf children and the application of research to the development of new teaching methods, new materials, and new devices. It could happen that different approaches, materials, and devices will have to be developed for different groups of deaf children. Some of these children, especially those who acquire speech coding, might simply need special uses of the materials and methods developed for hearing children. Others might need special materials and methods adapted to various forms of visual-manual English and perhaps some of the techniques of teaching English as a second language. Still others might need to receive information in some visual form other than printed English (e.g., videotaped ASL). If this materializes, a major research and educational problem will be to determine which approach is best for which child, and since the determination will need to be made very early in life, it will be an extremely knotty problem indeed. The alternative, however, is even worse: to swing from one basic language to another (whether oral English, manually coded English, or ASL) for *all* deaf children and base one set of reading approaches on the language of choice. The low reading performances of deaf children attest to the lack of validity of this approach and argues for more diversification of reading techniques based on the various language and communication approaches. Finally, there is also the question of whether the teaching of the reading of print is feasible or a productive use of time at all for some, as yet undetermined, portion of the population of deaf children.

Chapter 4

Current Practices in Reading Instruction with Deaf Children

Given the importance of reading to the educational process and the spectacular lack of success in achieving even minimal levels of literacy (i.e., fifth grade) by most deaf children, it is surprising that (1) relatively little is known about current instructional practices for teaching deaf children to read, and (2) there is little research being conducted to determine the effects of various instructional methods. In sharp constrast, a fairly substantial body of polemic writing is available in which various spokespersons argue for specific approaches and prescribe specific instructional practices which they believe should be used.

In this chapter, current instructional practices in teaching reading to deaf children are examined. The chapter is organized according to the three major sources from which information is available—descriptive research on current practices; experimental research on the efficacy of various approaches; and descriptive polemic prescriptions of approaches and techniques. The advantages and limitations of each major source are identified and discussed. The following topics are covered: (1) survey studies; (2) observational studies; (3) experimental studies; (4) polemic discussions of instructional practices; and (5) a summary of available information and directions for needed research.

SURVEY STUDIES

Much of the available information on current instructional practices in reading with deaf children comes from survey studies. Five such studies have been conducted in the last 10 years (Coley & Bockmiller, 1980 [see also Bockmiller & Coley, 1981]; Hasenstab & McKenzie, 1981; Lanfrey, 1975; LaSasso, 1978a; Marshman, 1974). LaSasso (personal communication, May,

1984) is in the process of updating her 1978 survey. Unfortunately, the final report of this study was not available. Some preliminary results of the study, however, are reported in Chapter 6.

For the most part, the survey studies provide consistent data. Therefore, the information is presented within the following categories: (1) teacher preparation; (2) teachers' beliefs about reading; (3) approaches to reading instruction; (4) perceived needs and directions for future research and materials production; (5) instructional strategies and organizational plans; and (6) students' beliefs, habits, and interests. Before discussing these topics, a brief synopsis of the advantages and limitations of survey studies is provided. At the end of the section, a summary of the information obtained from surveys of reading programs for deaf children is provided.

Advantages and Limitations of Survey Research

Survey studies primarily provide indications of the beliefs of educators about practices and goals for reading instruction. Such studies provide needed data bases on which observational and experimental studies can be built (Glaser, 1979). The advantages of conducting instructional research via survey include the following: (1) the ease of data collection; (2) the ease in quantifying and analyzing the data; (3) the limited time needed for respondents to complete a questionnaire; and (4) the size of the sample that can be examined. The limitations include (1) the use of forced-choice questions which may hinder or influence responses; (2) the inability to determine how respondents interpreted the questions and how much care they used in filling out the questionnaire; and (3) the inability to predict or determine how the information on unreturned questionnaires might have affected the results. Survey studies are also limited in generalizability to the population from which the sample was selected. Several of the surveys of deaf children have focused on residential schools only (Coley & Bockmiller, 1980; Lanfrey, 1975; Marshman, 1974). Therefore, the results of these studies cannot be generalized as widely as those of LaSasso (1978a) and Hasenstab and McKenzie (1981), who included both day and residential programs.

The most important limitation of survey studies, however, is the lack of correspondence between survey data and information gained from direct observation of the instructional setting. Hook and Rosenshine (1979) reviewed 11 studies from a variety of disciplines (i.e., not limited to reading instruction), which compared survey results with observational data. They concluded

> In practice, one is not advised to accept teacher reports on specific behaviors as particularly accurate. No slur is intended; teachers do not have practice in estimating their behavior and then checking against actual performance. There appears to be some value in teacher reports when behaviors are grouped into dimensions, but one has no way of knowing, a priori, which dimensions will correlate with actual practice.
>
> (Hook & Rosenshine, 1979, p. 10)

In the field of reading, an example of discrepancies between survey and observational data is reported by Mason and Osborn (1982). They compared teacher beliefs as reported on surveys with observational data on whether there is an instructional shift from "learning to read" in the early elementary grades to "reading to learn" in the later elementary grades. They concluded "a shift from learning to read to reading to learn is a belief that teachers share but do not practice" (p. 39). Therefore, since surveys of teachers' beliefs about reading instruction do not always coincide with observations of what occurs in the classroom, care must be taken not to attribute too much significance to survey data. This seems to be an especially important point given that surveys are the primary source of information regarding reading instructional practices with deaf children.

On the other hand, survey data constitute a starting base on which a comprehensive instructional research program can be built. Further, most of the survey studies reported herein have not addressed the types of instructional issues on which there is great discrepancy between survey and observational studies. For example, information on teacher preparation is perhaps best gained through survey research. The need for comparative studies of survey data, observational data, and experimental data is greater when issues such as instructional strategies or grouping practices are the object of study.

Teacher Preparation

Information about teacher preparation for teaching reading is reported by Coley and Bockmiller (1980) and Bockmiller & Coley (1981). More than 20% of the teachers surveyed had had only one or no courses in reading, and almost 40% of the teachers had had no graduate courses in reading instruction. These figures seem low considering that only teachers directly responsible for teaching reading were included in the survey, so it is likely that preparation for teaching reading is even lower among the general teaching population.

Given the results of this study, it might also be wondered how many teachers of deaf children consider themselves teachers of reading. Each school was asked to identify the number of reading teachers, and that number of questionnaires was then sent to the school. The average number of teachers per school who were identified as reading teachers was five (543 forms were distributed to 122 schools). Although information was not provided as to the number of teachers at each school, nor whether the identification of "reading teachers" was determined by the administration or was self-determined, this number seems extremely small, especially given the common prescription in textbooks on deafness that all teachers of deaf children are teachers of language and reading.

More encouraging evidence of teacher preparation in teaching reading is provided by Marshman (1974). She found that 61% of the administrators and 48% of the teachers in her study had had three or more courses in reading. Also, approximately 15% of both administrators and teachers had had three or more courses specifically in teaching reading to deaf children. The study, however, also found evidence of inadequate preparation in that 18% of the administrators and 22% of the teachers, like those in the Coley and Bockmiller study, had had no or only one course in teaching reading. This study also included teachers who had been identified as reading teachers only.

Another aspect of teacher preparation deals with teachers' perceptions of their own abilities in teaching specific aspects of reading. Bockmiller and Coley (1980) found that teachers with more training did not use a wider range of techniques than teachers with less training. The most often used techniques, however, were those for which teachers felt best prepared. For example, basal readers were used to a much higher extent than packaged kits (such as the SRA Reading Lab or Project LIFE). Correspondingly, a higher percentage of teachers felt more comfortable using basal readers than packaged kits. Only 10.9% of the teachers felt less than adequately prepared to use the basal readers, whereas 31.4% felt less than adequately prepared to use the packaged kits.

The degree of confidence in using a specific technique correlated with greater use of that technique. For example, among those using basal readers more than 50% of the time, only 4 of 163 felt poorly prepared to use such materials. Among the techniques teachers felt most poorly prepared to use were multilevel questioning (26%), word banks (38%), and study techniques such as the SQ3R (75%). Most teachers (88%) felt well prepared to develop their own materials for teaching reading (Coley & Bockmiller, 1980).

Teachers' Beliefs About Reading

Although it is common to hear teachers state that their instructional practices are atheoretical (Harste & Burke, 1977), recent studies have found evidence of the impact of theoretical views on classroom behaviors (Harste & Burke, 1977; Stansell, Moss, & Robeck, 1982). Of the survey studies with teachers of deaf children, only Lanfrey's study (1975) examined the theoretical orientations of teachers as evidenced by their beliefs about the reading instructional process. The overwhelming majority of the respondents (93.6%) preferred a meaning-emphasis approach, rather than a code-emphasis approach, to beginning reading.

However, just as with teachers of hearing children, there appears to be a dichotomy between teachers who support top-down approaches and those who support bottom-up approaches to reading. This can be seen in the responses to Lanfrey's questions regarding whether individual letters or whole words are the appropriate focus of initial instruction. Forty-eight percent of Lanfrey's respondents recommended that the "initiation of printed forms" be accomplished through the introduction of whole words, whereas another 48% thought that printed forms should be introduced through letters of the alphabet. Teaching of letter names versus whole words also resulted in a split of teachers, with 59.3% supporting the position that whole word names be taught before letter names almost always or frequently, and 28.3% supporting the practice of teaching letter names before whole words.

The importance of forming and being aware of one's own beliefs about reading cannot be overstressed. Harste and Burke (1977) discuss how theoretical orientation affects all aspects of the learning environment from the goals and strategies of instruction to diagnostic procedures, to the use of learning materials, and to the criteria used as evidence of reading success. Further study of the beliefs of deaf children's teachers is needed. Gove (1983) provides a helpful questionnaire, the *Conceptual Framework of Reading Interview*, which teachers can use to help clarify their own beliefs about reading and reading instruction. The *Reading Comprehension Interview* is also available to help teachers gain insight into their students' perceptions of reading (Wixson, Bosky, Yochum, & Alvermann, 1984).

Approaches to Reading Instruction

LaSasso (1978a) examined the use of four basic approaches to teaching reading in programs for deaf children—basal reader approach, language-experience approach (LEA), programmed instruction approach, and individualized approach (defined as the use of library books with students selecting their own books). She further studied whether each approach was used as the primary or a supplementary approach. The data were reported separately for four levels of instruction—primary (ages 5 to 8); intermediate (ages 9 to 12); junior high (ages 13 to 15); and senior high school (ages 16 to 18).

Overall, the two approaches that were cited most frequently as the primary or supplementary method were LEA (83.5% of the programs) and the basal reader approach (73.5%). The other two approaches were used to lesser extents: individualized approaches, 41.7%; and programmed instruction approaches, 36.1%. Advocates of the individualized approach explained that they were using that method because they had not found appropriate regular instructional materials for their students. Detailed information on specific materials used in teaching reading to deaf children is provided in Chapter 6. In this chapter, it will suffice to note that the majority of reading and language texts used with deaf children are those designed for hearing students (Clarke et al., 1982; Lanfrey, 1975; Takemori & Snyder, 1972). In a survey of language methods, King (1983) found a split among teachers of deaf children between those who preferred not to use materials designed for *deaf* students (30%) and those who preferred not to use materials designed for *hearing* students (45%).

Particularly interesting in LaSasso's data is the shift in the *primary method* for various levels of instruction. LEA methods were the strongest at the *primary level* (79.7%), after which the use of basal readers becomes more predominant at the intermediate and junior high levels. Use of basal readers as the primary method of teaching reading at the high school level remained fairly high (15.2%), especially considering the mismatch between the interests of high school students and the content of materials designed for children of a much younger age.

A surprising result in regard to the use of basal readers with deaf children is that 25–30% of the respondents at the primary level were not using basal readers at all (Bockmiller & Coley, 1980; LaSasso, 1978a). This result contrasts with studies of reading instruction with hearing children in which only 7% of the teachers in grades two through five never used basal readers (Mason & Osborn, 1982).

Directions for Future Research and Materials Development

The surveys of current instructional practices in teaching reading to deaf children identified several major directions for future research and materials development. LaSasso (1978a) identified three major foci for future reading research: (1) development of linguistically controlled materials (46% of the respondents); (2) research on the efficacy of various instructional strategies for teaching reading to deaf children (29%); and (3) development of diagnostic procedures which can be used to identify the reading skill needs of deaf children (22%).

Hasenstab and McKenzie (1981) focused on respondents' suggestions for reading materials specifically designed for deaf children. The three most frequent suggestions were (1) controlled and sequential development of vocabulary; (2) appropriate, systematic progression of language development; and (3) the inclusion of supplementary materials for reinforcement. In a more general study, Prickett and Hunt (1977) found that the development of more academic materials designed specifically for deaf children was perceived as the thirtieth priority in desirability and the thirty-second priority in likelihood.

Marshman (1974) identified specific needs in terms of training, personnel, and materials. The five major concerns were lack of materials, lack of appropriate tests, limited time available for instruction, lack of specialized personnel, and lack of training. Eighty-one percent of the teachers in the study indicated that reading specialists for consultation or diagnosis are never available or that availability was unknown. Fifty-two percent indicated that availability of in-service training was unknown or that such training was "almost never" available.

Instructional Strategies and Organizational Plans

Identification of specific instructional strategies was investigated in only two of the survey studies (Lanfrey, 1975; Marshman, 1974). The following topics are representative of the issues addressed: methods of grouping students for instruction; amount of time devoted to reading instruction; assessment techniques used; numbers of books in classrooms; and reports to parents on reading achievement and instruction.

Grouping Arrangements and Teaching Strategies

Marshman (1974) found that 45% of her respondents (reading teachers in residential schools for deaf children) had only a single group for reading instruction. Sixty-four percent always or frequently taught reading to the whole class. There also appeared to be little grouping across classes at the same age or ability level (14% always or frequently) and little use of a resource room as the major instructional plan (0% always; 7% frequently). Fewer than one quarter of the teachers had more than two reading groups. When grouping occurred, students were assigned to groups largely on the basis of skill needs. The student's previous reading record, intellectual ability, and age or grade level also contributed to the decision. A vast majority of the teachers were satisfied with their organizational structure for reading instruction, with 87% indicating that their organizational plan was excellent, very good, or satisfactory.

The lack of cross-class grouping is somewhat surprising since 78% of the respondents indicated that there was more than one class being taught at the level they taught. The use of a single reading group also contrasts with the general trend in reading instruction with hearing children in which *all* teachers at the second grade level grouped students for reading and 90% of the teachers in third through fifth grades grouped their students (Mason & Osborn, 1982). Although this difference may be due in part to smaller class sizes for deaf children, it would be interesting (1) to determine whether the organizational patterns noted more than a decade ago by Marshman reflect current practices in residential schools for deaf children; and (2) to make comparisons of such data with data from day programs for deaf children, in which a more heterogeneous grouping within a single classroom might be expected. Comparisons of survey and observational data are also needed.

Lanfrey (1975) gathered information concerning a variety of beliefs and strategies concerning the teaching of reading to deaf children. She found that 73.8% of the teachers in her study supported the early introduction of silent reading with deaf children. Eighty-seven percent always or almost always preceded reading with some type of discussion. More than half (55.8%) wanted a general outline of activities in the teacher's guide, rather than a step-by-step outline of what to say and do.

Instructional Time

P. Cunningham (1983) notes that the amount of time devoted to formal reading instruction actually reflects only a portion of reading-related activities during a school day. However, data on formal reading instructional time are useful indicators of the priority given to the subject. Marshman found that the vast majority (82%) of teachers of deaf children taught reading five days a week and that 79% spent one half to one and a half hours per day in formal reading instruction. The teachers of the older students spent more time in formal instruction than did teachers of younger students.

Additional studies are needed to determine (1) the amount of time students spend reading discourse-level materials during the school day (e.g., in content area classes), and (2) the amount of time students spend reading outside of the classroom. Both surveys and observational studies would be helpful.

Assessment Techniques

More than two thirds of the teachers of deaf children (69%) reported that they used informal tests to evaluate their students' progress rates and ability levels. Seventy-seven percent of the teachers indicated that these informal tests were teacher-made always or frequently (Marshman, 1974). This contrasts greatly with the use of informal reading tests with hearing children (approximately 8 to 14% of the teachers for second to fifth grade; Mason & Osborn, 1982), and it seems to indicate a distrust in using commercial reading tests with deaf children. Additional support for this hypothesis comes from responses to the query about "availability of test instruments for assessing student achievement and progress"—only 6% of the teachers thought the availability was excellent; 29% rated it as fair (one score less than satisfactory); and 20% felt availability of test instruments was poor.

On the other hand, however, standardized achievement tests were used by 49% of the teachers for deaf children between 5 and 7 years of age; 75% for 8 to 10 year olds; and 93% for deaf children 11 years of age and older. Here, direct comparison with hearing children is not possible. Marshman requested information on the administration of such tests, whereas Mason and Osborn requested information on the usage of test results for grouping purposes. It can be assumed, however, that most schools for hearing children administer general achievement tests. More detailed information on assessment procedures with deaf and hearing students is found in Chapter 7.

Equipment and Materials

Both teachers and administrators were generally satisfied with the *equipment* available for reading (e.g., captioned movies; language masters; overhead projectors). However, there was a much lower level of satisfaction with the major and supplementary reading *materials* available. Lack of appropriate materials was a major problem reported by administrators and teachers (Marshman, 1974). Details concerning problems with specific materials are discussed in Chapter 6.

Two measures that Marshman used to indicate breadth of available materials are of interest here. Eighty-five percent of the programs had a separate library for elementary students, and 90% had a librarian for these students. (The discrepancy is accounted for by programs that had a general library for the entire school population.) The percentages of teachers whose classrooms had 50 or more books increased with the increasing age of the students: 44% of the classrooms for 5 to 7 year olds; 50% for 8 to 10 year olds; and 63% for 11 year olds and older students. It would be informative to compare these data with data from teachers who are not identified as reading teachers and with data from teachers of hearing children.

Involvement of Administrators and Parents

In Chapter 2, it was noted that there was a positive correlation between the participation of administrators in reading instruction programs and high quality programs (Venezky & Winfield, 1979; Weber, 1976). Although such correlations have not been determined for reading programs for deaf children, some data are available regarding administrative participation. Forty-eight percent of the administrators in Marshman's study of residential programs for deaf children indicated that they were involved in locating, securing, and distributing materials for teacher examination and in working directly with teachers, including the interpretation of test results. These administrators were sensitive to the teachers' dissatisfaction with available instructional and testing materials. However, there were some discrepancies in the data provided by teachers and administrators. For example, administrators listed in-service as a top priority in assistance to teachers, yet 52% of the teachers marked "never" or "unknown" regarding the availability of in-service training for reading-related topics.

Most of the programs (81%) indicated that the teachers reported reading achievement results to the parents, but in only 40% of the programs did teachers provide parents with reports of how the school taught reading or of how parents could assist in that process. It should be noted, however, that Marshman obtained this information from the administrators and thus the results might have been different had individual teachers been polled on this question. We might also wonder what effect, if any, Public Law 94-142 has had on involvement of parents in reading instruction. There does appear to be a growing trend for schools and professional organizations to encourage greater parental involvement in reading instruction. For example, the International Reading Association has published many pamphlets, books, and articles on ways parents can contribute to their child's reading development (e.g., Grinnell, 1984). Similarly, some schools for deaf children are encouraging greater parental involvement. One such school, the Western Pennsylvania School for the Deaf, has a bimonthly newspaper called *Partners in Reading*, which focuses on suggestions for parents (Garrity, 1981). A useful resource for parents and teachers is Trelease's *Read-Aloud Handbook* (1982). In this book, Trelease presents a comprehensible discussion of how and why people should be reading *to* children. Half of the book is devoted to an annotated "Treasury of Read-Alouds."

Students' Views

Views Toward Reading and Reading Instruction

There are virtually no published reports in which the views of deaf students toward reading, reading instruction, or reading assessment were systematically examined. Some information, however, is available from anecdotal reports and studies designed for other purposes. Two brief examples are provided. McCarr (1973) found that many deaf students in junior and senior high school tend to overestimate their reading abilities. Ewoldt (1983) reported that, when asked what they did upon encountering an unknown word, the majority of deaf students responded with "ask my teacher" as their sole strategy. Investigation of deaf students' perceptions and beliefs about reading and reading instruction is fertile ground for study. With some modifications, the *Reading Comprehension Interview* (Wixson et al., 1984) mentioned earlier in this chapter might be a useful tool for such study. Studies on the attitudes and beliefs of hearing children could be used as models for such research. Hoffman, Kastler, Nash, and Daly (1982) provide a useful study of the beliefs and attitudes of hearing students toward oral reading instruction (also see Summers, 1977, for a bibliography on reading attitudes).

Reading Habits and Interests

Several survey studies are available regarding the reading habits and preferences of deaf individuals (Andrews, 1978a; Blatt & Sulzer, 1981; McLaughlin & Andrews, 1975; Stoefen & Holmze, 1979). The first three studies addressed the reading habits of deaf adults. Andrews (1978a) found that the reading habits of deaf college students resembled those of hearing college students more closely than they did the habits of deaf non-college students. The influence of educational level was stressed. The study also confirmed an earlier finding of McLaughlin and Andrews (1975) in that a movie-book relationship was found in the choice of books. All three groups read at least some books about movies they had seen or planned to see. Andrews (1978a) suggested that books about movies be used in junior high and high school reading classes.

The major purpose of Blatt and Sulzer's study (1981) was the identification of media habits (reading and television) for deaf adults. Their sample included 1745 hearing-impaired adults. They found that 80% of the subjects read the newspaper every day. Twenty-five percent read major news magazines every week. Reading habits were associated with educational level. Fifty percent watched the *ABC Captioned News* two or more times each week. The inconvenient time for the newscast (usually late at night) was the major reason it was not viewed more often.

Stoefen and Holmze (1979) compared the reading interests of deaf children with those of hearing children. Like hearing children, deaf children tend to prefer to watch television shows on specific topics rather than read about those same topics. Both male and female deaf children between the ages of 9 and 12 rated social empathy stories highest. Both groups rated excitement stories lowest. Stoefen and Holmze noted "it is difficult to detect clear sex differences in the content interests of hearing-impaired children" (p. 145). In contrast, content interests for hearing children show clear sex differences.

Summary of Survey Studies

It is apparent that there is a great deal of information available from survey studies. Generally, teachers may not be as well prepared to teach reading as is desirable. Given that approximately 20% of the "reading teachers" of deaf children have had only one or no courses in teaching reading, examination of preparation for teaching reading among teachers not designated as reading teachers would likely indicate that the problem is even greater than that reported herein. Also, despite an overwhelming belief in meaning-emphasis programs, instructional practices appear to reflect the more traditional dichotomy between bottom-up (letters first) and top-down (words first) approaches to beginning reading instruction. Additional study of this phenomenon and dissemination of information on the interactive theory of reading is needed within the field of deafness.

The surveys clearly indicate that the major instructional approaches used with deaf children are basal readers and language-experience approaches. The materials most frequently used are those designed for hearing students. From the little information that is available, it can be conjectured that instructional practices are fairly similar to practices as they occur in classrooms for hearing children. A few notable exceptions are less use of basal readers in programs for deaf children at the primary level, and greater use of a single reading group in programs for deaf children. Generally, there appears to be a fairly high level of dissatisfaction with current instructional and testing materials. Marshman (1974) reports that 74% of the administrators in residential schools for the deaf are dissatisfied with their overall reading programs. Details concerning the views of teachers on specific materials are provided in Chapter 6.

The major focus of the available survey studies appears to be descriptions of general approaches and materials. Relatively little is known about instructional strategies and organizational structure. Only two studies were found that attempted to determine specific instructional and organizational plans for teaching reading to deaf children. Research in this area should be a major priority in the near future. Other areas in need of greater research efforts are (1) studies of deaf students' perceptions and beliefs about the reading process; (2) studies of deaf students' reading habits and interests; and (3) comparisons of survey data with data from observational and experimental instructional research.

OBSERVATIONAL STUDIES

An extensive literature search revealed only two observational studies of reading instruction with deaf children (Howarth, Wood, Griffiths, & Howarth, 1981; Mogford, Gregory, & Keay, 1978). The first of these compared individual reading instructional sessions for deaf and hearing children, and the second examined interaction patterns in early parent-child reading sessions. Although each study examined only a single aspect of the instructional setting, the results of these studies are reported in detail since they provide models for needed research in this area. It should be noted that the focus of discussion in this chapter is identification of *instructional techniques* rather than description of reading behaviors. Studies of the reading behaviors of deaf children in noninstructional (testing) settings (e.g., Andrews, 1983; Ewoldt, 1981b; Livingston, 1981; Maxwell, 1980; Quinn, 1981) are not included.

In this section, the advantages and limitations of observational studies are discussed first, followed by the available observational studies of reading instruction with deaf children. General studies of classroom observations with deaf children are also reported. The results of two observational studies of reading instruction with hearing children are reported for comparison purposes and as potential models for future research on instructional techniques with deaf children.

Advantages and Limitations of Observational Research

The most notable advantages of observational studies relate to the limitations of survey studies. In other words, the major advantage comes from the ability to directly observe behaviors in the context of naturally occurring reading instruction sessions rather than relying on reports of behaviors, which may be colored by the requirement to estimate averages for activities that vary greatly in range, by inaccurate recall, and by attempts to idealize performance. Observational studies of reading instruction come within the general rubric of ethnographic studies, which take as their task the description of sociocommunicative behaviors within a particular context. Detailed discussion concerning ethnographic approaches to instructional research can be found in J. Green and Bloome (1983) and Flood (1984a). Logan (1982) provides a historical perspective on classroom observation systems used in reading instruction research.

The limitations of observational studies are well stated by Doyle (1981):

> First, the observational tools and analytical tools of teaching effectiveness research tend to fragment teaching processes into discrete and narrowly defined variables (praise, questions, qualities of teacher talk, etc.) and to freeze the actions of classrooms. The result is a list of characteristics or conditions associated with higher achievement or more positive attitudes. But it is difficult to ascertain from this information how these conditions associated with effectiveness are brought into

being and sustained over long periods of time in classrooms. . . . Second, the conceptual framework of teaching effectiveness research tends to be individualistic. As a result, evidence concerning specific process-product relationships often is interpreted as if the interaction occurred between a teacher and a single student. But classrooms are collective settings and teacher "treatments" are administered to groups of students.

(Doyle, 1981, p. 3)

Further limitations on observational studies are noted by Duffy (1983), who found that students sometimes appeared to be engaged in an academic task whereas in fact they were not attending to the task. He identified such behaviors as "mock participation" and noted that almost all students engage in mock participation at some time, with some students apparently engaging in mock participation nearly all of the time.

Two other limitations of observational studies should also be kept in mind. First, observational studies provide information only about *what is* and are of limited value in determining *what should be* in terms of instructional practices. Second, the outcomes of observational studies are limited to identification of *correlational* relationships rather than *causal* ones. Too often, researchers and practitioners assume that a causal link exists between events when no such relationship has been established.

Parent-Child Reading Sessions

Useful information about instructional techniques for teaching reading can be obtained from observations of parent-child interactions with books during early childhood. Unfortunately, few studies of this type have been conducted with deaf children. Mogford et al. (1978) examined parents' "reading" of picture books with hearing-impaired and hearing children at ages 18 and 24 months. Although no differences were apparent in terms of the time spent in book reading or turns per dialogue at 18 months of age, significant differences were found between the hearing and hearing-impaired children at two years of age. The investigators found that exchanges between mothers and their hearing-impaired children were more highly structured than those between mothers and hearing children of the same ages. Mothers of hearing-impaired children were also less likely to direct their child's attention away from the book to draw connections between the child's environment and the book. The same tendency for relatively higher levels of control has been shown to exist in other language interactions between hearing-impaired children and their caregivers (e.g., Craig & Collins, 1970; see the discussion in the next subsection).

The importance of the study by Mogford et al. for instructional purposes is twofold. First, knowledge of the disruptions that occur in interpersonal relationships between hearing-impaired children and others is an initial step toward finding ways to minimize or remedy such disruptions. Second, knowledge of the types of utterances used by the mothers in "reading" picture books can be used by the resourceful teacher to provide similar and supplementary types of experiences in the preschool environment. The major types of utterances included the following:

attentional vocatives ("Look!")
queries ("What are these?")
feedback ("Yes, they are rabbits")
labels ("That's a kitty cat")
qualifiers ("It's pretty")
invitations to vocalize ("Say" or "You say it")
encouragement for child to relate concepts to own environment
  ("Those are shoes. Where are your shoes?")
expansions within the book context
  ("Cows. Those cows are being milked")

(Mogford et al., 1978)

Additional studies of this type are needed; they produce information on useful approaches to reading instruction as well as information on emerging patterns of reading behavior in very young children. Although there are several published reports of the successful emergence of reading in deaf children prior to formal instruction (Henderson, 1976; Maxwell, 1980; H. Schlesinger & Meadow, 1972), systematic study of the development of concepts about print and orientation toward reading as they occur in the typical preschool deaf child is needed. Andrews (1983) provides this type of information for one group of deaf children. Observational studies of instructional practices are also needed. The following are useful resources for information on emergent reading behavior in hearing children and on research designs that might be used to examine instructional practices and emergent reading behaviors with deaf children: Clay (1979), Goldfield and C. Snow (1984), Mason (1984), and Resnick and Weaver (1979). Andrews and Mason (1984) provide a model of emergent reading in deaf children that is based on earlier work by Mason (1977).

General Studies of Classroom Communication with Deaf Students

General communication patterns in classrooms for deaf children have obvious relevance to the description of instructional practices in reading. Therefore, a brief synopsis of such research with deaf children is provided here. The studies cited include classroom contexts in addition to the reading instructional setting.

Studies of classroom communication patterns in classes for deaf children have typically shown that communication is teacher-dominated and teacher-controlled (e.g., Craig & Collins, 1970; Crandall & Albertini, 1980; T. Kluwin, 1983; Lawson, 1978; Wood, Griffiths, Howarth, & Howarth, 1982). Craig and Collins (1970) found that teacher-initiated communication occurred much more frequently than student-initiated communication (a ratio of 11 to 1). Similarly, Wood et al. (1982) found negative correlations between the amount of adult control through questioning and the initiative and participation of deaf children in conversations. They also found that conversations between deaf children and their teachers more often resembled didactic teaching sessions than egalitarian conversations.

As noted earlier in this chapter, such studies are important since recognition of disruptive interaction patterns is necessary before such patterns can be changed. The reported studies, however, have not addressed *causal* relationships among the variables. It might be asked, "Which came first— the child as a reluctant communication partner or the controlling behavior of the adult?" Although final resolution of this question may be as elusive as the solution to the "chicken or the egg" question, a recent study by H. Wood and D. Wood (1984) would seem to indicate that teachers can influence the conversational abilities of deaf children through changes in their conversational styles. H. Wood and D. Wood (1984) examined seven conversations in three groups, each consisting of a teacher and the same two students, to discover the effects of teachers consciously attempting to bias their contributions to the conversations in one of five ways. The conversation styles included (1) requests for the students to say it again "properly"; (2) closed questions (yes-no questions or forced-choice wh-questions); (3) open questions; (4) contributions of personal experiences; and (5) phatic responses (sitting back and nodding; acknowledgment-type responses).

The major conclusion of this study is that the communication behaviors of deaf children can be shaped by the teacher's conversational style. Positive and negative consequences of each conversational style are discussed at length by H. Wood and D. Wood. They conclude "no single strategy produced unambiguously successful results, rather the advantages of the different moves seem to complement one another. . . . it is clear on an intuitive level that the best conversations—where enthusiasm, thematic cohesion and 'relevance' are all high—are ones where the teachers have managed to tip the *balance* [italics added] of power first one way and then the other–introducing topics whilst still giving their children the opportunity to contribute and develop their own ideas along the theme" (H. Wood & D. Wood, 1984, p. 60).

Two additional studies of classroom communication with deaf children are noteworthy. Huntington and Watton (1981, 1982) examined the relationship between the linguistic complexity of "teacher talk" and "pupil talk" and found that higher levels of complexity in teacher talk were *associated* with longer and more complex language on the part of the students (no causal link was established). T. Kluwin (1983) looked at the discourse structure of teaching episodes in four classrooms of deaf children. He discusses four factors that he identified as important variables in the effectiveness of the teaching episodes: (1) task persistence; (2) high cognitive demands; (3) linguistic facility; and (4) cohesion. Kluwin's data were also correlational rather than causal.

Observations of Classroom Reading Instruction

The work reported by Howarth et al. (1981) is the only study that has been focused on observations of formal reading instruction with deaf children. These researchers conducted a comparative study of the reading lessons of deaf and hearing primary level students in England. The variables of interest included time spent in reading; number of words actually read; frequency of stops initiated by teacher and child; and reasons for the stops (derived from the teacher's interpretation of the child's failure). Deaf and hearing students were matched based on the use of a particular story selection in their reading texts. The investigators used an ecological matching procedure in that they selected lessons that were part of the normal instructional process rather than requiring students to read stories that were not part of their regular lessons. An individual reading session with the teacher was the instructional mode chosen for this study. Group reading sessions were not studied.

The results indicated that there were marked differences between the reading lessons of deaf children and of hearing children using the same materials. Deaf children stopped reading or were stopped by their teachers more frequently than the hearing children (a mean of 17.6 stops for deaf children; 8.9 for hearing children). In fact, half of the deaf students were being stopped, on the average, every four words or fewer! An examination of the reasons for stops revealed that the major cause of more frequent stops for the deaf children was for meaning failure (lexical stops). "The deaf children's teachers spent much more time teaching children the meaning of words they were encountering in the text. . . . When we looked at stops which were made to praise and encourage the child, however, the pattern was reversed. Here hearing children were more likely to encounter such a stop" (Howarth et al., 1981, p. 158).

Examination of reading times also revealed some interesting differences between the reading lessons of deaf and hearing students. Although both groups read the same number of words, the deaf students took significantly longer to read the passages. The differences were accounted for by the higher frequency of stops for the deaf children. Measures of reading rate (words per minute with stops excluded) indicated that the range of reading rates for deaf and hearing children were comparable. Some qualifications on this result, however, are necessary. In a post hoc examination of the reading rates, Howarth et al. found that all of the deaf children from one of the two schools in the study (school B) were reading at rates below 40 words per minute, which was taken as the cut-off for speech at an intelligible rate (normal extempore speech occurs at a rate of approximately 160 words per minute, J. Kelly & Steer, 1949). Two major conclusions were based on the slow reading rate of the deaf children. First, it is doubtful that students from school B "were deriving much sense from the structure of the text" (p. 161). The second conclusion is of major importance and is quoted at length from the original study:

The two schools differed in their general philosophy about teaching the deaf child how to read. . . . School B attempted to use the written word as a vehicle not only for teaching reading but also [for] language itself. . . . School A on the other hand argue [*sic*] that the child cannot learn to read until he has mastered enough vocabulary and grammatical knowledge to enable him to translate the printed code into a phonetic one. Thus the fact that children at school A had had a similar length of reading teaching as those in school B and yet read more advanced texts faster *suggests* [italics added] (but no more) that the early experiences of the children in school B may not be adding to their reading development. . . . However, because the children in school A were also older, the schools' difference is confounded with mental age which also correlates with reading speed.

(Howarth et al., 1981, p. 161)

A final concern of Howarth et al. was the relationships among reading rate, text difficulty, and student age. They found that the use of more advanced texts was associated with faster reading rates and that this relationship held for both deaf and hearing students. Thus, teachers of deaf children and hearing children appear to use the same logic in matching the demands of the text with the child's reading rate. Comparisons of text difficulty for the two schools for deaf children revealed that the child's mental age was correlated with the use of more difficult texts. Thus, even though students at the two schools had been reading for comparable lengths of time, the older students in school A were using more difficult texts.

Although the study by Howarth et al. was the only such study found that dealt with deaf children, a fairly substantial literature is available comparing the reading lessons of good and poor hearing readers. Of these, Allington's work (1977, 1980, 1984) with hearing children most closely parallels the study by Howarth et al. with deaf children in that interruption behaviors are a major focus. Allington's results are also similar to those for deaf children; that is, poorer readers are interrupted more often than better readers. Other research has compared the instructional strategies teachers use with low ability and high ability groups of readers (see Hiebert, 1983, for a review of this literature). Differences between the two groups were found in almost all aspects of classroom dynamics. Students in low ability groups spend less time practicing reading and more time acquiring skills. Low ability groups also receive more emphasis on word identification.

Allington's question (1977), "If they don't read much, how are they ever gonna get good?" is an important question because it forcefully draws attention to the need for poorer readers to read more and with fewer interruptions. We would hope, however, that educators will not take this information as evidence that current practices (i.e., teacher interruptions) are all bad and thus go to the opposite extreme (i.e., no interruptions). Allington (1980) offers a balanced view:

It is unlikely that the resolution of this question will be found in an "all or none" proposition. Most likely, there exists a curvilinear relationship between teacher interruptions and the development of effective and efficient reading abilities. . . . *either* [italics added] persistent interruptions *or* [italics added] consistent disregard of oral-reading errors would seem to lead to the development of less than optimal reading strategies.

(Allington, 1980, p. 375)

Also, as with the relationship between the reluctant student and the controlling teacher, it is not at all clear what the causal relationship is between teacher behaviors and student performance. Duffy (1983) discusses possible relationships and suggests that current knowledge in this area "provides hypotheses but few answers" (p. 292).

Summary of Observational Studies

Although available observational studies on reading instruction with deaf children are limited in number and in scope, it seems appropriate to note two general findings. First, differences do exist between reading lessons for deaf and hearing children using the same stories. Deaf children are interrupted more often and take longer to read a passage. The story time deaf children share with their parents is more structured than similar times for hearing children. The dyadic communication between a deaf child and his or her parent is also less likely to include nonbook-related discussion or links between the book and personal experiences. Similar differences are found between hearing children who are good readers and those who are poor readers. Additional research is needed to determine the causal relationship among student behaviors and teacher behaviors. Second, it is clear that the classroom is a complex context in which teacher behaviors, student behaviors, communication patterns, and situational tasks all interact and influence each other. Recognition of this complex environment must be a major aspect of all future instructional research. Mosenthal (1984) provides a comprehensive discussion of the theoretical and research design factors that must be considered in such research.

It is apparent that greater efforts toward determining *what is* in classrooms for deaf children are needed. To that end, the results of two observational studies with hearing children are discussed (Durkin, 1978-1979, 1984). These studies are important, not only as models for future research, but also as indications of general practices in teaching reading comprehension.

Durkin reported on her observations of classrooms that were designed to determine the extent of time devoted to comprehension instruction. She defined *instruction* as "Teacher does/says something to help children understand or work out the meaning of more than a single, isolated word" (Durkin, 1978–1979, p. 488). Comprehension *assessment* included activities in which the teacher determined if students have comprehended the passage. An example will serve to differentiate the two. Imagine that students were reading a story in which the following paragraph occurs (example from Durkin, 1980):

Paul drives a blue Chevrolet. *That's* what I bought, but I wanted a red *one*.

The teacher asks, "What kind of car did the author of the story buy?" One student gives an incorrect response. The teacher that uses an *instructional* activity helps the student to identify the referent for "That's" and shows the student how to figure out the meaning of similar anaphoric devices (words that refer back to previous words, statements, or concepts in the language of the text). The teacher that uses an *assessment* activity asks another student. At the conclusion of the assessment activity, the first student knows that he or she gave the wrong answer but has no idea of how to attack similar problems in the future. Durkin's results showed that, in 300 hours of observation, less than 1 percent of the time was devoted to comprehension instruction. The point is made that more time needs to be devoted to *teaching* children to comprehend rather than *testing* their comprehension.

Durkin's second study (1984) compared the prescriptions of teacher's manuals from basal series with the activities of teachers in using those manuals and basal readers. Pearson (1984a) provides a concise summary of the study and the implications of Durkin's two studies:

> Durkin's two studies, taken together, reveal a picture of virtually no direct instruction in comprehension. Instead, teachers seem to spend most of their classroom discussion time asking students questions about stories they have read and giving assignments. Regarding comprehension skills—such as main idea, sequence, fact-opinion—manuals provided little guidance concerning how the skills ought to be presented to students. Teachers apparently provide little guidance to students about how they ought to solve problems and/or answer questions exemplifying these skills. The prevailing wisdom is to provide massive doses of unguided practice. Nor is there much evidence, either in manuals or classrooms, that students receive substantive feedback that would allow them to evaluate how well they are performing a task or, more important, what inappropriate strategies they might be adopting. The student who is not doing well on a particular comprehension skills seems to have little help to look forward to, save additional opportunities to improve performance on his or her own through practice.
> (Pearson, 1984a, pp. 8–9)

It is clear that these studies provide useful information for the teacher trainee, the in-service teacher, and the researcher. Studies with deaf children that would allow direct comparison with Durkin's data would be helpful.

EXPERIMENTAL STUDIES

Experimental and quasi-experimental studies of reading instructional techniques fall into one of three major categories: (1) manipulation of text-based variables, such as vocabulary, text structure, and format; (2) examination of reader-based techniques that can enhance comprehension (i.e., metacognitive strategies); and (3) examination of instructional techniques (i.e., situation-based, classroom teaching strategies). Much of the experimental research on reading instruction with deaf children fits within the first category. These studies are reviewed in Chapter 5, along with other research on reading materials. Studies in the other two categories are discussed in this chapter. First, an overview of experimental designs is presented, followed by discussion of the advantages and limitations of experimental research on reading instruction. Next, experimental and quasi-experimental studies of instructional techniques are discussed. The major focus is studies with deaf children. Several studies with hearing children are also included for comparison purposes and as potential models of future instructional research with deaf children. A summary is provided at the end of the section.

Experimental Designs

Although detailed discussion of experimental design is beyond the scope of this book, a brief orientation will likely be useful in helping readers to comprehend the results and implications of experimental studies. Experimental studies are designed to determine *causal* relationships among variables (Borg & Gall, 1979). Observational studies, such as those reported in the last section, can show that some type of relationship exists between, say, controlling behavior by teachers and children as reluctant communicators. However, causal links cannot be assumed to exist unless one of the variables is manipulated systematically to determine the effects on the other variable (i.e., unless an experiment is conducted). *True experimental studies* require (1) that a control group be used, and (2) that subjects be randomly selected from the target population and randomly assigned to the experimental and control groups (Borg & Gall, 1979). These conditions often are not or cannot be met in educational settings (Calfee, 1982). Campbell and Stanley (1963) use the term *quasi-experimental studies* to refer to studies in which one or both of the conditions are not met.

It is important to be aware of the difficulties inherent in trying to establish causal links between variables in complex social settings (e.g., reading classrooms). Calfee (1982) provides a succinct synopsis:

> The body of reading research since 1960 is impressive for its size alone. . . . In spite of considerable time, energy, and money, it appears to many that we have little coherent advice to offer for policy makers or practictioners about "how to teach reading." What, for instance, has been learned from large-scale social experiments on reading instruction, like the First-grade Reading Study (Bond & Dykstra, 1967) and Planned Variation in Follow-through (for a technical history and list of the voluminous documentation, see Villaume & Haney, 1977)? The answers are not too inspiring:
>
> • The "method" does not seem to make much difference.
> • Spending time teaching reading is better than spending time doing something else.
> • Teachers make a difference, though why and how are not altogether clear.
> • Most of the variance in student performance can be predicted by background characteristics.

• Growth in reading (as presently measured) does not depend greatly on program variables.

(Calfee, 1982, p. 1)

Dissatisfaction with current techniques for conducting experimental studies on instructional processes in reading is fairly widespread (e.g., Pearson, 1984a; Tuinman, 1979). One example of this dissatisfaction is seen in concerns about differences that exist between the results of experimental studies conducted in the "laboratory" and of studies conducted in "naturalistic classroom settings" (see the review in Mosenthal, 1984). Venezky (1979) provides a powerful example of how instructional techniques and students' skills that exhibit specific characteristics in the laboratory setting are manifested quite differently in the classroom setting:

> Elkonin (1963), Zhurova (1963), D. Bruce (1964), and various others proved conclusively that children before some magic age—6 in Bruce's study, 7 in Zhurova's, and so on—could not perform certain tasks that involve manipulating abstract sounds. The children in these studies couldn't segment words, or repeat the first sound of a word, or do other sound processing tasks before 6 or 7 years of age.... The great shock comes when you take these tasks, or slight modifications of them, into a classroom with the same age children and start doing these things day after day. You soon discover that almost all kids from kindergarten up can be taught all these tasks without tears or frustration, given repeated practice and appropriate sequencing of tasks. There is a world of difference between the ongoing, day-by-day activities of the classroom and the laboratory.
>
> (Venezky, 1979, p. 280)

R. Snow (1974) uses the term *ecological validity* to represent the degree to which the results of experimental studies translate to actual classroom settings. Ecological validity is thought to be highest when the regular classroom environment and routine are held intact, lower when an outside experimenter impinges on the classroom environment for either pull-out and within-class activities, and lowest when a noninstructional, laboratory setting is used (Mosenthal, 1984).

A final concern regarding the implications of experimental studies is the possibility of overrelying on *statistical significance*. The *educational significance* of the results is of equal or greater importance. The following questions can be helpful in judging whether results are educationally significant:

1. Regardless of the statistical significance of differences between pretest and posttest scores, are the scores sufficiently different in terms of educational goals? For example, a difference of one or two points on a 100 point test may be statistically significant, but likely is not educationally significant.

2. Are the effects of the experimental technique greater than what might be expected under "normal" instructional conditions? For example, if the experimental technique shows gains equal to typical gains for students at that age, the technique may be useful, but it does not produce results that are (educationally) significantly better than other approaches.

Advantages and Limitations of Experimental Research

The major advantage of experimental studies over other forms of instructional research relates to the ability to make causal links between instructional practices and the performance of students. However, as occurs with experimental research in other social sciences, experimental instructional research faces some unique challenges in establishing conclusively that causal links exist and in determining exactly what those links are. Calfee (1982) lists five major problems: the number of factors that are likely to influence the situation; the limited theoretical guidance for choosing variables; the common occurrence of interaction among variables; the ethical and social limits regarding what can be manipulated and controlled; and the hierarchical nature of social systems.

Difficulties in definitively establishing causal links are even greater in quasi-experimental studies. Because no control group is used, the experimenter may *assume* that the experimental treatment was the cause of any observed changes between the pretest and posttest scores. "There is always some chance, however, that one or more extraneous variables brought about all or part of the change noted between the pretest and posttest scores" (Borg & Gall, 1979, p. 539).

Various researchers have attempted to define the extraneous variables that influence the results of experimental and quasi-experimental research in education. Examples include (1) maturation, (2) instruction other than the experimental treatment, (3) a Hawthorne or novelty effect, (4) experimenter bias, (5) interaction among variables, (6) differences between experimenters (teachers) in the study, (7) instrumentation problems (e.g., nonparallel pretests and posttests), (8) preexisting differences between the groups prior to the experiment, and (9) the effects of attrition during the study if there is a consistent pattern among dropouts (Borg & Gall, 1979; Campbell & Stanley, 1963).

In a review of experimental research on teaching reading comprehension, Tierney and J. Cunningham (1980) note four major problems that result in "making it virtually impossible to attribute causation to any specific teaching practices" (p. 55). Paraphrased, these include the following:

1. Failure to equate the experimental and control groups on relevant skills at the beginning of the experiment and to consider whether the groups were developmentally "ready" for the skill which was to be taught.
2. Failure to adequately define the treatment "so as to rule out the possibility that practice in reading alone would effect the same gains as treatment" (Tierney & J. Cunningham, 1980, p. 56).
3. Failure to apply treatments for a sufficient duration to provide information about long-term effects and to include transfer tasks as part of the experimental treatment.
4. Failure to use multiple measures in order to be sensitive to a range of training effects and to look at the treatment effects on these measures separately and in combination.

Tierney and J. Cunningham (1980) also criticize instructional research in reading because of what has been described as a "single shotgun approach." They recommend that cohesive lines of research be developed which include replication, modification, and extension. The research of Frase (1967, 1968) is cited as exemplifying a comprehensive approach to reading research. The line of research by Raphael (1984) and associates discussed later in this chapter is another good model of comprehensive research.

True Experimental Studies

Most of the true experimental studies on reading instruction with deaf children focus on the effects of various types of materials (e.g., Anken & Holmes, 1977). These studies are reviewed in Chapter 5. Only a few studies with deaf children were found in each of the other two categories: reader-based strategies and instructional techniques. These studies and several studies with hearing children that focus on the same techniques are reported here.

Studies of Reader-Based Strategies

Deaf children. G. Long and Conklin (1979) conducted a series of experiments to determine the effects of teaching hearing-impaired college students to use semantic networking as a strategy for comprehending and retaining information from reading materials. Experimental groups of students were trained to construct graphic representations of five basic relationships among ideas in written prose: characteristics, definitions, examples, consequences, and comparisons and contrasts. An example of a network for a prose passage is shown in Figure 1. Control groups of hearing-impaired students read the passages but were not involved in network training or construction. Comprehension tests were given to both groups. The results were generally supportive of teaching networking to deaf college students in that the experimental groups usually had higher levels of performance. Better performance by the experimental groups was associated with tasks requiring long-term retention rather than immediate recall and with un-cued questions (tell me all you know) rather than cued questions (e.g., multiple choice; fill in the blank).

Long and Conklin attempted to ferret out the relationships among the variables by eliminating extraneous variables. For example, one possible explanation for the higher performance of the experimental groups is the depth of processing encouraged by the networking activity. If this were the case, however, similar results might be predicted whether the networking process were written out or just thought out. The results did not bear out this hypothesis. Performance was higher when networking was written out on paper.

Hearing children. Dansereau et al. (1979) examined the use of semantic networks with hearing college students and found the same facilitative effect

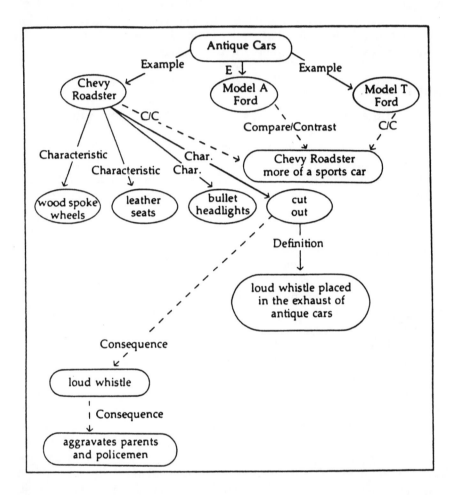

Figure 1.   Semantic network for a prose paragraph. From Long, G., & Conklin, D. (1979). The implementation and evaluation of a technique for improving the prose comprehension of a technique for improving the prose comprehension of deaf college students. In G. Propp (Ed.), *1980's schools . . . Portals to century 21. Selected papers* (pp. 158–170). Silver Spring, MD: Convention of American Instructors of the Deaf. Reprinted with permission.

as that obtained with deaf college students. We must be cautious, however, in generalizing these results to younger children. Research is needed to determine whether these techniques would help or hinder deaf and hearing children who are at earlier stages of reading development. Other approaches to diagramming the patterns of ideas in texts include mapping (T. Anderson, 1978), flowcharting (Geva, 1983), and rhetorical structures (B. Meyer, 1975).

Experimental studies of other reader-based strategies with deaf children are virtually nonexistent. There is, however, a fairly extensive base of studies with hearing children. Some of the studies that relate to the development of inferential and metacognitive strategies were discussed in Chapter 2. The research cited here focuses on some additional instructional techniques for teaching children to effectively use reader-based strategies.

Raphael (1984) provides a synopsis of a line of research that she and associates conducted on teaching students to identify the relationship between questions and their answers as a strategy for comprehending text. Children were taught to determine explicitly whether questions could be answered based on information *right there*, whether the questions required students to *think and search*, or whether a student had to find the answers "*on my own*." These three strategies were based on the three levels of question-answer relationships (QARs) discussed by Pearson and D. Johnson (1978)—textually-explicit questions, textually-implicit questions, and scriptually-implicit questions. An example is shown in Figure 2.

Experimentation with the QAR technique was carried out with hearing children in fourth through eighth grades. The research involved several studies, each of which focused on one or a few aspects of the phenomenon. The first study (Raphael, Winograd, & Pearson, 1980) was descriptive in nature to determine the abilities of students to answer the three levels of questions without training. This research confirmed that *on my own* questions were indeed more difficult than the other types of questions and that ability to answer the three types of questions differed depending on the abilities of students. A series of training and instructional experiments was conducted to determine whether training students to determine the source of the answers to questions would be effective in improving performance on questions.

The training study (Raphael, 1981; Raphael & Pearson, 1982) involved training by the experimenters. This study confirmed that the technique resulted in higher performance on passages where students explicitly identified QARs. For high ability students, improved performance was seen only on the *on my own* questions since performance on the other two types of questions was already at the ceiling on the test. One of Raphael's subjects offered a probable reason: "Someone should have told me about QARs long ago. I have a lot of information in my head—I just didn't know I was allowed to use it!" (Raphael, 1984, p. 306). Low ability students, on the other hand, had significant gains on *right there* and *think and search* questions, but did not improve on *on my own* questions. One of these subjects stated: "I know

Three Kinds of Questions

Type 1

Where is the answer found?   Right There

The answer is in the story, easy to find. The words used to make
the questions and the words that make the answer are Right There,
in the same sentence.

Type 2   Think and
Search

The answer is in the story, but a little harder to find. You would
never find the words in the question and words in the answer in
the same sentence, but would have to Think and Search for the
answer.

Type 3   On My
Own

The answer won't be told by words in the story. You must find
the answer in your head. Think: "I have to answer this question
On My Own, the story won't be much help."

Figure 2.   Question-answer relationships (QARs). From Raphael, T. (1982). Question-
answering strategies for children. *Reading Teacher*, *36*, 186–190. Reprinted with permission.

this is an On My Own question and I went to my head, but there was nothing there" (Raphael, 1984, p. 306).

Two instructional studies were designed to determine (1) whether the technique would be effective in ecologically valid instructional settings (i.e., with the regular teacher), and (2) whether QAR training would transfer to other reading comprehension tasks. Additional objectives were to determine the amount of in-service training needed to help teachers in using the QARs and the amount of training that was optimal for students at various levels of reading ability.

The effectiveness and transferability of the technique were confirmed in all studies (Raphael, 1984). Raphael and Wonnacott (1981) found that a half-day inservice training session in which the technique was explained and materials that teachers could use in training students were given was sufficient. Follow-up with the researchers going into classroom to observe and provide feedback was deemed unnecessary. The greatest differences occurred between low ability groups whose teachers received in-service training and low ability groups whose teachers did not receive such training. Raphael and McKinney (1983) found that the optimal amount of training depended on the grade level of students.

> In fourth and fifth grades, there should be 1 week of intensive training followed by approximately 6 to 8 weeks of practice on maintenance passages. By sixth grade, the week of training appears to be sufficient, while in eighth grade, a 10-minute orientation is as effective as a longer training period.
>
> (Raphael, 1984, p. 310)

Additional research on the effects of the QAR technique is ongoing. Given that most deaf children read at levels below the fourth grade, it cannot be assumed that this technique will be equally effective with them or with hearing children below a fourth grade level. Raphael (1984) indicates that she has attempted to implement QAR training in second grade classrooms for hearing children. Preliminary results indicate that changes in the approach are necessary for this age group.

Several investigators have examined the effects of teaching children to use a story grammar outline (see Chapter 2) as a strategy for comprehending and recalling text. An example of an exercise used with hearing children is shown in Figure 3.

Experimental studies with intermediate grade readers (fifth grade and above) have essentially shown that such instruction is not necessary (Dreher & Singer, 1980; Sebesta, Calder, & Cleland, 1982). The studies have found no differences on amount recalled or the pattern of recall between groups who received such instruction and those who did not. Neither were differences found between good and poor readers, indicating that the two groups did not differ in their knowledge of story structure. The only positive effect of the training was on ability to place sentences from a story into a story chart (see Figure 3). The instructed group correctly placed 82.7%

Fill in the sentences from the story that fit in each part of this chart.

1. Setting
   Where does the story take place?
   Who are the main characters of the story?
   When does the story take place?

   _____

   Is there any other information that helps us get the picture of what things are like at the beginning of the story?

   _____

   _____

2. Goal
   What is the main *goal* or purpose of the main character?

   _____

   Is there any other information about the main character's goal? Maybe the story explains the reason the main character wants the goal.

   _____

   _____

   _____

3. Plot
How does the main character try to get the goal?

A. First try
   Something happens.

   _____

   What does the main character do?

   _____

   How did it turn out?

   _____

   Is there any other information about the *first* try?

   _____

   _____

B. Second try
   Main character makes a new plan to get the goal.

   _____

   Main character tries new plan.

   _____

   How did it turn out?

   _____

   Is there any other information about the *second* try?

   _____

   _____

4. Ending
Did the main character get the goal?

_____

Is there any other information about the way the story ended?

_____

_____

Figure 3.   Exercise for teaching story structure. From Dreher, J., & Singer, H. (1980). Story grammar instruction unnecessary for intermediate grade students. *Reading Teacher*, 34, 261–268. Reprinted with permission.

of the sentences in the correct place, as opposed to only 19% correct placement for the uninstructed group (Dreher & Singer, 1980). The evidence seems to indicate that explicit knowledge of the categories of story grammar likely is not necessary for students to effectively use their implicit knowledge of story structure (assuming that they possess such knowledge). This conclusion is in agreement with the case for language (i.e., explicit knowledge of English syntax is not necessary for effective use of the language). On the other hand, explicitly teaching story grammar structures may be useful for hearing children who do not already possess knowledge of story structure (see the discussion in Tierney & J. Cunningham, 1984). Such instruction may also be helpful for deaf children. The Rhode Island School for the Deaf (Zarcadoolas, 1981) uses a simplified story structure to teach basic plots to deaf children. No published reports are available regarding the effectiveness of the technique.

Studies of Instructional Techniques

Deaf children. The results of Iran-Nejad et al. (1981) on deaf children's comprehension of metaphors were discussed in Chapter 3. The training component of that study (which included feedback to students) is of interest here. These researchers compared deaf children's comprehension of metaphors following a training session of four practice items with feedback (the experimental group) with the comprehension of other deaf children without the training session (the control group). Subjects receiving the training performed at significantly (statistically and educationally) higher levels on a metaphor test than those without the training (63% and 20% accuracy, respectively). Iran-Nejad et al. are appropriately conservative in making inferences about definitive causal links between their experimental treatment and higher levels of performance. They also discuss possible extraneous variables which might account for the data. "Whether it is feedback itself or practice alone that is so effective is addressed not directly by this experiment, but indirectly" (Iran-Nejad et al., 1981, p. 554). The researchers express the belief that the feedback was the causal factor since deaf children without the training did not improve during the test as a result of practice.

Maeder (1979) studied the effectiveness of written questions inserted during reading, signed questions inserted during reading, and no questions during reading as related to performance on a postreading test that was composed of half new items which none of the subjects had seen and half items which subjects in the inserted questions conditions had seen while reading the 1,500 word passage. Subjects were 36 deaf students from a high school program. The 18 "good" readers had an average reading grade level of 6.9; the 18 "poor" readers had an average reading grade level of 3.5. No feedback was given to subjects in the experimental groups regarding performance on the inserted questions.

On the total scores for the postreading test, there were no differences among the three conditions (no inserted questions, inserted print-questions, inserted sign-questions). Differences did emerge between the groups with inserted questions and the control group for literal comprehension questions (i.e., *right there* QARs; see discussion earlier in this chapter). Expected differences also were found between the scores for better and poorer students. It would have been interesting to compare the groups' performances on the questions that the experimental groups had seen and those they had not seen. The author, however, did not conduct this comparison, and data from the study are insufficient to allow for a post hoc analysis. Maeder suggested that further study of the role of questions is needed with larger groups, longer treatments, a larger variety of question types, and longer texts.

Andrews (1983) examined the effects on reading development of weekly story-time sessions with young deaf children. The instructional approach for story-time focused on (1) establishment of the link between signs, words, and referents, (2) practice with a fixed set of vocabulary in storybooks, and (3) drills of word cards with a sign drawing on one side and the printed word on the other. This study is rich in detail on the emergence of reading in young deaf children, and it provides useful tools for assessing prereading skills. The experimental aspect of the study, however, suffers from major methodological flaws. First and foremost, it is unclear what degree of difference actually existed between instruction in the experimental treatment and the instruction that the control groups received at two other schools for deaf children. Andrews (1983) makes the following statement:

> In general, all 3 participating schools made extensive use of manual signs and fingerspelling to teach alphabet letters and printed words during reading instruction. Then, how was the experimental treatment in this study different from typical reading instruction? *The fundamental difference was that the experimental training made more explicit the meaningful relationship between the single, lexical sign and the printed word in reading materials which limited letter and word knowledge to a fixed set of words and phrases. Further, by training the children to recite short, 6 to 15 content item stories, they were able to acquire important notions about story structures.*
> (pp. 37–38, italics in original)

It is also likely that Andrews' data were contaminated in that several of the children in the control group were participants in the experimental group for another study (which was designed to determine the effects of computer-assisted vocabulary drill [Prinz, K.E. Nelson, & Stedt, 1982]). Other difficulties included differences between the experimental and control groups at the beginning of the experiment; the short duration of the experimental treatment (although it occurred over a period of seven months, there were only 12.5 hours of contact time in the story-reading sessions); and the lack of control for (or attention to) possible extraneous factors that also could have accounted for the results.

Before it is assumed that this study has little value, it must be stressed that the problems relate only to the experimental aspect of the study. The noted problems are those which Tierney and J. Cunningham (1980) identified as common in instructional research. Similar problems are also found in the quasi-experimental studies reported in a later section in this chapter. A major strength of Andrews' study lies in the descriptive data base on emergent reading behaviors in deaf children.

Hearing children. Discussion of the voluminous body of research on reading comprehension with hearing children is beyond the scope of this book. Tierney and J. Cunningham (1980, 1984) provide a review of much of this literature. Several other major textbooks are also excellent references (Flood, 1984a, 1984b; Pearson, 1984b). The present discussion focuses on three instructional issues: (1) feedback to students during oral reading, (2) questioning strategies, and (3) methods of teaching vocabulary.

A fairly substantial number of studies have addressed the issue of teacher feedback during oral reading lessons. Two representative studies are discussed. L. Meyer (1982) studied the effects of word analysis (phonic) feedback to learning disabled and educationally handicapped children in comparison to the effects of word supply feedback. She found no differences on posttest performance on reading tests nor on the percentage of words missed during reading of a story. Subjects in this study were in fourth through seventh grades.

A second study, that of Hoffman, O'Neal, and Clements (1982), focused on the effects of feedback on the performance of nonhandicapped children in second grade classrooms. No data were provided on reading level. It is likely that at least some children were reading above a second grade level since only students from the highest reading group were selected. The study is quasi-experimental in that a control group was not included, but it is discussed here because of its relevance to feedback mechanisms. Three feedback conditions were studied: terminal (word supply); sustaining graphophonic (focusing attention on orthographic features); and sustaining content (focusing on surrounding structures and meanings). Feedback was also varied as to whether it occurred immediately after a miscue or was delayed until the first sentence break following the miscue. Feedback was given only for a selected list of target words.

The major conclusion was that no differences were found between the number of miscues on the target words or total miscues for any of the experimental treatments. The profiles of miscues were also similar for the three feedback conditions: Mispronunciations were most common, followed by hesitations and substitutions. Omissions, insertions, and calls for help were not considered due to low frequency. Differences emerged when the effects of immediate and delayed feedback were compared. The low ability group (defined as the bottom half of the subject pool) tended to hesitate rather than mispronounce in the immediate graphophonic feedback conditions. Opposite results were shown for the context feedback conditions: immediate feedback led to more mispronunciations and delayed feedback led to more hesitations. Hoffman et al. (1982) concluded that differences in the teacher's verbal feedback did not affect the *quantity* of miscues but did affect the *quality* of student performance during oral reading.

The issues of when and how to question students about reading selections are among the most hotly debated and least resolved issues in the reading field. Several reviews of research on these issues are available (e.g., R. Anderson & Biddle, 1975; Andre, 1979; Memory, 1982; Tierney & J. Cunningham, 1980, 1984). In this chapter, discussion is limited to two aspects: when to ask questions and what types of information to ask questions about. Two related issues are discussed in Chapter 7: (1) whether reading can or should be divided into separate subskills, and (2) what type of questions to ask in terms of linguistic features (e.g., vocabulary and syntax) and format (e.g., multiple choice or wh-questions).

Various researchers have addressed the issue of whether it is most effective to ask questions before reading, during reading, after reading, or at some combination of these times. Much of the research on this topic is complicated by the use of students of varying levels, varying types of materials, and varying measures of comprehension. For example, two reviews of literature came to different conclusions regarding the effects of questions inserted during reading. Anderson and Biddle (1975) examined studies conducted with older (high school and college) students and concluded that questions inserted during reading had a positive effect on posttests for both questioned and unquestioned literal information. Memory (1982) examined studies conducted with younger (middle grade) students and found that the use of inserted questions enhanced recall of questioned information and reduced recall for unquestioned information. These differences clearly point to the need for considering the students' levels in determining the effects of instructional practices on student performance (Memory, 1982).

Harris and Sipay (1980), among others, summarize current beliefs on questioning practices during reading instruction for elementary school students. Questions asked before reading tend to restrict the incidental learning of textual information that is not needed to answer the questions. Qualifications on this main conclusion, however, are needed. Memory (1983) found that *why* questions regarding the main idea of passages presented prior to reading helped low-average sixth graders, but not good readers, to understand the main idea while at the same time not interfering with the learning of other information. He concludes

> Despite the findings of some previous research, teachers do not have to assume that a guiding question given before the reading of a selection will necessarily detract from the learning of significant information not directly related to that question. If the guiding question focuses on the main idea of a cause-effect passage, then it can enhance understanding of that main idea by low-average readers without hindering learning of other important passage information.
>
> (Memory, 1983, p. 46)

In terms of questions asked during reading, Tierney and J. Cunningham (1984) concluded that "research seems to bear out teachers' intuitions concerning the facilitative effect of inserted questions" (p. 623). This conclusion was based on studies with intermediate level readers and those with higher skills. Beginning readers and less able readers, however, may actually be distracted by answering questions during a story and consequently may not process concepts central to the story (Kurchak, 1977).

Some researchers have focused on *who* is to ask questions rather than *when* questions are to be asked. Palincsar (1981) and Brown and Palincsar (1982) studied the effects on comprehension of training seventh grade students to generate their own questions. Subjects for the study were good decoders but poor comprehenders. Results indicated that students who received training improved in their ability to answer comprehension questions. McNeil (1984) provides practical suggestions of how to implement this strategy in the classroom.

Other studies have focused on the effects on learning of questions asked about different aspects of text information. Wixson (1983) reports on two studies with fifth grade students that were designed to determine interactions among reader, text, and question form. In the first study, students read a passage and then each of four groups was asked only one type of question (*right there, think and search, on my own,* or text-irrelevant questions). The second study used the same design but the types of questions were differentiated by level of importance as rated by adult judges. The results showed that students' learning from passages (based on free recall one week after reading the texts) was significantly related to the types of questions that had been asked immediately following reading. The study clearly shows the importance of the types of questions that teachers ask.

The implications for the correct balance of questions to ask, however, are less clear. Teachers might be tempted to assume that higher order (more important, more abstract, *on my own*) questions should be the only or major type of questions asked. The folly of such a conclusion is clearly shown by Andre (1979) and Memory (1982), who indicate that low ability students do not benefit from practice with higher order questions when the answers require background information that the poor readers do not have.

Roser and Juel (1982) studied the effects of vocabulary instruction on children's knowledge of words and comprehension of stories. These researchers provide a summary of the research literature on methods of teaching vocabulary to hearing students and abstract three major principles for successfully teaching vocabulary from that literature:

1. The teaching of vocabulary must be direct and systematic.
2. Instruction should help the learner draw the relationships between words to be learned and the learner's own background, needs, and interests.
3. Instruction should provide in-depth work with vocabulary words rather than cursory attention.

(Roser & Juel, 1982, p. 111)

Roser and Juel used these three principles to design the instructional treatment in a comparison of the effects of vocabulary instruction versus no vocabulary instruction. Two conclusions of the study are important here. First, prior to instruction, children in first and second grade *recognize* (in print) slightly less than half of the words that are identified as "new" in the teacher's guide for a story and *know the meanings* for just slightly more than half of these words. Second, vocabulary instruction did not influence word recognition but had a significant influence on word meanings. Roser and Juel concluded

> While children appear to be successfully learning to identify words by simply reading those words in the basal story context, they do not appear to be as successfully learning the meanings of words through story context. Rather, direct instruction in word meaning prior to story learning appears especially helpful. In particular, there is an indication that low reading group children profit from direct word meaning instruction.
>
> (Roser & Juel, 1982, p. 114)

Vaughan, Castle, Gilbert, and Love (1982) addressed the issue of the form vocabulary instruction should take. In a comparison of a definition-based approach, an experience-based approach, and no instruction, Vaughan et al. found that the experience-based approach was superior in terms of the effects on both comprehension and vocabulary knowledge. Since previous studies had not shown a positive relationship between vocabulary instruction and comprehension, it might be conjectured that an important factor in the study by Vaughan et al. was the way in which words were selected as targets for vocabulary instruction. Selection was based on the relative importance of words to the story plot, rather than being based on words assumed to be unknown to the students. The classification system of Graves' (1978) is also suggested as a potential system for teachers to use in determining words which should be taught prior to reading (see the discussion in Graves, 1984). The four types of vocabulary include the following:

> Type One Words—words which are in students' oral vocabulary but which they cannot read
> Type Two Words—new meanings for words which are already in the students' reading vocabulary with one or more other meanings
> Type Three Words—words which are in neither the students' oral vocabulary nor their reading vocabulary and for which they do not have an available concept but for which a concept can be easily built.
> Type Four Words—words which are in neither the students' oral vocabulary nor their reading vocabulary, for which they do not have an available concept, and for which a concept cannot be easily built.
>
> (Graves, 1984, pp. 246–247)

It is important to note the limitations of vocabulary instruction as well as the benefits. Nagy and Herman (1984) outline these limitations and stress that even the most intensive word-by-word approach to vocabulary instruction will be ineffective as a sole method of teaching vocabulary. They conclude

> A chief goal [of vocabulary instruction] should be *to teach strategies which will allow readers to cope with unfamiliar words, and become better independent word learners* [italics added]. Other attainable goals might include increasing comprehension of specific texts through intensive instruction on the meanings of a few difficult but *important* [italics added] words, and bringing words into students' speaking or writing vocabularies. *No one method of instruction will be the best for all of these goals* [italics added].
>
> (Nagy & Herman, 1984, p. 32)

Quasi-Experimental Studies

Quasi-experimental studies include those studies which did not use a control group or did not randomly select subjects and assign them to experimental and control groups. A few representative studies with deaf children are reported here. Studies with hearing children are not included. At the outset, it should be noted that the majority of quasi-experimental studies suffer from methodological flaws that, to paraphrase Tierney and J. Cunningham (1980), make it impossible to determine what effects, if any, the experimental treatment had on students' performance.

Studies of Reader-Based Strategies

Only one quasi-experimental study of reader-based strategies that involved deaf subjects was found. This study (G. Long & Aldersley, 1982) is an extension of the G. Long and Conklin (1979) study discussed earlier in this chapter. The objective of the study was to determine whether the higher performance exhibited on passages that students had networked would transfer to other passages on which students had not used the technique. An eight week training session on semantic networking was provided between a pretest and a posttest measure of comprehension for two passages. On the posttest, students generated a semantic network for only one of the passages. Posttest performance on both passages was significantly higher than pretest performance, indicating that the effects of semantic networking transferred to non-networked texts. G. Long and Aldersley note that the results may have been confounded by the use of the same passages for the pretest and posttest, but they reject that possibility because of the ten week period between testing sessions and the use of a testing procedure during which the texts were available. Their explanation seems logical. In fact, the use of the same passages may strengthen the study in that current popular procedures for matching texts (i.e., readability formulas) do not ensure that passages are indeed equivalent (DiStefano & Valencia, 1980).

Studies of Instructional Techniques

Lieding and Gammel (1982) examined reading instruction for preschool deaf children. Their program incorporated four major components: story-reading sessions, primer reading sesssions, vocabulary development, and phonics instruction. An important aspect of the program was parental involvement in the weekly story-reading sessions. Subjects were five preschoolers with severe to profound hearing losses (mean = 81 dB; chronological age = 4 years 4 months to 5 years 6 months). No formal pretest measures were administered. Teachers judged the students to be nonreaders. At the end of a year, students were functioning on grade level or better (first through third grade) on the *Gates-MacGinitie Reading Test* and the *Peabody Individual Achievement Test*. Although the authors ascribe the students' performance, at least in part, to the instructional program, no such conclusions are warranted. Studies such as that of Lieding and Gammel, in which only posttests are administered,

> have poor internal validity. . . . The students' scores on the posttest could be accounted for by their regular school instruction or by maturation, as well as by the treatment. . . . Without a measure of change, it is impossible even to determine whether the students' achievement improved over time, regardless of whether this change was due to the treatment or to some other variable.
>
> (Borg & Gall, 1979, p. 538)

Serwatka, Hesson, and Graham (1984) studied the effects of indirect intervention (informational services to parents, teachers, and dormitory teachers) on reading improvement in deaf adolescents (chronological age 11 years to 16 years). A part of the *Right to Read* effort, this study examined more than 250 students over a three year period. Only students who were thought to have the poorest prognosis for success participated. The *Stanford Achievement Test-Hearing Impaired Version (SAT-HI)* was used to measure reading achievement. During each year of the study, statistically significant gains were shown on at least some subtests. Grade equivalent scores on the Reading Subtest A increased from 2.1 to 2.4 during the second year. Average grade equivalent gains on all reading-related subtests for the third year were in the .2 to .4 range. The authors attributed these gains to the indirect intervention techniques (*Right to Read* Project), although they did state that further study was needed before a cause-and-effect relationship could be established.

The major difficulty with the study revolves on the question of whether the results are really *educationally significant*. We are struck by the similarity in the average gains (.2 grade level per year) to the average gains for a large portion of the deaf school-age population (Di Francesca, 1972). On the one hand, it might be argued that, since only students with the poorest skills were involved, attainment of average scores for a large group of deaf students did indeed indicate educationally significant gains. On the other hand, there is some evidence that gains in the .2 grade level range for deaf students on the *SAT-HI* might not reflect educational gain but rather might be attributable to testing error (Allen, White, & Karchmer, 1983; see Chapter 7 for further discussion). Although it cannot be attributed conclusively to either variable at present, the results of this study do clearly show the need for experimenters to consider educational significance as well as statistical significance.

McCarr (1973) studied the effects on reading performance of an individualized reading instruction program and direct feedback about test results for a group of older deaf adolescents. Details on the experimental aspect of this report are sketchy. Average yearly gains prior to the "experiment" were .3 to .5 grade level per year. At the end of the first year, average gains were 1.3 grade levels for all 7th through 12th grade classes. It is apparent that such gains are educationally significant. It cannot be assumed, however, that a *causal* link exists between the reading program and student gains.

A study by Johnson, McLaughlin, and Hunsaker (1982) shows some of the difficulties in establishing causal links between the variable being manipulated (in this case, free reading time in a regular classroom) and improved reading performance (based on programmed reading materials in a resource classroom). Baseline data were collected for ten days, during which the student completed zero to five pages of work. For each successive ten day period, a criterion was set at 7 pages of work, then 10 pages, and then 14 pages (all with 90% accuracy), after which the student was permitted to leave the resource room for free reading time in a regular classroom for hearing students. The student's work output and accuracy level met or exceeded the criterion throughout the three ten day periods. The implications of the study, however, are somewhat clouded. What caused the increase in performance? Was it the reinforcer (free reading time), the establishment of a criterion (i.e., clear teacher expectation or the challenge), a combination of these two factors, or some other extraneous variable? The authors attributed it to both factors with major emphasis on the reinforcer. The results, however, can only *suggest* these conclusions since definitive evidence of a causal link was not established. More definitive answers might have been obtained had the authors used a multiple-baseline research paradigm in which the variable of interest (i.e., free reading time) was systematically introduced and withheld (Hersen & Barlow, 1976; Kazdin, 1982). Halle, Stoker, and Schloss (1984) provide a comprehensible discussion of how multibaseline techniques can be used in conducting instructional research as it applies to the education of deaf children.

It should be noted that the value of the cited quasi-experimental studies, like that of Andrews' work (see page 102), is not determined solely by the experimental aspects. Each of the studies cited is rich in detail of current practices in teaching reading to deaf children, and thus they are likely very useful sources of ideas for practitioners. None of the studies, however, prove the effectiveness of the specified techniques, nor do they establish causal links between the teaching techniques and student performance.

Summary of Experimental and Quasi-Experimental Studies

The studies discussed in this section have focused on a wide variety of instructional issues. The best way to summarize them, perhaps, is to return to Calfee's statement presented at the beginning of the section: "We have little coherent advice to offer for policy makers or practitioners about 'how to teach reading' " (Calfee, 1982, p. 1). The truth of this statement becomes especially clear when we consider that most of the experimental and quasi-experimental studies that have shown positive effects have been conducted with middle grade students, often with a minimal reading level of fourth grade. We must be careful in generalizing these results to the deaf population as a whole, because only a small percentage of deaf students achieve reading levels of fourth grade or above (Furth, 1966a; Trybus & Karchmer, 1977). And yet, although this somewhat pessimistic view accurately reflects the general situation (Pearson, 1984a), it is possible to identify some promising instructional strategies that warrant further investigation.

First, the studies cited in this section have demonstrated the effectiveness of teaching certain reader-based strategies (semantic networking and QARs) to specific age populations. The ineffectiveness of story grammar instruction was shown for students at the fifth grade level and above. In contrast, positive results have been shown for students who do not already have knowledge of story structure. The results on these strategies, of course, cannot be generalized to other groups without prior experimentation to determine the effects. For example, it may be that the typical young deaf child with a first or second grade reading level may benefit from techniques that have been shown to be ineffective at other levels and may not benefit from techniques that have been shown to be effective at other levels. The child's age, developmental stage, and reading ability must be considered in any decisions to teach specific reader-based strategies. The studies reported here and in Chapters 1 and 3, however, clearly show the effectiveness of training deaf individuals to perform cognitive and reading-related tasks with which they have difficulty (e.g., Belmont et al., 1976; Iran-Nejad et al., 1981). Study of reader-based metacognitive strategies appears to be a fruitful goal for future instructional research.

Second, studies on feedback during oral reading indicate that teachers' responses do influence the quality, if not the quantity, of students' errors. Although the exact nature and composition of "effective" feedback are not yet known, it is encouraging to note that teachers' behaviors can and do influence student performance. With feedback strategies, as with interruption behaviors, it seems worthwhile to heed Allington's (1980) advice that an "all or none" approach need not be taken. Some combination of the various types of feedback—graphophonic feedback, context feedback, encouragement, and comments about the story—will likely prove to be most effective.

Third, direct teaching of vocabulary seems necessary, especially for beginning readers (Hoffman et al., 1982). Techniques that focus on drawing links between the readers' background experience and new words seem most effective. D. Johnson, Toms-Bronowski, and Pittelman (1982), among others, provide a review of methods for teaching vocabulary.

Fourth, the timing and type of questions asked about reading selections have a major impact on students' comprehension and recall. Specific guidelines about when and what to question, however, are not possible from the current research base. Maeder (1979) found that written or signed questions inserted during reading (without feedback) did not enhance comprehension for deaf students reading at or above a third grade level. Neither, however, did the inserted questions have a negative impact. Additional research is needed on the effects of various timings for questions (i.e., before, during, or after reading, and combinations thereof). In terms of the types of questions, it is clear that students' learning is related to the topics about which teachers ask questions. Wixson (1983) has shown that fifth grade hearing students recall questioned material better than unquestioned material, regardless of the importance of the two types of materials or of their relationship to the main concepts in the reading selection. Recall is also associated with the level of questions asked. Literal questions (*right there* QARs and some *think and search* QARs) tend to elicit learning of literal facts, whereas inferential questions (some *think and search* QARs and *on my own* QARs) tend to elicit learning of inferential information. However, asking inferential questions for which students do not have the appropriate background does not lead to better comprehension.

Finally, it should be apparent that much additional experimental research is needed before any definitive conclusions can be formed about effective instructional practices for teaching deaf children to read. Only experimental research can establish causal links between instructional techniques and student performance and yet it is experimental research that has received the least attention in the field of deafness. Comprehensive plans of research, like that described by Raphael (1984), are needed; single shot-gun approaches will likely be ineffective.

POLEMICS AND READING INSTRUCTIONAL ISSUES

A Brief Definition

The dictionary defines *polemics* as "an argument or controversial discussion" (Guralnik, 1970, p. 576). In other words, the purpose of polemic presentations is to argue for or against particular ideas, techniques, or philosophical views. Applied to reading instruction, this means that *all* presentations that attempt to prescribe how reading *should be* taught are, at least in part, polemic in nature. The term *polemics* is often contrasted with the term *research* since the first depends largely on logical argument and opinions while the second is based on systematic and objective study. The dichotomy of polemics versus research is an important precept since it helps people to evaluate the available evidence that is used as a support base for ideas presented in the professional

literature (i.e., people give greater credence to ideas that have been studied·
systematically and objectively).

At the same time, of course, it must be remembered that the dichotomy
(something is either polemic argument or objective research) is not perfect,
especially in the social sciences. Thus, although the importance of the
distinction between polemics and research cannot be overstressed, it is equally
important for readers to remember that conclusive determination of a causal
link between a specific instructional technique and improved reading abilities
is rarely possible (see the discussion beginning on page 94). Owing to the
complex nature of the reading instructional setting and the vast number
of variables that can influence a child's performance, definitive conclusions
often cannot be made; rather we must rely on the preponderance of the
available evidence. This process, by definition, necessarily includes some
logical argument and opinion.

Polemics and Reading for Deaf Children

As noted at the beginning of this chapter, the polemic literature on
suggested methods of teaching reading to deaf children is fairly extensive.
Appendix B provides a selected bibliography of published references on
suggested methods of teaching deaf children to read. Most of the references
in this bibliography are polemic in nature; however, the bibliography is not
restricted to such references. Rather, selection of research references for
inclusion in Appendix B was based not on whether the publications included
polemic discussions but rather on whether the reports had been discussed
extensively in other parts of this textbook. For example, the study by
Howarth et al. (1981) discussed previously in this chapter is not in Appendix
B. Readers will need to consult both Appendix B and the general
bibliography of this book to have a comprehensive list of published reports
regarding suggested methods of teaching reading to deaf children.

Polemic writings, while outside the realm of instructional research, are
discussed in this chapter because they focus on major instructional issues
that have not been addressed by research. Also, whether topics have been
researched or not, it is important to be aware of the opinions of spokespersons
and practitioners in a field since their opinions have major influences on
current instructional practices. The present discussion does not attempt to
provide a comprehensive coverage of the instructional issues that must be
addressed in relation to teaching deaf children to read. The purposes of
this section are (1) to outline the major issues, (2) to stress the need for
research efforts to address these issues, and (3) to present a perspective on
instructional choices which—rather than reflecting a view of these choices
as either-or decisions—supports a view that various instructional techniques
should be carefully balanced and varied according to the specific goals of
an instructional session, the different needs of individual children, the
differing needs of specific children given different tasks, and the specific level

of competence attained by the students (i.e., beginning, intermediate, skilled reading). At the outset, it should be noted that this perspective is not a new concept, nor is it one that is totally missing in the professional literature on reading and deafness. It is, however, an attitude that seems to be missing in some of the polemic writings regarding suggested methods for teaching reading to deaf children.

Advantages and Limitations of Polemic Writings

The most useful functions of polemic writings are the following: (1) they provide general overviews and orientations to a subject for individuals new to a field and for those in related fields; (2) they encourage sharing of ideas among professionals; and (3) they provide a forum for the development of theoretical models, research plans, and instructional plans. Researchers, practitioners, and theoreticians all need and benefit from avenues for communication whereby ideas can be shared, discussed, and shaped without the rigor required in descriptive and experimental research (such rigor is needed, of course, before we can assume that specific instructional techniques are helpful in improving students' reading abilities).

Limitations found in existing polemic writings include (1) vehement arguments accompanied by little or no supporting evidence; (2) presentation of the authors' opinions as facts; (3) inappropriate conclusions based on the data (e.g., assumption of causal links when correlational data are presented); and (4) rigid either-or positions in comparing various approaches and strategies. A further limitation results from polemic writings. Some polemic presentations, in their emphasis on specific aspects of the reading process that are neglected in current practices (e.g., an emphasis on semantics), often result in current practices (e.g., an emphasis on syntax) being pronounced "unacceptable" or "of limited value." Such pendulum swings are unfortunate in that the positive aspects of current practices are usually forgotten while the negative aspects of the new practices are often unrecognized until the next pendulum swing. Although the authors of polemic writings may or may not intend to create disjunctive breaks (Farhady, 1979) from current practices, it is exactly this consequence that typically occurs (Chall, 1977).

Testimonials (i.e., I tried it and it worked!) suffer from several additional limitations. One is the difficulty of generalizing from a single or a few *selected* success stories. All instructional programs show success for at least some children, and in all instructional programs some children fail. More rigorous evidence than testimonials is needed before the effects of specific instructional techniques can be established. A second limitation of testimonials is the possible influence of personal or emotional involvement by the individuals providing the testimonials. Although personal involvement does not necessarily deter objective analysis, its possible influence should be of concern to individuals attempting to evaluate the described programs. Readers should also be critically aware of the possible influences of emotional involvement on objectivity in the outcomes of research and its influence on the arguments used in polemic discussions for or against specific approaches. For example, the emotional nature of the age-old oral-manual debate often inhibits objective study of the issue.

A final major limitation of polemic writings to be discussed here regards polemic prescriptions by spokespersons for a field. Such writings have the potential for possible misrepresentation of the beliefs and practices of the field at large. Lanfrey (1975) addressed this issue in her survey study of the opinions and beliefs of educators of deaf children; she found some inconsistencies among the views of educators in the field and those of spokespersons for the field.

Instructional Issues

In this section, some major instructional issues in teaching reading to deaf children are identified and a historical account of the views of professionals in the field of deafness is provided regarding four representative issues. Major questions that teachers of deaf children have asked and are asking are presented to provide an impetus for greater discussion, observation, reflection, and research efforts to address these issues. Answers to the questions, however, are not provided. In fact, definitive answers to most of these questions are not available. Although most professionals in the field of deafness have formed at least preliminary opinions of answers for questions posed in this section, actually very little is known about the effectiveness of any of the suggested methods, nor is much known about the relative use or acceptance of these suggested methods of teaching within the field at large. As Clarke et al. (1982) note, "the current state of methodology is one of confused eclecticism" (p. 65). Further, it seems unlikely that global answers to these questions can be discovered given that (1) the questions are posed as either-or choices, the format of which assumes that at least one of the alternatives will be rejected, and (2) global answers would imply that instructional techniques can be applied to any given instructional goal, any level of instruction, and any type of learner. The primary purposes of this section are (1) to stress the need for research on these issues, and (2) to propose a perspective which, rather than asking either-or questions, redefines the questions to focus on determining (a) which students will benefit from a specific instructional technique, (b) when and where the specific technique will be useful, (c) when and where that same technique, in use with the same child, will be ineffective, and (d) which techniques are most suitable for specific types of reading goals and reading materials.

The following list of either-or questions has been gathered from the professional literature, workshops, professional meetings, and pre-service training programs. The questions are posed as either-or questions since that is the form in which they are usually addressed in polemic discussions (i.e., there is a belief that there is a "best" choice among the alternatives proposed in the question). After the list, a brief historical account of answers that have been proposed by various spokespersons for the field of deafness is presented for four of the posed questions (these questions are indicated by asterisks). The either-or questions on these topics are then redefined into several open-ended questions to reflect the perspective that a balance of diverse methods is needed to meet the various goals of reading instruction and the various needs of individual children. Readers are encouraged to redefine the other questions posed here in a similar manner.

1. Can reading be taught *or* can it only be "caught?" (i.e., is it a teacher's job to teach reading *or* to encourage its [natural] emergence?)

* 2. Should language be established before beginning formal reading instruction *or* can language be learned through the reading process?

3. Should early reading instruction focus on developing readiness skills (e.g., cognition, language, verbal and auditory discrimination) *or* on providing informal exposure and orientation to print? (a balanced approach to this question is provided by Mason, 1984)

4. Should the child's language *or* the teacher's revisions of the child's language be used in reading lessons using the language-experience approach? (see the discussion on pages 157–158 in Chapter 6)

* 5. Should initial reading instruction focus *either* on decoding *or* on meaning?

* 6. Should semantics (meaning) *or* syntax (form) be the primary consideration in the preparation of materials and lessons for a non-reader's first formal (i.e., instructed) experiences with print? In lessons and materials for readers at higher stages of reading development?

* 7. Do exercises that focus on components of the reading process (e.g., vocabulary) or reading skills (e.g., getting the main idea) in reduced-context environments help *or* hinder an individual's progress in learning to read and reading to learn?

8. Should reading be broken into subskills *or* should it be viewed only as a holistic process? (this is a more general statement of question 7; also see the discussion on pages 201–202 in Chapter 7)

9. Should special materials be prepared for and used with deaf children *or* should regular instructional materials for the general school population be used? (see the discussion on pages 154–157 in Chapter 6)

10. Should instructional materials (regular or special) be used or should only naturally written literature for children be used? (see the discussion on pages 153–154 in Chapter 6)

11. Should the emphasis in reading activities be on the development of reading and language skills *or* on conceptual development? During reading class? During language class? During content-area classes such as science and social studies?

12. Should new vocabulary, syntax, and concepts be pretaught or should new language and concepts always be encountered in contextual reading? (see the discussion on the direct teaching of vocabulary on pages 105–106 in this chapter)
13. Should questions be asked during reading *or* should questions that intervene during the reading process be avoided? (see the discussion on pages 104–105 of this chapter)
14. Should reading instruction focus *either* on oral reading *or* on silent reading? (see page 79 in this chapter for views on this question by educators of deaf children; also see Taylor & Connor, 1982, for a view that supports the "rational instructional use of both processes" [p. 420 in Taylor and Connor])
15. Should teacher feedback during oral reading focus *either* on meaning *or* decoding? (see the discussion on page 103–104 of this chapter)
16. Should reading ability be assessed by controlled measures (e.g., open-ended and multiple-choice questions) *or* by free measures (e.g., free recall)? (see the discussion on pages 203–206 in Chapter 7)
17. Should a form of manual communication be used or encouraged during oral readings of English print *or* should oral communication be used? (i.e., the oral-manual controversy)
18. Should a sign system that uses English markers (e.g., Signing Exact English) be used during readings of English print *or* should Pidgin Sign English be encouraged (i.e., conceptual signing)?
19. Should any features of ASL (e.g., directionality, reduplication, nonmanual signals) be allowed or encouraged during readings of English print *or* should word-by-word signing be encouraged? (see Wilbur, 1979a, for descriptions of ASL features)
20. Should invented signs be allowed or encouraged during readings of English print *or* should the development of fingerspelling be encouraged?

Language Before Reading OR Reading Before Language

For hearing children, reading development is built onto a fairly extensive existing language base (see the discussion in Chapter 2). Most deaf children, however, do not have a well-developed language base before the usual age at which reading instruction is begun. This difference, then, forces educators in the field of deafness to make a decision as to whether reading can be used to develop initial language competence or whether some minimal level of language competency is needed (regardless of how long it takes to acquire that competence) before formal reading instruction should begin.

Educators' views. In the field of deafness, reading has been viewed traditionally as a primary vehicle for the development of language in deaf children. Belief in this view can be traced back at least to Ponce de Leon in the 1500s (Bender, 1960). In 1929, Alexander Graham Bell indicated his support for teaching language through reading with the following statement:

I would introduce into the very youngest classes the practice of reading, *regardless of the fact that the children may not understand the meaning of the words on the printed page before them....I would have a deaf child read books in order to learn the language, instead of learning the language in order to read books.*

(Bell, 1929, pp. 193-195)

Belief in the early introduction of reading to teach language has continued into the present time (see the quotation on page 89), although it appears limited to a small number of programs. Thus, although most educators of deaf children today would likely support the view that reading can be *helpful* in teaching language, these educators (at least as represented by views expressed by spokespersons for the field) reject the view that reading is an effective vehicle for learning language during the beginning reading stage. Instead, there is fairly widespread support for the belief that there needs to be a close match between the child's language and the language in materials used for initial reading instruction (Groht, 1955; Hargis, 1970; D. Ling & A. Ling, 1978; Quigley & King, 1981, 1982, 1983, 1984; Quigley et al., 1976; Truax, 1978).

A balanced approach. The present view held by many educators of deaf children reflects a balanced approach in that, while a basic language competence is considered necessary for initial reading instruction, reading and language are also seen as integrated skills. This view is clearly seen in Streng's (1965) suggestion that "every language lesson is a reading lesson and every reading lesson is a language lesson" (p. 31).

The question of reading first or language first, however, does not address other issues, which are equally relevant to the discovery of an appropriate balance in the relationship between reading and language. The question "How much of the language in reading materials should be known by the reader?" is of great importance, and it is one that continues to be of importance well beyond the beginning reading stage. Therefore, it is suggested here that the either-or question (number 2 in the list given earlier) be redefined to the following:

- How much language ability is needed before students can or should be exposed to formal reading instruction?
- How much familiarity with the language in reading materials is needed by beginning readers who are said to be in the "learning to read" stage and who must struggle with acquiring decoding skills as well as processing meaning?
- How much familiarity with the language in reading materials is needed by readers who are moving into the "reading to learn" stage, during which decoding skills are automated?
- How can the language in reading materials be structured such that the progression from "learning to read" to "reading to learn" can be made smoothly and efficiently?

Research. There is some preliminary support in the literature for the view that a "too early" introduction to reading may be detrimental to the development of effective reading abilities (e.g., Howarth et al., 1981; see page 89 in this chapter). Research efforts have also been directed toward determining what the minimal language level should be. Browns's study (1979) of young deaf readers indicates that reading instruction has been initiated with deaf children with language levels as low as 36 months. This level is obviously much lower than the 60 month language level (i.e., 5 years of age) at which the typical hearing children begins learning to read. However, Browns's study in no way settles the controversies concerning the minimal language level at which formal reading *should be* introduced. Indeed, Browns (1979) describes 13 factors in addition to language that were correlated with success in beginning reading instruction.

This issue of when to begin formal reading instruction is a major one that concerns most teachers of deaf children. It is abundantly clear that the decision must be based on criteria more stringent than any one of the criteria that have been proposed thus far (i.e., the child's age, the child's cognitive and motor readiness, the child's language abilities). Research efforts are needed to address these issues. The work of Mason (1984), among others who are studying early reading with hearing children, will likely be a major resource for such efforts. Mason's work is also important in that she presents a balanced approach to the either-or choice between readiness approaches and orientation-to-print approaches to early reading instruction. Mason suggests that problems are inherent in the use of either approach as the sole instructional technique to the exclusion of the other. She also outlines three major tasks that a non-reader must master: learning the function of print, learning the form of print, and learning the conventions of print. Early reading instruction that focuses on all three of these tasks is most likely to be successful.

Meaning Emphasis OR Code Emphasis in Beginning Reading Instruction

Educators' views. The strong support for meaning-emphasis approaches to reading instruction among educators of deaf children is clearly shown in the data presented in Lanfrey's survey (1975) of teachers' opinions on instructional issues in reading (see pages 76–77). This emphasis is likely due to the recognition that "deaf children and other 'difference readers' [i.e., readers who do not possess a basic knowledge of the language they are learning to read] frequently develop adequate decoding skills and are able to identify the words in a passage in a word-by-word fashion without comprehending the whole" (Quigley & King, 1981, p. 8). In contrast, the major view of hearing children's teachers has been that a code-emphasis approach is superior (e.g., Chall, 1967; also see Barr, 1984, for a comprehensive review of the major issues). However, using either extreme to the exclusion of the other approach is unnecessary. Either total concentration on decoding skills without regard for meaning or total concentration of developing meaning without sufficient attention to decoding skills is likely to be ineffective.

A balanced approach. Chall (1977) notes the difficulties in taking *either* decoding *or* the acquisition of meaning as the sole goal for beginning reading. She describes what occurred following her 1967 finding that code-emphasis programs tend to produce better results than meaning-emphasis programs:

> In their enthusiasm, many authors, publishers, and teachers may be extending the decoding practice too far, and students may be spending too much time on it. . . . Thus, stories and books, the true vehicles for reading for meaning, may be neglected in the zeal for mastery of decoding.
>
> (Chall, 1977, p. 12)

In her earlier work, Chall (1967) had carefully discussed qualifications to her findings and had clearly indicated that reading for meaning should not be abandoned. Yet, the result was "a dangerously inaccurate oversimplification of a complex problem" (Harris & Sipay, 1980, p. 67).

It would be equally tragic if the current swing back toward meaning-emphasis programs resulted in a total neglect of decoding. Given that enthusiasm for new methods often has the effect of causing current methods to be abandoned, this concern is a serious one. The authors of this book are very supportive of meaning-emphasis programs, yet they see danger in any program that excludes either meaning or decoding. Chall's conclusion to the above quotation seems applicable to both extremes: "Moderation here, as in all of life, should be valued" (1977, p. 12).

Redefinition of the either-or question of meaning-emphasis versus code-emphasis (number 5 in the list above) would result in the following questions:

- What is the proper balance between meaning-emphasis and code-emphasis approaches at the various stages of reading development (i.e., beginning reading, intermediate reading, skilled reading)?
- How can it be determined which type of instructional techniques (i.e., emphasis on meaning or decoding) is most appropriate for specific reading goals, reading tasks, and types of readers?

Syntax OR Semantics

Educators' views. Presentation of specific educators' views on the issue of syntax versus semantics is difficult in that polemic discussions on this topic usually do not argue for the exclusion of one or the other of these aspects of language. Instead, they are intended as a means of increasing awareness of the importance of one aspect. In other words, most educators recognize the importance of both aspects (syntax and semantics); the problems emerge in determining how to balance these two important aspects. The purpose here is to reemphasize that exclusive focus on either aspect is inappropriate.

Recently, interest in the semantic and pragmatic aspects of language has increased dramatically (see the review of trends in linguistic theories in Quigley & Paul, 1984a). Reviewing the literature reveals discussions of "semantics: the forgotten component" (e.g., Hasenstab & Bevilacqua, 1980) and much attention being directed toward developing methods and materials for teaching these aspects of language. This shift in the focus of interest accompanies an increase in the knowledge base concerning semantic and pragmatic aspects of language, and it is an important step toward more comprehensive coverage in language instruction. Unfortunately, whether authors intend it or not, a common consequence of writings that stress the importance of one aspect (e.g., semantics) is that the importance and contributions of the other aspect is depreciated or forgotten. It is this either-or choice that the present authors oppose.

   A balanced approach. Clark and Sewell (1979) present a balanced approach to the question of syntax *or* semantics in their reaction to an article by Gormley and Franzen (1978), which emphasized the importance of semantics.

> Our concern is that in attempting to stress the importance of semantic considerations the authors are, in a sense, in danger of "throwing the baby out with the bath water." Both semantics and syntax are important in achieving full control of the reading process. *An approach which seeks to integrate these, at a level suitable for the individual child, would seem to hold the most promise* [italics added]. The relative emphasis placed on either semantics or syntax will depend on the demands of the reading task and on the individual requirements of the child.
> (Clark & Sewell, 1979, p. 848)

This view recognizes and applauds the contributions of Gormley and Franzen (1978), but it also sees the danger of having the pendulum swing from too much emphasis on syntactic structure to too much emphasis on semantics. Thus, it is suggested here that, rather than asking "should semantics or syntax be the primary consideration in lessons and materials for readers at various stages of reading development?," the question be redefined to the following:

- How can the focus on semantics and syntax be balanced to achieve an integrated approach to reading and language instruction that recognizes the importance of both aspects?
- How can we determine which aspects (structure, meaning, or some combination) should be of major concern in preparing lessons and materials for specific reading goals, reading tasks, and types of readers?

Research on these questions should produce greater benefit than having advocates of syntax or semantics square off to determine *the* superior approach.

Reduced-Context Tasks—Help OR Hindrance?

   Educators' views. Most educators of deaf children recognize the facilitative effects of context on deaf children's comprehension of text passages. Indeed, the importance of providing massive amounts of reading practice and of teaching deaf children to use contextual information cannot be overstressed.

   There is debate, however, within the field as to the role of reduced-context tasks such as preteaching vocabulary, syntax, and concepts or teaching skills such as "getting the main idea" from sentence-level or short paragraph materials. This debate relates both to the question of the relative importance of syntax and semantics and to the question of whether reading is a holistic process or one that can be divided into skills. The first question was discussed in the last subsection; the second question is discussed on pages 201–202. The purposes of the discussion here are (1) to present the view that the goal of developing contextual reading skills does not necessarily exclude the use of reduced-context tasks, and (2) to stress the need for *teaching* deaf children to use the context rather than expecting them to develop these skills through practice alone.

Gormley and Franzen (1978) make the important point that "deaf children require extensive experience of reading passages rather than single sentence material" (Clark & Sewell, 1979, p. 848). Likewise, Ewoldt (1982b) criticizes the common practice of helping "the reader digest the material a sentence or a word at a time" (p. 26). These criticisms are valid points which all teachers would do well to heed. Problems emerge, however, if we goes to the opposite extreme of *always* "let[ting] children read whole stories [without help] and trust[ing] them to interact with the author in a meaningful way" (Ewoldt, 1982b, p. 27). For example, Gormley and Franzen (1978) argue that, in reading contextual passages, "intersentence redundancies may be available to allow the reader to revise falsely interpreted sentences, such as passive sentences, without knowing that particular grammatical construction" (p. 546). Although this point is well taken, it is insufficient support for the exclusion of sentence-level or other reduced-context tasks. Although Gormley and Franzen do not argue for excluding an emphasis on syntax or sentence-level tasks, such exclusion is a possible extrapolation of their arguments. Even though a child may revise falsely interpreted sentences, "it is also feasible that the child will *not* deviate from an early hypothesis and will interpret the remainder of the passage in such a way as to be consistent with the initial hypothesis" (Clark & Sewell, 1979, p. 848). Obviously, some balance is needed between relying on the use of context and recognizing potential problems which a child will have in reading a text and taking steps to avert those problems.

Ewoldt (1982b) hints at such a balance in noting that the

> redundancy [in a text] alone is not sufficient if readers cannot draw from their previous experiences to deal with concepts in the story. . . . This means that we must not only provide readers with the opportunity to read whole stories that are sufficiently redundant, but also that we be sure that readers have had related experiences *prior* [italics added] to reading so that they can draw from those experiences. . . . It is important, then, that teachers know which concepts to pursue and which to ignore.
>
> (Ewoldt, 1982b, p. 27)

How to achieve a balance, however, is less clear.

A balanced approach. Studies of the decision-making processes that teachers use daily in helping their students interact with texts will likely contribute greatly to knowledge of how a balance can be obtained between contextual reading (without interruption) and reduced-context tasks, which focus on developing comprehension of smaller units of language (e.g., words, sentences, paragraphs). An important point to be made here is that *either* sole use of reduced-context tasks *or* sole use of unassisted contextual reading practice will likely result in less than efficient readers. The best answer to the question of "are reduced-context tasks a help or hindrance?" likely is that they can be a help *if used appropriately*. Determination of appropriate conditions, then, will become a major goal of research efforts.

- For what purposes are reduced-context tasks appropriate?
- What teaching strategies are effective in *teaching* students to utilize contextual information?
- Should the goals of comprehension at the word level, sentence level, paragraph level, and text level be balanced differently for readers at various stages of reading development?

Summary of Polemics and Reading Instructional Issues

In this section, *either-or* approaches to instructional decisions were criticized as being overly simplistic approaches to the complex process of matching appropriate instructional techniques to the needs of individual students. The four representative issues discussed herein largely focus on the relative importance of form and function. It was concluded that either extreme, to the partial or total exclusion of the other aspect, will likely result in the development of less than optimal reading strategies. The manner in which the various goals of reading instruction can be balanced and the appropriateness of specific techniques as tools in reaching specific goals have not yet been determined. These should be major foci of future research.

An instructional emphasis on form and one on function need not be mutually exclusive, but rather these should be complementary processes in the reading instructional setting. Thus, *using known language to develop reading skills* and *using known reading skills to develop language abilities* are both appropriate goals at different times and for different purposes in the reading instructional setting. Similarly, *focusing on meaning* and *focusing on decoding* should be complementary processes. Here, perhaps, the best instructional lead can be obtained from studies of young children who learn to read before formal instruction. Maxwell (1980) reports on the reading activities of a young deaf child, Alice, who flips back and forth between "telling the story" (largely ignoring the printed words) and "reading the print" (without great concern for the meaning). Recognition that seemingly opposite approaches are appropriate at different times and for different purposes is an important concept for professionals involved in the educational process. *Emphasis on syntax* and *emphasis on semantics* also need not be mutually exclusive goals. How to balance the importance of these two goals is not at all well understood. However, it does seem clear that a focus on either aspect to the exclusion of the other results in the possibility of "throwing the baby out with the bath water." Finally, *reduced-context tasks* can be viewed as supplementary and complementary to *contextual reading* rather than as a hindrance. Exclusive or predominant use of reduced-context tasks, on the other hand, is inappropriate. Excessive use of such tasks is likely to be the major reason that some educators advocate excluding reduced-context tasks completely. However, the opposite extreme, expecting students to acquire efficient reading strategies exclusively through practice in contextual reading, is equally inappropriate.

The criticism expressed herein of either-or decisions, however, should not be taken as an indictment of the views presented by authors of various polemic writings. Obviously, the dissatisfaction with current methods that leads to shifts in the focuses of interest (e.g., from syntax to semantics and pragmatics in the language field or from views of reading as text-based to recognition that reading is text-based, reader-based, and task-based) provides an important impetus toward developing better teaching methods and greater understanding of the language and reading domain as a whole. Indeed, the enthusiasm for and concentration on new areas may well be essential to teachers' continued morale, given the slow progress of many deaf children. The period of dissatisfaction that accompanies shifts in methods may even be instrumental in reawakening the field to the problems inherent in current practices.

The major points made here relate to the futility of an either-or argument and to the need for an awareness of historical trends in understanding the pendulum swings that occur as the difficulties of specific techniques are identified. It is the authors' hope that (1) zeal for new methods will not blind educators to the problems inherent in these methods; and (2) enthusiasm for the these new methods will not lead to an either-or choice with total rejection of other methods. At the same time, however, discovery of such new methods is *essential* to the continued evolution and development of knowledge of the reading process and effective teaching strategies that can lead to successful reading. The educational field must be open to new ideas and as fully cognizant of the limitations and problems inherent in present practices as possible.

A major step forward in the approach to reading instructional research will come from the redefinition of either-or questions to questions that reflect an awareness of the differing needs of readers at various stages of reading development and of the differing needs related to specific goals of reading instruction. Recognition that an instructional technique (e.g., teacher interruptions) is neither all bad nor all good will also do much toward achieving a balanced approach to reading instruction. Finally, the goal of discovering the conditions under which various techniques are useful–as opposed to the goal of proving the superiority of specific techniques–must be shared by researchers and practitioners alike if any real progress is to be made.

SUMMARY

In this chapter, four major sources of information on current methods of teaching reading to deaf children were examined: survey studies, observational studies, experimental studies, and polemic presentations. Each of these major sections has an extensive summary and discussion of the implications of the information gained from that source. These summaries are not repeated here. Instead, the major tenets of this chapter are reiterated: (1) relatively little is known about current practices in teaching reading to deaf children, (2) there is a paucity of research being directed toward determining the effects of various approaches, and (3) there is a great need for systematic study to determine "which methods, and balance among those methods, will be most effective for specific children using specific materials and being asked to perform specific reading tasks?" In addressing this question, intensive research efforts at all developmental reading levels are needed. Single shot-gun approaches, in which isolated aspects of the reading instructional setting are studied, will likely be ineffective; comprehensive and cohesive plans of research are needed. Correlational, observational, quasi-experimental, and experimental studies are needed to determine the conditions under which various instructional techniques will be most effective. Major efforts must also be directed toward determining decision-making processes that lead to an appropriate balance among various instructional techniques and among the various goals of reading instruction. Study of the extensive polemic base regarding suggested instructional methods is needed. Survey and observational studies are required to explore more deeply the beliefs and practices of the field at large and to determine whether the field at large agrees with the views and suggestions made by its spokespersons.

Finally, it seems likely that three attitudes on the part of researchers and practitioners will be needed to obtain useful information from studies on the effectiveness of reading instructional techniques with deaf children. These are (1) awareness of the myriad complex variables that influence reading and of the difficulties of separating out causal relationships among these variables; (2) awareness of historical trends and theoretical frameworks for suggested instructional approaches; and (3) the perspective that instructional issues are not either-or propositions; relative emphasis on various aspects of the reading process will change with demands of the task and with children's individual needs.

Chapter 5

Reading Materials I: Research

The major purpose of this chapter is to identify variables that make texts more or less difficult to comprehend. The following topics are covered: (1) text difficulty, (2) linguistic and conceptual analyses of instructional reading materials, (3) experimental studies of adaptation and simplification, (4) text-based variables that influence text difficulty, (5) reader-based variables that influence text difficulty, and (6) a summary of the major conclusions that can be drawn from existing data on various types of materials. The information presented in this chapter provides an important knowledge base for individuals who are involved in selecting, writing, or rewriting reading materials. At the outset, it should be noted that only a few studies have directly investigated the relationship between text difficulty and *deaf* children's comprehension of these texts. Therefore, much of the information presented in this chapter is based on studies with hearing children. Research on deaf children's comprehension of various types of texts to obtain such data is needed.

TEXT DIFFICULTY

Traditionally, estimates of text difficulty have been based solely on text-based variables such as vocabulary difficulty and sentence length. Recent work in the reading field, however, shows that the difficulty of a particular text does not reside in the text alone. Rather, it is the interaction between a reader and text that determines how difficult the text is. The task (e.g., free recall, answering questions) that is selected to measure a reader's comprehension also influences an individual's perception of how difficult a text is for that particular reader. It is important to keep these three factors—the text, the reader, and the task—in mind while reviewing the methods used to measure text difficulty.

Readability Formulas

Readability research began in the 1920s and was designed to develop objective measures of text difficulty (Chall, 1984). Since that time, more than 100 variables that influence the difficulty of a text have been identified. These variables include such things as vocabulary, sentence length and structure, concept density, text organization, abstractness, and physical characteristics of the text. A given readability formula, however, includes only a few of these variables. Usually only those variables that contribute most strongly to the prediction of a text's difficulty (i.e., vocabulary difficulty and sentence length) are included. Readability formulas are quite popular, as indicated by their widespread use among professionals in the reading field. Publishers use them to guide materials production and to indicate the level of difficulty of published reading materials. Writers and adaptors use the formulas as aids in controlling and reducing the complexity of texts. Chall (1984) notes that teachers rarely use the formulas themselves, although they do use the results of the readability formulas as aids in selecting appropriate reading materials for children. This appears to be the case with educators of deaf children as well. LaSasso (1978a) found that only 18.1% of the teachers in her survey used a formal means of measuring text difficulty. LaSasso conjectured that the low percentage might be attributable to unfamiliarity with the formulas or wariness about their appropriateness for deaf children. An additional explanation is that nonuse reflects the general trend of teachers to use the results but not the formulas themselves. Information on teachers' reason for not using the formulas will be available in the update survey by LaSasso (personal communication, March, 1985).

Despite their popularity, however, readability formulas as the major means of determining a text's difficulty have come under severe criticism in recent years. The criticism has focused on four major points. Readability formulas (1) provide inconsistent results for the same text; (2) are frequently used for purposes for which the formulas were not designed; (3) are often not validated or are validated only in terms of other readability formulas; and (4) do not include all of the factors necessary to account sufficiently for the difficulty of a text (B. Bruce et al., 1981; Davison, 1981; Davison et al., 1980; Harrison, 1980; Klare, 1974-1975, 1976, 1984; Rubin, 1981; Tamor, 1981).

The first three criticisms focus on problems inherent in readability formulas. Thus, even if the factors that are currently included in the formulas were sufficient to provide a comprehensive index of text difficulty, these problems would still need to be addressed. One major difficulty is that different readability formulas provide different scores for the same text (Klare, 1974-1975, 1976, 1984). A related problem is that a single readability formula will produce different results when different portions of the same text are used to calculate reading level (Fitzgerald, 1981; Bradley, 1976). In describing variability in the levels of difficulty of a given text, Bradley and Ames (1976) concluded "there is no way of knowing which part of a book is predicted by an instructional reading level short of measuring all of its contents for readability" (p. 104).

The next criticism focuses on how readability formulas are used. Although the selection and production of materials appear to be the most valuable and most common contexts in which they are used, the formulas were not designed for these purposes. B. Bruce et al. (1981, pp. 9–10) list six major conditions that must be met for readability formulas to provide valid information. Paraphrased, these include the following:

1. The material must have been written to satisfy a communicative goal and not to satisfy a readability formula.
2. Higher level text structures are irrelevant in determining the difficulty of a text.
3. No time limit is imposed on reading of the materials.
4. Differences in the purpose for which the material is to be used (skimming, pleasure, etc.) are not relevant.
5. Useful information about the appropriateness of a given text for a specific individual can be obtained from statistical averages of the difficulty of texts and of the reading levels of individuals.
6. Readers with whom the materials will be used are the same as the readers on whom the readability formulas were validated.

It is obvious that adherence to these conditions excludes readability formulas from most of the contexts in which they are presently used. Yet, if the conditions are not met, the formulas are invalid.

The procedures used in validating readability formulas have also been questioned. A common practice in the validation of new readability formulas is to show positive correlations between the scores of the new formula with scores of older, established formulas. This practice, however, may be circular (Davison et al., 1980), and the validities of the early formulas have also been questioned (e.g., B. Bruce et al., 1981). Further, only about half of the studies that have directly compared readability scores with measures of reader performance (reading speed and comprehension) have shown positive correlations between the two (see the review in Klare, 1976).

The final point is the one most debated among advocates and critics of readability formulas. Critics note that the traditional readability formulas use only text-based variables and ignore reader-based variables (Kintsch & Miller, 1984). These critics focus on the need for readability formulas to (1) describe a text's difficulty sufficiently in terms of the many variables within the text itself, and (2) provide an index of text difficulty that reflects the interaction between a reader and text (Kintsch & Vipond, 1979). Obviously the difficulty of a scientific article, which contains much jargon, will be of one difficulty level for the scientist and another difficulty level for the layperson.

The insufficiency of current readability formulas is also shown in "incomprehensible texts" being rated at low levels of difficulty. For example, Gordon (1980) applied readability formulas to *Parmenides* by Plato, a text with simple language and very complex ideas. Philosophical scholars differ about the meaning of this text, "the ordinary person will be hard put to it to discover any meaning at all" (Hamilton, 1961, cited in Gordon, 1980, p. 60), and yet the readability scores for *Parmenides* range from fifth to eighth grades on one formula and from sixth to tenth grades on another.

On the other hand, advocates of readability formulas, while recognizing that the formulas do not adequately *describe* all of the factors that influence text difficulty, focus on the ability of the formulas to *predict* text difficulty. Thus, they argue that readability formulas can provide helpful information if used by a person who is aware of the limitations and appropriate uses of the formulas (Chall, 1984).

Alternative Measures of Text Difficulty

Although it is clear that there are many problems in using existing readability formulas as the sole measures of text difficulty, alternative measures do not provide a complete description of text difficulty either (e.g., see Chall, 1984; Davison, Lutz, & Roalef, 1981; Tamor, 1981). For example, some text-based measures of text difficulty focus on syntax (e.g., Botel & Granowsky, 1972; Dawkins, 1975; Endicott, 1973; Richek, 1976); others focus on coherence and ideation depth and density (Kintsch & Vipond, 1979); and still others focus on relationships between sentences with overlapping references (Gourlay & Catlin, 1978) or other textual structures (Templeton, Cain, & Miller, 1981). Similarly, reader-based methods that measure a text's difficulty behaviorally by the number of oral reading errors (Leslie & Osol, 1978) or by the number of correct substitutions in cloze passages (Aquino, Mosberg, & Sharron, 1969; Bormuth, 1968; Henk, 1982; Pikulski & Tobin, 1982) have also been criticized as being insensitive to the full range of text-based and reader-based variables (e.g., Leu, 1982; Richaudeau, 1981; Shanahan & Kamil, 1982, 1983; Tamor, 1981). Thus, most of the available measures of text difficulty do not cover all of the possible factors that can contribute to the comprehensibility of text.

Recently, several researchers have proposed subjective, checklist-type approaches to determine the relative difficulty of materials (Irwin & Davis, 1980; Armbruster & T. Anderson, 1981; Rubin, 1981). These approaches probably provide the most help in selecting appropriate reading materials for given students since they address a variety of factors that contribute to text difficulty. However, they are difficult to operationalize for use in research that assesses the effects of text adaptations, and their use as reliable measures of text difficulty has not been established.

Thus, although there are many ways to measure a text's difficulty level, none seems to be completely satisfactory. It is clear, however, that there are at least three major variables that must be considered—the text, the reader, and the task or testing situation (Klare, 1976). At present, there appears to be no single best approach to determining how comprehensible a given text will be for specific individuals. Yet, if an individual wishes to examine the effects of differences in the difficulty of texts on reading comprehension, some measure of text difficulty is needed. In examining the research on the effects of various types of texts on reading comprehension, it should be remembered that (1) no matter what measure of text difficulty was used, it likely does not provide a complete picture of the text's difficulty, and (2) factors other than the one being manipulated can and do contribute to the relative difficulty of a text.

LINGUISTIC AND CONCEPTUAL ANALYSES OF READING MATERIALS

In recent years, there have been many reviews, critiques, and comparisons of instructional reading materials. Much of this work has been done by major research centers such as Center for the Study of Reading at the University of Illinois (see the summaries in R. Anderson, Osborn, & Tierney, 1984, and in Pearson, 1984a) and the Learning Research and Development Center at the University of Pittsburgh (Beck & McCaslin, 1978; Beck, McKeown, McCaslin, & Burkes, 1979). These institutions, among others, have examined various aspects of materials used in teaching reading and have identified a number of potential problems with such materials. For the most part, the studies reported in this section consist of linguistic and conceptual analyses that were designed to determine the current state of materials used in teaching reading and to establish a base for empirical research. These studies have provided many examples of potential problems and of useful strategies that can aid individuals who write materials for children. The results of such linguistic analyses, however, must be treated as logical conjectures that are in need of verification. Kane (in T. Anderson, Armbruster, & Kantor, 1980) stresses that empirical research demonstrating that the perceived problems do indeed cause difficulty is still needed. The existing body of experimental studies is reviewed in the next section.

Linguistic and conceptual analyses of instructional materials have focused on almost all types of materials. Both regular reading instructional materials (e.g., basal readers; Beck et al., 1979) and special reading instructional materials (e.g., adaptations; Davison et al., 1980) have been examined. Also examined were instructional materials for subjects other than reading (e.g., science; T. Anderson et al., 1980). Other researchers have focused on directives for instruction as exemplified in the teacher's guide and workbook components of reading materials (e.g., Durkin, 1981; Osborn, 1981, 1984). Still others have attempted to identify hierarchies of skills, such as reading comprehension, within specific materials (e.g., Mason et al., 1977) or compared conventions in oral and written language (Schallert, Kleiman, & Rubin, 1977).

Virtually every possible linguistic and conceptual aspect of reading materials has also been explored and critiqued. For example, Beck et al. (1979) examined the previous knowledge assumed by texts as well as the vocabulary levels of the texts and the instructional directives provided in materials accompanying the reading texts. G. Green et al. (1980) discuss text analysis in terms of the lexical, syntactic, and discourse features of the text. They also consider illustrations and other physical features of the text. Each of these aspects is considered individually later in this chapter. The purpose here is to provide an overview of the major problems that have been identified.

Instructional Reading Materials

Paradoxically, critiques of instructional reading materials have focused on both ends of a spectrum. On one hand, examples of aspects that can cause difficulty for young readers are noted. On the other hand, materials are also criticized frequently as unchallenging. Examples of both types of criticism are presented here, followed by a proposed resolution to the conflict offered by Beck et al. (1979).

Criticism of the materials as being both too difficult and too easy is based on the linguistic constraints in instructional reading materials. The inadequacy of current methods for controlling difficulty in regular instructional materials is clearly seen in the following examples of problems. Critics judge existing materials as too easy, as too difficult, and as possessing non-systematic progressions in difficulty. And these judgments are made in relation to the same set of materials.

Instructional materials are too easy—(1) instructional materials do not prepare children for all types of story structure (B. Bruce, 1981; Steinberg & B. Bruce, 1980); (2) over 50 percent of the stories in instructional materials are bland narratives of children carrying out everyday activities (Blom et al., 1970); and (3) simplified sentence structure may reduce the amount of redundancy and cohesion in the text (G. Green, 1984).

Instructional materials are too difficult—(1) limited vocabulary can result result in roundabout language that is more complex than more conceptually demanding words (Beck et al., 1979; Davison et al., 1980); (2) some materials require inferences that young children do not have the background experience to provide (R. Anderson, 1981); and (3) the sentence structures used in instructional materials are at a higher level than those used in oral communication by young children (e.g., Quigley et al., 1976; Strickland, 1962).

Instructional materials are not systematic in their progression of difficulty—(1) there is a great deal of intra-book variability in the complexity of instructional materials (Bradley, 1976); (2) progressions in complexity are not always systematic (e.g., Kachuck, 1981; Quigley et al., 1976); and (3) there is no systematic increase in the underlying logical structure of stories (Templeton et al., 1981).

Most critics of instructional reading materials emphasize the need for meaningful and interesting materials in teaching children to read. This is an important precept that all individuals involved in teaching reading should remember and one that cannot be stressed too strongly. However, some critics of instructional reading materials advocate the exclusion of any materials that are designed specifically to teach reading (Bettelheim & Zelan, 1981; K. Goodman, Olsen, Colvin, & Vanderlinde, 1966). Such an approach strongly de-emphasizes basic decoding and comprehension skills, and R. Anderson (1982), among others, takes exception to such a practice.

> In their emphasis on the importance of meaning in teaching a child to read, and their de-emphasis of reading skills, they may be swinging the pendulum too far. There are technical flaws in our methods for assessing the difficulty of children's reading, to be sure. At the same time, though, you need some means for ensuring that the reading material we give youngsters is appropriate to their ages and abilities. We can't just assume that meaning will carry them along, and give them *War and Peace*.
>
> (R. Anderson, 1982, p. 114)

R. Anderson's position is that instructional materials are a necessary component in teaching children to read. However, he also recognizes that present criteria for controlling the difficulty of instructional reading materials are too simplistic. Thus, rather than excluding specific types of material, a major thrust of research should be to determine how best to provide a balance of easy and difficult materials. One possible solution is offered by Beck et al. (1979):

> The notions of easy materials and the need for challenge would seem to leave us with conflicting recommendations. We believe this conflict may have a resolution in the development of a two-track system of reading instruction to consist of daily reading assignments of fairly easy material combined with regular presentation of conceptually more difficult materials grouped around the same knowledge domain. The easier selections would provide children with the reading practice necessary to build fluency while the more difficult material would help to build students' knowledge structures. (p. 133)

Both helpful and disruptive strategies on the part of materials producers have been identified in the linguistic analyses of regular instructional reading materials. The following examples of a "misdirective" context and a directive context for the introduction of new vocabulary are illustrative.

A Misdirective Context

His lips were parted in a wide smile of victory.

"He sure has beautiful teeth," said Sally *grudgingly*.

"Look at him *strut*. You'd think he was on television doing a toothpaste commercial."

The theme of smiling, teeth, and toothpaste commercials could lead a student to expect that the word *strut* concerns some activity centered around the mouth, such as *grin*. Thus, we believe that children are likely to receive incorrect impressions of the words *grudgingly* and *strut* from this context.

(Beck et al., 1979, p. 72)

A Directive Context

I suppose the earth sneezed, or shook itself, or the bottom dropped out of something. Anyhow there was a shake and a roar and a general *stramash*, and I found myself miles away underground and wedged in as tight as tight.

With clues such as "earth sneezed," "shook," "bottom dropped out," "shake," and "roar," the meaning of *stramash* is discernible; a disturbance or crash.

(Beck et al., 1979, p. 74).

Adaptations and Simplified Materials

The use of adaptation or simplification to convey information to less skilled readers or language users is a frequent strategy of teachers and other individuals involved in the dissemination of information. For example, high interest-low vocabulary materials are often used with poor readers. In a similar manner, special reading materials for deaf children have been prepared to meet their specific language difficulties (see Chapter 6), and captions for televised shows are sometimes simplified to meet various presentation and language constraints (Shulman & Decker, 1981). Adaptations are often used for other language-different (Honeyfield, 1977; Madsen & Bowen, 1978; Shuy, 1979) and language-delayed (Frostig, 1973; Stowitschek, Gable, & Hendrickson, 1980) populations as well. There also is a growing trend toward "plain English" documents for the general population, which has resulted in increased efforts toward determining ways to make text more comprehensible (e.g., Felker, 1980).

Much research, both linguistic and empirical, has been directed toward this issue, and a number of books and other resources are available that detail the results of these research efforts. In this section, the major conclusions of *linguistic* research, which is based on logical analyses, are presented. Perhaps the most comprehensive linguistic analysis of adaptations is that conducted by Davison et al. (1980). They summarize the study as follows:

In an attempt to characterize factors not measurable by current objective readability formulas, we compared four texts that were adapted for younger readers, with their originals, in order to see what kinds of changes adaptors had made, and to assess the effectiveness of the changes. . . . We present in this paper a taxonomy of the adaptive changes and a discussion of the possible motivations behind the changes with our evaluations of the changes in particular cases.

Changes were found to be interdependent and influenced by factors such as assumed background knowledge, definition of the discourse topic, logical ordering of ideas, and syntactic structures, as well as limitations imposed on passage length, sentence length, and vocabulary choice. *Adaptation was found to be most successful when the adaptor functioned as a conscientious writer rather than as someone trying to make a text fit a readability formula* [italics added].

(Davison et al., 1980, p. 1)

These researchers noted various adaptation strategies, some of which they perceived as helpful and others as disruptive to children's reading. These strategies influenced all levels of text structure, from the individual word to the discourse-level organizational structure. At the word level, strategies included the use of word lists to substitute more frequent words for less frequent ones, lexical changes, thematic changes, and complex changes that involved other levels of the text structure. At the sentence level, the strategies included splitting sentences, merging sentences, and changing word order and syntactic properties of sentences. At the discourse level, elaborations, deletions, changes in organizational information, and changes in connectives and referential connections were all noted. Shifts in style of writing (from colloquial to formal language) and changes in other rhetorical devices were also seen. Whether a particular strategy was viewed as helpful or disruptive depended to a large extent on the context. Two examples of syntax level adaptations are provided:

The following example from DAYTON (the original text) places the resultative clause first, contrary to the more usual order:

(15) DAYTON

O[rig] We had water to drink after that. We set out basins and caught the raindrops.

A[dapt] We set out basins to catch the raindrops so that we would have water to drink.

Note also that the relationship between the conjoined clauses of the second sentence of O(riginal) must be *inferred*, since *and* has a number of possible purpose clauses. In this way clause merger can explicitly state relationships which are only implicit in the original text.

The deletion of a conjunction or the use of a vague one may obscure and make it harder to comprehend causal relations.... For example:

(16) DAYTON

O[rig] "I'm going down to the contract," said Jack, "to see that everything is all right."

A[dapt] "I'm going down to the building project," Jack said. "I have to see if everything is all right."

In example (16), the meaning of purpose is not really expressed by the assertation of obligation in the adapted version, where the counterpart of the *to* purpose clause is a separate sentence without an overt conjunction.

(Davison et al., 1980, pp. 25–26)

Davison et al. concluded that "a tension is inherent in the adaptation betweeen the need to shorten, and the need to clarify, between the need to simplify structure and lexicon, and the need to add indications of cohesiveness to the text. Therefore, no one of these strategies can be employed in isolation" (p. 31). Readers are referred to the original work for greater detail and examples of the various strategies.

The study by Davison et al. is representative of a large body of linguistic and experimental research on the effects of adapting and simplifying texts. The major conclusion of such studies is that writing to meet a formula does not necessarily result in the reduction of text difficulty. Rather, a conscientious intent to convey information combined with a solid knowledge of the many factors that can contribute to text difficulty appear to be the best tools for any writer. Researchers from fields as diverse as psycholinguistics, cognitive psychology, ergonomics (human factors), and typography have all added to the knowledge base of the most efficient strategies for designing documents to improve comprehensibility (Felker, 1980). Critique and linguistic analyses of adaptations and rewriting have also come from the field of deafness (Carter & LeNard, 1982; Ewoldt, 1983, 1984; LaSasso, 1982b; Luetke-Stahlman, 1982; Zarcadoolas, 1981).

EXPERIMENTAL RESEARCH ON ADAPTATIONS

In this section, *general* studies of adaptations and text difficulty are discussed. Such studies either did not describe the exact manipulations that were involved in the adaptations or were designed as general studies of adaptation strategies and text difficulty. Studies that have attempted to manipulate *specific* text-based or reader-based characteristics are described in the next two sections of the chapter.

One topic of interest here is the comparison of individuals' perceptions of difficulty with objective measures of text difficulty. Alvermann and Boothby (1982) present one such study on children's perceptions of text difficulty. In finding that fourth graders could identify differences between expository and narrative texts, they also discovered that interest was an important factor in the perception of a text as "easy" and that familiarity with the content was not. Alvermann and Boothby also asked the children if hard words and longer sentences (the variables used in readability formulas to determine text difficulty) made something hard to understand. Forty-three percent said yes, 24% said no, and 33% were unsure. The variety of children's opinions indicate that readability formulas and children themselves do not necessarily use the same variables in determining text difficulty. A second study compared junior high school students' perceptions of the difficulty of adaptations and originals of the same story. The results were mixed in that not all of the adaptations were perceived as easier, but the order of presentation significantly contributed to perceived difficulty: "when an original story was read first, that version was rated as much more difficult than its adapted version" (Mitchell, Bradley, & Ames, 1982, p. 79).

LaSasso (1982a) compared estimates of text difficulty based on teacher perceptions and readability formulas with objective measures of deaf children's comprehension (comprehension questions). She found that the teachers' judgments and the readability measures predicted the same order of difficulty for four texts. However, that predicted order was not confirmed by the measures of the children's comprehension. The text predicted as easiest was actually the most difficult. In her discussion, LaSasso stresses that this result may have been influenced by the type of comprehension measure used and does not necessarily mean that teachers are not good judges of text difficulty.

Other studies have been designed to determine how adaptations made to reduce word difficulty and sentence length affect measures of text difficulty. For example, Trapini and Walmsley (1981) used three objective methods of adaptation (synonym substitution for difficult words, shorter sentence length, and synonym substitution plus shorter sentence length) and one subjective method of adaptation (making a list of the main ideas of the original and rewriting in the adaptor's own words). The subjective method was better in lowering readability scores than the objective measures that manipulated the variables that produce the readability scores.

Another group of studies examined the effects of adapted texts on comprehension. These studies used intuitive or subjective methods of adapting texts and looked at both adapted and original versions of texts. With college level texts and subjects, L. Johnson and Otto (1982) did not find easier comprehension on adapted texts. However, one stylistic factor was thought to be important: sentence structure. R. Charrow and V. Charrow (1979) also found no significant differences between adapted and original instructions written for one group of jurors. In a later study with a group whose educational level was lower than the first group, however, they found that the students' paraphrase ability was about 50% higher on the rewritten instructions than on the original instructions (V. Charrow, 1981).

Cohen and Stover (1981) had gifted sixth and eighth graders intuitively rewrite mathematical word problems and then varied experimentally the three major factors which the gifted students had modified to make the word problems easier (use of a diagram, reduction of extraneous information, and matching the order of presentation in the problem with order of needed arithmetic operations). They found large differences between average sixth graders' comprehension of the easier (adapted) and harder (original) problems.

Results of studies of the relationship between oral reading errors (miscues) and text difficulty have been mixed. Hittleman and Robinson (1975) used the oral miscues of ninth graders as indications of text difficulty and then rewrote the texts, modifying those aspects that caused oral miscues. The use of reader miscues to guide adaptation, however, did not result in more readable texts. On the other hand, Tamor (1981) found that second, third, and fifth grade children exhibited different profiles of miscues depending on whether texts were easy or difficult.

As noted previously, there are only a few studies of the effects of special or adapted materials on the comprehension of deaf individuals. Anken and Holmes (1977) compared the use of adapted classics, not with the originals but with the use of basal readers. Substantial and statistically significant differences in achievement on word meaning and paragraph meaning subtests were found between the group using the adapted classics and those using basal readers. The classics used in this study were adapted largely on an intuitive level. Later, however, Layton, Schmucker, and Holmes (1979) examined the adapted classics and basal readers to determine differences between the two. Basically, they found that three major factors differentiated between the adapted classics and the basal readers: (1) text length; (2) linguistic complexity; and (3) the number and types of kernel sentence patterns. Several studies that addressed the influences of manipulating specific, rather than general, text features on the comprehension of deaf students are discussed in the next section (S. Anderson, 1978; Drury & Walter, 1979; Noretsky, 1981).

A study by Heine (1981) provides some data on the efficacy of special basal reading materials designed for deaf children. In this study, Heine used several stories from Level 5 of *Reading Milestones* (Quigley & King, 1982b) to investigate the influence of higher order (more important) and lower order ideas on the comprehension of deaf children. Although he did not find the expected difference between recognition of higher order and lower order ideas, Heine did find that deaf children comprehended literal information in the passages *as well as or better than* a comparison group of hearing children. Given that deaf children typically have much lower comprehension of regular materials than hearing children, this result gives at least preliminary support to the belief that the use of linguistically controlled reading materials can positively affect comprehension.

Finally, information about the effects of adapted materials on the comprehension of deaf individuals comes from studies of television and film captions (e.g., Braverman, 1981; Braverman, Harrison, Bowker, & Hertzog, 1981; Braverman & Hertzog, 1980; Caldwell, 1973; Getson, 1979; Montandon, 1982; Murphy-Berman & Jorgensen, 1980; Seidenberg, 1981; Shulman & Decker, 1981). The results are somewhat mixed in that the language level of captions sometimes affected comprehension and sometimes it did not. However, it seems clear that captions written at lower language levels do have a facilitative effect on some measures of comprehension and on some types of televised material. These research efforts have also succeeded in identifying many of the variables that influence the comprehension of captioned broadcasts. Seidenberg (1981) describes five such factors: display conventions, sentence structure cues, global structure cues, lexical choice, and genres. Additional research on the comprehension of syntactic structures in context was done by Wilbur, Goodhart, and Montandon (no date). The results indicated that "even by eighth grade reading level, various syntactic structures of English have not been completely mastered by deaf students....In general, the performance of the students in this study confirms the findings of Quigley et al. (1976) that deaf students do not understand a large portion of the syntactic structures present in reading materials written for hearing children and underscores the need for continued research toward the development of linguistically controlled reading materials especially designed for hearing-impaired students" (Wilbur et al., no date, p. 44). The guidelines for writing materials for deaf children, which were produced by the Multi-Level Captioning Project (Shulman, 1979; Shulman & Decker, 1981), are described in Chapter 6.

TEXT-BASED VARIABLES THAT INFLUENCE TEXT DIFFICULTY

Earlier in this chapter, it was explained that text difficulty involves both text-based and reader-based variables. In addition, text difficulty can be influenced by characteristics of the task used to assess comprehension and by instructional practices, such as preteaching of vocabulary, providing questions to guide reading, and teaching students specific strategies for monitoring their comprehension. These last factors are discussed in other chapters (task-based [assessment] variables in Chapter 7 and instructional techniques in Chapter 4). Therefore, the discussion here is limited to text and reader variables. In this section, the following text-based variables are addressed: (1) vocabulary; (2) syntax; (3) discourse-level structures; and (4) format. Additional information on these variables can be found in Chapters 2 and 3. Also, in analyzing the research presented here, the reader should recall that factors other than the one being manipulated can and do contribute to the relative difficulty of texts.

Vocabulary

Substantial correlations between individuals' vocabulary knowledge and reading comprehension skills have been found (Thorndike, 1973). Vocabulary is usually a primary variable in determining text difficulty in readability formulas (Klare, 1976) and a primary control in the construction of special and regular instructional materials. In attempting to discover whether difficult vocabulary *causes* lower reading comprehension, various researchers have attempted to manipulate the difficulty of vocabulary in texts. In a review of such studies, Klare (1976) found that changes in vocabulary difficulty generally did not affect reading comprehension of texts.

Marks, Doctorow, and Wittrock (1974) and Wittrock, Marks, and Doctorow (1975) found that reading comprehension was lowered when 15% of the high frequency words in a text were replaced by rare synonyms (low frequency words), whereas Jenkins, Pany, and Schreck (1978) found no decrease in reading comprehension with more difficult words. Freebody and R. Anderson (1981, 1983) investigated this issue further. They used three measures of comprehension—free recall, summary recall, and sentence recognition—with sixth grade students, and they found that a high rate of difficult vocabulary (one third of high frequency words being replaced by rare synonyms) was necessary before there was a reliable effect on comprehension. Second, they examined the placement of difficult vocabulary. Their question was "if the difficult words occurred in important propositions [ideas], was the effect on comprehension greater?" A greater effect of difficult vocabulary in important propositions was seen only on the summarization measure of comprehension. Thus, there is some limited evidence that increases in difficult vocabulary result in some decrease in reading comprehension, but a high proportion of difficult vocabulary is needed before such an effect is seen. Conversely, reductions in difficult vocabulary (substituting easy words for difficult words) appear to result in better comprehension (Kameenui, Carnine, & Freschi, 1982).

In addition to the proportion and placement of difficult vocabulary, the type of vocabulary has also been shown to affect reading comprehension. For example, Edwards (1974) found that increasing amounts of idioms in passages had a detrimental effect on the reading comprehension of eighth grade students. (Recall that idioms and other figurative language features in isolated sentences have been shown to be difficult for deaf children [Conley, 1976; Giorcelli, 1982; Payne, 1982.]) In another study of specific types of vocabulary, Duffelmeyer (1979) found that replacing abstract nouns and verb nominalizations with concrete nouns or full verbs had a positive effect on the reading comprehension of poor readers but little or no effect on the comprehension of average and good readers.

Studies of instructional techniques designed to improve vocabulary knowledge, while not measuring directly the effects of difficult words on comprehension, have provided some information about ways in which comprehension of difficult vocabulary can be enhanced. For example, D. Johnson et al. (1982) identified three types of information in a story that aid identification of unknown words: direct explanation, appositives, and contrast.

Syntax

Sentence length is usually considered to be an indirect measure of syntactic complexity in readability formulas, yet research studies that have manipulated this factor have shown no effects of sentence length on comprehension (e.g., Pearson, 1974–1975; see also the reviews by Klare, 1974–1975, 1976, 1984). On the other hand, manipulation of other measures of syntactic complexity has been shown to affect reading comprehension.

The work of Chomsky in the 1950s and 1960s sparked great interest in the syntactic aspect of language, which resulted in many attempts to determine the progression of complexity of various syntactic structures and the effects these had on oral and reading comprehension. Early reading studies found that (1) texts that used structures occurring frequently in a child's oral language were easier to comprehend than texts that used low frequency oral patterns (Tatham, 1970), and (2) texts which had been simplified to remove some syntactic transformations (e.g., passives, relative clauses) were easier to understand than texts that included such syntactic transformations (Coleman, 1964; Evans, 1972–1973). Improved comprehension of simplified texts was also shown to be strongest with poor readers (e.g., twelfth graders with seventh to eighth grade reading skills; Evans, 1972–1973).

Progressions in the complexity of other syntactic structures were also developed. Most of this research was done with single sentences or short groups of sentences and was discussed in Chapters 2 and 3 (see also Goetz, 1975, for discussion of differences and similarities in studies in which either sentences or connected discourse was used as the unit of study). Several formulas or systems for determining the syntactic complexity of connected text have been developed (e.g., Botel & Granowsky, 1972; Christensen, 1965; Dawkins, 1975; Endicott, 1973), and various studies have been conducted to determine if differences in syntactic complexity as measured by these systems affect reading comprehension. For example, using Christiansen's work in rhetoric to assign sentence weightings, DiStefano and Valencia (1980) grouped seventh and eighth grade students according to whether they read a baseline passage at a frustration, instructional, or independent level. The results indicated that changes in the syntactic complexity of texts had a substantial effect on the reading comprehension of students reading at their instructional level, but no effects were found for students at frustration or independent levels.

Another area of interest has been the effects of conjunctions and other connectives between and within sentences on reading comprehension. Early studies seemed to indicate that simple conjunctions with "and" between sentences did not affect reading comprehension (Coleman, 1962) and that the occurrence of complex conjunctions such as "because" reduced reading comprehension (Bormuth, Manning, Carr, & Pearson, 1970; Stoodt, 1972). More recent studies, however, have challenged these results (Pearson, 1974–1975; Pearson et al., 1979; Irwin, 1980). Specifically, these researchers have found that when complex conjunctions and connectives are manipulated, "either comprehension is equally efficient across forms or else the more subordinated and longer sentence forms elicit better comprehension" (Pearson, 1974–1975, p. 189). In assessing the applicability of these studies, however, it must be noted that they were undertaken with intermediate level children; Pearson (1974–1975) used third and fourth grade subjects; Pearson et al. (1979) used second graders who read on third and fourth grade levels; and Irwin (1980) used fifth grade subjects. As such, the results may not be directly applicable to younger or less skilled readers, especially those who have not acquired linguistic control of the structures being used. Thus, it may be that the results of the earlier and more recent studies on connectives do not contradict each other, but instead reflect differences in the linguistic abilities of the subjects. Support for this interpretation is provided by studies such as those of Amidon (1976) and Distad and Paradis (1983), which indicated that some temporal and conditional connectives were still not well understood by hearing children at ages five, seven, and nine.

A final area of interest in the effects of syntax on hearing children's comprehension relates to the use of repetitive sentence patterns in children's books. The use of such materials has long been advocated by various professionals (e.g., Kendall Demonstration Elementary School, 1981; Pickert, 1978) and has recently been the focus of experimental manipulation. Bridge, Winograd, and Haley (1983) compared the effects on the learning of target and nontarget sight words of the use of conventional preprimers versus stories with repetitive patterns in them. Significant differences were found in favor of the patterned language books on both the target and nontarget words. Additionally, some of the children in this group changed their major strategy for dealing with unfamiliar words from asking for help to the use of context to determine the meaning. Bridge et al. offer a list of structured language books that are helpful in teaching reading through this approach.

Some studies of the effects of syntactic complexity on the comprehension of deaf individuals were discussed earlier in this chapter. These studies varied vocabulary and content as well as syntactic complexity. Drury and Walter (1979) held vocabulary and content constant and had hearing-impaired college students complete cloze passages written at three levels of syntactic complexity. They found that comprehension, as measured by the cloze scores on passages, decreased as syntactic complexity increased. Thus, as with the early studies with hearing subjects, increases in syntactic complexity were shown to have a negative effect on reading comprehension.

Two other studies with deaf subjects, however, did not show better comprehension with simplified syntax. S. Anderson (1978) studied the effects of eliminating passives, subjunctive clauses, nominals, and ellipsis (deletions) on deaf high school students' performance on a cloze test and a set of multiple-choice questions. She found that, while scores were higher for the modified stories, the differences were not significant. Noretsky (1981) also found no significant differences between the performance scores for hearing-impaired college students on materials that had been simplified by eliminating certain forms of complex syntactic structures. Several explanations can be offered to explain these results: (1) the passages were either too easy (Noretsky) or too difficult (S. Anderson) even with the modifications, (2) the lack of results was due to the use of formula-like substitutions without consideration of the text as a whole, which research with hearing subjects has shown to be ineffective in reducing text difficulty (e.g., Trapini & Walmsley, 1981), or (3) syntactic modifications do not result in decreases in text difficulty. Additional research is needed in this area.

Discourse-Level Structures

Recently, there have been many advances in knowledge about the structure and organization of texts at the discourse level. Researchers have focused on three major aspects of discourse (reviewed by G. Green et al., 1980, and by Tierney & Mosenthal, 1982). These are (1) cohesion (Halliday & Hasan, 1976); (2) organization and importance of conceptual information (e.g., Kintsch, 1974; Frederiksen, 1975); and (3) structural characteristics of narrative and expository texts (e.g., Brewer & Lichtenstein, 1980; Mandler & N. Johnson, 1977; B. Meyer, 1975; Stein & Glenn, 1979; Thorndyke, 1977; Warren, Nicholas, & Trabasso, 1979).

The concept of cohesion in terms of connectives was explored under syntax. Other forms of cohesion, such as anaphora (words that refer to previously mentioned things in a text), also affect reading comprehension (Nash-Webber, 1977, 1978). For example, Barnitz (1979, 1980) found that pronouns (a form of anaphora) that refer to single nouns or noun phrases were easier to comprehend than pronouns that refer to clauses or sentences. Kameenui and Carnine (1982) found that replacement of pronouns with their referents resulted in better comprehension of expository texts, but not of narrative texts.

Beck, McKeown, Omanson, and Pople (1984) looked at the effects of revisions in a basal reading story that improved coherence. The revisions were "applied 'creatively,' by which we mean not treating each instance of a specific text feature in a standard, algorithmic way, but, rather, considering the role of each instance of problematic features within the context of the entire story" (Beck et al., 1984, p. 275). The performance of both skilled and less skilled readers was enhanced on the revised text.

The informational organization of texts has also been shown to affect reading comprehension. For example, clear and early statements of themes and main ideas make texts easier to understand (e.g., Belmore, Matthews, Bridge, Moskow, & Cohen, 1982; Fishman, 1978; Kieras, 1978, 1980). Similarly, increases in the number of word concepts (e.g., decreases in how often a specific concept is repeated) adversely affect comprehension, even when the number of propositions (ideas) is held constant (Kintsch, Kozminsky, Streby, McKoon, & Keenan, 1975). Vande Kopple (1980), among others, found that texts that use old information as the topic of sentences are more readable than texts that do not follow this convention.

Results on the effects of various structural characteristics of narrative and expository texts on reading comprehension have differed according to the type of text and the specific system used to describe the text's structure. However, the studies have consistently shown that the discourse-level structure of a text affects comprehension. For example, stories that present events (e.g., setting, character introduction, consequence) in the expected order as defined by a story grammar are recalled better than stories that deviate from the expected grammar (Mandler & N. Johnson, 1977; Stein,

1978; see also the discussion in Chapter 2). B. Meyer, Brandt, and Bluth (1980) showed that explicit signaling of the organization of problem-solution expository texts enhanced the comprehension of underachieving readers.

McGee (1982) conducted an interesting study in which the text structure (problem-solution) was held constant. She found that the text's difficulty influenced how well students were able to use text structure for recall. "Easy" texts, which were defined by comparing readability estimates of text difficulty with the reading level obtained from standardized tests for the subjects, were comprehended better than "difficult" texts.

Studies of the effects of discourse-level variables with deaf children are almost nonexistent. This area is fertile ground for research. One study that was designed to assess the effects of higher order (more important) and lower order propositions on the comprehension of deaf children (Heine, 1981), however, failed to show any difference; possibly this means that deaf children may be less sensitive to discourse-level cues that indicate the relative importance of ideas within a text. The study of Gaines et al. (1981) might also be interpreted similarly (see the discussion in Chapter 3, page 67).

Comparisons of deaf children's comprehension of syntactic structures in isolation and in context (e.g., McGill-Franzen & Gormley, 1980) were reviewed in Chapter 3. The conclusion reached there was that context can indeed facilitate comprehension, although the effects may be related to familiarity. In a further investigation of this issue, Nolen and Wilbur (1984) have shown that the facilitative effects of context are not limited to familiar materials nor to a specific reading level, being applicable to reading grade levels two through six. The generalizability of this effect to all syntactic structures, however, cannot be assumed, since it was found that students at the lower reading levels scored higher on isolated passive sentences than those presented in context. Thus, additional research is needed to determine the exact relationship between isolation and context in deaf children's comprehension of various syntactic structures. It may be that this result, like those discussed earlier, is simply reflective of differences between younger, less able readers and those with higher reading abilities.

Format

Up to this point, it has been shown that word-level, sentence-level, and discourse-level variables within a text all can influence reading comprehension. However, reading comprehension can also be affected by the format in which the text is presented. Format variations have typically included one or more of the following: (1) use and placement of illustrations; (2) legibility of print type; (3) attention-directing devices; and (4) variations in text layout—correspondence between the ends of sentences and lines, use of justification, and chunking of linguistic units. Format features of captions are considered within the last category (variations in text layout).

Illustrations

Statements about the efficacy of using illustrations in reading materials must remain tentative (Hayes & Readence, 1982; Schallert, 1980). Although early studies typically found that illustrations interfered with comprehension, more recent studies have shown that pictures in agreement with the text usually improve children's comprehension (Peeck, 1974; P. Wilson & Dixon, 1980). Five major factors have been identified that can affect reading comprehension: (1) artistic stylization; (2) amount of detail and relation to text; (3) shifts in perspective from one picture to the next; (4) the size and completeness of the picture; (5) proximity of the pictures to the related text; and (6) whether or not the picture is placed within text (Beck et al., 1979; P. Wilson & Dixon, 1980). P. Wilson and Dixon (1980) found that, after a week's time, children's recall of a story in which pictures contradicted the text was more influenced by the contradictory pictures than by the printed words.

In a study of the effects of varying amounts of verbal and pictorial information on comprehension of procedures for operating machinery, Reynolds and Booher (1980) found that deaf college students' best performance on operating the machinery occurred when the material was mostly pictures with some verbal description. All verbal and mostly verbal texts resulted in low error rates in operation but longer task completion times. The authors stress that these results are likely to be task-dependent and may not be generalizable to other types of tasks and that the results should be generalized only to people who have achieved at least a fourth grade reading level.

Perhaps the most convincing argument for the use of illustrations in materials for deaf children comes from a study conducted by Thompson in 1925 (Thompson, 1927, 1964) in which supplemental materials were designed to teach the meaning of words. For the experimental group, an explicit attempt was made to link words to picture referents. After eight months of instruction, standardized reading achievement tests revealed that the children in the experimental group, who were in first through third grades, achieved close to the reading level of hearing children at the end of first grade. In comparison, the achievement of the control group "was only a small fraction of that amount, particularly on paragraph meaning" (p. 350). This appears to be strong support for the concept that pictures can be helpful in beginning reading instruction and that attention need not be directed to the text alone.

Print Legibility

Standard orthography. Watts and Nisbet (1974) provide a comprehensive review of the effects on comprehension of various type sizes, type fonts (styles), amount of leading (distance between lines), length of print lines, and other legibility factors. Although the results are somewhat equivocal as to the best or most readable type, it is generally accepted that, for beginning readers, type should fairly large (14 or 18 point type; $^{14}\!/_{72}$ or $^{18}\!/_{72}$ inch) and clear (usually sans serif—without extensions on letters). Text lines of approximately 3¼ to 3⅓ inches are also recommended for beginning readers (K. Goodman et al., 1966). Weiss (1982) found that preferences for various type sizes, type styles, and illustration positions varied according to children's reading ability, age, and sex.

Alternative forms of orthography. In a study of nonstandard orthography (print) for English, Jackson (1980) found that sign-print, such as that used in the *Signed English Readers* (Bornstein et al., 1973–1984) was meaningful in isolation to deaf children with third grade reading levels who had been exposed to signs. Robbins (1983) and Andrews (1983) also found that the addition of sign-print to standard orthography was helpful to beginning readers. These studies appear to provide support for the suggestion that the method of initial reading instruction must be tied to the internal language mediating system of the child.

Prinz and K. E. Nelson (1984) are exploring the use of a computer in teaching reading (and writing) to deaf children. In their system, picture symbols, graphic representations of signs, and whole words and phrases can be associated with a single key on the computer. The system also uses animated sequences to illustrate the sentences that the deaf children form. Preliminary analysis of the data revealed that deaf children as young as two years of age demonstrated significant gains in word recognition and reading after ten weeks of instruction. Similar results have also been seen with CARIS (Computer Animated Reading Instruction System; Geoffrion & Goldenberg, 1976) with deaf children as young as four years old. A description of CARIS and of a deaf child's first encounter with the system is provided by Goldenberg (1979).

Attention-Directing Devices

Headings, captions, abstracts, and summaries are some additional format features that are thought to aid comprehension. Although some of these features can also be considered as discourse-level structures, they are considered here since they they fit within the general category of attention-directing devices. General conclusions are presented here. A detailed review can be found in J. Cunningham and Tierney (1984).

The results of studies on such devices are mixed. In a review of 32 studies on advance organizers (abstracts of the article to be read), Barnes and Clawson (1975) found that fewer than half supported the use of such devices. However, in a study of the effects of "previews" (abstracts) of difficult short stories on the comprehension, recall, and attitudes of low ability junior high school (hearing) subjects, Graves, Cooke, and LaBerge (1983) found that the use of such devices had positive effects on all three measures.

Although some studies indicate that the presence of headings and other nonprose devices can result in lack of comprehension or recall of text aspects not covered in the attention-directing devices, most studies indicate some positive effects on comprehension (Harrison, 1980; Watts & Nisbet, 1974). The addition of titles to texts that are potentially ambiguous also leads to better comprehension in that the title activates the correct framework or schema from the possible alternatives for the ambiguous text (Bransford & N. Johnson, 1972; Christopherson, Schultz, & Waern, 1981).

Use of typographical variations, such as **bold print**, <u>underlining</u>, and *italics*, has been shown to affect comprehension (Harrison, 1980). Furthermore, some studies have shown that the use of glosses (definition or summaries in the text margins) positively influences comprehension (Otto, White, & Camperell, 1980). This technique has also been used with computerized text in which the use of gloss is regulated by the reader, with such self-regulation resulting in improved comprehension (Blohm, 1982). Richgels and Hansen (1984) and Richgels and Mateja (1984) offer strategies and guidelines for teachers wishing to construct glosses for use in teaching reading.

Variations in Text Layout

The final format variable to be considered has to do with manipulations of the physical text that have been shown to affect comprehension. For example, it has been shown that young children typically associate the end of a line with the end of a sentence and that texts in which sentences continue onto a second line may be difficult for beginning readers to comprehend (reviewed by Raban, 1982). Also, the use of unjustified text (without a straight right margin) along with use of one sentence per line has been suggested for beginning students (Harrison, 1980; Streng, R. R. Kretschmer, & L. Kretschmer, 1978). Some teachers and researchers also recommend that beginning and poorer readers be given texts in which the line breaks (ends of lines) correspond with phrasal boundaries (Harrison, 1980; Streng et al., 1978). Research on this point, however, indicates that line breaks that "pre-cue" the reader that more of the sentence is to follow can also aid comprehension (Raban, 1982).

The use of spaces or slashes between phrasal units—"chunking"—has been shown to be effective in increasing comprehension (see examples in Chapter 6), at least for poor readers (Cromer, 1970; Mason & Kendall, 1978; Oaken, Weiner, & Cromer, 1971; Stevens, 1981). Gregory (1981, 1982) has established that the use of a similar technique, underlining the phrasal chunk, was effective with deaf children. Two researchers, however, did not find significant effects of chunking on the comprehension of either hearing children (Carver, 1970) or deaf children (Osgood, 1977). Interest in the chunking phenomenon has reemerged recently in the reading literature (Amble & Kelly, 1979; Brozo, Schmelzer, & Spires, 1983; Gerrell & Mason, 1983; O'Shea & Sindelar, 1983). All of these studies have shown beneficial effects on the comprehension abilities of good and poor readers. One study found greater benefit for the group of poorer readers (Amble & Kelly, 1979).

The effects of "cued text," a system of glossing text with visual cues to pronominal referents, were examined in relation to the ability of deaf students to comprehend various texts (Campbell, 1984). Three examples of cued text are provided:

Ⓣ   T
Tina sat down at the table. She was hungry.

Ⓜ   Ⓑ   M   b
Mike saw the boy stumble and fall. He ran over and helped him up.

Ⓜ   Ⓑ   M,B
Mom and Brian went out for pizza. They didn't get home until late.

(Campbell, 1984, p. 410)

Unfortunately, experience with such "cued texts" did not appear to significantly influence the ability of deaf children to comprehend the texts as measured by posttests. Further research on the effects of manipulating the physical characteristics of text on the comprehension of deaf students is ongoing (Campbell, 1984).

In another study of the physical characteristics of text, Braverman, Egelston-Dodd, Hertzog, Quinsland, and Austin (1980) found that the addition of diacritical marks aided deaf college students in improving their knowledge of word meanings. Further investigations of format variables are needed. For example, it would be illustrative to know if the form of the materials (i.e., soft cover, hard cover, chart paper) influences the comprehension of text. Such factors may be especially relevant in the education of deaf children since a large portion of materials are teacher-made (King, 1983).

Captioned films and television programs are a major form of reading materials for deaf individuals. Therefore, knowledge of the most advantageous formats for these materials is of major importance. The Captioning Center at WGBH-TV in Boston, among others, is conducting research on the format features of captions (see the summary by Braverman, 1981). Shulman and Decker (1981) also discuss format considerations for captioning films and television scripts. They cite research showing that an average presentation rate of 120 words per minute is appropriate for caption viewing. They also recommend that longer viewing times be provided for captions which accompany strong action segments and that captions should not be displayed over shot changes in the video portion of the message. In terms of caption placement, there are no research findings to support any specific placement techniques. Shulman and Decker provide some useful examples of captions being placed on or near the person who is speaking. Chunking of long captions into smaller segments has been shown to be more effective than presenting long, three-line captions. Research on the influences of various special effects for captions (movement, color, type style, overlays) is ongoing.

There is some evidence that the format of captions might need to be varied for different portions of the deaf population. For example, the average rates of 120 words per minute may be too high for many deaf individuals who read at a second or third grade level (Shroyer & Birch, 1980). The heterogeneity of the deaf population is also the reason for multilevel linguistic guidelines being used for captioning. Results of research on linguistic variations in captions were presented earlier in this chapter.

READER-BASED VARIABLES THAT INFLUENCE TEXT DIFFICULTY

Researchers have investigated the effects of five major reader-based factors on comprehension of texts rated at different levels of difficulty: familiarity, knowledge, interest, motivation, and purpose. Although these factors are related, it also is important to be aware of the differences among them. For example, familiarity and knowledge might be distinguished as follows: An American's and an Englishman's contacts with a topic such as football represent differences in familiarity, whereas an enthusiast's and a nonenthusiast's understanding of football represents differences in knowledge. Interest can be distinguished from knowledge by comparing a football coach and rookie football player: both might have high interest in football, but their knowledge will likely vary. Motivation and purpose can be distinguished by their source, with motivation, for example, being created from external forces such as remuneration or threat. Purpose can be defined as being created from either external or internal forces, but as influencing the strategy used in reading (e.g., skimming for general information purposes and slow, concentrated reading for studying purposes).

Familiarity

Only one study has been found that manipulated both text difficulty and familiarity (P. Johnson, 1981). In this study, Iranian college students (learning English as a second language) and a control group of American college students read adapted and unadapted English versions of stories from Iranian folklore and American folklore. Both groups recalled significantly more about the stories from their own culture. However, adaptation of the stories had different effects on the two groups. Iranian students recalled more of the adapted version of the American folktale than the unadapted version but showed no differences between adapted and unadapted versions of the Iranian folktale. The American students, however, recalled more of the unadapted versions on both the American and Iranian folktales. Thus, adapted text increased reading comprehension of unfamiliar texts for less fluent English users but had a negative effect on reading comprehension of both familiar and unfamiliar texts for the native English users.

Other studies have examined the effects of familiarity (without concomitant variations in text difficulty) on comprehension. The McGill-Franzen and Gormley study (1980) cited previously was designed to determine the effects of familiarity on deaf children's comprehension. Gormley (1981, 1982) further studied the issue. Not surprisingly, deaf children who scored on reading tests at a second grade level, when reading third grade materials that were technically too difficult for them, recalled familiar stories better than unfamiliar stories. Gormley emphasized the need to use familiar materials in introducing new skills. A variation of this principle is seen in the advice which some spokespersons for the field give to educators of deaf children: Use familiar syntax to introduce new words and use familiar vocabulary to introduce new syntax (Lanfrey, 1975). The idea of having only one new element in introducing a new topic is also reflective of a general teaching principle in any and all disciplines.

Knowledge

High knowledge of content has been shown to "wash out" the effects of "easy" texts (Funkhouser & Maccoby, 1971; Klare, Mabry, & Gustafson, 1955; Voss, Vesonder, & Spilich, 1980). (Note that text difficulty in these and the following studies was determined by readability estimates.) When knowledge is high, there are no differences in comprehension between easy and hard texts. When knowledge is low, however, differences in comprehension favor the easy or more readable text.

Interest

A reader's interest interacts with text difficulty (Denbow, 1973). Subjects learned more from the adapted (easy) versions of both high interest and low interest texts, but the amount of information gain was higher for low interest texts. Thus, text difficulty is less important when interest is high and more important when interest is low. The results obtained by Alvermann and Boothby (1982) (see the discussion earlier in this chapter) would seem to indicate that interest may be of greater importance than knowledge in its effects on comprehension.

Motivation

Motivation, in the form of threats or payments, has also been shown to influence comprehension of easy and difficult texts. McLaughin (1966) varied both the presence or absence of threats and the difficulty of the text. Subjects who were highly motivated (under threat) comprehended both easier and harder versions equally well, whereas subjects who were not as motivated comprehended significantly more from the easier version. Similar results were found with payment as motivation (Klare, 1974-1975). Mothner (1980) and LaSasso (1983a), among others, discuss techniques for motivating deaf children to read.

Purpose

No specific studies of the interaction among reading purpose, text difficulty, and reading comprehension were found. This may have been because most studies were done in experimental settings, and thus the experimenters (and subjects) perceived the purpose of reading as obtaining the maximal amount of information possible. However, it would be interesting to investigate whether text difficulty and reading purpose would interact in situations in which both variables were manipulated. For example, would deaf (and hearing) students be able to comprehend more difficult materials if their purpose was limited to attainment of a specific concept? Research with hearing children tends to support the idea that a narrow purpose does enhance the learning of that particular bit of information (with some qualifications based on subjects' ages), but to the detriment of learning or remembering other information presented in the text (see the discussion in Tierney & J. Cunningham, 1984).

SUMMARY

Three major conclusions can be drawn from the research on reading materials. First and foremost, although research has identified a great number of variables that can contribute to text difficulty, there is not yet a complete picture of what makes a specific text difficult or of how text difficulty can be changed. Information on the interactions between and relative contributions of various text-based and reader-based variables is needed. Although researchers have attempted to manipulate variables individually, it is not always possible to determine which variables actually cause increases in difficulty or improved clarity in individuals' comprehension of texts (Klare, 1976). The use of different definitions of text difficulty and reading comprehension by various researchers has also clouded the picture of the relationship between text difficulty and comprehension.

Second, although reduction of the complexity of texts through adaptation either has no effect on or affects negatively the comprehension of older and more proficient readers (R. Charrow & V. Charrow, 1979; L. Johnson & Otto, 1982; P. Johnson, 1981), the effects of adaptations are generally positive for individuals with low reading or language skills (Armbruster, Echols, & Brown, 1982; Beck, Omanson, & McKeown, 1982; P. Johnson, 1981). With average reading levels of below fifth grade, many deaf children fit the description of less proficient readers. Also, some studies with deaf children have shown positive benefits from the use of specially prepared and adapted materials (Anken & Holmes, 1977; Heine, 1981). Although Heine's study was not designed to assess the efficacy of special materials, the fact that the deaf subjects comprehended the materials at the same level as hearing children seems to be especially strong evidence that the use of special materials can be helpful. The lack of positive results for simplified materials in two studies with older deaf children and adults (S. Anderson, 1978; Noretsky, 1981) is consistent with the general trend for hearing individuals.

Third, adaptations and other materials designed for reading instruction can actually be more difficult than the original material, as well as uninteresting, if the sole purpose of the writing process is to attain some level of difficulty as measured by readability scores. The best adaptations and regular instructional reading materials are those that are guided by the desire to communicate meaningfully and by a thorough understanding of language and its uses. It should be also be noted that the problems in existing materials appear to result from incorrect or uneven balancing between controlling difficulty and exposing children to more difficult material, which in turn results from limited knowledge about how to manipulate all of the relevant variables simultaneously, rather than a lack of attention to the importance of meaningfulness. Manuals on writing materials for children have always stressed the need to provide contextual information (Colby, 1967). Early work on readability (Horn, 1937, cited in Chall, 1984) also clearly stated that readability formulas should not be used as writing guides.

One issue not yet addressed in research is the question of how difficult materials *should* be (Crismore, 1981). Just because a specific aspect of text is shown to be difficult for a given individual or group does not necessarily mean that that aspect should be limited or excluded in instructional reading materials. Conversely, just because the difficult aspect of text should not be excluded in reading materials, it does not mean that any and all types of language and concepts can be presented indiscriminately in beginning reading materials. Rather, a careful balance is needed between controlling or systematically introducing difficult aspects of texts and exposing children to challenging or difficult texts. At the present time, there are not any easy or complete answers as to how such a balance can be achieved or maintained.

Chapter 6

Reading Materials II: Description, Selection, and Use

In this chapter, the various materials currently used in reading programs for deaf children are examined. A major purpose of the chapter is to provide readers with information concerning available materials. The view that no single type of material should constitute the entire reading instructional program is proposed. The following topics are covered: (1) types of reading materials; (2) issues in selecting reading instructional materials; (3) descriptions of materials used in reading programs with deaf children; and (4) guidelines for materials evaluation and production.

TYPES OF READING MATERIALS

A major objective of any reading program—for deaf or hearing children—is to enable students to read the literature of the general population (Clarke et al. 1982; Quigley, 1978). The types of materials used in reaching that goal can be categorized according to the amount of linguistic and conceptual control and sequence that the authors use in constructing the materials. Figure 4 presents a graphic representation of the various types of materials used in teaching reading. The ways in which six major text variables are controlled and sequenced are noted: content, vocabulary, syntax, figurative language, inference, and discourse structure. Descriptions of materials that fit into each of the categories in Figure 4 are provided in later sections of this chapter.

Comprehensive reading programs should include a variety of types of materials at all levels of the instructional program. Within that instructional program, then, the proportion of use for a specific type of material might vary from a read-to condition only (i.e., students would not read directly from the type of material) to that type of material being one of the primary

TYPE OF MATERIAL		CONTENT	VOCABULARY	SYNTAX	FIGURATIVE LANGUAGE	INFERENCE	DISCOURSE	BEGINNING READING ⟶ ⟶ ⟶ ADVANCED READING
LITERATURE	GENERAL	*	*	*	*	*	*	
	AGE-RELATED	C	L	L	L	L	V	Children's Literature · Adolescent Literature · Young Adult Literature
REGULAR INSTRUCTIONAL MATERIALS	Reading	C	S	L	L	S	C	
	Content	C	L	L	L	C	V	
SPECIAL INSTRUCTIONAL MATERIALS	Reading	C	S	S	S	S	V	
	Content	C	C	C	C	C	V	
SPECIAL/ADAPTIVE MATERIALS		C	C	C	C	C	V	
TYPE OF MATERIAL		CONTROLS						BEGINNING READING ⟶ ⟶ ⟶ ADVANCED READING

Figure 4. Representation of varying levels of linguistic and conceptual sequence in reading materials. KEY: * = not controlled or sequenced; L = some control, controlled to a limited extent; C = strictly controlled; S = sequential, controlled development; V = varies in different materials within that type of material.

sources of reading materials. As stated in Chapter 5, relatively little is known about what the difficulty of materials *should be* for maximal benefit in instructional settings, and current research efforts provide few clues as to how a balance should be achieved between the goals of providing materials at the students' level and at a level that will challenge students to improve and grow. It does seem likely, however, that the balance between the different types of materials will vary according to the student's stage of reading development (beginning, intermediate, advanced readers), according to the individual needs of students at the same stage of reading development, and according to specific goals for reading lessons.

ISSUES IN SELECTING INSTRUCTIONAL READING MATERIALS

Several of the *either-or* questions posed in Chapter 4 focus on determining whether specific types of materials are appropriate for use as instructional reading materials (questions 9, 10, and 11 on page 115). These questions are discussed here: (1) instructional materials or children's literature, (2) regular or special instructional materials, and (3) the child's language or the teacher's language in language experience materials. At the outset, it should be remembered that an either-or choice between the types of available materials is an oversimplification of a complex problem. Educators need to be aware of the advantages and limitations of the materials they use. Using a variety of types of materials should help ensure that the limitations of one type are counterbalanced with the advantages of another. The difficult task is finding a way to balance use of the various types of materials as well as finding instructional time to address all the various needs of students.

Instructional Materials OR Children's Literature

Blackwell, Engen, Fischgrund, and Zarcadoolas (1978) provide a useful summary of the debate regarding whether instructional reading materials or children's literature should be employed as the major type of materials in instructional reading programs. These authors present a strong argument for the inclusion of children's literature as a prominent and integral part of the reading and language program. Their viewpoint defines "literature" as materials that are written for aesthetic value, that use artistic language, and that contain "a combination of authenticity and wonder of life through language" (p. 33). Authors of instructional reading materials have dual goals: (1) providing interesting, meaningful text, and (2) systematically introducing and reinforcing various aspects of the text language. In balancing these goals, such materials do not always possess the aesthetic characteristics of "literature." Although Blackwell et al. do not go to the extreme of suggesting that instructional reading materials not be used at all, other spokespersons for general education have made such suggestions (Bettelheim & Zelan, 1981; also see K. Goodman et al., 1966).

Blackwell et al. (1978) indicate that the view toward using literature within the field of deafness traditionally has been "to accept what is being said about the vitality of literature and yet, because of language and reading delay, [to] discount its possibilities in the curriculum for the hearing impaired" (p. 33). This statement is probably a valid representation of current practices in the field. However, at the same time, evidence of the desire for including literature as a component in reading programs for deaf children can be found in much of the professional literature. Bell (1929), for example, made recommendations that prominence be given to literature, especially fairy tales, in reading programs for deaf children (also see Appendix B for other references). The fallacy of using only instructional materials or only literature seems obvious (see the quotation by R. Anderson on page 131).

Regular OR Special Instructional Materials

Special instructional materials for exceptional learners have typically taken one of three approaches: (1) rewriting, or adaptation, of materials to an "easier" level; (2) modification of instructional techniques used with available materials; and (3) writing of original materials to meet the needs of specific learners (Stowitschek et al., 1980). Regardless of the specific approach, however, the use of such special materials and techniques has been controversial in many areas of special education. The following quotations adequately illustrate the opposing viewpoints on the use of special materials:

> No one questions the need for adapted materials for children with physical or sensory deficits.
>
> (L. Goodman, 1978, p. 93)
>
> . . .it is [not] advisable to simplify written materials.
>
> (Kachuck, 1981, p. 375)

Professionals in the field of deafness have debated whether to use special materials since the education of deaf children began. Two major groups can be identified: (1) supporters of the use of special materials, and (2) critics of special materials. Although the delineation of two major groups actually masks many positions between the two poles, the dichotomy simplifies the discussion of educators' viewpoints to be presented here.

Support of Special Materials
The first special reading book for deaf children in the United States may have been a book produced by Thomas Hopkins Gallaudet in 1817 (M. Nelson, 1949). Since that time, many special reading materials have been prepared for deaf children. Most advocates of these special reading materials rely on two major factors as evidence for the need for special materials: (1) the mismatch between the deaf child's linguistic, inferential, and experiential background and the background that is presupposed by regular reading materials; and (2) the belief that beginning readers and good readers differ

in their approaches to reading and that beginning readers need special help in learning to meaningfully decode printed words.

Support of special reading materials is based on the belief that the mismatch between the language skills of deaf children and the language used in regular reading materials is so great that "reading books produced for ordinary [i.e., hearing] children are, on the whole, unsuitable for the needs of deaf pupils" (Redgate, 1973, p. 2). Advocates of special reading materials for deaf children have typically focused on research on the syntactic aspect of English for support of their position regarding a mismatch between the child's language and the text language (see Chapter 3). Other text-based and reader-based aspects of the reading task, however, are also considered. Support for controls of vocabulary, background experience, and inference is usually based on studies that have demonstrated that deaf children (1) have smaller English vocabularies than hearing peers; (2) do not make the same inferences from English texts as their hearing peers; and (3) frequently have restricted world knowledge or experience (see Chapter 3 for further discussion).

With regard to differences between beginning and good readers, advocates of special materials usually agree with the limited capacity theory of reading (LaBerge & Samuels, 1974; see Chapter 2 for further discussion). This theory states that there is a limited amount of attention and memory that can be used in the reading process, and thus attention and memory must be split between lower level skills (such as decoding) and higher level comprehension processes. According to this viewpoint, a child's attention during the beginning reading stage is largely consumed by the new skill of "cracking the code." Therefore, the use of special reading materials which require the least attention to other aspects of the text (such as vocabulary, syntax, inference, and experiential background) is considered necessary for beginning readers who do not have adequate control of standard English. In this way, maximal attention can be directed to "cracking the code" and "obtaining meaningful information from print."

In summary, advocates of special materials believe that the experiential, linguistic, and inferential deficits of deaf individuals and the special needs of the beginning reader (both for meaningful stories and for decoding practice) make the use of special materials a necessary component of a comprehensive reading program. Most of these advocates, however, do not recommend the use of special materials to the exclusion of regular instructional materials or general literature (Quigley & King, 1981, p. 4). Survey data regarding the views of teachers toward special reading materials are presented in Chapter 4 (see pages 77 and 78).

Criticism of Special Materials

Criticism of special reading materials for deaf children has been around as long as the special materials themselves. For example, in 1915, Buell stated, "Let us open up a new field of thought in our reading by using readers used in the public schools" (p. 4). More recently, criticism of special materials has come from proponents of the psycholinguistic approach to reading, which is based on the work of K. Goodman and associates (K. Goodman, 1967, 1976; K. Goodman & Y. Goodman, 1978; Y. Goodman & Burke, 1976, 1983). Basically, the psycholinguistic approach is a top-down theory of reading that stresses the constructive nature of the reading process within the reader while deemphasizing the need for exact decoding of the text (see Chapter 2 for further information).

The criticism of special reading materials by advocates of the psycholinguistic approach stems from the belief that a student's world knowledge plus the contextual information in the text "offers more support for learning to read...than the controlled, simplified text of rewritten material" (Carter & LeNard, 1982, p. 11). These proponents of using regular instructional materials with deaf children do not deny the significant linguistic problems experienced by deaf children, but they do not think that special materials can solve these problems (Carter & LeNard, 1982; Ewoldt, 1983, 1984; Gormley & Franzen, 1978; Luetke-Stahlman, 1982). In criticizing the control of syntax and vocabulary in special reading materials, these individuals feel that too much emphasis has been placed on the role of the text in reading and too little emphasis on the role of the reader. There are three major criticisms of special materials: (1) syntactic and vocabulary controls are unnecessary because the reader does not read every word in a story and he or she can rely on the redundancies of the text and on his or her own world experience to disambiguate unknown words and language structures (Ewoldt, 1981b, 1984); (2) reading materials with controlled vocabulary and syntax offer little or no contextual information and may be fragmented (Carter & LeNard, 1982; Luetke-Stahlman, 1982); and (3) "explicit control of specific syntactic structures at the sentence level may not be in fact necessary for the deaf child to understand material at the passage level" (Gormley & Franzen, 1978, p. 545).

In addition to those who state emphatically that special reading materials are not needed for deaf children, further critique of special reading materials comes from spokespersons who see merit in the use of special materials (LaSasso, 1982b; Zarcadoolas, 1981). For example, LaSasso (1982b), while indicating that rewriting is a "theoretically defensible strategy" (p. 165), thinks that it is based on an assumption that meaning resides solely in the text and, as such, rewriting in and of itself may not be enough.

> Simplification of vocabulary or syntactic structures will not automatically insure increased comprehension....It would appear that the "acquisition" of meaning is a function of all the reader's previous concepts and knowledge, knowledge of the rules of language, beliefs about what he or she should be deriving from the text, willingness to read a particular selection for stated or perceived purposes, and so forth.
>
> (LaSasso, 1982b, p. 165)

Zarcadoolas (1981) also indicates that rewriting is sometimes necessary for students with poor reading abilities, but, on the other hand, she is critical of all materials designed for use in teaching reading to young children. Specifically, Zarcadoolas states that rewritten "literature" is preferable to the use of "reading systems" that place controls on the types of language that can be used.

A Perspective

Although each of the three criticisms of special reading materials makes a valid point, together they do not appear to be a sufficient argument for excluding the use of special reading materials as a component in a comprehensive reading program. First, insisting on an either-or dichotomy between regular and special instructional reading materials is unnecessary. Second, research on the issues raised in the criticisms does not provide definitive support for the view that special instructional reading materials are inappropriate. The fact that redundancies in text aid readers in acquiring the meaning does not exclude the use of special materials—redundancies can be found in special materials too. The view that special materials are unnecessary because readers do not read every word has been questioned. Based on recent eye-movement studies, McConkie and Zola (1981) conclude that readers fixate on virtually every content word. Evidence of fragmentation in both special and regular instructional materials was reviewed in Chapter 5. This fragmentation results from a lack of knowledge of how to balance the importance of text structure and text content rather than from inattention to contextual information. As Armbruster and T. Anderson (1984) state, "easy reading is damned hard writing" (p. 3). Increasing research efforts toward the goal of balancing the importance of text structure and text content would seem to be more productive than the suggestion to eliminate the use of special instructional materials altogether. In terms of the effects of context, the research base (see Chapters 3 and 5) does not provide definitive evidence that deaf students can bypass syntax in comprehending text. Although it is possible, it also is possible that a student's difficulties in understanding language at the word and sentence levels can diminish the effectiveness of contextual skills (see the discussion in Chapter 4). Either way, however, it seems clear that reading teachers must *teach* their students strategies for using contextual information—whether those materials are special instructional materials or not.

Language-Experience Materials—Whose Language?

Although much of the present chapter is devoted to commercially available materials, the importance of teacher-made and child-made materials in reading programs for deaf children should not be minimized. Evidence of their role is clearly seen in the high percentage of programs for deaf children that use the language-experience approach (LEA) (LaSasso, 1978a). What exactly is meant by "language-experience approach," however, needs to be clarified within the field of deafness. In the field of reading, the term "language-experience materials" usually refers only to child-dictated stories (Stauffer, 1970). Indeed, the use of the child's own language is the major cornerstone of LEA. Educators of deaf children, however, appear to have several definitions for the term. Some restrict the meaning to child-dictated stories only; others expand the definition to include child-dictated stories that have been modified by the teacher to reflect standard English patterns; and others still expand the definition to also include teacher-written chart stories that were not child-dictated (see the list of references in Appendix B).

For the purposes here, LEA is considered to include child-dictated stories, whether modified or not. Surprisingly, only three of the articles on the language-experience approach in Appendix B address the question of whose language should be the base of language-experience materials (LaSasso & Heidinger, 1983; LeBuffe, 1979, 1982). The issue is succintly stated by LaSasso and Heidinger (1983):

> Many teachers of deaf children who use LEA are faced with a dilemma when the language of their students deviates from standard English. They wonder whether they should record verbatim the language of the student, as recommended by most proponents of LEA (who take the position that to do otherwise reflects a lack of respect for the student and his language), or whether they should modify the child's language to correspond to English.
>
> (LaSasso & Heidinger, 1983, p. 8-9)

Part of the dilemma can be resolved through redefinition of the either-or question to a question that recognizes that the two approaches (using the child's language and making revisions) can be complementary to each other. Increased research and discussion of this issue are needed. Major objectives of such activity will be determination of (1) how to balance respect for the child's language with exposure to grammatical English, and (2) how to achieve a balance among LEA materials, commercial materials (children's literature and regular and special instructional materials), and teacher-made materials.

The remainder of this chapter is devoted to descriptions of existing materials that are currently used in reading programs for deaf children. The categories of materials to be discussed (from Figure 4) include both commercially available materials and reading materials prepared by teachers and students. Discussion is limited to commercial materials since teacher-made and student-made materials would be classified in various categories, depending on the controls the author applied in constructing the materials.

The concentration on commercial materials in this chapter should not be interpreted as an indication of their relative importance in comparison to noncommercial materials. Indeed, informal observations of classrooms for deaf children clearly show that a substantial proportion of materials being used are teacher-made and student-made materials that are not available commercially. Evidence of the prominence of such materials is also shown in a survey of language methods and materials. The results revealed that teacher-made materials are used an average of 53% of the time in preschool programs, 45% in primary programs, 35% in intermediate programs, and 29% in junior high and high school programs; usage ranged from 0% to 100% (King, 1983).

Student-made materials include both child-dictated stories and the students' own writing. The use of student writing as reading material is an important component in any reading program. Recognition of the interrelationships between reading and writing is a bridge that needs to be built early in the language arts program. In this book, teacher-made and student-made materials are addressed through (1) discussion of existing sets of guidelines for preparing reading materials for deaf children from the professional literature (this chapter), (2) an outline of suggested steps for use in preparing reading passages for deaf children (Appendix A), and (3) a list of resources on the interrelationships between reading and writing (Appendix C).

GENERAL LITERATURE

The *literature of the adult, general population* includes things such as newspapers, magazines, and books. The authors of these texts do not attempt to control or sequentially develop linguistic aspects of their messages since they assume basic reading skills in their readers. Attention is directed, of course, to principles of good, clear writing and to the provision of interesting information.

Authors of *age-related literature* (e.g., children's literature, adolescent literature, young adult literature) also typically pay little or no attention to controlling the linguistic form of their messages. Attention is paid, however, to controlling the concepts that are presented to meet the interests and cognitive abilities of their readers. A major objective of children's literature and other age-related literature is the transmission of cultural and aesthetic values. Again, basic reading skills and language competence are assumed.

Use in Instructional Programs for Deaf Students

General Literature

It seems safe to assume that the general literature, especially popular literature such as newspapers and magazines, is used in most reading programs with deaf children. LaSasso (1978a) indicated that, of programs taking an individualized approach to reading instruction, 81% used newspapers as part of that approach. The polemic literature contains frequent mention of the use of newspapers and popular literature in reading programs (see Appendix B). However, only a few articles (e.g., LaSasso, 1983b) are devoted exclusively to discussion of such use.

Age-Related Literature

As noted previously, support for the use of age-related literature, especially children's literature, can be found in many resources on reading and deafness. Such support is seen in curricular guides (Kendall Demonstration Elementary School for the Deaf, 1981), articles (Ernest, 1982), and textbooks (Blackwell et al., 1978). Although survey data on the proportion of programs that use children's literature are not available, LaSasso's data (1978a) can be used to abstract a general trend regarding the inclusion of literature as a component in formal reading programs. LaSasso defined an individualized approach to reading instruction as constituting "an approach where instruction takes place with library books and other materials the child selects himself " (p.22). Making the tentative assumption that programs that selected this option might also include an emphasis on literature, we find that the individualized approach is selected as the primary or a supplementary method by between 27.6% and 43.6% of the programs at the various levels. It seems likely that programs others than these would also include some emphasis on literature.

Selected Resources

Many resources are available on children's literature. Most universities offer courses on this topic, which provide extensive coverage of children's literature and its contributions to a comprehensive program in instructional reading. Texts for such courses are useful resources (e.g., Huck, 1976). Another major resource is the list of Children's Choices (i.e., "best loved books"), which is published in *The Reading Teacher* each October. The International Reading Association, among others, also has produced several textbooks that address uses of literature in reading programs (e.g., Roser & Frith, 1983). Some additional resources that we have found useful are listed in Appendix C under the topic *Age-Related Literature*. Three subcategories are also presented: picture books, predictable books, and books categorized by plot structures. The references in these sections are bibliography lists that teachers may find useful.

REGULAR INSTRUCTIONAL MATERIALS

Regular instructional materials, which are designed for the general school population, typically involve control or sequence of content and linguistic form. The control of vocabulary typically is the major concern, with some attention being directed toward controlling sentence length. Content is usually controlled, as is the inference level. Syntactic complexity and discourse structure, however, are rarely controlled or developed sequentially (see Chapter 5 for details).

Two distinct types of regular instructional materials can be identified: *instructional reading materials* and *content area textbooks*. Although the distinction is not an exact one, perhaps the easiest way to differentiate between the two is based on whether the materials were designed for "learning to read" or "reading to learn." Content-area texts, which are designed for "reading to learn," are similar to age-related literature in that they assume basic reading skills. Intructional reading materials, on the other hand, specifically attend to taking a child from a nonreading status to some intermediary level of competence. Providing a progression of difficulty within a set of instructional reading materials is of major importance.

Use in Instructional Programs for Deaf Students

Regular Content-Area Texts

Regular content-area texts are used extensively in programs for deaf children. This is confirmed by classroom observations as well as by a few survey studies (King, 1983; Takemori & Snyder, 1972). For example, the respondents to King's questionnaire listed a total of almost 600 different texts that were used in teaching language to deaf students. The vast majority of these were regular content-area texts.

Regular Reading Instructional Materials

Most programs for deaf children also use regular instructional materials in reading classes. The prevalence data on such use was reported in Chapter 4. In this chapter, the purpose is to describe specific materials that are popular among programs for deaf children and to outline identified strengths and weaknesses of such materials (Hasenstab & McKenzie, 1981; LaSasso, 1978a).

Basal readers. Survey studies of materials used in reading programs for deaf children indicate that approximately 36 to 40 different basal reading series are used (Hasenstab & McKenzie, 1981; LaSasso, 1978a; Marshman, 1974). The most frequently cited series are: (1) basal series by the Scott Foresman Company (Reading Systems, Open Highways)—40%; (2) basal series by the Ginn Company (the 360 and 720 series)—12-19%; and (3) the Bank Street Readers—24% in 1978, 7% in 1981.

Strengths and weaknesses of these basal series for use with deaf children were identified in two of the survey studies (Hasenstab & McKenzie, 1981; LaSasso, 1978a). LaSasso's data are presented here (see Table 5).

Some differences in opinions among educators of deaf children can be seen in the data in Table 5. For example, in 46% of the programs, educators thought that the vocabulary in the Scott-Foresman Reading Systems series was too difficult for 9 to 12 year old deaf children, 54% thought it was not too difficult. There appears to be a fairly strong belief, however, that the identified basal series are appropriate for use with modification with most hearing-impaired children (67% to 95% of the respondents agreed with this statement).

It should be noted that the particular basal series identified as most

Table 5.   Strengths and Limitations of Basal Readers Used with Hearing-Impaired Children

	Primary Level 5–8 years			Intermediate Level 9–12 years			Junior-Senior High School Level 13–older		
	Reading Systems (Scott Foresman) %YES	Bank Street Readers (Macmillan) %YES	Ginn 360 (Ginn and Co.) %YES	Reading Systems (Scott Foresman) %YES	Bank Street Readers (Macmillan) %YES	Ginn 360 (Ginn and Co.) %YES	Reading Systems (Scott Foresman) %YES	Bank Street Readers (Macmillan) %YES	Ginn 360 (Ginn and Co.) %YES
1. Vocabulary is too difficult or abstract	36	31	41	46	37	58	42	33	54
2. Insufficient repetition of vocabulary	66	31	43	68	41	56	73	39	57
3. Syntax is too complicated	44	40	55	54	52	68	44	61	45
4. Heavy idiomatic or figurative expression load	43	36	47	58	45	65	68	32	64
5. Interest level of stories is appropriate	92	86	74	76	73	67	56	55	68
6. Phonics emphasis is too heavy for most hearing impaired children	44	30	51	42	40	49	38	47	45
7. Conceptual load is appropriate	78	72	62	70	65	65	70	63	76
8. Supplementary materials are helpful	93	88	83	89	82	82	82	79	85
9. Diagnostic tests provide useful information	70	59	53	60	57	51	64	39	58
10. Can only be used with linguistically competent children	26	26	44	35	27	48	38	44	62
11. Can be used with modification with most hearing impaired children at this level	88	90	78	90	95	75	82	82	67
	N=124	N=75	N=59	N=118	N=68	N=61	N=152	N=27	N=110

Numbers given are percentages of programs responding YES to the question.
N = number of programs reporting use of the particular basal reader at each level.
From LaSasso, C. (1978a). National survey of materials and procedures used to teach reading to hearing-impaired children. *American Annals of the Deaf, 123,* 22-30. Reprinted with permission.

appropriate or most frequently used in programs for deaf children will likely vary over time. For example, LaSasso (personal communication, March, 1985) indicates that, based on preliminary results of her current survey, some changes in the specific series being used have occurred since her original survey in 1978. It is recommended that readers refer to these new data when the study is published.

Programmed instruction materials. LaSasso (1978a) identified 16 different programmed instruction materials in use in reading programs for deaf children. Project LIFE was the most frequently cited material in this category. (This program was developed for handicapped children and is discussed under *Special Instructional Material.*) The next most frequently cited materials were the Sullivan Programmed Reading and the SRA Reading Laboratory. Educators using these materials considered them to be successful with profoundly deaf children (87% and 94% of the programs, respectively). Use of such materials, however, was limited to a small percentage of the surveyed programs (6.7% and 3%, respectively).

Other reading instruction materials. A great number of other types of reading materials (e.g., skills kits, library books) are available. The degree to which such materials are used in programs for deaf children can be inferred from the data provided by Bockmiller and Coley (1981). Sixty-six percent never use reading kits; 26% used them up to one fourth of the time; and 8% used them more frequently.

Selected Resources

Numerous publications have been devoted to discussions of regular instructional reading materials. Most introductory reading texts, for example, include discussions of popular materials. Educators of deaf children also have compiled lists of regular materials that they find helpful in teaching reading. These resources are provided in Appendix B. Of the resources listed there, the Browns and Arnell guide (1981) is likely the most comprehensive and up-to-date. These authors also provide a useful set of questions that can be used as criteria for evaluating reading materials.

SPECIAL INSTRUCTIONAL MATERIALS

Special instructional materials differ from regular instructional materials in the amount of control or sequence applied to the linguistic form of the message. Such materials typically are designed for special populations, such as deaf individuals, disabled readers, learners of English as a second language, learning disabled individuals, mentally retarded individuals, and individuals with language delay. The major text variables that authors of special materials manipulate are vocabulary and syntax. Other variables (e.g., figurative language, content, inferential demand, background experience, and specific reading skills) are also controlled or sequenced (Quigley & King, 1981, 1982, 1983, 1984). Materials so constructed are sometimes referred to as "linguistically controlled materials," although this usage does not denote similarity with the "linguistically controlled materials" that focus on controlling the phonological aspect of language (e.g., Nan can fan Dan; see the description on pages 101–105 in Harris & Sipay, 1979). Special instructional materials can consist of rewritten or adapted materials, or the materials may be original and designed to meet the needs of specific learners.

These materials, like instructional materials for the general school population, can be divided into two types. *Special instructional content-area texts* typically focus on the development of knowledge in a specific content area. "Reading to learn" is the primary objective of such materials. The use of linguistic controls is seen as a vehicle for making information more easily accessible, and the objectives of teaching children to read or increasing language skill are usually not stated and may not be intended.

Some special content-area materials are "instructional" in that a progression of conceptual difficulty within a single content area is developed (e.g., *The Controlled Syntax Science Series*, Fleury, 1979). Other materials might better be labeled "informational" in that there is no progression in linguistic or conceptual difficulty. Plain English documents (Flesch, 1979)—which are designed to reduce the linguistic complexity of legal, medical, and government documents—fit within this category. Multilevel captions for hearing-impaired people are another example. Linguistic features in these materials are controlled for informational rather than instructional purposes. (Note: References on the reading component in the use of captions are provided in Appendix B.)

Special reading instruction materials, on the other hand, have as their major objective "learning to read." The use of linguistic controls in these materials is seen as a vehicle for reducing the load on the beginning reader so that attention can be directed to "learning to read." Control and systematic progression of linguistic complexity (as opposed to the limitation of linguistic complexity) are considered to be of primary concern. Reading systems are included in this category, as are supplementary reading texts and reading skills materials.

As noted previously, special materials can be designed for any population. In this chapter, the major focus is on materials specifically designed for deaf students. Although programs for deaf students use materials designed for other special population, descriptions of such materials and their uses with deaf students are already available in the literature (e.g., Crosby, 1948). Lists of special high interest-low vocabulary materials are also available from the International Reading Association, among others. A compilation and description of materials specifically designed for deaf students, however, is not available. Such a work is an objective of this chapter.

Use in Instructional Programs for Deaf Students

The survey of reading methods and materials currently being conducted by LaSasso (personal communication, March, 1985) contains questions regarding the use of special reading materials in programs for deaf children. Preliminary data from the survey indicate that 46% of the respondents using basal readers used *Reading Milestones*. This was, far and away, the most frequently cited series. Satisfaction was also high (87%). From these data it seems likely that educators in many programs for hearing-impaired students are using at least some, and likely a great deal of, special materials.

Resources—Materials Designed for Deaf Students

Special Content-Area Texts

A list of linguistically controlled content-area texts specifically designed for deaf individuals is presented in Table 6. The list accurately reflects currently-available, commercial materials known to the authors, but some others may have been missed. It can be seen that much variety exists in the special reading materials developed for deaf children; many different content areas and topics are covered, and there is a wide range of levels for which the materials have been prepared—from preschool to adult. It is also interesting to note that many of the materials have been published since the late 1970s.

The information on linguistic controls in the last column of Table 6 is based on authors' descriptions that accompanied the materials. No attempt was made to infer the existence of controls if the authors of the materials did not describe such controls. An informal analysis of the materials, however, revealed differences in the complexity of the content and language used in the materials for a given level. For example, the linguistic controls used in one set of materials for deaf students at an intermediate level may or may not be similar to the linguistic controls used in another set of materials for the same type of students. In the following discussion, general statements are provided concerning the ways in which special content-area texts are designed. The discussion is limited to text-based variables because it is these that materials developers can manipulate directly.

Although most of the materials control syntax and vocabulary primarily, the specific ways in which syntax and vocabulary are controlled differ. For example, developers of some materials use research data to select "acceptable" syntactic patterns (based on linguistic complexity or on the language acquisition of deaf or hearing children or both); others use intuition or judgments of the difficulty of texts based on professional experience with deaf children; and still others use a combination of research data, professional judgments, and intuition. Regardless of the exact method for controlling syntax, however, the materials are similar in that the limitation of difficult syntax, rather than systematic introduction of syntax, is of primary concern.

In terms of vocabulary, material developers frequently use a vocabulary list to aid in the selection of words to use in the materials. Different lists appear to be preferred by different materials developers. Differences also

Table 6.   Content-Area Texts Written for Deaf Students

Author and Date	Title	Level of Topic	Description of Materials
Fleury, 1979, 1982	*Controlled Language Science Series*	Primary–inter-mediate Science	Controlled syntax, vocabulary; exclusion of figurative language and idioms
Doblmeier, 1981	*Environmental Science*	Secondary Science	For students with "language difficulties"
Pfau (Assistant Director), 1963–1974a	*Programmed Assistance to Learning (PAL–Project LIFE)— Science Series*	5th–9th Grade Science	56 filmstrips; text passages; no details on controls
Slater, 1981	*History – Economics – Political Science*	Junior high–high school Social Studies	Simple sentence definitions; 2.0–4.5 grade reading level; increasing difficulty
Boyd, 1982	*Industrial America*, teacher guide, student workbook	Secondary Social Studies	Fourth grade reading level
Carter & Kearney, 1982, 1983	Syntactic Structures Series *Young American Adventurers, Folk Tales from Around the World, Great Escapes*	Secondary Social Studies	Controlled language reading books, focusing on passives and relative clauses
Volta Bureau, 1974	*World Traveler* (2 packets) (16-page full color magazine, photos from *National Geographic*)	Inter-mediate–high school Social Studies	High interest–low vocabulary; third grade reading level; magazine 1969–1974
Harrison, Keener, & O'Brien-Smith, 1981	*Controlled Syntax Biography Series*	Inter-mediate–high school Social Studies	Syntax controlled; vocabulary glossary; second grade reading level
LeBuffe, 1981	*Roots*, teacher guide, student workbook	Secondary Social Studies	Easy-to-read adaptation of *Roots*, activities
Carroll, 1980–present	*World Around You: A Magazine for Deaf and Hard of Hearing Youths*	Secondary Social Studies	No details on controls

Table 6.   Content-Area Texts Written for Deaf Students (continued)

Author and Date	Title	Level of Topic	Description of Materials
Pfau (Assistant Director), 1963–1974b	*Programmed Assistance to Learning (PAL–Project LIFE)—Social Studies Series*	5th–6th grade Social Studies	40 filmstrips; text passages; no details on controls
Carter, 1981b	*Interaction: True Stories and Directions*	Secondary English	Controlled vocabulary and syntax; biographies
Carter, 1981a	*Interaction: Made-Up Stories*	Secondary English	Controlled vocabulary and syntax; fables, myths
Carter, 1983a	*Interaction: Information*	Secondary English	Controlled vocabulary and syntax; encyclopedias, etc.
Carter, 1983b	*Interaction: Word Play*	Secondary English	Controlled vocabulary and syntax; idioms, figurative language
Walker, 1981	*Getting a Job*, teacher guide, student workbook	Secondary Careers	Controlled vocabulary
Maeder, 1982	*Career Exploration*, teacher guide, student reading book	Secondary Careers	No details on controls
Maeder, 1981	*Career Awareness*, teacher guide, student workbook	Secondary Careers	Controlled syntax, progression of vocabulary
Veatch, 1982	*How to Get the Job You Really Want*	College Careers	No details on controls
Husak, Pahre, & Stewart, 1976c	*The Work Series*	Inter-mediate Careers	Controlled syntax
Husak, Pahre, & Stewart, 1976b	*The Money Series*	Inter-mediate Careers	Controlled syntax
Kearney, 1981	*Loans and Credits*	Secondary Life Skills	Fourth grade reading level
Gochnour & Smith, 1977, rev. 1981	*The Language of Life*	Secondary Life Skills	No details on controls
Olsen, 1984	*Skills for Living*	Secondary Life Skills	Third grade reading level

Table continued on following page.

Table 6.   Content-Area Texts Written for Deaf Students (continued)

Author and Date	Title	Level of Topic	Description of Materials
Husak, Pahre, & Stewart, 1976a	*The Health Series*	Intermediate Health	Controlled syntax
Malcolm, 1983	*A Workbook in Library Science for NTID Students*	College Library Skills	Controlled syntax; specific to NTID library but useful guide for library skills
Star, 1980	*We Can!* (31 biographies of oral deaf adults)	Intermediate Deafness	Fourth grade reading level
Toole, 1981a, b	*Successful Deaf Americans, Courageous Deaf Americans*	High School Deafness	High interest–low reading; no details on controls
Bowe & Steinberg, 1973	*I'm Deaf Too, Twelve Deaf Americans*	Deafness	No details on controls
Alexander & Gannon, 1984	*Deaf Heritage* (student text and workbook)	Intermediate– High School Deafness	No details on controls
Talcove, 1981	*Resource Guide for Hearing-Impaired Students*	Secondary Deafness	Information on deafness; no details on controls
Wilson, 1974	*Noah and the Rainbow*	Intermediate Religion	Sign-print; no details on controls
Duncan, 1975	*Samson, the Strongest*	Intermediate Religion	No details on controls
World Bible Translation Center, 1975	*New Testament. English Version for the Deaf*	Intermediate Religion	No details on controls
Russo, 1980	*Made by Hand; A Catechesis for the Deaf*	Secondary Religion	Picture dictionary; comic book style

exist in how strictly the list is used, how frequently words are reinforced, and how and when important words are introduced. Similarities among the materials in their controls of vocabulary can also be identified: a basic sight-word vocabulary is usually presumed by the authors of all of the materials, and the development of vocabulary for the specific content area is of prime importance. The controls on inferential demand, background experience, and figurative language are usually intuition-based. Figurative language and idioms are frequently excluded or are very limited.

Reading Instruction Materials

A list of linguistically controlled materials specifically designed for reading instruction with deaf students is presented in Table 7. Many of the materials in Table 7 are similar in many ways to those listed as content-area texts in Table 6. The distinction here is based on their use. Materials in Table 7 are used in instructional settings that focus on teaching reading. Most of these are supplementary materials (a single book or a few general reading books or a large group of books, all written at the same basic level). A few of the entries in Table 7, however, are major reading systems (i.e., materials that are designed to take students from some beginning level through some higher level of skill). One of these is *Reading Milestones* (Quigley & King, 1981, 1982, 1983, 1984), which is the only basal-type reading series developed for deaf children. A second is the Project LIFE materials. The history of Project LIFE is provided in the references in Appendix B. Two other reading systems that were planned but have not been published are described by LaGow et al. (1979) and Bornstein (1978). Not all of the materials listed in Table 7 provide detailed information about the linguistic controls used in their development. Indeed, some of the materials may not have controlled linguistic features to the extent described herein. The basis for the information provided here is descriptions of controls in the materials identified as reading systems in Table 7.

Like the linguistically controlled content-area texts, the major controls in special reading systems are syntax and vocabulary. Usually research data, professional judgments, and intuition all play a role in determining the linguistic controls. However, the developers of such materials usually use research data as their primary resource to provide a systematic sequence in the introduction of new syntax and vocabulary. The research of Quigley et al. (1976) seems to be the primary reference for syntactic controls. *Reading Milestones* uses a scope and sequence chart based on that research. The materials from the Tennesee School for the Deaf use a scope and sequence chart provided by Hargis (1977). A slightly different chart was proposed by LaGow et al. (1979). Despite minor differences in the exact order in which specific syntactic structures are introduced and in the terminology used to refer to those structures, there is general agreement as to which structures are difficult and which are easy.

In terms of vocabulary, developers of special reading systems use one or more vocabulary lists to aid in the selection of words to use in the materials. However, rather than a basic sight-word vocabulary being presumed, as with content-area texts, development of a basic reading vocabulary is of prime

Table 7.   Instructional Reading Texts Written for Deaf Students

Author and Date	Title	Level of Topic	Description of Materials
Clarke School Faculty, 1978	*Trips and Treats*	Primary-Intermediate General	Second to third grade reading level
Volta Bureau, 1910	*The Raindrop*	Secondary General	Fairy tales and stories; no details on controls
Paris & Tracy, 1982	*Fables/Myths*	Inter-mediate –high school General	Simple syntax; glossary for vocabulary
Cole, 1979	*Apple Tree Story Books*	Elementary General	Controlled syntax and vocabulary
Crocker, Jones, & Pratt, 1966	*Language Stories and Drills*	Inter-mediate –high school General	No details on controls; books designed for use in language lessons
Gadzuk & Rosenbloom, 1981	*Reading Sampler (Book One)*	Secondary General	Simplified language; 1st–2nd grade reading level
Carter, 1981e	*Reading Sampler (Book Two)*	Secondary General	Simplified language; 3rd–5th grade reading level
Norris, 1982, 1984	*Jean's Christmas Stocking In Our House*	Elementary Sign-Print	140 to 150 word vocabulary; sign-print included
Johnston, 1984	*Popsicles Are Cold*	Elementary Sign-Print	No details on controls
Andrews, 1978b	*Ed's Off Day*	Secondary Sign-Print	Key vocabulary in sign-print; comic book format
Maupin, 1981	*Deaf Eagle and the Bank Robber*	Secondary Sign-Print	Comic book format; basic sentence structures
Kendall Faculty, 1981	*Coloring Book Classics*	Elementary Sign-Print	"Streamlined" difficult language of originals
Miller & Paul, 1984	*Educational Coloring Books*	Readiness Sign-Print	Word level materials; signs, fingerspelling, and print
Caccamise & Norris, 1973–1974a–d	*Community in Signs, Animals in Signs, Home in Signs, Food in Signs*	Readiness Sign-Print	Word level materials; signs, print, "primers"

Table 7. Instructional Reading Texts Written for Deaf Students (continued)

Author and Date	Title	Level of Topic	Description of Materials
Scherer & Hayward,1975	*Transitional Reading Series for Hearing-Impaired Children*	Preschool Sign-Print Reading System	Controlled vocabulary and developmental language
Bornstein, Saulnier, & Hamilton, 1973–1984	*Signed English Series* (Levels I, II, and III) —12 beginning books, 15 stories and poems, 21 growing up books, 3 posters, 1 record, 3 reference books	Preschool Sign-Print Reading System	Sign-print; original and adapted stories; no details on language controls
Schoolfield, 1974	*Phonovisual Launch—The Phonics Program*	Beginning Reading Skills	Workbooks, reading books, tests, classroom aids, vowel and consonant charts
Rush, 1977	*The Language of Directions*	Elementary Reading Skills	Workbook on following directions
Roppelt & Mowl, 1982	*Tomorrow, We're Taking a Test*	Elementary Reading Skills	Workbook on test-taking skills
Walter, 1971; Peter, 1973, 1974, 1978	*The Jack and Julie Series*	Elementary Reading Skills	Sequencing cards, building stories with pictures
Pfau (Assistant Director), 1963–1974c	*Programmed Assistance to Learning* (PAL-Project LIFE)—Prereading Series	Readiness Reading Skills	Visual memory, classification pattern analysis, shape discrimination, 51 filmstrips
DiSomma & McTiernan, 1985a–c	*Simple English Adapted Classics Series—Black Beauty, Little Women, The Prince and the Pauper*	Inter-mediate Adapta-tions	Controlled vocabulary and syntax
Newby, 1984a–e	*Simple Language Fairy Tales* (5 soft-cover books)	Beginning Reading Adapta-tions	Controlled vocabulary and syntax
Myborg, 1981a–c	Reading Classics: *Hans Brinker, The Fir Tree, Legend of Sleepy Hollow*	Secondary Adapta-tions	"Easy-to-read"; basic sentence patterns

Table continued on following page.

Table 7.   Instructional Reading Texts Written for Deaf Students (continued)

Author and Date	Title	Level of Topic	Description of Materials
Worden, 1973	*Beowulf*	Secondary Adaptations	No details on controls
Olson, 1974	*Song of Roland*	Secondary Adaptations	No details on controls
Quigley & King, 1981b–1984	*Reading Milestones* (Levels 1–8), 10 reading books, 10 workbooks, 1 teacher's guide at each level	Beginning Reading— 4th grade Reading System	See references and chapter text for details
Tennessee School for the Deaf, 1980	*Tennessee School for the Deaf Language-Based Reading Curriculum*	K-12 Reading System	Picture inventory, print inventory, story samples, recreational reading stories, adventure stories, figurative language materials
Pfau (Assistant Director), 1963–1974d	*Programmed Assistance to Learning (PAL–Project LIFE)— Reading/Language Series (Levels 1–3)*	Elementary Reading System	9 sets of filmstrips in each level, sentence-level materials
Pfau (Assistant Director), 1963–1974d	*Programmed Assistance to Learning (PAL–Project LIFE)— Reading/Language Series (Level 4)*	Elementary Reading System	72 filmstrips, paragraph-level materials, Social Studies topics
Pfau (Assistant Director), 1963–1974	*Programmed Assistance to Learning (PAL-Project LIFE)— Reading/Language Series (Level 5)*	Elementary Reading System	64 filmstrips, paragraph-level materials, Science topics
Pfau (Assistant Director), 1963–1974	*Programmed Assistance to Learning (PAL–Project LIFE)— Reading/Language Series (Reading Experiences)*	Elementary Reading System	Storyland—28 filmstrips, Holidayland—21 filmstrips, Great People—12 filmstrips

importance. Controls on vocabulary in these materials usually take one of two forms: (1) limiting the percentage of unknown words in a given amount of text, usually 3 to 5 percent in 100 words of running text (Hargis, 1970; La Gow et al., 1979), or (2) strictly controlling the number of new words for a story, ensuring that all other words have been introduced in previous stories, and reinforcing new words as frequently as possible (Quigley & King, 1981, 1982, 1983, 1984).

As with content-area texts, content, background experience, inferential demand, and figurative language were controlled largely on an intuitive basis. However, some guidelines for these aspects of text were used in the construction of the reading systems. For example, research on the interests of young children (Oliver, 1977) was used to guide selection of content in *Reading Milestones* (Quigley & King, 1981, 1982, 1983, 1984). Similarly, research and professional judgments about the experiential background of deaf children contributed to how authors of these materials controlled the knowledge and experiences expected of individuals who would read the materials. The amount of inference required by a text was also controlled, with a progression in complexity from earlier materials to later materials. Again, this progression was largely intuition-based, although some guidelines were available (Wilson, 1979a, 1981).

Figurative language and idioms were usually excluded at the beginning levels of the special reading systems and then systematically introduced at higher levels. Content largely determined the order in which figurative language and idioms were introduced, but some direction was provided by various handbooks on idioms (Boatner & Gates, 1975; Cowie & Mackin, 1976) and by research on the abilities of deaf children to comprehend idioms (Coley, 1976, and preliminary findings from Giorcelli, 1982, and Payne, 1982). Finally, in addition to linguistic controls of text, guidelines for the systematic and sequential introduction of reading comprehension skills were provided for two of the sets of materials (La Gow et al., 1979; Quigley & King, 1981, 1982, 1983, 1984).

The other reading instruction materials in Table 7 share most of the features just outlined. Although there is some variation in the linguistic controls and in the sources used in selecting those controls, the systematic introduction and reinforcement of linguistic features (such as syntax, vocabulary, and inference) appear to be a shared goal of most of these materials.

Two features that characterize some of the materials listed in Table 7 are especially noteworthy. Some of the materials use "sign print," which consists of picture representations of signs, along with the standard English orthography. (Note: Research on the use of sign print was reviewed in Chapter 5. Additional references relating to nonstandard orthography and on the use of sign language in teaching reading can be found in Appendix B.) An example of sign print, as it is used in the *Signed English Series* (Bornstein, Saulnier, & Hamilton, 1973-1984), is presented in Figure 5. The use of sign-print is actually similar to the use of talking books with young hearing children (Gamby, 1983) in that a representation of the child's internal language is used to help build the association between printed words and the concepts they represent.

Reading Milestones (Quigley & King, 1981, 1982, 1983, 1984) also has a

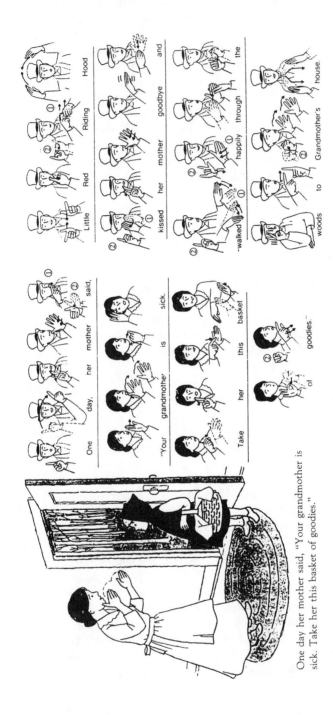

One day her mother said, "Your grandmother is sick. Take her this basket of goodies."

Figure 5. Sample of sign-print in the *Signed English series*. From Bornstein, H., Saulnier, K., & Hamilton, L. (1980). *Little Red Riding Hood* (3rd ed.). The Signed English series. Washington, DC: Gallaudet College Press. Reprinted with permission.

unique format feature. "Chunking" of sentences into their phrasal constituents is used in the first three levels of the series. The research support for this technique was reviewed in Chapter 5. Preliminary results from LaSasso's recent survey (personal communication, March, 1985) has shown that 82% of the respondents who use *Reading Milestones* considered the chunking to be a satisfactory technique. An example of the chunking technique is provided in Figure 6. The format shown in Figure 6 is used in the first three levels of *Reading Milestones*. It is not continued into the fourth level and beyond. Students are expected to internalize the process of reading materials in chunks (phrases) rather than word by word.

Reading Milestones is also unique in two other features. First, lists of important syntactic structures, vocabulary words, idioms, and inferences are provided in the Teacher's Guides for Levels 4 to 8. These lists of important linguistic features in a story are provided to help teachers identify potentially difficult or new aspects in stories and allow them to use this information more easily in teaching reading. Second, the editors and authors of *Reading Milestones* used the resources of the Center for the Study of Reading extensively in their planning and production of the materials. As has been mentioned frequently in this book, the Center for the Study of Reading has produced numerous reports, which include research results on the abilities of children to comprehend various types of texts, discussions of the reading process and reading theories, and descriptions of existing materials with comparisons among materials and approaches as well as identification of potentially problematic aspects of materials used to teach children to read. These reports were very useful in providing at least general guidelines for areas that otherwise would have been controlled largely by intuition.

From Tables 6 and 7, it can be seen that the number of special instructional materials specifically designed for deaf students has risen dramatically in the last decade. Many different types of materials are being prepared. There are some differences in the purposes for which the materials are constructed and some differences in the linguistic controls used in writing them. However, there also is one strong and central similarity among the materials—the goal of reducing the linguistic and conceptual complexity of reading materials.

Selected Resources—Materials Designed for Other Special Populations

As noted previously, there are many descriptions available of special instructional materials designed for other special populations. Appendix C contains selected references under the heading *Books for Special Populations*. These resources are mainly bibliographies or lists of materials. For greater detail, readers are referred to the professional literature regarding groups

The wolf   blows   hard!
The house of sticks   falls   down.
The little pig   runs   fast!

Figure 6. Sample of chunking of phrasal units from a story in Level 3 of *Reading Milestones*. From Quigley, S., & King, C. (Eds.) (1981). Level 3, Book 1. *Reading milestones*. Beaverton, OR: Dormac. (Book authors: Stuckey, P., & Quigley, S.) Reprinted with permission.

such as disabled readers, learners of English as a second language, the learning disabled, language disordered, and language delayed populations, and the mentally retarded population. A discussion of similarities between the reading and language problems of these children and those of deaf children is provided in Chapter 8.

SPECIAL-ADAPTIVE MATERIALS

Special-adaptive materials differ from both regular and special instructional materials in that they do not share the goal of preparing individuals to read the general literature. Instead, the goal is to transmit information to the targeted individuals. No attempts are made to "instruct" the individuals toward better reading and English skills. The use of ASL videotapes as described in Chapter 2 fits into this category. Other examples include (1) the use of Sutton's Sign Writing (Center for Sutton Movement Writing, 1983), in which a graphic symbol is used to represent signs, and (2) the use of audiotapes with adult nonreaders. Standard captioning techniques do not belong in this category since they use standard orthography in their presentation.

Use in Instructional Programs for Deaf Children

Little is known about the extent special-adaptive materials are used. It seems likely that, if they are used in instructional settings, such use is seen as a complement to, rather than a replacement for, teaching deaf children to read English.

Selected Resources

Only a few resources are available that address the use of special-adaptive materials. The Sutton Movement Organization publishes a monthly newsletter that is written with Sutton sign writing (some English print is also used). Some institutions (e.g., California State University at Northridge) are captioning films with sign language inserts rather than English print (R. Jones, Murphy, & Perrin, 1979).

GUIDELINES FOR EVALUATING AND PREPARING READING MATERIALS

In this section, resources that are helpful in evaluating and preparing reading materials for deaf children are identified. The major focus is directed toward describing the tools that are available to aid evaluators and writers in the process of materials evaluation and preparation. An outline of suggested steps for the process of evaluating materials is provided in the text of this chapter. A similar outline for the process of preparing materials is provided in Appendix A.

Guidelines for Evaluating Texts

Checklists

Numerous checklists are available for evaluating reading texts. These can be found in introductory reading texts, in curricular guides, in journal articles, and in brochures from some publishers of reading materials—to name a few sources. Two which we have found to be helpful are those presented by Browns and Arnell (1981) and Irwin and Davis (1980). These checklists are actually lists of questions that the evaluator asks in relation to the text he or she is evaluating.

Three major considerations are important in determining which of the many available checklists are the most appropriate. These are (1) the type of text to be evaluated, (2) the purposes for which the text will be used, and (3) the types of learners with whom the text will be used. Individual preference will also likely play a role in the evaluator's selection of checklists. It should be noted that the large number of available checklists is testimony to the tendency for new evaluators to pick and choose aspects of several different checklists and then compile a new tool. The process of selecting or creating evaluation checklists is extremely important, and it is recommended that individuals who are interested in evaluating reading texts devote sufficient time to this task. The following is a list of steps that might be used during this process:

1. Brainstorm a list of text characteristics which you consider important in selecting texts. Be sure to include text-based variables, reader-based variables, and task-based variables (also see the list of variables in Appendix A).
2. Collect available evaluation checklists and expand your list of text characteristics, if possible, by examining the items on these checklists.
3. Compare each of the evaluation checklists against your list of important text characteristics.
4. Select, for further evaluation, a few checklists that you consider the most appropriate. If needed, devise a new checklist that combines those features you consider most important.
5. Evaluate the checklists that you selected or devised in step 4. (Note: If a new checklist is devised, make sure to also select at least one other checklist for this step.) Select existing texts about which you have already formed an opinion, having based that opinion, of course, on experience in using the texts with students. Use the checklists to evaluate these

texts, keeping a particular class of students and a particular purpose for the reading lesson in mind during the evaluation.

6. Compare the results on the checklist with your preestablished opinion. Determine which checklist(s) provides the most accurate reflection of that opinion.

7. Use the best checklist(s) from step 6 in evaluating texts about which you have not yet formed an opinion. You may need to use different checklists for different types of materials. Continue evaluating the checklists as you gain experience in their use for evaluating texts. Modify them as needed.

Measures of Text Difficulty

Determining the difficulty of texts is a major component of any evaluation of reading materials for instructional purposes. Reviewed in this section are some of the measures of text difficulty that have been used in programs for deaf children. (Recall, however, that most teachers of deaf children do not use formal measures of text difficulty; LaSasso, 1978a.) If a teacher chooses to use formal measures of text difficulty, it is important to recognize that such measures give only a general idea of relative difficulty. Thus, too much significance should not be attributed to small differences in the text difficulty scores for different texts. This is true regardless of the specific text difficulty measure that is used. For example, if one text is rated (by a readability formula) to be at a 3.8 grade reading level and another text is rated at a 4.1 grade reading level, differences between the difficulty of the texts (at least as measured by the readability formula) are likely to be insignificant.

Readability formulas. Fry's Readability Graph (1968, 1977) is the formula used most often in programs for deaf children (LaSasso, 1978a). Such formulas are easy to apply and are useful as gross measures of text-based difficulty (however, see the criticisms of the formulas in Chapter 5). Many computer programs are available, which simplify the computational aspect of the formulas (see L. Geoffrion & O. Geoffrion, 1983, p. 195, for a list of commercial programs). An example from one of these programs, applied to a passage from Level 8 of *Reading Milestones* (Quigley & King, 1984), is shown in Figure 7.

Syntactic formulas. Perhaps the best known readability formula that is designed to measure the syntactic complexity of texts is that developed by Botel and Granowsky (1972). Basically, this formula assigns counts of zero to three points to various syntactic structures in a text. The counts for all sentences in the text are calculated and then averaged. The complexity scores are not grade equivalents. Dawkins (1975) provides examples of how this information can be used both in evaluating and in preparing reading materials. Streng et al. (1978, pp. 154–157) provide a modification of the Syntactic Complexity Formula for use in programs for deaf children. Figure 8 presents the application of this modified formula to several sentences from

Primary Analysis

Words not on the Easy Word word list	21
Spache Grade Level	3.5
WHEELER-SMITH	Second Reader
Fry Readability Graph	3.1

Display Words > 2 Syllables

3	fisherman
3	happily
3	fisherman
3	fisherman
3	several
3	fisherman

Complete Statistics

# of sentences	17	# words	162
# characters	625	# words/sentence	9.5
# chr/word	3.8	# syllables/word	1.2
# words > 2 syllables	6	# syllables/100 words	122.222
# syllables	198	# sentences/100 words	10.4938

Minimum Grade Level	5.2
Highest Grade Level	9.6
Average Grade Level	6.8
Estimated Dale Index	9.6
Fog Index	5.2
Flesch Grade Equivalent	5.6
Smog	6.3

Figure 7.   Sample of computer-assisted readability analysis.

the same story from which the 100 word sample in Figure 7 was drawn. The numbers in front of each sentence in Figure 8 give the complexity count for the sentence; the numbers above the sentence refer to the number of points given for the marked structure and the rule number from the formula. For example, 1-21 means that one point is given for "set expressions," rule 21. For the entire story, 420 points were given for 116 sentences or an average complexity count of 3.6 for each sentence.

In comparing the readability analysis in Figure 7 and the syntactic analysis in Figure 8, we can see differences between the two types of measures. The readability measures range from second grade to the middle of third grade on the primary level formulas and from a grade level of 5.2 to 9.6 on formulas designed for more advanced materials. The results of the Syntactic Complexity Formula, however, indicate that the text is written at a fairly simple level (as a comparison, the average score for the *Reader's Digest* is 6.8 [Botel & Granowsky, 1972]).

At present, there are no computer programs that simplify the process of computing the Syntactic Complexity Formula. There are, however, several programs available that analyze word-level and sentence-level aspects of language samples. (Note: Such programs were not designed as readability measures.) For example, programs are available that calculate total word and frequency counts for individual words in given texts (e.g., *Grammatik*, Aspen Software Company, 1981). Other programs determine the frequency of specific syntactic structures in texts (Levitt & Newcomb, 1978; Miller & Chapman, 1982; Mordecai, Palin, & Palmer, 1982). These tools are likely to be of greater benefit to the writer of reading materials than to the evaluator. They are mentioned here, however, since they are tools that provide quantified measures of text difficulty.

Discourse-level analyses. Several methods are available for quantifying a text's difficulty at the discourse level (see the discussion in Chapter 5). Several reviews of these systems are available (B. Meyer & Rice, 1984; Tierney, Mosenthal, & Kantor, 1984). The purpose here is to give an example to familiarize readers with such systems. The systems are complex and require a more detailed discussion than can be presented in the limited space of this chapter. Figure 9 presents an example of the propositional analysis system developed by Kintch and Vipond (1979); this system was used by Heine (1981) in his study of deaf children's comprehension of higher order and lower order ideas in texts.

Summary. The limitations of measures for text difficulty are described in detail in Chapter 5. Two of these are repeated here because they are important cautions for potential users of the tools identified in this section. First and foremost is recognition that these measures are at best gross measures of text difficulty. No one measure covers adequately all of the text-based, reader-based, and task-based variables that contribute to text difficulty.

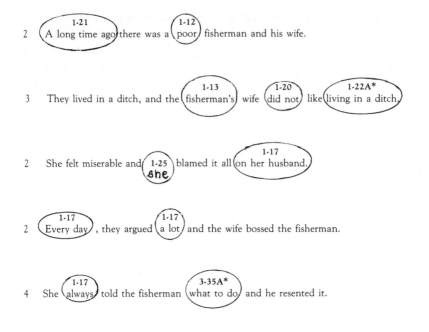

2   A long time ago there was a poor fisherman and his wife.

3   They lived in a ditch, and the fisherman's wife did not like living in a ditch.

2   She felt miserable and she blamed it all on her husband.

2   Every day, they argued a lot and the wife bossed the fisherman.

4   She always told the fisherman what to do and he resented it.

*   The formula in Streng et al. (1976) was further modified to provide one point for gerunds in object position (rule 22-A) and three points for clauses in object position (rule 35-A).

Figure 8.   Application of the modified Syntactic Complexity Formula. Story from Quigley, S., & King, C. (Eds.) (1984). Level 8, Book 5. *Reading milestones*. Beaverton, OR: Dormac. Reprinted with permission.

Second, the difficulty level of a text fluctuates throughout. Measures of text difficulty, however, usually are applied only to a small portion of a text. The concept of text difficulty that is formed from these text samples might be akin to the concept of "elephant" a group of blind people, without other information, would form from touching different parts of the animal. Recognition of these limitations is an important attribute for users of these tools. To paraphase Chall (1977), the limitations of text difficulty measures are minimized when their application is based on informed use.

Guidelines for Preparing Texts

"How to" suggestions for writers can be found in a myriad of resources. This includes texts on general writing, texts on writing for children, texts

Text: More than 100 years ago, there was a gold rush in California. Someone found gold and became very rich. Then people from all over America rushed to California. They wanted to find some gold and become rich, too. There were many people in California, and they were all looking for gold.

Text Base

1. (POSS.: CALIFORNIA, GOLD RUSH)
2. (TIME: OF, 1, 100 YEARS AGO)
3. (QUALIFY, 2, MORE THAN)
4. (FIND, SOMEONE, GOLD)
5. (QUALIFY, GOLD, SOME)
6. (BECOME, SOMEONE, RICH)
7. (QUALIFY, RICH, VERY)
8. (CAUSE: 6, 4)
9. (RUSH, PEOPLE, CALIFORNIA)
10. (QUALIFY, PEOPLE, FROM ALL OVER AMERICA)
11. (WANT, PEOPLE, GOLD)
12. (WANT, PEOPLE, BECOME RICH)
13. (PURPOSE: 11, 12)
14. (LOOK, PEOPLE, GOLD)
15. (NUMBER OF, PEOPLE, MANY)
16. (LOCATION: PEOPLE, CALIFORNIA)
17. (LOOK, PEOPLE, GOLD)
18. (PURPOSE: 16, 17)

Level [of Importance]

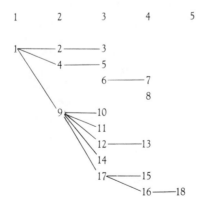

Figure 9. Sample propositional analysis. From Heine, M. (1981). *Comprehension of high and low level information in expository passages. A comparison of deaf and hearing readers.* Unpublished doctoral dissertation, University of Pittsburgh. Reprinted with permission. Text from Quigley, S., & King, C. (1982b). *Reading milestones. Level 5.* Beaverton, OR: Dormac.

that focus on general document design, texts that critically analyze existing instructional materials, texts that focus on adaptation strategies, and texts that focus on the use of instructional materials with special populations. Examples of such resources, which we have found useful, are provided at the end of the outline of steps for preparing reading materials in Appendix A.

A list of references that give suggestions on the preparation and use of reading materials with deaf children is found in Appendix B. Several of the references in that list provide general principles for materials preparation (e.g., Golladay, 1979; Hargis, 1978; Holmes, 1982). Principles for materials preparation can also be found in descriptions of the guidelines used in constructing special instructional materials for deaf children (e.g., LaGow et al., 1979; Quigley & King, 1981, 1982, 1983, 1984). In addition, there are four major sets of guidelines that provide examples of the process of writing for deaf children and that outline specific procedures and controls for use in preparing reading materials for deaf children. These four references, and one additional resource that was not designed specifically for deaf individuals, are described here.

Captioning Reference Manual

The *Captioning Reference Manual* (Shulman, 1979) is the first edition of the multilevel guidelines developed by the Captioning Center at WGBH-TV in Boston. The manual focuses on three major text-based variables: vocabulary, syntax, and inference. Special captioning concerns are also addressed. The chapter on vocabulary contains a chart of word lists that can be used to control vocabulary demands. Multiple meanings and idioms are also discussed. Two suggestions for improving contextual support for vocabulary in captions are given: use of video support and definition. The chapter on syntax (Wilbur, 1979b) outlines the syntactic structures that can be used in materials for three levels of complexity, which are based on the research of Quigley et al. (1976). Linguistic characteristics of major syntactic structures and acquisition patterns by deaf and hearing children are also summarized briefly. The chapter on inference (K. Wilson, 1979b) discusses the role of inference in language comprehension and provides examples of four categories of inferences (word inference, syntactic inference, contextual inference, and thematic inference). Examples from captioned programs are used to demonstrate how to deal with inferences in preparing materials for deaf people. The chapter on special captioning considerations addresses text-based variables (readability, visual format, spatial placement), reader-based variables (reading rate, reading skill), and task-based variables (timing, special effects, overlays). Examples are given of how these aspects influence and interact with the content of captions.

Readable English for Hearing-Impaired Students

The book by Shulman and Decker (1981) is the second edition of the multilevel guidelines discussed above. The three major chapters on vocabulary, syntax, and inference are maintained (Wilbur, 1981; K. Wilson, 1981), although each of these has been revised to reflect new research. Additional strategies for dealing with the various aspects of captions are also discussed. The chapter on captioning considerations (Decker, 1981) is expanded to include the application of the guidelines to the editing of news reports, reading instructional materials, and instructional documents (e.g., driver's manuals). *Readable English for Hearing-Impaired Students* essentially replaces the earlier edition (*The Captioning Reference Manual*).

Guidelines to Writing and Rewriting Materials for Deaf Students with Special Emphasis on Syntax

The book by Rosenbloom (1981) presents the guidelines used by the Model Secondary School for the Deaf (Washington, DC) in preparing many of the materials listed in Tables 6 and 7. The text variables which are addressed in this manual include syntax, vocabulary, and idioms. The issue of rewriting-versus-writing is discussed, and a general outline of steps in preparing reading materials is provided. Four levels of text difficulty are suggested. Appendices for this text provide summaries of the syntactic structures permitted at each of these levels, organized by syntactic structures and by level. The guidelines for syntax are based on the research of Quigley et al. (1976). Examples of rewriting a paragraph at different syntactic levels are also provided.

Adapting Written English for NTID Students

The book by Crandall (1979) is an instructional module that is designed to provide (1) basic guidelines on preparing materials for deaf college students, and (2) practice in preparing such materials. Nine general guidelines are given for sentence structures; three guidelines are given for vocabulary. The guidelines are designed for students with scores on reading achievement tests of seventh grade in vocabulary and eighth grade in reading comprehension. Most of the document is devoted to practice texts provided for analyzing and adapting passages (suggested analyses and adaptations are provided on fold-out pages following the practice pages). These exercises were designed for use in a workshop setting with a skilled person to provide explanations and clarifications.

The Document Design Project

The Document Design Project is conducted by the American Institutes for Research (1055 Thomas Jefferson Street, NW, Washington, DC 20007) in conjunction with Carnegie-Mellon University and a private firm, Siegel and Gale, Inc. The publications of this project are important resources for individuals involved in any type of document design. Relevant research from six major disciplines is reviewed in a volume edited by Felker (1980); the six disciplines are psycholinguistics, cognitive psychology, instructional research, readability, human factors, and typography-graphics. This research is the basis for *Guidelines for Document Designers* (Felker, Pickering, Charrow, Holland, & Redish, 1981), a set of "25 principles for making documents easier to read and understand" (p. 3). Important prewriting steps are outlined. A separate section is provided on each of the 25 guidelines. These contain (1) explanation and illustration, (2) related principles, (3) qualifications, and (4) a summary of what research says about the principle. The Document Design Project also produces a newsletter, *Simply Stated*, which contains articles related to producing Plain English documents.

In this section, descriptions were provided for five major sets of guidelines for preparing reading materials for deaf people. These guidelines are important resources for teachers of deaf children. Other reference texts that are equally important are listed in Appendix A. Such references were not discussed in this section only because of space limitations, not because they are of lesser value than the five described here.

SUMMARY

In this chapter, uses of reading materials are discussed. The suggestion is made that a comprehensive reading program for deaf children include *all* of the following types of materials: general literature, age-related literature, regular content-area texts, regular reading instruction texts, special content-area texts, and special reading instruction texts. Special-adaptive materials might also be used, either as a supplement to the reading program or as a separate component in the overall curriculum. References to resources that provide detailed information about various types of materials are included in this chapter and in Appendices B and C. Lists of materials specifically designed for deaf students are provided in Tables 6 and 7.

The second half of the chapter focuses on guidelines for evaluating and preparing reading materials. Major resources for these activities are identified. It is recommended that readers critically review the various evaluation checklists that are available and choose those that best fit their purposes. Brief synopses are also provided for five sets of guidelines for materials preparation. These, along with the information in Appendix A, should prove helpful to teachers and others who wish to write for deaf people. Finally, it is suggested here that the quality of text evaluation, preparation, and use depends primarily on having professionals (1) who are knowledgeable about the factors that influence the reading process (text-based, reader-based, and task-based variables), and (2) who are knowledge-seekers—individuals who recognize the positive and negative attributes of the methods and materials they use and who continue seeking to expand and increase their knowledge.

Chapter 7

Reading Assessment

The discussion of reading assessment is organized under the following topics: (1) definitions; (2) views of reading assessment; (3) characteristics of good assessment tools; (4) general issues in reading assessment; (5) performance of hearing-impaired individuals on assessment tasks; and (6) current practices, major problems, and promising directions in reading assessment with hearing-impaired individuals. The sixth topic is subdivided into separate sections for three major types of reading assessment tools.

DEFINITIONS

Reading assessment tools are classified here into three major categories: (1) formal tests, (2) informal tests, and (3) unobtrusive measures and dynamic assessment data collected during the instructional process. The major types of assessment tools in each of these categories are presented in Figure 10. The first two categories include situations in which assessment is separated from instruction (i.e., traditional testing). The division between these two categories is somewhat arbitrary, and there is overlap between them. However, for the most part, assessment tools in the two categories do differ on several dimensions (commercially-produced or teacher-made; most frequent use by administrators, reading specialists, or classroom teachers; degree of analysis of the test's characteristics, and so forth). Also, the two categories differ in that (formal) survey tests frequently place students one to one and a half years higher than do informal assessment procedures (Fry, 1972; Miller, 1978). The third category differs from the first two in that it involves assessment that occurs during the instructional process.

Formal Tests

Most formal reading tests include only two subtests: vocabulary and comprehension (Duffelmeyer, 1980). Alternatively, reading tests may focus on a single function or aspect of reading (e.g., reading readiness, study skills,

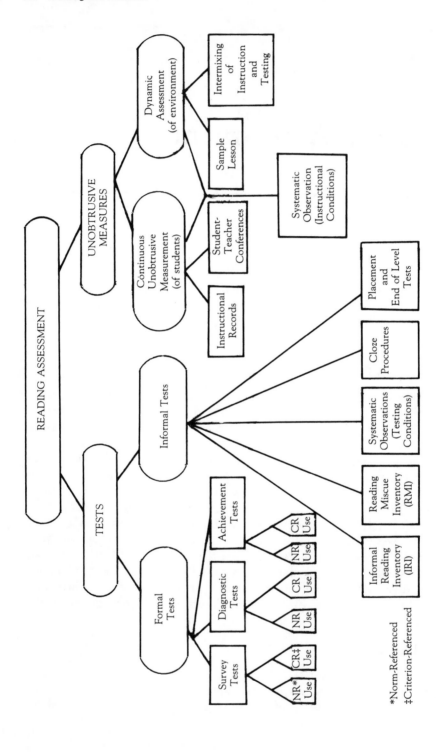

Figure 10.   Graphic representation of types of assessment tools.

decoding). Formal tests are discussed here as a single class. This seems justified on the basis that teachers of hearing-impaired children appear to use few formal reading tests (other than general achievement tests) (LaSasso, 1978a).

The subclasses under formal reading tests in Figure 10 are the traditional categories. Detailed discussions of the formats of, advantages of, and differences among these can be found in most introductory reading texts. A second major way in which formal tests are classified is according to their use: for comparison (norm referenced [NR]) or for diagnosis (criterion referenced [CR]). Although recent work indicates that the statistical underpinnings and test development process should be different for tests designed for these two uses (NR and CR), this simply is not the case in existing assessment tools (Wardrop et al., 1982). Thus, although "proponents of criterion referenced tests tried hard to create a dichotomy with the so-called norm referenced tests, . . . we now have criterion referenced tests with norms and criterion referenced interpretations of norm referenced tests" (Karlsen, 1981, p. v). Second, although the literature is replete with attempts to show the superiority of one over the other, these two approaches have their respective places in a comprehensive assessment and need not be mutually exclusive.

Informal Tests

The major informal testing techniques listed in Figure 10 are perhaps the classroom teacher's most useful and most often used tools for assessing the reading abilities of students. The *cloze procedure* has two formats: open cloze (generation of a missing word) and limited cloze (maze; selection of a missing word). *Informal reading inventories (IRIs)* and *reading miscue inventories (RMIs)* both use oral reading and some type of comprehension measure as their main components. These two techniques differ in that the IRI is designed for a simple frequency count of oral reading errors whereas the RMI is designed to make a qualitative distinction between significant and nonsignificant miscues (Y. Goodman & Burke, 1976). The distinction, however, is not a perfect one. There have been suggestions to synthesize the two approaches (Siegel, 1979; Tortelli, 1976; Williamson & Young, 1974), so there are IRIs with RMI features (qualitative analysis of the oral reading errors) and RMIs with IRI features (use of the independent, instructional, frustration reading level categories). The comprehension measures on IRIs and RMIs typically include either a short set of questions (Betts, 1946; Johnson & Kress, 1965) or retelling of the story, alternatively followed by probes or questions or both (Y. Goodman & Burke, 1976; LaSasso & Swaiko, 1983). *Placement tests* and *End-of-Level tests* may differ from this basic format, depending on the basal series for which they were designed. The majority of such tests, however, use an IRI or RMI format (King & Quigley, 1984). *Systematic observations* have likely always been an important component of the assessment techniques used by the classroom teacher. Recently, recognition of teacher observation as an important assessment tool is increasing in the literature. For example, P. Cunningham (1982) describes the process of "diagnosis by observation," and Johns (1982) discusses the "inner ocular technique," which is a term he invented "in hopes that this pseudoscientific abbreviation might help teachers legitimize something they have always done: use observational skills to help determine whether their instruction is producing the desired results" (Johns, 1982, p. 2). Evidence that teacher observations are valid measures of student ability as measured on standardized or informal tests is also emerging (Lovitt & Fantasia, 1980).

The advantages and disadvantages of each subclass of informal tests are discussed in the last major section of this chapter. Step-by-step procedures for constructing and administering these tests are not given. References are given to basic texts that provide this information. For now, the major point is to distinguish between the use of these tools in testing (i.e., no feedback) as opposed to the use of observation, oral readings, and other techniques in instruction. Obviously, the teacher is assessing students' abilities in both situations, but the types of feedback permissible vary greatly between an informal testing situation and an informal assessment during instruction.

Unobtrusive Measures and Dynamic Assessment

Assessment tools that are used during the instructional process are typically designed for one of two purposes: (1) continuous data collection rather than periodic evaluations (Tyler & White, 1979), and (2) determination, not of the student's static abilities, but of the conditions under which the student can learn.

Unobtrusive Measures

Unobtrusive assessment (term from Tyler & White, 1979) is conducted during instruction. It is like testing in that the objective of unobtrusive assessment is measurement of the child's static abilities. It differs, however, in that the "test" factor is eliminated (i.e., help can be given to the students). In a report on future trends in testing, Tyler and White (1979) use a metaphor of the measurements used in team sports to describe unobtrusive measures in educational settings. This metaphor is important since it demonstrates that the concept of unobtrusive assessment (without a parallel obtrusive measure) is possible in a real world environment.

Professional ball players, for example, rarely take a batting test or a pitching test. Instead, statistics are collected based on observations from ongoing play. Thus, the assessment does not intrude on the ongoing event. Some of the data collected are used to *change ongoing events* (a pitcher has walked several people; the coach therefore decides to put in another pitcher), whereas other data that had been collected during the game are used after the fact *to make placement decisions* (with regard to first, second string, and so forth) and *to make remedial and diagnostic decisions* (as in reviewing a baseball videotape to plan future practice sessions).

In Tyler and White's analogy, the teacher in educational settings is the equivalent of the coach in the sports example. Thus, a teacher's professional observational skill becomes a very important aspect of the assessment process. Furthermore, just as coaches uses tools such as videotape recorders to aid them in making observations, teachers use various tools to aid them in making their observations (e.g., checklists, anecdotal reports). One of the tools with the most potential for aiding teachers in the collection of a continuous stream of data is the computer. For our purposes here, an example of existing unobtrusive assessment should suffice.

McConkie and his associates at the Center for the Study of Reading at the University of Illinois at Urbana-Champaign (R. Anderson, 1981) are using a computer with a touch screen to teach prison inmates to read. When the person comes to a word he or she does not know, the reader touches the screen and the computer speaks the word. The computer keeps a record of the number of requests for help and the specific words being requested. Over a span of time, then, this data base provides a rich source of information about the person's performance—information that is probably a more valid and reliable indication of true ability than data collected outside of the instructional process and at specific, discrete points in time (i.e., pretests and posttests). McConkie (1984) has now made this computer system available commercially, and it is being used in beginning reading instruction programs. L. Geoffrion and O. Geoffrion (1983) also describe how a computer can be used in teaching reading.

Dynamic Assessment

The objective of measuring the environment, or conditions under which students can achieve their highest potential, has variously been called dynamic assessment (Cioffi & Carney, 1982), zone of proximal development (Brown & French, 1979; Vygotsky, 1978), and learning potential assessment (Feuerstein, Rand, & Hoffman, 1979). Much of this work has been done in the intelligence testing field, but the concept is now being applied to other areas, including educational assessment of deaf individuals (Braden, 1984; Carlson & Dillon, 1978; Keane, 1984). Also, although the emphasis on assessing the environment instead of the child is relatively recent, the concept of intermixing assessment and instruction is not. Thus, the concept of a "sample lesson" as a diagnostic procedure in reading (i.e., trial teaching) likely is as old as education itself. Harris and Sipay (1980) suggest five methods of using sample lessons for diagnosis in their introductory text on reading methods. These two concepts, then—evaluation of the environment and intermixing of instruction and assessment—distinguish dynamic assessment from the other categories discussed.

VIEWS OF READING ASSESSMENT

In recent years, there has been much criticism of assessment in general and of reading assessment in particular. For example, the Council on Exceptional Children and the National Education Association have called for a moratorium on testing (Singer & Dreher, 1983). Criticism also comes from many researchers who indicate that the functional limits of psychometric (statistical) measurements have been reached and other methods of designing and validating tests must now be devised (Lumsden, 1976; Johnston, 1983; Tuinman, 1979; Wardrop et al., 1982). These viewpoints are important since they indicate that reading assessment is in a state of flux and that there will likely be many changes in the ways reading and other skills are assessed in the near future.

However, it is equally important to be aware of the viewpoints of those most directly affected by assessment and assessment results: teachers, parents, and the students themselves. Generally, the public approves of testing. Many parents, business people, and legislators want more testing—both as an index to students' achievements and as an accountability measure of teachers' skills (Madaus, 1981). This general approval of testing is also shown in the increased use of standardized tests over the past 30 years—from a market of $7 million in 1948 to one of $42 million ($24 million when corrected for inflation) in 1976 (Resnick, 1981). In special education, Public Law 94-142, which stipulated that an individual educational plan (IEP) be developed for each child, also mandated the use of testing and other evaluation techniques (*Federal Register*, 1977). Similar trends toward mandatory testing have also begun to emerge in general education (Edelman, 1981).

In contrast, the views of educators toward tests are at best mixed. Several opinion polls have indicated that teachers often have ambivalent attitudes toward standardized tests. In California, 92% of teachers did not favor the use of standardized tests, yet 84% indicated that they would be unable to teach effectively without the results of standardized tests (Takeuchi, 1978). Similarly, in a national survey, the National Education Association found that 84% of the teachers believed that standardized test scores could be biased or misleading, yet 90% thought that such testing was appropriate if the results were not used in isolation (National Education Research, 1978). In reference to a mandatory testing program in Los Angeles, 92% of the teachers believed that the same information would be available with fewer tests and 90% thought that the benefits from the testing were not equal to the financial and time costs. Higher acceptance of specific tests appeared to correlate with awareness of the philosophy and limitations of the test (Edelman, 1981).

Most teachers seem not to be opposed to testing per se. For example, only 16% of 3500 teachers from a national survey agreed with the call for a moratorium on testing, which is supported by the Council on Exceptional Children and the National Education Association (Stetz & Beck, 1980). There is also some evidence of a dichotomy among teachers with regard to their views of testing. On the one hand, some teachers rely too heavily on standardized test results. These teachers do not alter placement levels that were based on test results (Rosenbaum, 1980; Weinstein, 1976), and they tend to rely heavily on standardized reading test scores to select materials and to place students in reading groups (Schell, 1982). On the other hand, many teachers place more confidence in their own observations than in formal test results (Singer & Dreher, 1983). These differences may reflect two different types of teachers, or they may simply reflect ambivalent feelings toward tests on the part of many teachers. Shannon (1983) sheds some light on this subject by showing that teachers' dependence on commercial materials is at least in part due to their beliefs that they are fulfilling administrators' expectations.

Educators of hearing-impaired children appear to have similar types of concerns and attitudes toward testing as do their counterparts in regular education. Differences exist, however, in that there may be an even higher degree of concern about the appropriateness for deaf children of generally available assessment tools. For example, Marshman (1974) found that 54% of the administrators and 49% of the teachers in her sample felt that the assessment tools available in reading were unsatisfactory for hearing-impaired children. Similar or higher levels of dissatisfaction with testing procedures for hearing-impaired children have also been noted in other domains, such as intelligence testing (Vernon, 1968; Levine, 1974; see also Chapter 1).

With regard to students' views of reading assessment, there are few published studies. As might be expected, however, better readers generally have more positive attitudes toward testing than do poorer readers. Shannon (1980) found that, regardless of how well or how poorly a student does, counseling students about the testing can increase positive attitudes. Students' attitudes reflect the general population's positive attitude toward testing in that the group who did not take a reading test responded more positively on the attitude scale than the groups who took the test but who did not receive counseling about the nature and purpose of the tests (i.e., these students received either only a score report or no information at all). There appear to be no published studies of how hearing-impaired children view testing.

CHARACTERISTICS OF GOOD ASSESSMENT TOOLS

Accurate assessment in reading is especially difficult since the *process* of comprehension is not directly observable. Rather, a teacher often must judge whether an individual has comprehended a specific passage based on *products* of that comprehension (e.g., responses to questions, free recall). As with all other subject areas, however, methods are available to aid in determining the appropriateness of specific assessment tools and in determining how much confidence to place in the results of the assessment.

The issues of validity (how well an assessment tool measures what it is meant to measure) and reliability (how well the assessment tool provides the same type of information across test items, over time, or between examiners) are primary concerns in assessment. The issue of practicality is also important. In relation to the first two, this presentation supports the recommendation of Sheehan and Marcus (1977) that validity and reliability be reported for the entire assessment tool *and* for each subtest if decisions are made on the basis of individual subtests. More detailed descriptions of testing theory and practices can be found in Thorndike and Hagen (1977). Wardrop et al. (1982) also offer useful descriptions and critiques of current assessment practices.

Validity

Validity is the most important consideration in evaluating specific assessment tools. It is defined in the following question, "Does this assessment tool measure what I want to measure, all of what I want to measure, and nothing else but what I want to measure?" Generally, five types of evidence can be presented to support the validity of assessment tools: (1) criterion-related validity, (2) predictive validity, (3) content validity, (4) construct validity, and (5) face validity.

Criterion-Related Validity

The validity of an assessment tool can be supported by showing that a substantial correlation exists between that tool and other tools used to assess similar skills. Thus, when a new test is devised, the developers normally calculate correlations between the results of that test and of other, established tests that address the same domain. If there is a substantial correlation (indicating agreement in the way the two tests rank order a group of students), this is taken as evidence that the new test is valid. This type of validity is addressed by most developers of reading tests. However, although this type of information supports the idea that two assessment tools are providing the same type of information, it does not directly address whether they are accurately measuring what they purport to measure. Further, criterion-related validity does not tell us whether the two tests indicate the same level of ability for a given student, but only that they rank a group of students in the same order.

Predictive Validity

Predictive validity is perhaps the most important type of validity since it attempts to show the relationship between performance on an assessment tool and later performance in a real world environment. For example, in evaluating a placement test for a specific reading series, a teacher wants to know "To what degree does the placement test predict how students will read the stories in the level at which the placement test predicted was the best for them?" Unfortunately, published reading tests (especially informal placement tests) often do not address predictive validity. However, whether the test provides such information or not, all test administrators should address this issue in their use of reading tests. Thus, the teacher should use systematic observations of students' performance in real world reading tasks to help in determining the predictive validity of test results.

Content Validity

Content validity is sometimes referred to as rational or logical validity since it entails a comparison of the content on the assessment tool with specific domains (e.g., reading) or with specific course content (e.g., a school's curriculum). Typically, the manuals for published reading tests provide information about the classification of reading skills or the theory of reading that was used as the basis for test construction as evidence of content validity. They may also indicate that professionals in reading were consulted to confirm the appropriateness of test items.

Final determination of content validity, however, rests with the individual using an assessment tool. Thus, a teacher will want to compare the content of the assessment tool with his or her own reading curriculum and objectives. Jenkins and Pany (1976) demonstrated that, although standardized reading achievement tests are not meant to correlate highly with any one curriculum, some of these tests are biased toward one or another basal series. These researchers compared the vocabularies of several basal series with the vocabulary items on standardized reading achievement tests and marked as correct only those words that were introduced in the basal series. When the constructed scores were compared, differences were found among the scores for the different basal reading series. Jenkins and Pany present an especially powerful example of the effects of this possible bias on a teacher's decisions about a student based on the test results.

> Suppose that a child is new to a school as a second grader. In September his new teacher administers the SORT [*Slosson Oral Reading Test*] so that a placement in Macmillan can be made. The child, having read Books 1-7 of the Sullivan Programmed Readers at his former school[,] scores a grade equivalent of 1.1. Other students in the class (who finished the Macmillan first grade readers) receive on the average a grade equivalent of 1.9, close to grade level. The teacher might conclude that the new child is a non-reader, and that s/he will not "fit" with the rest of his/her second grade...However, if the same child were given a WRAT [*Wide Range Achievement Test*], a grade equivalent of 2.0 would indicate that he, too, is reading at grade level, and is only a little behind his classmates who, given their Macmillan background, could be expected to obtain a WRAT score of 2.3. In this case, the teacher would probably assume the child could safely be placed in a "middle" reading group, beginning a 2^1 reader.
>
> (Jenkins & Pany, 1976, p. 12)

Educators of special students (including hearing-impaired children) must also be aware of another type of content validity—that relating to the appropriateness of the assessment tool for the specific population. Federal law specifically states that any assessment tools used in the education of special students (1) must have been validated for the purpose for which they are used; (2) must not be racially or culturally discriminatory; (3) must be administered by trained personnel; and (4) must be presented in the native language or mode of communication whenever possible (*Federal Register*, 1977).

Construct Validity

Construct validity examines the degree to which a specific assessment tool reflects some theoretical construct (Ventry & Schiavetti, 1980). Imagine that a theory of reading predicted that determining the main idea of a passage would be more difficult if there were no direct statement of the idea than if the main idea were explicitly stated (e.g., "The main point of this story is..."). If a specific assessment tool verified that this variable (explicit-implicit statement of the main idea) did indeed influence comprehension, agreement between the theoretical construct and the assessment tool (i.e., construct validity) would be established. Although statements of the theory that guided the development of the tests are usually made, construct validity is rarely addressed by published reading tests. The ways in which construct validity can be used in test development are discussed by T. Anderson et al. (1978).

Face Validity

Face validity refers to the degree to which the individuals taking the test view it as appropriate for them. Obviously, if test-takers view an assessment tool as either too easy (resulting in a cavalier attitude) or too difficult (resulting in an attitude of futility), the results of that assessment may be invalid. It should be noted, too, that face validity is a separate issue from whether or not the assessment tool is in fact of appropriate difficulty for the students. The important consideration is the students' attitudes toward the assessment procedure. All aspects of the test, from its format to its content, can influence the face validity of an assessment tool. For example, primary type (large print) and primary level content on a test used with high school students will likely not have face validity. This is an important consideration for educators of deaf children, given that even at ages 17 and 18, more than 40% of hearing-impaired students take a primary level test of a standardized achievement test battery (Trybus, 1978).

Reliability

Measurements of the reliability of an assessment tool give us an indication of how accurately the instrument measures whatever it is supposed to measure. It should be noted, however, that validity is the more crucial consideration in determining the appropriateness of a particular assessment tool. This is clearly shown in the following quotation:

> Reliability is important only as a necessary condition for a measure to have validity. . . . A test must measure something before it can measure what we want it to measure. . . . The converse of [this] relationship does not follow. . . . A test may measure something with the greatest precision and still have no validity for our purposes. Thus we can measure head size with a good deal of accuracy, but the measure is still useless as an indicator of intelligence. Validity is something over and beyond mere accuracy of measurement.
>
> (Thorndike & Hagen, 1977, pp. 87–88)

Examiner Reliability

Reliability can be based either on the examiner(s) who administer the assessment tools or on the assessment tool itself. Reliability of examiners is important for informal measures, such as oral reading errors, in which the results are based on the examiner's observations. *Inter-rater reliability* is the degree of agreement between independent examiners looking at the same assessment data, whereas *intra-rater reliability* is used to determine the consistency of a single examiner across several sets of assessment data.

For the assessment tool, four major types of reliability are available: (1) internal consistency, (2) parallel forms, (3) standard error of measurement, and (4) test-retest. All of these measures, however, are affected by variations among the scores of the subjects who take the test. Thus, these reliability measures can be used only with assessment tools that are designed to differentiate among students. If an assessment tool is constructed so that there is little variation among the students (i.e., all students get all the items correct or they get all items wrong), these measures are not appropriate (Schell, 1982). Also, if the population with whom the test will be used differs from the group used to establish reliability, published reliability figures cannot be used as evidence that the test is reliable for the new group of students. Indeed, Sheehan and Marcus (1977) state that reliability should be determined locally with the students who will take the test.

The first three reliability measures listed are affected by test length. There are two sides to this issue: (1) the more items in a test or subtest, the more the examiner can rely on the results; therefore, undue importance should not be attached to scores based on small numbers of items, and (2) reliability measurements can be inflated simply by increasing the length of a test.

Internal Consistency Reliability

Internal consistency reliability depends on the consistency of an individual's performance across items. Of the various types of reliability, published reading tests most frequently report this type of reliability. Internal consistency reliability is based on the performance of a single group of individuals with a single test administration. Performance of the students on one part of the test is correlated with their performance on another part of the test. Three major statistics are available: Spearman-Brown Prophecy Formula, Coefficient Alpha, and the Kuder-Richardson Formulas (KR-20 and KR-21). An internal consistency coefficient of .90 to .95 is needed to be considered adequate for making decisions about individual students.

Parallel Forms Reliability

When more than one form of an assessment tool is available, parallel forms reliability is frequently reported. Parallel forms reliability coefficients indicate the degree of agreement between the two forms, or, in other words, whether the two forms would place a group of students in the same rank order. The reliability coefficient alone, however, is insufficient for determining the equivalence of parallel forms. Test users should compare the content and item format on the parallel forms to ensure that the forms are indeed parallel. This is an especially important concept for teachers of hearing-impaired children since Brill (1974) reports that scores may vary by two or three years when hearing-impaired children are tested on two successive days with parallel forms of the same test.

Standard Error of Measurement Reliability

Standard error of measurement (SEM) provides an indication of intra-individual consistency (variation in scores that might be expected if an individual takes a test many times under the same conditions). This is an important concept for determining how accurate a given individual's score might be. For example, imagine that the SEM for a given test was 3 points. If an individual got 55 correct of a possible 90 items on a test, his or her score would be between 52 (score − SEM) and 58 (score + SEM) two in every three times if he or she were to take the test again and again.

This range of scores (actual score ± SEM), then, gives an idea of the variation that might be expected in one individual's scores. The SEM also provides information about how much confidence can be put in differences between a student's scores on different subtests or between the scores of different students. Thus, if Peter received a score of 55 and John-Allen a score of 58 on the test just described, the teacher would not have much confidence in the idea that John-Allen actually did better than Peter.

The standard error of measurement is especially important when growth over time is slow. Allen, White, and Karchmer (1983) indicate that the standard error of measurement for hearing-impaired students on the *Stanford Achievement Test—Hearing Impaired Version (SAT-HI)* is approximately equal to the average yearly growth for these students. Thus, the test, like other standardized achievement tests, does not have sufficient reliability to measure changes in the reading abilities of hearing-impaired students over short periods of time (Jensema, 1978), nor is it sufficiently sensitive to detect year-to-year gains for many hearing-impaired students (Allen et al., 1983). (Note: The *SAT-HI* is the only standardized achievement test with current norms for hearing-impaired individuals. It is discussed later in this chapter; see Allen et al., 1983, for a history of its development and discussion of the new 1982 edition.)

Test-Retest Reliability

Test-retest reliability is another measure of intra-individual consistency. This involves administering the same test to a group of individuals on two different occasions. Thus, test-retest reliability provides a measure of the test's stability over time. In interpreting this type of data, the examiner must be aware that the students' recall of how they responded on the first administration may result in higher correlations than those found in parallel forms reliability studies. Second, the students' attitudes toward repeating the test may also influence the results. This influence should be of special interest to teachers of deaf children since they are well acquainted with students who say "finished...finished" when presented with materials more than one time.

It is also important to be aware of the influence of students' recalling items and of their attitudes toward use of the same test since many hearing-impaired students take the same level of an achievement test battery year after year. For example, Rawlings and Allen (1980) found that over 25% of a group of hearing-impaired students in Texas took the same level achievement test in each year of a three year study. In addition, the national percentages of hearing-impaired students taking the same level test year after year are likely even higher, given that 70.6% of all hearing-impaired students who take the SAT-HI take the Primary Level I or Primary Level II test (Trybus, 1978).

Practicality

Although validity and reliability are the major issues in the selection of specific assessment tools, practicality in terms of cost, time, and ease of administration and scoring are also important variables. The importance of cost is evident to any administrator or teacher who has had to purchase materials and assessment tools. Similarly, the amount of time needed to administer and score tests is important to the busy teacher and administrator. Short administration time, however, is sometimes a false economy—short assessment tools often have lower reliability and may not offer the breadth of assessment needed to make appropriate diagnostic decisions.

On the other hand, administering longer tests or additional assessment tools may not the answer either. Venezky (1974) suggests that the value of an assessment tool should be measured in terms of its *unique* contribution to a decision. Following this suggestion, teachers would ask, "Will the information gained by administering this test add to the knowledge needed to make an instructional decision and does my decision require additional precision?" Thus, if a program has four instructional procedures, an assessment that groups students into ten levels may be too precise. Venezky states, "Almost all standardized survey and diagnostic tests for reading produce finer classifications than can be utilized for instructional decision making" (Venezky, 1974, p. 11).

Ease of administration and scoring are also important issues. Assessment tools should be easy for teachers to administer and for students to take. Computer-based scoring of reading and other achievement tests has contributed to the relative ease of this process. However, the separate answer sheets often needed for such scoring sometimes create administration difficulties, especially for younger children. Still, computer-based testing appears to be a promising direction, especially with the growing availability of microcomputers in schools. Two versions appear especially useful: (1) computer-based test administration whereby a child takes a test at the computer and the computer provides either a summary of the results or a detailed item analysis of the child's responses, and (2) computer-based scoring whereby a teacher enters a student's responses (or errors) and the computer handles the time-consuming scoring and mathematical calculations; the computer also looks up score conversions that the teacher would normally do by hand. The first version is especially exciting since this would allow for individualization in the assessment process. In other words, the computer could determine the items to administer based on the child's responses to earlier questions (Johnston, 1983).

Finally, Venezky's recommendation (1974) that the amount of assessment an individual receives should be proportional to his or her needs is important; a program that uses a standard battery of assessment tools for all students likely is not meeting the students' individual needs. Although this may actually lessen the practicality factor in that the management of individual assessment profiles is obviously more complicated and time-consuming than a standard battery, the need for individualization obviously should be the overriding factor; indeed, an individualized educational plan is mandated by law for all handicapped children (*Federal Register*, 1977).

GENERAL ISSUES IN READING ASSESSMENT

Some general issues of importance in reading assessment are (1) determination of what to assess; (2) selection of assessment tasks; (3) construction of assessment tools; (4) administration of assessment tools; (5) scoring of assessment tools; and (6) utilization of assessment results.

Determination of What to Assess

An examination of currently available assessment tools in reading reveals little agreement among educators and test developers concerning what should be assessed in reading. Three general issues have been identified. The first two issues are examples of either-or approaches to assessment. The view taken here is that an either-or approach is simplistic and that accurate assessment will involve both factors. The third issue results from the recent awareness of the contributions of background knowledge to the reading process and recognition that it is an appropriate area for assessment.

Real World Versus Reduced Context Tasks

Critics of available assessment tools often focus on the need for assessment to be related to reading in a real world environment. For example, there is much concern that many assessment tools measure only tangential skills, drills, and rules, which are unrelated to fluent reading (Smith, 1973). Other critics have focused on the form of the tasks being used to measure reading. Pikulski and Shanahan (1982) criticize assessment tools that focus on *encoding* (e.g., circling the printed word pronounced by a teacher) because such behavior has little to do with the regular reading process, which requires *decoding*. Mosenthal and Na (1980) and Mosenthal (1984) indicate that children may perceive assessment tasks as special tasks and therefore respond in ways that are different from their typical reading behavior.

These criticisms are important. They alert users to the limitations of traditional assessment tools. Obviously, assessment during realistic reading sessions probably does provide the best picture of a student's abilities. However, there are also situations in which assessment should be done out of context (i.e., in a reduced-context environment; term from Luetke-Stahlman, 1984). Taking an example from language development, if a teacher wishes to determine a child's comprehension of language, it is impossible in a context in which he or she has a box of cookies in your hand and asks, "Do you want a cookie?" Given this context-rich environment, in which the child can see the cookie, he or she does not need to comprehend the language to be able to respond appropriately. Similarly, in reading, it is possible for a child to understand the gist of a story without being able to recall specific sequences within the story or without having adequately developed strategies for dealing with unknown words.

Thus, ecologically valid tasks (i.e., in context) and reduced-context tasks need not be mutually exclusive, but rather should be complementary. Information from both sources is needed for a better understanding of an individual's reading abilities.

Comprehension—Holistic Process or Discrete Subskills?

A second major issue in determining what to assess is whether reading comprehension can be divided into components. Even among those who support dividing comprehension into subskills, there is little agreement as to what those skills should be. For example, in a review of reading tests, Schell (1981) states "no two tests include identical subtests. In fact, several tests. . .for the same level were more different than alike" (p. 5).

Various researchers have attempted to identify, statistically or logically, unique subskills related to reading comprehension (Baker & Stein, 1978;

Davis, 1944, 1968, 1972; Spearitt, 1972). Although these studies have identified discrete skills, there has been little consensus on the number or type of relevant factors. Opponents of separating comprehension into subskills use similar studies to show the holistic or unitary nature of comprehension (Drahozal & Hanna, 1978; Thorndike, 1974). Researchers have concluded recently that there is no clear evidence to support or validate a hierarchy of discrete subskills in reading comprehension (Johnston, 1983; Mason et al., 1977; Tuinman, 1979).

Johnston (1983) discusses the issue at length and identifies six major problems with the subskills or holistic research that he indicates "have made it difficult to adequately defend either position" (p. 4). These problems include difficulties in test construction, differences in the subskills that may be related to specific developmental stages, and attempts to find independent skills without sufficient reason to support the notion that the skills should be unrelated. Johnston goes on to indicate that the two positions (reading as holistic reasoning or as a series of subskills) need not be incompatible, but rather can be viewed as complementary.

Once again, an either-or approach—holistic process or subskills—is deemed unnecessary. The following quotation from Pearson and D. Johnson (1978) adequately describes this issue:

> reading comprehension is at once a unitary process and a set of discrete processes. It is unitary in three senses. First, . . . comprehension is a process of building bridges between the *new* and the *known*. Second, the ability to deal with any one of these relations is likely to be highly related to the ability to deal with any of the other relations we have discussed. Third, . . . there is much overlap. [For example, t]ime relations are often causal relations in disguise. . . . Reading comprehension must also be regarded as a set of discrete processes. The simple fact is that you cannot deal with the universe of comprehension tasks at once. . . . [W]e recognize that, for the sake of instructional convenience and sanity, you have to start somewhere and move toward something else.
>
> (Pearson & D. Johnson, 1978, p. 227)

Despite the difficulties in identifying an exact set of subskills, there appears to be support for the assessment and teaching of separate skills. Johnston (1983) cautions, however, that much additional work is needed before we will be able to identify a defensible set of (theory-based) subskills. In any case, people who are involved in choosing and administering tests need to evaluate carefully the basis on which test developers choose the subskills they include in tests and to make professional judgments as to the appropriateness of the subskill categories and of the items in a specific category. A selected list of resources on reading skills is provided in Appendix D.

Passage Dependence

A final major issue in determining what to assess is whether or not to assess prior knowledge. In most reading assessment tools, an effort is made to remove any items that are passage-independent—that is, questions that could be answered correctly without reading the passage. This practice is supported by many introductory reading texts (e.g., Harris & Sipay, 1980) and is based on research by Tuinman and others (Farr & Tuinman, 1972; Hanna & Oaster, 1978; Pyrczak, 1975-1976; Tuinman, 1974). Recent research, however, has shown that even text-explicit questions (those that are based on information within the passage) can be affected by background information (Johnston, 1983). These researchers contend that, rather than removing all passage-independent items from assessment tools, reading tests should be designed such that the influences of prior knowledge on the reading process can be measured. By deliberately including some passage-independent questions, then, the examiner would be able to determine whether an individual had the requisite background knowledge and whether he or she used it in comprehending the text. Methods for distinguishing between the availability of background knowledge and the selection of appropriate background knowledge (i.e., recognizing that available knowledge is relevant and using it in comprehending the text) will need to be developed (Spiro, 1980).

Selection of Assessment Tasks

A major factor that impacts the selection of assessment tasks is the theoretical orientation of the individuals involved in the selection process. In a review of reading tests, Schell (1981) notes

> A factor that complicates the selection and interpretation of a diagnostic and/or criterion-referenced test that can't be reviewed in a publication like this is the user's notions or beliefs about reading. There is a great controversy among reading educators as to whether reading is primarily a global, unitary entity or one comprised of numerous discrete subskills. Those who hold the former belief may be uncomfortable with many of the tests and reviews in this book because they disagree that reading can be fractionated in these ways or that these are the most important skills and processes to be diagnosed. Other educators have no such qualms and will find that many of these tests mirror their assumptions about what reading is and how it should be measured and taught. The point is that tests, in and of themselves, may not necessarily be good or bad, appropriate or inappropriate. Rather, one's point of view as to what constitutes reading and reading instruction may ultimately be more important in evaluating and choosing a test than is the test itself. This requires test users to determine what they believe reading and reading instruction are and then to choose a test [or tests] that best matches this definition rather than merely comparing one test with another.
>
> (Schell, 1981, p. 8)

A second major factor that influences the selection of assessment tools is the type of tasks. Assessment tasks in reading, as in other areas, can be divided into two major categories: free measures and controlled measures. These categories transcend the formal, informal, and unobtrusive categories to be discussed later in this chapter. For example, informal assessment tools might utilize both free and controlled measures. Therefore, these two task types are discussed here as a general issue in the development and use of assessment tools. At the outset, it should be noted that these two types of tasks are not mutually exclusive, but rather are complementary. There are advantages and limitations in each task type.

Free Measures of Reading

Free recall, in which an individual retells a story or the information from a read article, is the most common free measure in reading assessment. To a lesser extent, open-ended questions, probes following free recall, and cloze exercises can also be considered free measures in that, although the focus of the recall is controlled, the individual's responses are not constrained to a specific set. Such tasks can be regarded as both controlled and free because the test-takers provide *free* responses to a *controlled* task presented by a test-giver. The tasks, then, can also vary along a continuum from free to controlled (e.g., "What else do you remember?" to "What caused _____ to happen?").

Advantages. One advantage of free recall as a measurement of reading ability relates to the ease of preparing such assessment tools. For free recall, the person administering the reading assessment tool simply chooses the reading selection to be used.

Free recall also allows the examiner to assess aspects of the individual's comprehension strategies that might not be exhibited in controlled measures. For example, Livingston (1981) noted that several of her hearing-impaired subjects used syncretistic reasoning in inferring causative links between events in a story (e.g., because birds later ate the crumbs that Hansel and Gretel left on the trail, the children must have intentionally dropped the crumbs for that purpose). Although an awareness that children make such inferences would allow assessment of this feature in a controlled task, this awareness must be built from data from studies that do not constrain the child's responses.

A final advantage to be discussed here is that free recall allows the individual to organize the information in whatever manner is easiest for him or her. Thus, inferences can be made about the individual's knowledge of discourse-level structures and about the retrieval strategies the reader uses.

Limitations. The advantages of free measures of reading are also a source of limitations of such measures. Thus, Johnston (1983) notes that the "ease of preparation of the measure is inversely proportional to the ease of interpretation" (pp. 54–55). Indeed, the perceived difficulty in interpreting free recall measures leads many teachers to simply "eyeball" the data rather than going through a lengthy scoring and interpretation process (Pikulski & Shanahan, 1982). Also, without training, teachers may be unable to translate the assessment data into usable instructional goals.

Although free recall can provide data unattainable in controlled settings, the inverse is also true. An examiner cannot make any interpretations about what is left out of the recall protocol. For example, did the individual not comprehend a specific aspect of the story or article or did he or she simply not think it important enough to be included in the recall? Although probes can help in answering these questions, their use takes such tests out of the strictly free category.

In recall tasks, the effects of the production requirements on the individual's recall cannot be determined, nor can memory requirements. Production deficits or problems in retrieving information contribute to recall failure in ways that cannot be separated from comprehension failure.

The individual's perception of the task may also influence performance. For example, Harste and Burke (1979) have shown that a child's retelling to the teacher of a story that the child has just read orally to a teacher often differs dramatically from the child's telling of the story to someone whom he or she thinks has not read the story. In this case, the child's knowledge of a language convention (i.e., do not give unnecessary information; Grice, 1975) may actually work against the accurate assessment of reading (see Johnston, 1983).

Controlled Measures of Reading

Controlled tasks include the probes and open-ended questions discussed as having free responses, along with multiple-choice questions and other objective test items that control both the target information and the response choices. Cloze exercises can also be included in this task category when limited cloze (multiple-choice) is considered (J. Cunningham & P. Cunningham, 1978). Finally, confidence weighting, in which an individual estimates the probability of correctness for each alternative (Johnston & Pearson, 1982; Pugh & Brunza, 1975), is considered a controlled measure of reading. Johnston (1983) identifies the multiple-choice question as "the most researched, most maligned, most difficult to construct, most abused, yet most functional of all items (when properly harnessed)" (p. 59).

Advantages. Ease and objectivity in scoring are two advantages of controlled measures of reading. Controlled measures of reading also (1) permit the examiner to address specific aspects of the text that may not appear in spontaneous recall, and (2) reduce the production and memory requirements of the comprehension task. Additional advantages associated with the confidence weighting approach to controlled measures include the facts that (1) such an approach will force readers to process all the alternatives (which they otherwise might not do), and (2) readers could indicate their disagreement with all alternatives, rather than being forced to choose the least-wrong answer.

Limitations. First, controlled measures (probes and open-ended questions as well as multiple-choice questions) may encourage integration or further processing of information that otherwise may not have occurred (Johnston, 1983). Second, since controlled tasks tap recognition rather than production, inferences about the reader's ability to organize and structure the information on his or her own must be made cautiously, if at all. Thus, it is difficult to determine whether the reader got the item correct for the right reason, or merely by guessing, or through a process of elimination.

A third major limitation is the difficulty in generating appropriate probes and questions. Martuza (1977) describes the various approaches to choosing and writing questions which various reading specialists have advocated for use in assessing reading skills. For example, M. Johnson and Kress (1965) suggested that five questions be generated for each passage on an informal reading inventory. These questions were to be composed as follows: one vocabulary question, two factual (literal) questions, and two inferential questions. Others have advocated a linguistic transformation approach (R. Anderson, 1972; Bormuth, 1970), and still others have suggested that the questions tap only the most important concepts from the passage (Valmont, 1972). Peterson, Greenlaw, and Tierney (1978) found that existing guidelines (in this case, those suggested by M. Johnson and Kress, 1965) were insufficient to ensure reliability across examiners. In other words, a student's reading instructional levels on a passage varied according to which questions were asked as measures of his or her comprehension. This issue is further explored later in this chapter.

Lastly, and perhaps most importantly, the distractors used in controlled measures (excluding probes and open-ended questions) can greatly influence the picture that is obtained of an individual's reading ability. The influence of the typical hearing-impaired individual's limited English skills is of particular interest with regard to the appropriateness of distractors on controlled measures of reading ability.

King and Quigley (1984) discuss the issue of distractors in relation to a reading placement test designed for hearing-impaired children. In using distractors that tapped specific language patterns or reading strategies of hearing-impaired children, they note that "it may be that non-hearing-impaired children will perform at a higher level than their actual ability simply because the child may eliminate distractors which, because they were written for hearing-impaired children, may not seem plausible" (p. 12). Obviously, the reverse of this case also occurs; there are distractors on general reading assessment tasks that the hearing-impaired child eliminates as implausible; yet such distractors were written specifically because of their plausibility for hearing children. Specific examples of language patterns and test-taking strategies used by hearing-impaired individuals on reading assessment tasks are discussed later in this chapter (pages 224–238).

Construction of Assessment Tools

Much of the criticism of test construction in reading reflects general criticisms of classical testing theory and practices in general. The major criticisms focus on the dependence on statistical manipulations rather than the use of a theoretical base for the development of assessment tools. Wardrop et al. (1982) provide a detailed description of the many variables that influence test construction and the appropriate uses of assessment tools constructed according to different procedures.

First, classical testing theory supports the idea that there is an infinite number of test questions that can be generated about any given text passage. The test developer's job, then, is to choose a random sample of questions. However, it is now clear that a random selection technique is inappropriate for the reading domain since a person's ability to answer specific questions will be related to textual aspects, such as the relative importance of ideas within the text (B. Meyer, 1975). Similarly, reader-based variables, such as familiarity with the text genre (e.g., comparison-contrast), may influence the reader's ability to use that structure in comprehending the text. What is needed, then, is a rule-governed approach to item generation. Although attempts to generate such rules have been unsuccessful thus far, recent work by Pearson and D. Johnson (1978) appears to have promise for classifying the relationship between various question types and answers. This classification system is described in Chapter 4.

A second major criticism deals with the ways in which items and tests are revised during the test development process. Typically, those items that provide for the greatest differences among students are selected for inclusion in the final version of a test. Thus, an item that all poor students got wrong and all good students got right would be included on the test, whereas an item that all the students got right would be eliminated. Although such techniques generally are appropriate for tests designed to differentiate among students, a problem arises in that the same procedures are often used for assessment tools designed for diagnostic purposes. Also, Tuinman (1979) indicates that focusing on items with high discrimination indexes may result in questions that often are testing trivia and that tests designed this way may not provide an adequate coverage of all aspects of the reading domain.

A third major problem emerges in relation to methods currently being used to determine the reliability and validity of assessment instruments. Criterion-related validity and statistically derived reliability (described earlier in this chapter) are often the only tools used to establish validity and reliability for standardized tests. Major criticisms of such approaches are (1) correlations cannot be taken as evidence of a causal link; that is, tests that correlate with reading performance may not be those that reflect appropriate instructional strategies (Arter & Jenkins, 1978; Venezky, 1974); (2) sole reliance on statistical estimates of validity (criterion-related validity) is inadequate since it indicates only indirectly whether the assessment tool measures what it is supposed to measure (Wardrop et al., 1982); and (3) statistical estimates of reliability provide information only about how consistently the test differentiates among persons, rather than providing information about the repeatability of an individual's performance (Johnston, 1983; Wardrop et al., 1982).

Problems in establishing reliability and validity, however, are not limited to standardized tests. Diagnostic tests, whether criterion-referenced tests or informal assessment procedures, have similar problems. Validity for these tests is usually higher since the focus is on establishing mastery of specific aspects of reading rather than on differentiating among individuals, but problems arise in establishing acceptable levels of reliability. For example, a large body of research indicates that, even with training, there is frequent disagreement among examiners as to the reading level to assign to a student who has taken an informal reading inventory (IRI) (see Pikulski & Shanahan, 1982, for a review of the studies). Also, reliable judgments must be based on sufficient numbers of events. Spache (1976) indicates that 75 to 100 oral reading miscues are needed for a reliable diagnosis, yet most passages on IRIs are not of sufficient length to permit such numbers of miscues. The relatively low reliability of such informal testing is a major concern. Obviously, assessment tools must be *both* valid and reliable in order to be useful tools for determining an individual's abilities.

Administration of Assessment Tools

Administration procedures obviously affect the accuracy of assessment results. A major factor that contributes to that accuracy is the way in which the instructions are communicated (by the evaluator) and understood (by the student). The wording in the instructions, the variations in the tasks used, the child's familiarity with the task, the use of time limits and practice items, and the demonstration or teaching of the task are just a few of the possible factors that can change the results of assessment procedures. The influence of variations in the wording of instructions and in the task (i.e., creation versus selection in finding the main idea) can be seen in the following example: Using the instructions, "Make up just one sentence in your own words that says what all the sentences tell you," Otto, Barrett, and Koenke (1969) found that only 29% of their (hearing) second graders could perform the task. Yet, when Danner (1976) modified those instructions to "Find the one thing that the sentences in the paragraph tell you about," all of his second graders could perform the task at least 66% of the time.

For hearing-impaired individuals, accurate communication and reception of the instructions is complicated by the limited language and experiential base of the typical hearing-impaired individual. As noted in Chapter 1, difficulties in removing the verbal factor from assessment tasks are at least partially responsible for reported differences in the cognitive abilities of hearing-impaired and hearing children. In a review of research on test modifications, Bragman (1982a) identified seven major ways in which researchers have modified test administration for hearing-impaired individuals: "testing the limits, reinforcing responses, omitting verbal items, eliminating time limits, and demonstrating task strategies" (Bragman, 1982a, p. 339; see the citation list in the original work).

Practice items and the demonstration of task strategies basically have proven to be useful in helping hearing-impaired students to comprehend the task (e.g., Karchmer & Belmont, 1976; Rittenhouse & Spiro, 1979). Experience with a task also appears to have an effect on whether modifications in the instructions have a positive effect on the students' scores. Bragman (1982a) found differences among three types of instructions on an unfamiliar task, but no differences on a familiar task. When this is coupled with knowledge that the testwiseness abilities of hearing-impaired individuals are lower than those of hearing students and that they typically remain static despite increases in grade and reading level (McKee & Hausknecht, 1980; Stenning, 1979), the importance of providing experiences with assessment tasks (both for formal tests and for informal techniques such as retellings) and of teaching test-taking strategies is highlighted.

Some modifications in the administration procedure, however, appear not to be necessary. For example, the elimination of time limits does not seem to make a difference in the students' scores (Conrad, 1979; Garrison & Coggiola, 1980). In fact, Wood, Griffiths, and Webster (1981) found that hearing-impaired children attempted to answer more items than did hearing children in a comparable amount of time. As stated earlier in this chapter, the use of separate answer sheets can influence performance on standardized assessment tools. By the age of eight to ten years, however, it appears that hearing-impaired students have had sufficient experience with separate answer sheets so that there are no differences between their scores when answers are put on a separate sheet and when they are placed on the test form (Rogers, 1983).

Bragman (1982b) notes that that there are few attempts to standardize the modifications being suggested for providing instructions on assessment tasks to hearing-impaired students. And, when such attempts have been made (e.g., with the WISC-R), there are inconsistencies among the suggested approaches (Murphy, 1957; Neuhaus, 1967; Reed, 1973; Sattler, 1974). Bragman concludes that limited information is available regarding the most appropriate method(s) of conveying test instructions to hearing-impaired individuals.

The issue of modifying the linguistic characteristics (vocabulary, syntax, discourse structure, and so forth) in test instructions with hearing-impaired children has not been explored broadly. (However, see the discussion of linguistic modifications for test items later in this chapter and in Chapter 5 for test passages and other texts.) Indeed, the extent to which teachers modify the standard instructions and include additional examples during administration of formal tests is unknown. There is at least one school in which "standard" modified instructions are used for the *Metropolitan Achievement Test (MAT)* (i.e., a modified set of instructions is used in all classes). The administration guide for the 1982 *SAT-HI* also indicates that clarification of the instructions and additional examples are permissible (Center for Assessment and Demographic Studies, 1983).

There appear to be three major views on this practice. (1) Changes in the administration procedures invalidate the test for the purpose it was developed (i.e., the norms cannot be used) (Anastasi, 1976; Gerweck & Ysseldyke, 1975). Therefore, if changes are made, questions about the validity of the results must be raised (Gerweck & Ysseldyke, 1975). Given that federal law stipulates that tests used with special students must "have been validated for the specific purpose for which they are used" (*Federal Register*, 1977, p. 42496), the implications of this view are obvious. (2) Others believe that changes in the administration procedures invalidate only the normative uses of the data and focus on diagnostic uses (e.g., the school using modified instructions on the MAT focuses on criterion-referenced interpretations of the battery). (3) The third view is perhaps best illustrated in the following quotation from the administration guide for the 1982 *SAT-HI*:

> we realize that, to some extent, flexibility may compromise standardization. The use of norms presupposes that the testing situation is similar for the populations in which the test was standardized and in which the test will be used. Ironically, flexibility can both *ensure standardization* [italics added], if it ensures that the test is adequately understood, and can *undermine standardization* [italics added] if it unfairly assists students to detect correct answers.
> (Center for Assessment and Demographic Studies, 1983, p. 7)

Thus, although changes in the administration procedures are encouraged, these individuals believe that these changes need not invalidate the test nor the use of the norms.

Given the variety of communication contexts used in programs for hearing-impaired students and the variations in the academic and language abilities throughout the population, the logic of a flexible approach to test instructions seems persuasive. Indeed, in the manual for an informal placement test, King and Quigley (1984) recommend that teachers clarify, modify, and supplement the instructions as needed. However, the argument for flexibility is applicable only in so far as it ensures comprehension of the task. Extreme care must be taken to avoid teaching the test or (unintentionally) providing students with answers. Also, logic alone should not be taken as sufficient evidence of the effectiveness of encouraging flexibility in administration procedures. An experimental comparison of the two approaches (standard instructions and flexibility) would be helpful. This would seem especially important on formal tests and any assessment tools for which use of normative data is intended.

For any instructions (flexible *or* standard) to be effective, the personnel involved in the administration process must be trained in the use of specific assessment tools and well aware of the general functions and limitations of assessment. Although some teachers probably do possess these characteristics, a recent survey indicated that the average teacher in programs for hearing-impaired children has minimal training in reading (Bockmiller

& Coley, 1981; Coley & Bockmiller, 1980). Also, in a self-report study of the problems psychologists encountered in administering achievement and other tests to hearing-impaired individuals, a major problem noted was lack of training (Levine, 1974). The lack of training is a major concern, especially in light of PL 94-142, which clearly states that any assessment tools used in evaluating deaf and other special children must be administered by personnel *trained* to administer these tools.

Scoring of Assessment Tools

Appropriate scoring and interpretation of scores is an important issue in the use of reading assessment tools. Basic definitions of two types of scores are provided here and the problems associated with each type of score are described. A problem that relates to both types of scores—the weighting of items on an assessment tool—is also discussed.

Normative Data

Although norms are sometimes provided for informal assessment tools, normative data are most often associated with standardized assessment tests. They provide an indication of how a student's performance compares with the performance of a representative group of students. Perhaps the most common forms of normative scores are grade equivalents and percentiles. (A detailed discussion of types of normative reading scores can be found in Baumann & Stevenson, 1982.)

A *grade equivalent* of 5.2 means that the student performs like a typical fifth grade student in the second month of instruction (i.e., November; September is month 5.0). A grade equivalent of 5.2 on a third grade test, however, does not mean that the student can read fifth grade materials, but rather that the student scored as a typical fifth grader would have had the fifth grader taken the third grade test. In other words, there is no connection between measures used to grade materials and grade equivalent scores as measures of students' abilities on tests.

A *percentile* of 45 on a second grade reading test means that the student performed better than or equal to 45 percent of the second graders who took the test as part of the standardization process. It is important to recognize that percentiles show only the relative position of a student in comparison to a group of similar students (Singer & Dreher, 1983). Imagine viewing a student's percentile scores on two standardized tests, one administered while the student was in the second grade and one administered while he or she was in third grade, and that the student was at the 45th percentile on both tests. A lay person looking at such information might misperceive it as showing no improvement. However, in actuality, it is not possible to determine whether there was any improvement or not in the student's actual skills. All that can be determined from the percentile score is that the student has not made either more or less improvement than other students in his or her comparison group; i.e., the student has stayed at the same relative position within the group.

Recently, there has been increasing opposition to these types of scores (e.g., the International Reading Association has taken a stance against the use of grade equivalents in reading [IRA Resolution, April, 1981]). Some of the reasons for this opposition are the following:

1. Grade equivalents are less accurate for above or below average students (Karlin, 1973; W. MacGinitie, Kamons, Kowalski, R. MacGinitie, & McKay, 1978);

2. Increases in grade equivalents are not equal units (e.g., the difference between 2.2 and 3.2 is not the same as between 5.2 and 6.2);

3. Grade equivalents cannot be compared if based on different tests or different levels within a single test battery (i.e., a student who received a score of 5.6 on the second grade test does not have the same skills as one who received the same score on the fifth grade test); and

4. Small differences in the number of correct responses can result in large differences in grade equivalents (e.g., Harris & Sipay, 1980, indicate that an increase in four correct responses on one standardized test could move child from a grade equivalent of 2.9 to 3.6).

The last problem is especially apparent on any test on which there is little improvement above a given point—that is, where scores plateau—which is a frequent occurrence with hearing-impaired children. For example, in the normative table for these children on the 1972 edition of the *SAT-HI Primary Level 1 Test* (Office of Demographic Studies, no date), the difference between 29 and 30 correct items on the spelling subtest translates to a differences in grade equivalent from 4.2 to 6.3. Although this is an extreme example, it is a forceful demonstration of the problems inherent in normative scores when are there is a plateau effect. And, the problem is not unique to the *SAT-HI*—this same problem could be demonstrated with any test with any population for which a plateau effect occurs.

In addition, most reading achievement tests have a lower boundary such that, even if a student gets a minimal number of answers correct, he or she will get a higher grade equivalent than if he or she had gotten a higher percentage of the items correct on a lower level test (Harris & Sipay, 1980; Silverman, 1979). Also, there is opposition to percentiles because they do not allow for measurement of educational gain (Royer & J. Cunningham, 1978; Singer & Dreher, 1983).

The problems with specific types of norms, however, should not detract from the importance of comparative data. It is useful to be able to compare a student's performance against some type of standard (although this leaves open the question of who should be included in the reference group). Further, school personnel, parents, and students alike appear to want such information (Singer & Dreher, 1983). What is needed, then, are (1) users who are well informed of the meaning and limitations of normative data;

and (2) continued attempts to find normative measures that (a) do not focus attention on differences that are actually quite small, and (b) do allow for measures of educational gain. *Stanines* and standard scores are perhaps the most promising in terms of meeting these requirements. Stanines divide the scores of the normative group into nine equal levels. Differences of at least two stanines (e.g., a stanine of 5 and one of 7) are needed for the difference between two scores to be considered a real difference (Harris & Sipay, 1980). However, like grade equivalents, stanines cannot be compared across different levels of an achievement test battery. *Standard scores*, on the other hand, allow for comparisons across levels of a single battery (although still not across different batteries). Also, standard scores represent approximately equal units on a continuous scale. Since a difference of 10 scaled score points means the same thing across all levels of the battery, scaled (standard) scores can be used to measure educational gain from one year to the next. These scores, however, cannot be used to compare a student's performance in different content areas.

Diagnostic Data

Diagnostic data can take many forms, but the information is basically designed to provide an indication of a student's ability to perform specific tasks with reference to a level of mastery (i.e., criterion) in the task or skill, rather than in comparison to his or her peers. The data might consist of *percentages or numbers of correct responses on a test or subsets of items, analyses of a student's errors,* or *relative reading levels* (i.e., independent, instructional, and frustration reading levels).

As with all assessment data, diagnostic scores should be based on a sufficient number of items to allow for reliable decisions. Although the definition of "sufficient" will likely vary depending on the importance of the instructional decision that is being made and on the amount of other assessment data that will contribute to the decision, scores based on small numbers of items should be viewed cautiously. Furthermore, comparisons of percentage scores for different subtests are inappropriate if based on small numbers of items. This last point can perhaps best be illustrated by example. If we look only at percentage scores, we might assume that 66% and 80% were different enough to consider the 80% a higher score. However, if we are aware that the percentages are based on three and five items (i.e., 2/3 and 4/5) it becomes less clear that the student scored higher on the second subtest. Indeed, the number of items on each subtest is too small to make any reliable decisions.

Many tests that produce diagnostic data commonly designate some level, usually a percentage of items correct, as indicative of mastery of the given skill. Unfortunately, mastery levels are often set arbitrarily, and thus it is important for examiners to evaluate carefully the criteria used for various levels of mastery and to demand some form of rationale (preferably research-based) for the criteria chosen. Often, however, no rationale is provided for setting a mastery criterion at a certain level. For example, although one test developer may stipulate 80% accuracy as indicative of mastery, another may select 90% accuracy. The cut-off level could just as easily have been set at 81% or 89% or some other arbitrary value.

Difficulties with diagnostic data and mastery levels also emerge when a mastery level is given for comprehension tasks. Pearson and D. Johnson (1978) indicate that, although it may be defensible to have absolute states of mastery for basic decoding skills, absolute mastery is not possible in the comprehension domain. As an example, a teacher cannot stop teaching "finding the main idea" because a student has gotten eight of ten items correct on a test. As experienced teachers are well aware, a student's lack of mastery can always be demonstrated by increasing the conceptual difficulty of the passage or by eliminating a direct statement of the main idea. Furthermore, the use of a mastery criterion may not give adequate information about the student's strengths and weaknesses. Terwilliger (1972) points out that on a ten item test with an 80% mastery level there are 56 different combinations of correct items that will yield "mastery." Therefore, two students with "equal" mastery may actually have very different skills.

Thus, teachers attempting to use assessment results for student diagnosis must ask what mastery on a given test really indicates and what implications this will have for instructional practices. They will also want to carefully evaluate the rationale provided by the test developers as to the appropriateness of the scores chosen as the division lines between levels of mastery.

Weighting of Items

The determination of how to weight various types of items on assessment tools is an issue that has implications for both normative and diagnostic uses of these tools. An example is free recall protocols following oral or silent reading. Assigning weights to different types of items or bits of information from a story has intuitive appeal. It seems logical to give a child more credit for recalling the main idea of a story than for recalling a minor character's name. But, such weighting is inappropriate unless a systematic approach for determining the relative number of points to assign to any given type of item. Indeed, if an assessment tool assigns weights to different types of items, a rationale for that weighting system should be provided in the testing guide, and teachers would do well to determine whether there is sufficient justification for the weighting.

Use of Assessment Results

The major problems in the use of test results in reading assessment revolve around the ways in which results are reported and attempts to use results for purposes for which the tests were not designed. For example, Singer and Dreher (1983) criticized the form in which the results of standardized tests are reported. They found that a dramatic shift in teachers' attitudes toward testing occurred when (1) the same level of an achievement test was administered in two consecutive years to measure educational gain, and (2) content-bound information was added to the test reports (i.e., "the hardest passage the student could read was . . .").

A second major problem in the use of test results is due to the misperception that the areas assessed on a standardized test, which usually are selected because of their ability to predict future behavior, should be the areas used to determine instructional goals. For example, basic psychological and perceptual motor skills have been shown to correlate highly with later reading success, and some reading tests focus on the assessment of these basic processes (e.g., *Illinois Test of Psycholinguistic Abilities*; S. Kirk, McCarthy, & W. Kirk, 1968). However, there is little evidence that deficits in these underlying psychological processes *cause* reading difficulties. Most of the studies designed to show the effects of training in these basic processes have not shown a positive effect on reading abilities (Arter & Jenkins, 1978; Hammill & Larsen, 1978).

The third major problem also deals with standardized reading tests. The following quotation from Schwartz (1977) should suffice to describe this situation:

> The most blatant misuse of test results is the not infrequent practice of equating a grade level score with a graded reading level. . . the teacher erroneously assuming a connection between the grade level equivalency on the test and the level of difficulty of the reading text. No such connection exists! . . . [A] grade equivalent for a given score is simply the average score achieved by all children at that grade level in the standardized sample, and has nothing whatsoever to do with graded texts. As a matter of fact, the level of difficulty represented in a 3^2 reader is usually higher than the material which receives a third grade designation on a reading test. The poor youngster who is given a 3^2 reader on the basis of achieving such a score is surely in trouble.
>
> (Schwartz, 1977, p. 367)

This is not to say that the desire to match student ability as measured by standardized reading tests with some measure of text difficulty is inappropriate. As Pearson and D. Johnson (1978) note, however, at present these two measurements are not on the same scale and such comparisons cannot be made with any degree of accuracy or confidence.

Furthermore, the misuse of test data in matching students with levels of text difficulty is not limited to standardized reading tests. Pikulski and Shanahan (1982) note that many teachers use the grade level of a passage from an informal reading inventory to place students in materials graded by readability formulas. Yet the IRI was designed only to determine whether the student can handle the specific text from which the test passage was drawn. Since difficulty level can vary greatly even within a single text, even this use has been questioned. For example, Bradley and Ames (1976) found that 24 samples from a text were needed to provide a representative sample of a text's difficulty. Thus, the assumption that the difficulty levels of materials that are similarly graded are the same is indeed precarious (see the discussion in Chapter 5 on text difficulty).

Overreliance on test results is the final problem considered here with regard to the use of reading assessment tools. Evidence of such overreliance was cited earlier in this chapter. Here readers are simply reminded that all assessment procedures do no more than sample an individual's true abilities, and none can give a complete picture. Furthermore, factors within the reader, the text, and the task all interact in influencing the accuracy of assessment. Thus, it is useful to keep in mind that all testing is subject to error, and that this error factor must be considered in the interpretation of test results.

PERFORMANCE OF HEARING-IMPAIRED INDIVIDUALS ON ASSESSMENT TASKS

The accuracy of reading assessment can be influenced by differences in the tasks that are used to tap comprehension. In this section, research is reviewed that has been conducted to measure the influences of various aspects of reading assessment tasks. Specific test-taking strategies that many hearing-impaired individuals use are identified, and ways in which knowledge of task effects and reader strategies can be used in constructing assessment tools and in interpreting assessment data are discussed.

At the outset, readers should be aware that the generalizability of the reported research on task effects and test-taking strategies is limited by two factors: (1) many of the studies were conducted with hearing-impaired individuals with reading levels at or above the fourth grade level and, as such, may not necessarily reflect what would occur with younger or less able readers; and (2) some of the assessment tools used in the studies contained only a few items and thus the results of these studies must be viewed as tentative until further research can be done.

Task Effects

The aspects of the assessment task that are addressed include (1) the conditions under which the comprehension measure is collected; (2) the type of task; (3) the format of the task; (4) the type of information assessed; (5) the influences of reader-based variables; and (6) the influences of text-based variables.

Assessment Conditions

The influence of a look-back (reinspection) versus a no look-back condition on the performance of hearing individuals has been investigated by various researchers (e.g., Alessi, Anderson, & Goetz, 1979; Kender & Rubenstein, 1977). Similar studies of the peformance of hearing-impaired individuals have been conducted by Davey, LaSasso, and Macready (1983) and LaSasso and Davey (1983a). As might be expected, both groups of students perform at higher levels when allowed to reinspect the text while completing comprehension measures. The hearing-impaired students, however, appear to be less efficient than hearing children in using the opportunity to look back at the text (Davey et al., 1983).

What this means for assessment and instruction is not clear. Kender and Rubenstein (1977) argue that reinspection should be allowed to limit the memory factors inherent in recall tasks, whereas other researchers argue that the memory component of comprehension should be included in assessment measures (Johnston, 1983; Royer & J. Cunningham, 1978). The implications for hearing-impaired individuals are even less clear in that reinspection appears to encourage hearing-impaired children to use a visual matching strategy (LaSasso & Davey, 1983a; LaSasso, 1984, 1985; see the discussion later in this chapter). At present, there is no definitive answer as to whether reinspection should be allowed or not. As with other either-or issues, however, it likely is not an all-or-none proposition. In any case, recognition of the effects of reinspection should aid teachers in interpreting assessment data gathered under either condition. There also appears to be a need for teaching hearing-impaired children effective strategies for obtaining information from reinspection of a text.

Although the optimum conditions for the assessment of oral reading have not been investigated for hearing-impaired children, studies with hearing children have consistently shown differences in the performance levels of children based on the way in which the task is presented (e.g., Brecht, 1977; Gonzales & Elijah, 1975). The major focuses of these studies have been (1) whether the child should be expected to perform an oral reading on first sight or only after having read the passage silently, and (2) whether the same criteria should be used for establishing instructional reading levels under the two conditions. The most generally accepted answer to these questions has been that, since the original criteria were established based on oral rereading after silent reading (Betts, 1946) and since there are differences in performance between the two conditions, elimination of the silent reading component negates the use of Betts's criteria for independent, instructional, and frustration reading levels (Brecht, 1977). This issue needs much further study, especially in light of the fact that the silent reading component is not mentioned in the guides for many assessment tools that use oral reading even though Betts's criteria are used. Thus far, no one has adequately determined what changes in the criteria should be made if oral reading is done at sight.

Type of Task

Examination of the differences between performance on recognition and recall tasks has long been the focus of research in education and psychology. The basic result of this research has been that performance is usually higher under a recognition task (i.e., select the correct answer) than under a recall task (i.e., generate the correct answer). However, it has also been found that college-level deaf students do not appear to benefit as much as their hearing peers from being able to select, rather than generate, the correct answer (Osguthorpe, Long, & Ellsworth, 1977) and that, in some cases, there are no differences between the recognition and recall scores of college-level deaf students (McKee & Bondi-Wolcott, 1982). Thus, as in the look-back or no look-back condition, there appears to be a need for teaching specific test-taking strategies to deaf students so that they can better take advantage of information provided by the context of a test or text.

Davey et al. (1983) investigated the interrelationship between a task variable (recall or recognition) and a test condition variable (look-back or no look-back). They found that, for the hearing students, superior performance on recognition tasks occurred only in the no look-back condition. Thus, if the hearing students were allowed to reinspect the text, a free-response task resulted in better scores than a multiple-choice recognition task. Deaf students, on the other hand, had higher scores for the recognition task under both look-back and no look-back conditions.

Task Formats

Studies that have addressed the format of the task have focused largely on controlled response tasks (multiple choice, true-false, matching, and so forth). Researchers who have investigated this issue with hearing-impaired individuals have done so within varying contexts (e.g., a vocabulary test, a comprehension test) and with varying purposes (e.g., assessment of reading abilities or of subject matter). The results appear to be format-specific.

On a measure of vocabulary, Walter (1978b) found that there were no differences between the scores of hearing-impaired students related to whether the task was multiple-choice or matching. Similarly, McKee and Lang (1982) found no differences in the scores of college-level deaf students on a physics test related to whether the task was multiple-choice or true-false. They did note, however, that the students preferred the multiple-choice format and that there was a higher correlation between the multiple-choice test and the laboratory grades assigned (meaning that these two measures ranked the students in the same order).

On the other hand, Garrison, Covill-Servo, and McKee (1981) found differences in the results for hearing-impaired students on various forms of a psychological test that were parallel in content but different in item format (semantic differential, Likert-type scales, and so forth). LaSasso (1979) found that the format of forced-choice tests (wh-questions or fill-in-the-blank statements) on a reading comprehension task influenced the scores of hearing-impaired students. The results of this study (wh-questions received higher scores), however, must be viewed as tentative since the subjects' reading levels (grades 4.0 to 7.6 on the SAT-HI) are above average for the age population (14 to 18) and the difference between the scores on the two tests likely was not educationally significant (2.7 of 5 items for wh-questions and 1.8 for incomplete statements).

Other investigations of the multiple-choice format have focused on the form of the answers, the position of the correct answer, the number of options, and the order of items on the test. Based on data from a 1971 administration of the 1964 version of the *Stanford Achievement Test*, Trybus and Buchanan (1973) found that, if the correct answer was a negative response (i.e., none of the above, not given), hearing-impaired children were much less likely than hearing children to get the item correct.

Trybus and Buchanan (1973) also found that the position of the correct answer was related to whether hearing-impaired students got the item correct. Although the exact position that resulted in more correct answers varied from subtest to subtest, a general trend emerged in which more correct answers were made when the correct response was either the first or the last choice. McKee and Bondi-Wolcott (1982), in studying a group of college-level deaf students, found no position-related effects on a five option multiple-choice test while finding a strong position effect on an eight option test. The conflicting results on position effects for hearing-impaired individuals parallel the research on position effects for hearing individuals. For example, Cronbach (1950) found that multiple-choice tests were relatively free from position response sets whereas McNamara and Weizman (1945) and P. Jones and Kaufman (1975) found position-related effects.

The findings of the McKee and Bondi-Wolcott study are also important from another perspective: the researchers found one response-set in the test developer's placement of the correct answers (i.e., the correct answers were usually in the latter positions) and a different response-set in the test-takers' choice (i.e., in the first few positions). While finding a response-set on the part of the test developer is not unique in any way, it does highlight the importance of (1) being aware of possible response-set biases when constructing multiple-choice tests, and (2) developing testwiseness in students.

A final format variable that has been studied is the order of items. Deaf children, like their hearing peers, correctly answer more of the items at the beginning of a test than items at the end (DiFrancesca & Carey, 1972).

Type of Information

It seems logical that different proportions of literal and inferential questions on an assessment tool will produce different beliefs about a student's comprehension. For example, one explanation given for the failure of most deaf children to rise above a fourth grade reading level on standardized achievement tests is that the fourth grade test has a much higher percentage of inferential questions than does the third grade test (K. Wilson, Karchmer, & Jensema, 1978; see the discussion in Chapter 3).

Although there is little evidence to support the idea that a specific proportion of questions on assessment tools should be devoted to literal, inferential, or other types of information (see the discussion of question generation earlier in this chapter), knowledge of how hearing-impaired children perform on questions that elicit specific types of information is useful. Davey and LaSasso (1985, in press) have studied the effects on comprehension of whether test questions tapped textually-explicit or textually-implicit information. Textually-explicit questions tap information directly stated in the text, whereas textually-implicit questions tap the student's ability to integrate information from different parts of the text (e.g., linking a character's desires with later behavior). Scriptually-implicit questions, which require a student to integrate information from the text with his or her background experience, were not included in the study. Basically, these researchers found the expected better performance on textually-explicit items, although the results were complicated by interactions between relevant task and reader variables.

Reader-Based Influences on Test Item Responses

The reader-based variable that Davey and LaSasso (1985, in press) explored was cognitive style. They defined cognitive style in terms of the field independence of their subjects. Field independent individuals use internal referents and analytical strategies whereas field dependent individuals rely on external referents and react more globally to the total field. Earlier work had established that field dependence was related to the reading comprehension of hearing students (e.g., Annis, 1979; Gibson, 1984; Spiro & Tirre, 1980) and that deaf individuals were relatively more field dependent than hearing individuals (e.g., Blanton & Nunnally, 1964; Parasnis, 1983; Parasnis & Long, 1979). When the deaf subjects were placed into field independent (FI) and field dependent (FD) groups, no difference was found in overall reading comprehension scores. Differences did emerge on the scores for specific conditions (the FI scored higher on "no look-back" items) and for the type of information being assessed (FI scored higher on implicit information). Davey and LaSasso (1985) suggest that accurate interpretation of assessment data must include consideration of the effects of reader-based variables such as cognitive style.

Other reader-based variables that can influence performance on reading assessment are familiarity with the test format and content, knowledge of and interest in the content, motivation, and purpose for reading. The effects of these variables on reading in assessment and instructional settings are described in Chapter 5.

Performance on assessment tools is also influenced by reader-based variables, such as the socioeconomic status, cultural values, experiential background, and the dialect or language of the child (see Chapter 3 for a discussion of reader-based variables and achievement levels in deaf children). Difficulties in accurate assessment arise when there are differences in these factors between a minority population and the general population for whom the assessment tool was developed (i.e., different cultural values or different experiential backgrounds). For example, the Center for Assessment and

Demographic Studies (1983) identifies three subtests on the *SAT-HI* that may not be appropriate for all hearing-impaired children owing to their reliance on auditory experiences.

Johnston (1983) discusses three approaches that might be used to address the problems of differences in cultural background in relation to reading assessment. These are as follows:

1. carefully select texts and questions so as to eliminate those which might contain "biases";
2. assess in the language which is appropriate to the reader's subculture . . .;
3. assess in various contents and language structures but include assessment which will discriminate between background-induced problems and others.

(Johnston, 1983, p. 33)

Persons involved in test development typically have taken the first option and attempted to limit the influence of cultural background and background information by using short and often bland passages. Others have indicated that assessment procedures (and instructional materials) should be presented in the reader's native language only and be related to the reader's culture. Still others have argued for assessment in the standard language since it would be "flagrantly dishonest not to make minority children who are poor achievers aware that they have not mastered skills needed to participate and compete successfully in our society" (Harris & Sipay, 1980, p. 168). Although methods for clearly identifying *why* children are not successful on assessment tasks are in their infancy, the third option presented by Johnston certainly appears to be the preferred approach.

Text-Based Influences on Test Item Responses

Text-based variables of assessment tools include linguistic aspects of the test items and the linguistic nature of the test passages. The variables of interest range from individual words to the syntactic structures in the passage to the macro-level discourse structure of the passage.

Passage Difficulty on Assessment Tasks

The research on differences in passage difficulty, for both assessment and instructional purposes, is reviewed in Chapter 5. Only general findings that have implications for passage selection on oral reading tasks are presented here. Research has indicated that reading behaviors differed when children were reading easy versus difficult materials (e.g., Ewoldt, 1981a; Kibby, 1979; Leslie & Osol, 1978; Williamson & Young, 1974). Specifically, when dealing with materials at their frustration levels, individuals adhere more closely to the graphic characteristics of the materials. Also, the use of context may drop off by as much as 15% to 30% when an individual is dealing with frustration level materials (Pearson, 1978). Therefore, since the use of difficult materials taps different skills than do on-level or easy materials, the common practice in informal reading assessment of using materials that are one grade level above that which is usually assigned in class (Y. Goodman & Burke, 1976) appears questionable.

Linguistic Complexity of Assessment Items

Controlled measures of reading use an item stem (probe, question) to elicit responses. Since deaf children typically have poor English skills, the linguistic complexity of these item stems may lead them to miss an item when they might have gotten it right had the question or probe been stated in a different form. The linguistic complexity of the distractors might also influence a student's ability to choose the correct answer.

Trybus and Buchanan (1973) found that item difficulty on the SAT for a group of hearing-impaired children increased as the number of words in the item stem increased. Items with more difficult vocabulary or syntax, however, did not appear to be harder than those with easier vocabulary and syntax. They also found that hearing-impaired children appeared to have more difficulty with questions that accompanied more lengthy passages.

Rudner (1978) differentiated between item appropriateness and item bias in his analysis of the same data used by Trybus and Buchanan (1973). Inappropriate items were considered to be those that correlated poorly with the trait being measured. Item bias was defined as differential item difficulty between the performances of two different cultural groups (hearing and deaf). Rudner conducted a factor analysis of the data to determine which items had low correlations with the traits being measured on the test and then used a logical analysis of the item content to determine what may have caused these items to be different. He found that the following linguistic structures appear to be misleading for hearing-impaired students:

1. Conditionals (if, when);
2. Comparatives (greater than, the most);
3. Negatives (not, without, answer not given);
4. Inferentials (should, could, because, since);
5. Low information pronouns (it, something);
6. Lengthy passages.

(Rudner, 1978, p. 33)

In relation to these, it is worthwhile to note Rudner's admonition concerning the interpretation of his results: "these results are not to be interpreted as definitive. . . . Items containing one or more of these linguistic structures will not necessarily be inappropriate for use with the hearing-impaired" (Rudner, 1978, p. 39).

The results of the comparison of item difficulties revealed 26 items that were biased against hearing-impaired students. Content analysis of these items resulted in the items all fitting into one of the six categories based on the factor analysis. However, Rudner also found 22 items that were biased in favor of the hearing-impaired students (i.e., they did better on these items than did the hearing students). Although Rudner does not discuss these items, an examination of the item data presented by Di Francesca and Carey (1972) revealed that the incorrect choices for some items may not have been functioning to distract hearing-impaired children from the correct answer. Hearing-impaired children, for example, might not be as likely as hearing children to choose a distractor that is based on phonetic similarity. The item analysis of Di Francesca and Carey (1972) revealed that 86% of the hearing-impaired children correctly selected *know* for the following sentence: Do you _____ when Dad is coming home? (choices were *no* and *know*). Further discussion of this issue is provided in the section on test-taking strategies later in this chapter.

Rudner's study demonstrates a method that others can use to determine if specific items are biased. For example, logical analysis led Ewoldt (1982a, p. 88) to consider the following item to be culturally biased against hearing-impaired readers:

A famous composer who became deaf was not able to hear what he had composed. But he continued to compose in spite of his _____b_____.
[a.] speech   [c.] vision
[b.] handicap   [d.] age

She states that "a hearing-impaired reader with a positive self-concept is not as likely as a hearing reader to choose *handicap* as the appropriate response" (p. 88). Application of the methodology discussed by Rudner (1978) could determine if in fact this item were culturally biased. Linn, Levine, Hastings, and Wardrop (1980) offer a further explanation of methodology for determining item bias.

Bornstein (1971) argues that "the language used in multiple-choice achievement test items should be no more complex than is necessary to test the examinee's knowledge of the subject matter" (p. 44). He bases this argument on research in which he demonstrated that college-level deaf students performed at a higher level on a social studies test on which the item stems had simplified vocabulary and syntax than on a test with parallel content and unmodified vocabulary and syntax (Bornstein, 1971; Bornstein & Kannapell, 1971). The differences between the scores for the two versions of the test, although significant, were small. Therefore, although definitive statements cannot be made based on the results, the study is important in that it attempts to compare experimentally the effects of linguistic features of the items. Such studies offer more concrete evidence than logical analyses (Ewoldt, 1982a; Rudner, 1978). More research of this kind is needed.

Fischler (1983) examined the issue of contextual constraint on the performance of college-level deaf students on a cloze task. Although this study was not intended to determine the effects of linguistic complexity on performance, it is included here since it was the only study found that examined variables other than vocabulary and syntax. Fischler compared the deaf students' responses on items such as the following:

He mailed the letter with a _____.   (high constraint)
The police had never seen a man so _____.   (low constraint)

Surprisingly, the number of correct responses did not decrease as the contextual constraints decreased. This may have occurred because of a ceiling effect. Since the average percentage of items correct was 90%, the test may have been too easy for the subjects to demonstrate the expected effect of contextual constraint. The study, however, is useful in that it demonstrates that variables other than vocabulary and syntax must be examined in attempts to determine the influences of text-based variables on reading performance scores.

It has been demonstrated that there are differences among various reading comprehension tests in terms of discourse-level variables. Marr (1983) compared various discourse and readability features of three diagnostic reading tests. On the second grade versions of these tests, she found readability estimates ranging from 2.2 to 3.9; the number of idea units ranging from 20 to 50, and the number of text-based inferences ranging from 5 to 15. Statement of the main idea also varied. On one test, the main idea was included in the title; on the second, it was stated in the first sentence; on the third test, it was not stated at all. Research is needed to investigate the influence of these variables on performance scores.

Test-Taking Strategies of Hearing-Impaired Individuals

Hearing-impaired individuals appear to exhibit consistent test-taking strategies on reading comprehension tasks. Strategies that have been identified include (a) perseverence in question answering beyond ability level, (b) consistency in the answer selected by deaf children, (c) a word/idea association strategy, (d) a visual matching strategy, and (e) elimination of implausible distractors. Evidence of these strategies comes mainly from assessment tasks that elicit responses to probes and questions. Although these elicitation tasks have included both free responses (generating the answer) and forced-choice responses (selecting the answer), the test-taking strategies cannot, at present, be generalized to tasks that require the student to organize the presentation of information as well as to recall it. The lack of such generalizations, however, does not limit the significance of the results. The most common interaction in the classroom is teacher-controlled elicitation of students' responses (T. Kluwin, 1983), and so it is likely that the identified test-taking strategies have implications in the instructional setting as well as on assessment tasks. Further research is, of course, needed before that conclusion can be reached (Wolk & Schildroth, 1984).

In this section, little information on free recall tasks is presented. It should not be inferred from the concentration on controlled measures that deaf children do not exhibit consistent strategies on free measures or that such assessment tasks are less important. The lack of information simply reflects the fact that little experimental research has been done with free recall tasks.

Research using recall protocols has been limited to only a few doctoral dissertations (Ewoldt, 1977; Livingston, 1981) with only a few subjects in each case. Although these studies are suggestive of specific retelling techniques (e.g., the syncretistic strategy discussed earlier in this chapter), there have been no extensive studies of how deaf children organize retellings or of what information they include in such retellings. Work paralleling that of Stein and Glenn (1978; see the discussion in Chapter 3) is needed.

Question Answering Strategies

Webster, Wood, and Griffiths (1981) and Wood et al. (1981) conducted two studies of the test answering strategies of British hearing-impaired children. In the first study, they found that deaf children attempted to answer more of the questions (92%) on a limited cloze test than did hearing children (85%). The test required students to read a "cue sentence" and then to select one word from the sentence to fill a gap in an unrelated sentence. An example follows.

Pack the eggs in the box.   Hens lay _____.

(Webster et al., 1981, p. 138).

The researchers concluded that deaf children were likely to attempt to answer all questions on the test, while the (younger) hearing children tended to stop trying to answer the questions when they reached their reading ceiling. Wolk and Schildroth (1984) also found that deaf children were likely to attempt more items on the *SAT-HI* than hearing children. Webster et al. suggest the following interpretations of this phenomenon:

> Deaf children's perseverance long after their comprehension ceilings have been reached could be interpreted as a legacy of teaching practice: passive unquestioning styles of learning. It is also possible, however, that the nature of the Wide-span reading task itself, uncompromising as it is to the linguistic limitations of the deaf, forces such children into adopting strategies for solution which are unlikely to produce "correct" responses, but ones (like selection on the basis of spatial position) that might conceivably seem reasonable to the child testee. More research, using different tests to study the "reading" strategies of deaf children, is needed to explain why the deaf child continues to attack questions well beyond his measured reading ability. (p. 145).

In their second study, Wood et al. (1981) used a different standardized, limited-cloze test to examine the relationship between the difficulty of items and the likelihood that deaf and hearing children would attempt to answer the items. This time they found that, although their attempts resulted in lower percentages of correct answers, deaf children were much more likely than hearing children to attempt the more difficult items on the test. Seventy percent of the hearing students attempted to answer the most difficult item with 40% doing so correctly. On the same item, 81% of the deaf children attempted to answer it, but only 4% did so correctly.

Consistency in the Answer Selected by Deaf Children

Wood et al. (1981) also addressed the issue of whether the deaf children in their study were using a guessing strategy in attacking the larger number of items. *Not only did they show that deaf children were systematically choosing their answers on both correct and incorrect items, but they also found a high degree of agreement among the deaf children, whether right or wrong, as to what the preferred answer was.* On the other hand, the hearing children either selected the correct answer or did not answer the question. When errors did occur, there was little agreement in the choice selected by the hearing children who got the item wrong.

In contrast, Fischler (1983) found that the responses of deaf college students were more variable than the responses of hearing subjects on a free-response cloze task. Many possible interpretations of this difference in results could be suggested. However, it is interesting that, although Wood et al. (1981) found that deaf children converged on a single answer and Fischler (1983) found that the responses of deaf adults were more variable, both ascribe their results to the effects of "less familiarity with conventional patterns of English" (Fischler, 1983, p. 423). More research is needed on this question.

Word Association Strategy

In 1969, W. MacGinitie proposed the hypothesis that "deaf children do not understand the difference between similarities in meanings and close associational relationships" (Paul, 1984, p. 31). Recently, other researchers have investigated the use of associational relationships as a strategy for answering questions on reading tests (Webster et al., 1981; Wolk & Schildroth, 1984; Wood et al., 1981).

Wood et al. (1981) found that the most popular answer for specific items on the cloze test they used was the answer that could have been selected on the basis of associations among key words in the test sentence and the list of possible answers. Two examples, with the most popular answer underlined, follow:

Birds are covered with — trees   skirts   sky   <u>nests</u>   feathers
Careless driving leads to — happiness   <u>cars</u>   tractors
                            accidents   improvements

(Wood et al., 1981, p. 15)

Wolk and Schildroth (1984) used test data from the *SAT-HI* to investigate the use of the word association strategy by deaf children in the United States. Although this study is limited in that only six items on the Primary 2 level test were addressed, it also has an advantage in that data on 1900 hearing-impaired students were available. Large numbers of subjects allow for more definitive statements to be made about the generalizability of the findings. The study also extends the work of Wood et al. in that *SAT-HI* uses broader contexts than the single sentence format of the British reading tests. An abbreviated example follows:

A herring gull will pick up a clam and fly high into the air and toss it to the rocks to break its shell, then glide to earth to eat its meat. The laughing gull will follow a pelican and, when the larger bird catches a fish, the gull will sit on the pelican's beak and snap the fish away before the big bird can swallow it. There is no doubt that the gull family is an interesting group of birds.

The LAUGHING gull could be called a
playmate robber[1] friend   *joke*[2]

(Wolk & Schildroth, 1984, p. 138)

---

[1] correct answer
[2] word/idea association choice

Wolk and Schildroth found that the hearing-impaired students selected the incorrect word/idea association choice almost 2.5 times more frequently than the correct answer. The results for a group of hearing students were directly opposite—they were 2.5 times more likely to select the correct answer than the word/idea association choice.

The data provided here appear to be fairly powerful evidence that use of a word/idea associational strategy among hearing-impaired children is fairly widespread and that it may extend beyond the testing situation. However, the researchers note that their studies were based on post hoc analyses of data on existing tests, and thus a note of caution must be introduced. In other words, since the tests were not intentionally designed to determine the use of the word association strategy, generalizations based on these studies must await further research (Wolk & Schildroth, 1984).

Visual Matching Strategy

Various researchers have identified a visual matching strategy that is used by deaf children (Davey & LaSasso, 1983; K. Wilson et al., 1978) and deaf adults (Scouten, 1980). On multiple-choice tests, the strategy involves finding a key word in the item stem, finding the same key word in the passage, and selecting the alternative that has words in the closest physical proximity to the key word in the passage. On free-response questions or probes, the visual matching strategy involves matching a word or phrase in the question or probe with a sentence from the text that also contains that word or phrase. Then the student copies the entire sentence. A variation of this strategy occurs when the student (apparently) does not understand the task, but a written response is required. King and Quigley (1984) and LaSasso (personal communication, May 15, 1984) noted that some deaf children were copying part of the instructions rather than responding to the required task. Although it is conjecture that this behavior occurred because the student had no idea of what to do, it is an interesting phenomenon which merits further study.

LaSasso (1984, 1985) noted that the results of earlier studies were suggestive, rather than conclusive, since the tasks on which the visual matching strategy were observed were not designed to investigate visual matching and the numbers of observations of the strategy were small. She used a free-response task to assess whether 50 deaf and 50 hearing students would use a visual matching strategy in generating answers to questions on reading passages. The subjects were matched on reading ability grade equivalents, which ranged from 5.0 to 7.9. Only incorrect answers were analyzed since correct responses could not be differentially attributed to the visual matching strategy or to comprehension of what was read. LaSasso identified nine types of visual matching strategy which she used in classifying the data. Table 8 presents these nine categories with the examples from LaSasso (1985).

Although the deaf and hearing subjects had been matched on reading ability, there were large discrepancies between the two groups on their use of visual matching strategies. Approximately 41% of the total incorrect responses of deaf subjects suggested use of visual matching strategies, whereas only 4% of the hearing subjects' responses suggested such strategies. Deaf readers who were poorer readers and deaf readers who were better readers did not differ in their use of a visual matching strategy (LaSasso, 1985).

Elimination of Implausible Distractors

Elimination of implausible distractors is an efficient test-taking strategy in most cases, and deaf children's use of this strategy is no exception. The purpose here is not to show that deaf children use this strategy, but rather that they may not be responding to items in the same way as their hearing peers and that more research is needed to uncover some of the reasons for these differences.

The word/idea association strategy and visual matching strategy are just two of the strategies hearing-impaired children might be using to answer questions. Other strategies include (1) a position-related response (as shown by Trybus & Buchanan, 1973), (2) differential responses to items designed to assess phonetic confusion due to the influence of a word/idea association strategy, (3) selection or creation of responses that reflect the grammatical structures of the student's spontaneous language, (4) selection or creation of responses that reflect developmentally appropriate perceptions of the story based on the reader's age, cognitive maturity, or reading ability, and (5) selection or creation of responses that reflect the use of background experiences.

Examples of these strategies have been gleaned from published reports of data from the SAT-HI, from various research reports, and from experiences in the classroom. At the outset, it should be noted that these should not be taken as definitive strategies. They are offered to help readers recognize the difficulties of creating and interpreting assessment tools and to point out directions for future research. It also is important to note that interpretations of why a student selected a particular answer or stated an answer in a particular way should be based on solid evidence. The interpretations here are based on logical analysis but are largely conjecture. One of the purposes for presenting these interpretations is to point out the

Table 8. Examples of Visual Matching Strategy

TYPE 1: *Response contains key word(s) as well as language preceding or following word(s) in text. Often entire sentence containing key word(s) is written.*

Text (Partial):

> Lemonwood is very hard, but not hard enough to keep the string from cutting through it after the bow has been used several times. Therefore, a hard material is needed for the tips of the bow. The horns of South American oxen are best used for this purpose. Tips are cut to fit over the ends of the bow. *Then they are glued in place and notched for the string.*

Question:
What is *notched for the string?*

Response:
Then they are glued in place and notched for the string.

TYPE 2: *Response does not contain key word(s) but is within sentence containing key word(s) and is in direct vertical alignment to key word(s).*

Text (Partial):

> Have you ever dipped a thermometer in gasoline or chloroform and watched it while the liquid was evaporating, or drying off? If so, you will understand how the body is cooled. While the liquid is evaporating, the temperature falls very quickly. Often it falls from five to ten degrees in as many minutes. Nature has a similar method for cooling off the body. When little particles of water, called perspiration, are evaporated from the skin, the body is cooled to 98.6 *degrees.*

Question:
What is *perspiration* composed of?

Response:
98.6 degrees

TYPE 3: *Response does not contain key word(s) but is within sentence containing key word(s) and is horizontally aligned with key words.*

Text (Partial):

> Scientists can match rings in an old tree with those in trees cut and used by Indians who once lived nearby. By doing this, it will be possible to learn how long *ago Indians lived in various areas.*

Question:
How *long* do some turtles live?

Response:
ago Indians lived in various areas

Table continued on following page.

Table 8. Examples of Visual Matching Strategy (continued)

TYPE 4:   *Response does not contain key word(s), is within*
sentence containing key word(s), but is both vertically
and horizontally aligned with key word(s).

Text (Partial):

Einstein and other scientists believe that gravity is the explanation for the mystery spot. They believe that gravity is pulling
harder at that spot on both light rays and feet.

Question:

How would a person who is inside *the mystery spot* feel?

Response:

Einstein and other scientists believe that gravity is the
explanation

TYPE 5:   *Response does not contain key word(s), is within*
sentence containing key word(s), but is neither
vertically or horizontally aligned to key word(s).

Text (Partial):

Then the fish are easily harpooned and caught. It is only after
long rest and food that they are able to build up their ability to
shock their enemies again.

Question:

How do eels *build up their* electrical energy?

Response:

Shock their enemies

TYPE 6:   *Response does not contain key word(s) and is not within*
sentence containing key word(s) but is within two lines
of line containing key word(s) and is vertically aligned
with key word(s).

Text (Partial):

In order to overcome this difficulty, the Indians have devised
a very ingenious method of disarming the fish. Horses are driven
into the ponds and the eels expend their electrical charge on the
horses. *Then the fish are easily harpooned and caught.* It is only after
long rest and food that they are again able to build up their ability
to shock their enemies again.

Question:

How do Indians catch *eels?*

Response:

Then the fish are easily harpooned and caught.

TYPE 7:   *Response does not contain key word(s), is not within*
sentence containing key word(s), but is horizontally
aligned with key word(s).

Table 8. Examples of Visual Matching Strategy (continued)

Text (Partial):

> At one point during this voyage, men thought they saw an opening in the ice above them. The Nautilus tried to rise to the surface. *What they saw was not a real opening.* Instead, it was clear ice. The periscope of the Nautilus bent as the sub tried to pass through.

Question:
Why did the ship try to *surface?*

Response:
What they saw was not a real opening

TYPE 8: *Response does not contain key word(s), is not within sentence containing key word(s) but is both vertically and horizontally aligned with key word(s).*

Text (Partial):

> At one point during this voyage, men thought they saw an opening in the ice above them. The Nautilus tried to rise to the surface. *What they saw was not a real opening. Instead, it was clear ice.* The periscope of the Nautilus bent as the sub tried to pass through.

Question:
What happened to the ship's *periscope?*

Response:
What they saw was not a real opening. Instead, it was clear ice.

TYPE 9: *Response does not contain key word(s), is not within sentence containing key word(s) and is neither vertically or horizontally aligned with key word(s), but is within two lines above or below line containing key word(s).*

Text (Partial):

> The electric eel is a fish which is native to South America. It defends itself from *attacks of enemies* by a natural electric battery. A discharge from this battery is powerful. It can stun even the largest animals. In South America, roads often pass . . . .

Question:
How is the *eel* used by the Indians?

Response:
attacks of enemies

Adapted from LaSasso, C. (1985). Visual matching test-taking strategies used by deaf readers. *Journal of Speech and Hearing Research, 28,* 2–7.

dangers of ascribing specific causes for and interpretations of responses without sufficient evidence.

Items designed to assess phonetic confusions. The following items were taken from an item analysis of the responses of hearing-impaired children on the SAT Language Subtest, Primary II Battery (Di Francesca & Carey, 1972):

41. Do you 1 know when Dad is coming home?
        2 no

42. Janet and I walked 1 by the candy store.
          2 buy

45. Is the lady coming to 1 are house?
            2 our

The percentages of hearing-impaired children who got each of these items correct were, respectively, 86%, 40%, and 73%. From items 41 and 45, it might be inferred that most of the hearing-impaired children were impervious to the distraction of a phonetic confusion. (Although data are not available to confirm this hypothesis, it can be conjectured that these were two of the items which were biased in favor of the hearing-impaired children in Rudner's study [1978].) Given awareness of the test-taking strategies of hearing-impaired children, responses on item 42 could be interpreted as evidence of the word/idea associational strategy. Regardless of the interpretation, however, it seems apparent that hearing-impaired children may not be reacting to the distractors on standardized tests in the way in which the test developers expected the general population to react (i.e., to be distracted from the correct answer).

Responses that reflect grammatical features of spontaneous language. Most items on reading tests designed for hearing children do not include distractors that reflect the grammatical features of hearing-impaired children's spontaneous language. A list of distinctive structures that hearing-impaired individuals use in their spontaneous language and recognize on tests is provided in Table 9. These structures were identified by Quigley et al. (1976) and used in production of the *Test of Syntactic Abilities* (Quigley, Steinkamp, Power, & Jones, 1978) and the *Reading Milestones Placement Tests* (King & Quigley, 1984). Other test developers also might use these language patterns in writing items and distractors for forced-choice tests for deaf students. Such items help teachers in identifying specific syntactic, semantic, and pragmatic patterns and strategies used by their students.

Strategies based on the incorrect processing of English syntax occur during reading activities as well as during assessment tasks. During a classroom visit, one of the authors talked with a young deaf child who was reading a short story about unusual events. The child came up to the author to share something from the story that he found fascinating. The sentence was: "Not only do birds eat worms, but sometimes people eat worms too." The child was convinced that this sentence meant that birds do not eat worms, but people

Table 9. Distinctive Structures in the Language of Deaf Children and the Occurrence of these Structures in Other Populations

Distinctive Structure*	Environment	Example	Other Populations Using Structure†
Placement of negative outside sentence	Negation	No Daddy see baby.	First language learners (Bellugi, 1967); Spanish-speaking, Chinese-speaking (Dulay & Burt, 1972, 1974; Cancino, Rosansky, & Schumann, 1975)
Placement of negative inside sentence but not correctly marked	Negation	Daddy no see baby.	Same as above
Non-recognition of negative marker	Negation	Reads negative sentence as positive.	Not found in literature review
Object-object deletion	Conjunction	John chased the girl and he scared (her).	Learning English regardless of first language (all ESL) (Richards, 1974)
Object-subject deletion	Conjunction	The boy hit the girl and (the girl) ran home.	Not found in literature review
No inversion in questions	Question formation	What I did this morning? The kitten is black?	First language learners (Klima & Bellugi, 1966); Norwegian-speaking (Ravem, 1974); Spanish-speaking (Hernandez, 1972); all ESL (Richards, 1974); hearing children of deaf parents (Jones & Quigley, 1979)
Inversion of object and verb	Question formation	Who TV watched?	Not found in literature review
Overgeneralization of contraction rule	Question formation, Negation	Amn't I tired? Bill willn't go.	First language learners (Bellugi, 1967); Spanish-speaking (Politzer & Ramirez, 1973)
Noun copying	Question formation, Relativization	Who the boy saw the girl? The boy saw the girl who the girl ran home	Not found in literature review
Pronoun copying	Question formation, Relativization	Who he saw the girl? The boy saw the girl who she ran home.	Spanish-speaking (Politzer & Ramirez, 1973); Arabic-speaking. Persian-speaking, Japanese-speaking, Chinese-speaking (Schacter, 1974); language-delayed (Haber, 1977)

Table continued on following page.

Table 9. Distinctive Structures in the Language of Deaf Children and the Occurrence of these Structures in Other Populations (continued)

Distinctive Structure*	Environment	Example	Other Populations Using Structure†
Deletion of *by*	Verb processes	The boy was kissed the girl.	All ESL‡ (Richards, 1973); Arabic-speaking (Scott & Tucker, 1974)
Unmarked verb in sequence	Verb processes	The boy saw the girl and the girl kiss the boy.	All ESL (Richards, 1974); Arabic-speaking (Scott & Tucker, 1974); Spanish-speaking (Cohen, 1975)
Be + unmarked verb (*ing* missing; *ed* missing)	Verb processes	The boy is kiss the girl. The sky is cover with clouds.	All ESL (Richards, 1974); Spanish-speaking (Cohen,1975; Politzer & Ramirez, 1973)
Incorrect pairing of auxiliary with verb markers (confusion of tense markers)	Verb processes	Tom has pushing the wagon.	All ESL (Richards, 1974)
Omission of verb	Verb processes	The cat under the table.	Spanish-speaking (Cohen, 1975; Politzer & Ramirez, 1973); Arabic-speaking (Scott & Tucker, 1974)
Be-have confusion	Verb processes	The boy have sick. The boy is a sweater.	All ESL (Richards, 1974); Spanish-speaking (Politzer & Ramirez, 1973; Cohen, 1975); Arabic-speaking (Scott & Tucker, 1974)
Omission of *be* or *have*	Verb processes	John sick. The girl a ball.	Same as above.
Subject-verb agreement (third person marker missing)	Verb processes	The boy say "hi."	First language learners (Brown, 1973); All ESL (Richards, 1974); Spanish-speaking (Cohen, 1975; Lance, 1970)
Omission of conjunction	Conjunction	Bob saw liked the bike.	Spanish-speaking (Cohen, 1975); first language learners (pause instead of conjunction—Cohen, 1975)
Omission of determiners	Determiners	Boy is sick.	First language learners (de Villiers & de Villiers, 1978); all ESL (Richards, 1974); Spanish-speaking (Politzer & Ramirez, 1973; Cohen, 1975); Arabic-speaking (Scott & Tucker, 1974)
Confusion of determiners (non-recognition of definite-indefinite distinctions)	Determiners	The some apples...A best friend...He was the bad boy.	Same as above

Table 9. Distinctive Structures in the Language of Deaf Children and the Occurrence of these Structures in Other Populations (continued)

Distinctive Structure*	Environment	Example	Other Populations Using Structure†
Confusion of case pronouns	Pronominali-zation	Her is going home. This he friend.	First language learners (Menyuk, 1963b; Hatch, 1969); Spanish-speaking (Cohen, 1975; Politzer & Ramirez, 1973)
Wrong gender	Pronominali-zation	They packed our (their) lunch. Sue is wearing his new dress today.	Spanish-speaking (Cohen, 1975); First language learners (Cohen, 1975; Wilbur, Montanelli, & Quigley, 1976)
Relative pronoun deletion (Object-subject deletion)	Relativization	The dog chased the girl had on a red dress.	Arabic-speaking (Scott & Tucker, 1974); Persian, Japanese, and Chinese-speaking (Schachter, 1974); Spanish-speaking (Cohen, 1975)
Relative pronoun + possessive pronoun	Relativization	The boy helped the girl who her mother was sick.	Same as above
Noun phrases	Relativization	The boy helped the girl's mother was sick.	Not found in literature review
Extra for	Complemen-tation	For to play baseball is fun.	Not found in literature review
Extra to in gerund complement	Complemen-tation	Joe went to fishing.	
Infinitive in place of gerund	Complemen-tation	Joe goes to fish.	Spanish-speaking (Politzer & Ramirez, 1973); Arabic (Scott & Tucker, 1974)
Omission of to before second verb	Complemen-tation	Chad wanted go.	Spanish-speaking (Politzer & Ramirez, 1973)
Incorrectly inflected infinitive	Complemen-tation	Bill like to played baseball.	Spanish-speaking (Politzer & Ramirez, 1973); first language learners (Black English) (Bartley & Politzer, 1972)
Adjective following noun	Relativization	The barn red burned.	Spanish-speaking (Cohen, 1975; Politzer & Ramirez, 1973)

Table continued on following page.

Table 9. Distinctive Structures in the Language of Deaf Children and the Occurrence of these Structures in Other Populations (continued)

Distinctive Structure*	Environment	Example	Other Populations Using Structure†
For + Ving or For + V for infinitive	Complementation	The boy likes for fishing.	Arabic-speaking (Scott & Tucker, 1974)
Surface reading order strategy	Verb processes	The boy *was* kissed *by* the girl.	First language learners (Bever, 1970; Bell, Bird & Burroughs-Keith, 1977); French-speaking (Ervin-Tripp, 1972)
	Relativization	*The boy who the* girl ran home.	
	Complementation	*That the boy hit* the girl surprised me.	
	Nominalization	*The discussion of* the party bored Bob.	

* Adapted from Quigley et al. (1978). Each distinctive structure has been found in the language of deaf children and youth.

† Richards collected these errors from studies of English errors produced by speakers of Japanese, Chinese, Burmese, French, Czech, Polish, Tagalog, Maori, Maltese, and the major Indian and West African languages (Richards, 1974, pp. 173, 182–188).

From King, C. (1981). *An investigation of similarities and differences in the syntactic abilities of deaf and hearing children learning English as a first or second language.* Unpublished doctoral dissertation, University of Illinois at Urbana-Champaign. Reprinted with permission.

do eat them. When the author tried to explain the correct interpretation, the child continued to try to convince her of his interpretation. This example reinforces the importance of teachers being able to recognize common syntactic patterns and strategies used by hearing-impaired children (see Table 9).

Although most adults with native English skills may find the "Not only...but" sentence easy to understand, it should be noted that such sentences are likely to cause difficulty for hearing children as well. Look back at the sentence in italics on page 226. The difficulty in comprehending the meaning of the sentence seems to be related to the complexity of the sentence structure. This example may provide some insight into the difficulties of English syntax for hearing-impaired children and other language-impaired populations.

Developmentally-appropriate responses. Earlier in this chapter, an example from Livingston (1981) was presented that showed that hearing-impaired children, like their hearing peers, use syncretistic thinking, assuming that if an event occurs (i.e., birds eating the crumbs Hansel and Gretel left), then the event must have been planned (i.e., Hansel and Gretel dropped the crumbs for the birds). Obviously, awareness of such strategies and developmental patterns is useful in interpreting free-response tasks and in constructing forced-choice tasks. The following example, based on the story of *Sleeping Beauty*, shows how the information can be used in a multiple-choice item.

Why didn't the king invite the thirteenth fairy to the banquet?
a. because she was a mean fairy
b. because he didn't have a gold plate for her
c. because he didn't like her

Of the students who responded to this item during the development phase for the *Reading Milestones Placement Test*, 33% chose alternative *a* as the correct answer. Although these responses cannot conclusively be attributed to syncretistic thinking, a follow-up discussion with the student concerning his or her reasons for choosing certain answers could reveal whether this were in fact the cause.

Responses using background experience. Pearson and D. Johnson (1978) note that teachers are sometimes looking for specific answers to questions and may not recognize or accept the correctness of other answers. An example of an item from the *Reading Milestones Placement Tests* that was eliminated during the development phase illustrates this. Almost 50% of the students were distracted by alternative *c* on the following item. Although the authors had planned that distractor to tap a different strategy, upon reflection they realized that alternative *c* was a logical answer and therefore eliminated the item.

Why would Marion use a flashcube?
a. because the room was too dark   25%

b. because the camera was hot	25%
c. because her mother was in the house	48%
No response	2%

Context: Marion was taking a picture of her mother
Note: Numeric scores are the percentages of hearing-
               impaired students selecting the distractor.

Free-response items and retelling tasks can also elicit responses that indicate students are using their background experience. An example from data presented by Quinn (1981, pp. 157—159) illustrates this.

THE TEXT:
...."I am hungry," Nancy said. "Everyone is eating but I have nothing. I want to go home now."
   She walked through the yard. There was her cat! He was cleaning his face.
   "I forgot all about you!" Nancy said. She picked up her cat and hugged him. "We are together again! That dog is bad! He fights my cat...."

THE QUESTION:
Why did Nancy go home?

SOME ANSWERS:
Nancy go to home Because to Homework.
She went home because she help to food for animals.
Because they fight each other.
Because she ate her lunch.

Although no retrospective conclusion of the student's intent can be made based on these answers, it is likely that different teachers would respond to these answers in different ways. Quinn (1981) classified these responses as "anomalous" (inappropriate or indirectly related to the question). Others might want to argue that at least the second answer is a logical inference based on the text (Nancy picked up her cat so she was going to feed it as well as herself).

This example illustrates the difficulty of interpreting responses to open-ended questions and free recall tasks. While this difficulty should in no way deter teachers from using such tasks, the problem of reliability (agreement among different teachers and consistency of interpretation across different students for a single teacher) must be addressed.

CURRENT PRACTICES, MAJOR PROBLEMS, AND PROMISING DIRECTIONS IN READING ASSESSMENT WITH HEARING-IMPAIRED INDIVIDUALS

The issues discussed in earlier parts of this chapter are applicable, to some extent, to each of the three traditional classes of assessment tools: formal, informal, and unobstrusive measures of reading. In other words, the problems in reading assessment and the test-taking strategies discussed thus far transcend these categories and are not necessarily specific to any one type of assessment tool. In this section, the purpose is (1) to describe the extent to which the three major types of assessment tools are used with hearing-impaired children, and (2) to discuss specific problems and promising trends in such use.

Formal Tests

Current Practices

At the beginning of this chapter, it was noted that one way to categorize formal reading tests is based on the function or aspect of reading that is addressed by each test. In this section, information on current practices with general achievement tests is presented, followed by information on tests that address specific components of reading.

General achievement tests. The most common assessment tool used to determine the reading grade level of hearing-impaired children is the standardized achievement test, with between 50% and 65% of the programs using these tests (LaSasso, 1978a; Marshman, 1974). Buchanan (1973) found that the most popular test was the *SAT-HI*, with 57% of the programs using this test either alone or in combination with other tests. Seventy-seven percent of the hearing-impaired students were in programs that administered the *SAT-HI*.

Little is known about how or to what extent programs for hearing-impaired children use diagnostic reading tests. The lack of information is a reflection of the fact that recent surveys did not request information on these tests (LaSasso, 1978a), rather than that such tests are not used. Apparently, in the 1960s and early 1970s, the *Gates-MacGinitie Reading Test*, was popular among programs for hearing-impaired children and among researchers in deafness (Marshman, 1974). No recent information is available as to its current use in programs for hearing-impaired children, nor to the use of other diagnostic reading tests. (See, however, LaSasso's survey report when it is published [LaSasso, personal communication, March, 1985].) McCaughrin (1981) offers an annotated list of reading tests that might be used with hearing-impaired children.

Tests of individual reading components or functions. Some formal and informal tests focus on a single function or component of reading. For example, there are decoding tests, vocabulary tests, syntax tests, idiom tests, reading readiness tests, and study skills tests, to name a few. Other topics that have been the focus of separate tests include reading attitudes and interests (Summers, 1977), reading flexibility (Rankin, 1974), reading rate (Berger & Peebles, 1976), and testwiseness (Sarnacki, 1979). The extent to which these types of tests are used with hearing-impaired children has not been determined in any of the recent survey studies. Descriptions of most of the general tests from these categories can be found in any introductory reading text (e.g., Harris & Sipay, 1980). Only tests that have been specifically designed for deaf children and that are used in research or instructional programs with deaf children are discussed here.

Two major reading vocabulary tests have been developed for deaf children (Silverman-Dresner & Guilfoyle, 1972; Walter, 1978a). Neither of these, however, is available commercially. The test developed by Walter (1978b) was discussed in Chapter 3. The Silverman-Dresner and Guilfoyle test (1972) was designed to establish vocabulary norms for deaf children. Both tests have been criticized because of the complexity of the definitions that accompanied the vocabulary words. For example, the Silverman-Dresner and Guilfoyle test required students to match the word *boy* with the definition *a young male child*. Tests on idioms, multiple meanings, and figurative uses of language designed for deaf children are also limited to noncommercial tests used in research. Several of these tests appear to have potential as tests for general use (Conley, 1976; Giorcelli, 1982; Paul, 1984; Payne, 1982).

Two additional vocabulary tests have been developed for deaf children. These tests, however, are receptive language tests based on picture vocabulary and, as such, are not reading tests per se. The *Carolina Picture Vocabulary Test* (Layton & Holmes, in press) was normed on a population of 767 hearing-impaired children. It will be available commercially. The *SKI-HI Receptive Vocabulary Test* was developed by the SKI-HI project in Utah and is available from Tom Clark at Utah State University.

The only commercially available test that addresses the syntactic component of reading and language and that was specifically designed for deaf children is the *Test of Syntactic Abilities (TSA)* (Quigley et al., 1978). This test has a solid research base and has undergone rigorous test development procedures. The TSA requires students to read sentences and then to judge the grammaticality of the sentence, match it to another sentence with the same meaning, or choose the missing word that fits the sentence. A major advantage of this test is that the distractors (wrong alternatives) are based on the major grammatical patterns exhibited by deaf students (see Table 9). B. Jones (1984) provides an in-depth description of the TSA and its reliability and validity data.

Major Problems

Lack of standardization on the hearing-impaired population is the major problem reported with regard to formal reading tests. Attempts to remedy this situation have resulted in norms being established for hearing-impaired children on (1) unmodified standardized tests (Furth, 1966a; Office of Demographic Studies, 1973; Allen et al., 1983); (2) norms being established for modifications in administration procedures (R. J. Anderson & Sisco, 1977); and (3) norms being established for tests that were designed for special populations (Moog & Geers, 1980; Quigley et al., 1978). In the first category falls the *SAT-HI*, on which the items are unchanged, but the subtests have been rearranged and administration procedures modified. In the second category are IQ tests and in the third, language and reading tests developed for hearing-impaired children.

Criticisms of reading tests that address individual components of reading were discussed earlier in this chapter. Two major issues were identified: (1) holistic assessment versus assessment of individual components; and (2) context-rich versus reduced context testing. In regard to these issues, the view taken by the authors of this book is that division of assessment procedures into either-or dichotomies is a simplistic view of the reading process and a view that is overly restrictive in obtaining a comprehensive understanding of an individual's abilities. The remaining discussion in this subsection presents specific problems that have been identified in relation to the use of achievement tests with hearing-impaired students and the solutions to these problems which the Center for Assessment and Demographic Studies (CADS) has proposed.

Hearing-impaired students typically have uneven performance across the subtests of achievement tests such that correlations among the subtests are lower for hearing-impaired students than for hearing students (Trybus & Buchanan, 1973). This led CADS to rearrange the subtests within the SAT battery to resemble more closely the achievement patterns of hearing-impaired children and to include a screening test that allowed for placement within the battery (Allen et al., 1983) (in the 1974 version, children took a higher level mathematics test than reading test). Analysis of data from the 1974 SAT-HI resulted in the conclusion that two screening tests were needed, one for reading and reading-related subtests and one for mathematical computation and number concepts. This change is reflected in the 1982 version (CADS, 1983), which permits different, or the same, levels to be given in mathematics and reading.

Difficulties in administering the tests to hearing-impaired children led to practice tests being added and modifications in the instructions being made. Subsequent analysis resulted in identification of specific subtests on the SAT-HI that were inappropriate for some or all hearing-impaired children. Current practice is for individual schools to determine whether to administer these subtests based on a comparison of their curriculum and students with the objectives of the tests (CADS, 1983).

LaSasso and Davey (1983b) addressed the issue of whether the SAT-HI has criterion-related validity. They established that deaf children's performance on the SAT-HI correlated with performance on informal measures. Moderately high, consistent across task, positive correlations were found between performance on the reading comprehension subtest of the SAT-HI and performance on multiple-choice and free response question tasks, cloze tasks, and limited cloze tasks.

Three of the problems that CADS identified were not addressed in the revised SAT-HI (1) the mismatch between the interest of older hearing-impaired students and the interest level of the tests; (2) the use of test-taking strategies by hearing-impaired children that may make the distractors on standardized tests appear implausible; and (3) the fact that yearly growth in reading for hearing-impaired children and the standard error of the test are about equal, resulting in the inability of standardized tests to measure year-to-year growth.

Promising Directions

The Center for Assessment and Demographic Studies has made significant contributions to the use of standardized tests with hearing-impaired children. The continuation of this service is a promising direction in reading assessment for deaf children. The Center is collecting a rich data base that can be used to advance knowledge of the reading abilities of hearing-impaired children and of their test-taking abilities. Also, with the new 1982 edition of the SAT-HI, CADS will provide special scoring services that permit the generation and maintenance of local norms for programs. This, too, is a promising direction. The standardization of out-of-level testing (i.e., using tests other than the one for the grade in which a student is placed) is another encouraging movement. Programs for hearing students are also beginning to encourage the use of out-of-level tests (J. Long, Schaffran, & Kellogg, 1977). The experiences of CADS and the Psychological Corporation (the publisher of the SAT-HI) could be of help to those attempting to measure the effects of such testing with hearing children.

The development of tests specifically for hearing-impaired children is a second major positive direction in the use of formal tests with this population. These tests circumvent the problems of having incorrect alternatives on multiple-choice tests that do not distract students from the correct answer. They also provide avenues for assessing specific aspects and functions of the reading process. It seems likely that the three problems with formal tests that have been left unresolved may lead to additional special tests being developed to address specific problems in assessing the reading abilities of hearing-impaired children (Webster et al., 1981). This appears to be a promising trend since it should permit more accurate assessment. Caution, however, is needed to ensure that the trend toward special tests does not lead to the total rejection of assessment tools standardized on hearing children such that comparison of the performance of hearing-impaired children and hearing children is impossible. Only recently has there been a movement away from a belief that the language of deaf children is unique (V. Charrow & Fletcher, 1973; Myklebust, 1960) to one that recognizes similarities among different language-impaired populations and non-language-impaired populations (King, 1981; Quigley & King, 1982a; Quigley et al., 1976; Quigley & Paul, 1984b). If the creation and use of special tests for hearing-impaired children leads back to a view of the problems of hearing-impaired children as totally unique to that population, the promise of these tests may not be realized. Therefore, judgment concerning the promise of this trend toward special tests for hearing-impaired children must await the test of time.

Informal Tests

The cloze test differs greatly from the other informal assessment tools in its procedures and, as such, is discussed separately. The other assessment tools are addressed collectively since, although differing in purpose, they share many of the same procedures.

Cloze Procedure

Descriptions of how to construct and administer the cloze procedure as an assessment tool can be found in most introductory level textbooks on reading (e.g., see Harris & Sipay, 1979, pp. 199-201). A description of the process as it was applied in a study of the reliability and validity of the cloze procedure for hearing-impaired children is offered by L. Kelly and Ewoldt (1984).

Current practices. LaSasso (1978a) indicates that the cloze procedure is used infrequently in programs for hearing-impaired children as a means for determining the reading grade level of children (5.9% to 10.6% of the programs). It is more commonly used, however, as a means of determining a text's difficulty in terms of its suitability for a specific child. Although only a small proportion of programs use a formal measure of a text's difficulty to match students and texts (18.1% of the programs), cloze procedure is the second most popular approach (16% to 24%) for those programs that do use formal measures. The Fry Readability Formula (Fry, 1968, 1977) is the approach used most frequently.

Major problems. There are two major issues that are debated in relation to the cloze procedure as an assessment procedure: (1) whether cloze tests are sensitive to intersentential comprehension, given that scrambling the sentences in a passage often does not reduce the scores (Shanahan, Kamil, & Tobin, 1982), and (2) whether a cloze test should be scored for verbatim or synonymic responses (McKenna, 1976). The first issue is the focus of heated debate among reading researchers at present, and there appears to be no clear winner (Henk, 1982). However, the research cited in Chapter 3 (p. 59) appears to indicate clearly that cloze tasks measure different skills than standardized tests for hearing-impaired children. In other words, hearing and deaf children with the same scores on standardized tests exhibit different behaviors on cloze tests.

Acceptance of synonyms for the deleted word in a cloze task has intuitive appeal to most teachers. The demand for a verbatim response seems to unduly penalize students for not knowing an exact word. Research that has been done comparing verbatim scoring versus synonymic scoring has shown that verbatim and synonymic scores are highly correlated for the general school population (McKenna, 1976) and for ESL students (R. Anderson, 1972). Such comparisons have not been made with hearing-impaired children. McKenna (1976) argues for the use of verbatim scores since they appear to give the same type of information and are simpler to calculate. Pikulski and Tobin (1982) concur with McKenna, but for a different reason. They cite the low agreement among examiners as to what constitutes an acceptable synonym and also question whether the results can be used diagnostically.

McKenna's argument for verbatim scoring is applicable, however, only if a teacher is interested in rank ordering students based on cloze procedures. High correlations between verbatim and synonymic scoring indicate nothing about the relative level of the scores. So, the suggestion that verbatim and synonymic scoring provide the same diagnostic information seems unsupported. The use of logic in arguing for ease of calculation in verbatim scoring, although valid, could also be turned around to support the opposite argument (i.e., use synonymic scoring since it has greater face validity for the teachers using it). The issue of reliability, which Pikulski and Tobin (1982) discuss, is of much greater importance. As noted earlier in this chapter, reliability is a necessary, but not sufficient, condition for validity. If scoring by different individuals produces different results, both the reliability and validity of the measure are suspect. This issue will likely remain a problem for some time given the large body of research, which has failed for the most part to establish reliability for informal assessment tools (see Pikulski & Tobin, 1982, for a review of the studies).

Within the field of deafness, different researchers appear to have different concepts of the level of reliability needed. For example, L. Kelly and Ewoldt (1984) cited inter-rater reliability of 79% to 82% as sufficient for classification of cloze responses into the four categories they propose. Webster et al. (1981), on the other hand, declined to report on subcategories of test-taking strategies they had identified since inter-rater reliability was .81. This issue is in need of further investigation.

If cloze tasks are to be scored for synonyms, research will be needed to address the question of what constitutes the appropriate criteria for acceptable performance under the two conditions (synonyms and verbatim responses). Bormuth's (1966) criteria of cut-off scores for frustration, instructional, and independent levels on the cloze task (below 44%, 44%–57%, and above 57%, respectively) were established for verbatim responses. New criteria scores must be established if synonymic responses are to be scored as correct. Alternatively, other methods for determining acceptable levels of performance could be used (L. Kelly & Ewoldt, 1984).

Promising directions. Opinions as to the utility of the cloze procedure as a reading assessment tool in the education of hearing-impaired children appear to be split (L. Kelly & Ewoldt, 1984; LaSasso, 1978b, 1980a, 1980b). Further research is needed to resolve the issues. There does, however, appear to be value in the cloze procedure for at least some diagnostic purposes (L. Kelly & Ewoldt, 1984).

Other Informal Tests

Detailed discussions of the use of informal reading inventories (IRIs) and reading miscue analyses (RMIs) in the education of hearing-impaired children are provided by LaSasso and Swaiko (1983) and Ewoldt (1977, 1981a, 1981b). Harris and Sipay (1979) discuss the general procedures for constructing, administering, scoring, and interpreting IRIs. Y. Goodman and Burke (1976) provide a comprehensive discussion of the RMI for various populations.

Current practices. Results of a national survey showed that approximately 42% to 62% of programs for hearing-impaired children use IRIs (LaSasso, 1978a). Data on the use of RMIs are more difficult to obtain. LaSasso's survey form (1978a) did not provide a separate category for RMIs, although respondents could have written it under the heading "other." LaSasso (personal communication, March, 1985) indicates that only a small percentage of respondents did so.

The diagnostic procedures that accompany basal readers (i.e., placement tests and end-of-level tests) are used to a lesser extent than IRIs and RMIs in programs for deaf students. At the primary level, 38.6% of the total programs whose personnel responded to the questionnaire used such diagnostic procedures. Use was highest at the intermediate level, with 43.3% of the programs using the procedures. Use decreased at the junior high and high school levels, with 32.2% and 20.8% of the programs, respectively, using the diagnostic procedures that accompany basal readers (LaSasso, 1978a).

Major problems. Most of the problems related to the use of informal assessment tools have been discussed earlier in this chapter. In relation to the oral reading task of IRIs and RMIs, the major issues appear to be (1) whether oral reading should be scored quantitatively or qualitatively, (2) whether oral reading should occur on sight or after silent reading, (3) whether adequate inter-rater reliability can be established, and (4) whether a few passages from a text can adequately represent the difficulty levels in the text.

The problems with both free and controlled (prompted) measures of comprehension have also been described in earlier sections of this chapter. Research efforts are needed to examine the methods being used to score the retelling of stories by hearing-impaired children. The Kendall Demonstration Elementary School (KDES) *Language Arts Curriculum* (1981) recommends that the teacher assign 100 points to the major events in a story and then determine which of these were included in a child's retelling of the story. The description of how the points are to be assigned, however, is sketchy. Manson (personal communication, September 15, 1984) indicates that retelling protocols with points already assigned to various parts of the story are used within KDES. This improves the reliability of the story analysis. For other schools trying to use the guide, however, it seems likely that there are differences in the ways in which individual teachers assign points. Training and experience with propositional analysis (e.g., see Tierney & Mosenthal, 1982, and B. Meyer & Rice, 1984) will likely be necessary to develop reliability among individuals who determine the point values for various parts of the stories used to elicit retellings. Examination of inter-rater reliability for the scoring of the child's retelling is also needed. Again, it seems likely that different teachers may assign different point values to a child's retelling of a story.

Examination of the procedures for determining the difficulty level of the passages on IRIs and RMIs is also needed. The concept of readability and the problems inherent in measuring the difficulty of a text are described in Chapter 5. Earlier in this chapter, it was noted that the common practice of using texts written at levels higher than the reading grade level of the student on the RMI was questionable since different reading behaviors are exhibited on easy and difficult materials. Other means of determining a starting point likewise may not be appropriate for hearing-impaired children. For example, the utility of a word recognition task as an initial indication of the level of passages to assign appears to be limited, at least in application to hearing-impaired children. King and Quigley (1984) and LaSasso and Swaiko (1983) both note that such tests appear to overestimate the appropriate reading levels for hearing-impaired children. LaSasso and Swaiko also note that reading potential (i.e., listening comprehension) and silent reading comprehension abilities are often equal, since it is limited language and experience, rather than decoding per se, that are the major factors contributing to the reading difficulties of hearing-impaired children. This result is not surprising given the research that has indicated that hearing-impaired children appear to gain the most information from a reading task (see Chapter 3). From these studies, however, it should not be assumed that a reading potential task is unnecessary. Valuable information can likely be obtained from such tasks.

Promising directions. Increased use of these informal techniques is a promising avenue in reading assessment with hearing-impaired children. Such techniques are likely the most valuable in terms of providing diagnostic information that teachers can use in daily instruction. A list of resources on reading miscues and other informal testing procedures is provided in Appendix E. The major focus of future research on informal assessment tools should be on establishing adequate reliability.

Unobtrusive Measures and Dynamic Assessment

Current Practices

Teachers use unobtrusive assessment methods every day in their classrooms. Descriptions of the frequency of such methods, the specific procedures utilized, and the major problems associated with unobtrusive measures and dynamic assessment, however, have not received much attention in the research literature.

Major Problems

Recently, studies of the classroom environment have begun to uncover the characteristics that seem to distinguish "master" teachers who are good diagnosticians from those who are less able to assess their students' abilities adequately. Even with knowledge of the characteristics of good diagnostic teachers, however, the problem remains of how to teach others these skills. Often, when asked how they know a particular student can perform a given task, master teachers simply respond, "by observation." Most teacher trainers and trainees are well aware of the difficulties involved in developing skills in systematic observation.

A second major problem associated with unobtrusive measures relates to the reliability of the information gathered. As occurs with informal testing, different teachers may come to different conclusions regarding the skills of a student even though the same lessons were observed. Accurate recording of data collected via unobtrusive measures is also a concern. The major contribution of unobtrusive measures is related to the continuity of information that is gathered over a period of time. Without records, however, it may be difficult to remember how well or poorly an individual student performed on a given lesson.

Promising Directions

The major promising trend with regard to unobtrusive measures and dynamic assessment is the large amount of attention which has recently been directed toward such measures. Recognition that these are indeed legitimate techniques for assessment is a major step toward a comprehensive approach to reading assessment.

Additional research in this area will contribute to further development. Research on the characteristics of master teachers of hearing-impaired children is needed, along with systematic study of methods for preservice and in-service training of teachers. Models for research on teacher effectiveness are provided by, among others, Ruddell and Haggard (1982) and Rupley, Blair, and Wise (1982). Studies of the interaction patterns in classrooms for deaf children are also needed. Some studies of this type were reviewed in Chapter 4. Mosenthal (1984) provides a detailed review of the influences of classroom variables on the assessment of reading. Finally, close attention to developing reliability and accurate recording methods for these approaches will contribute to the continued view of unobtrusive measures and dynamic assessment as legitimate approaches to assessment.

SUMMARY

A vast amount of information on assessment in relation to the reading abilities of deaf and hearing individuals has been covered in this chapter. Three basic types of assessment tools are addressed: formal tests, informal tests, and unobtrusive measures. The views of educators, researchers, professional organizations, students, and the general public with regard to assessment are discussed. It seems likely that assessment techniques in reading or at least the procedures used in designing such tools will change dramatically in the coming decades. In this redesign, the field will need to be careful not to "throw the baby out with the dirty bath water." Assessment is a desirable goal, despite the validity of the criticisms that have been presented.

Desirable characteristics for assessment tools are discussed in this chapter. Five types of validity are defined: criterion-related validity, predictive validity, content validity, construct validity, and face validity. Six types of reliability are defined—two related to reliability between and within raters: inter-rater reliability and intra-rater reliability; and four related to reliability of the test instrument: internal consistency reliability, parallel forms reliability, standard error of measurement, and test-retest reliability. The need for practicality in terms of cost and of time and ease of administration and scoring is also stressed. Two suggestions are made: (1) assessment tools should be selected based on their relevance and unique contribution to the decision that is to be made based on the assessment; and (2) the amount of assessment an individual receives should be proportional to his or her needs.

Six general issues in reading assessment are covered. The view taken in this chapter is that either-or approaches to assessment (e.g., *either* real world, context-rich context tasks only *or* reduced context tasks only) are simplistic and that various types of assessment tools are needed to provide a comprehensive description of an individual's reading abilities. The advantages and limitations of free and controlled measures of reading are discussed. Again, both types of measures have a place in a comprehensive assessment program. Problems in the construction of assessment tools revolve around (1) the reliance on statistical methods for determining reliability and validity, and (2) the techniques used to generate, select, and revise items for assessment tools.

The administration of assessment tools is a major source of difficulty in the search for accurate assessment of hearing-impaired individuals. Practice items and the demonstration of test-taking strategies have been shown to be effective in helping hearing-impaired children comprehend the assessment tasks. Three diverse views on modifying administration procedures were identified: (1) any changes invalidate the use of a test; (2) changes invalidate only normative uses of a test, while not affecting criterion-referenced uses; and (3) changes do not invalidate normative uses so long as flexible administration procedures only ensure standardization without undermining it. Scoring of assessment tools is discussed in terms of the types of scores available (normative socres and criterion-referenced or diagnostic scores) and the limitations associated with each. The final general issue discussed is the uses of assessment results. Major difficulties identified include inappropriate use of test results (e.g., attempts to equate test scores and measures of text difficulty) and overreliance on assessment results. Readers are reminded that all assessment is simply an estimate of abilities; testing error (which occurs in all assessments) must be considered in interpreting tests. Two student-related activities that lead to better uses of assessment results are the following: (1) discussion of the test results with students since it leads to more positive attitudes (Shannon, 1980); and (2) discussion of the test items with students and probing for the reasons why students chose or produced answers since such discussion can lead to better understanding of the strategies a student is using in reading and test-taking.

The effects of various types of assessment tasks on the performance of a hearing-impaired individual are covered in the chapter. Basically, the effects of various tasks appear to be content-specific. Recognition tasks (e.g., multiple-choice questions) are generally easier than recall tasks (e.g., open-ended questions). Several studies point out that hearing-impaired individuals appear to be less efficient than hearing children in using appropriate test-taking strategies.

Five major test-taking strategies that hearing-impaired children use are identified. These include: (1) perseverance in question answering beyond ability level; (2) consistency in the answers selected among deaf children; (3) a word/idea association strategy; (4) a visual matching strategy; and (5) elimination of implausible distractors. Within the last category, the influences of the following factors are noted: (a) the grammatical features of the child's spontaneous language, (b) the child's linguistic and cognitive developmental stage, and (c) the child's background experiences and knowledge.

The final section of this chapter focuses on current practices, major problems, and promising directions in reading assessment with hearing-impaired individuals. The *SAT-HI* is the major achievement test used. Tests of individual reading components include measurements of vocabulary, syntax, and idioms, among other aspects. Major problems with formal assessment tools include (1) lack of standardization; (2) the uneven performance of hearing-impaired students across subtests of general achievement tests; (3) difficulties in test administration; (4) the mismatch between the interests of older hearing-impaired students and the interest level of the tests; (5) the use of test-taking strategies that may make the distractors on standardized tests seem implausible to hearing-impaired students; and (6) the fact that yearly growth and the standard error of measurement are about equal, resulting in the inability of standardized tests to measure year-to-year growth. The last three problems have not been addressed satisfactorily. Major promising trends include the work of the Center for Assessment and Demographic Studies and the development of special tests for hearing-impaired children. The final determination of the value of special tests, however, must await the test of time since it would be unfortunate if the outcome were that tests designed for hearing children would never be used. Important comparative data would thus be lost. Knowledge of what typical hearing children are capable of at specific ages is important information for teachers of deaf children to have to provide an appropriate balance of challenging and on-level instruction for their students.

Three major informal assessment tools are discussed: the cloze procedure, informal reading inventories, and reading miscue analysis. Issues concerning the cloze procedure include whether synonymic responses should be marked as correct and whether cloze tests are adequate measures of discourse comprehension. Whether the cloze procedure will be seen as a major assessment tool for deaf children remains to be determined. Opinions within the field are split as to its utility. The IRI and RMI approaches to informal assessment are used fairly frequently in programs for hearing-impaired children. The major difficulty associated with these techniques is the establishment of acceptable reliability. Both techniques—IRIs and RMIs— have merits and limitations. Still, these informal assessment tools are among the most valuable aids to the classroom teacher for diagnostic teaching.

Finally, unobtrusive measures and dynamic assessment are discussed. Major problems associated with these techniques are the difficulty of teaching others the skills that master teachers use and the difficulty of establishing adequate reliability among different evaluators. The recognition of unobtrusive measurement and dynamic assessment as legitimate techniques for assessment is seen as a positive trend.

In conclusion, accurate assessment of the reading abilities of hearing-impaired individuals requires three conditions: (1) trained personnel to select and administer the assessment tools, (2) appropriate assessment tools that provide valid and reliable information about the student's skills and potential, and (3) knowledgeable administrators, teachers, parents, and students who can interpret and make appropriate inferences based on the assessment results. Accurate assessment also requires a healthy lack of trust in any *one* assessment tool as providing all the answers about an individual's reading ability and knowledge of the variety of factors that can impinge on the assessment process. Reader-based, text-based, task-based, and situation-based variables must all be considered.

Chapter 8

Reading and Other Language-Variant Populations

Peter V. Paul, PhD

In this book, the correlates of the low reading achievement of deaf children and youth have been discussed within the framework of theoretical views of reading as an interactive process between the text and the reader. The intent in this chapter is to demonstrate that similarities exist between the reading problems of the deaf population and three other language-disordered populations: namely, students who have been classified as learning disabled, mentally retarded, and learners of English as a second language (ESL). It is shown that one of the major correlates of reading difficulty common across these populations is inadequate development in the target language (i.e., English).

First, the general requisites of reading ability are discussed briefly to provide a conceptual framework for some of the major correlates of reading disability. From this, it is argued that reading is related to the overall language comprehension process and thus is affected by inadequate language development. The quantitative and qualitative aspects of linguistic development are described to provide the focus of the comparisons of the language-variant populations under study with the deaf and the general populations. Following this, each of the three language-variant groups is considered separately, and a representative sample of research studies is presented and evaluated in each area. This task was difficult owing to incomplete descriptions of the populations and to lack of agreement on definitions in the research literature. In addition, the reader should be aware that (1) an exhaustive treatment of the reading difficulties of these groups is not attempted here, and (2) the groups, either together or separately, do not constitute homogeneous populations.

FACTORS RELATED TO READING ABILITY

The process of reading entails the interaction of the cognitive and linguistic skills of the reader with the linguistic aspects of the text (Rumelhart, 1977, 1980; Rumelhart & Ortony, 1977). Within this framework, the reader is said to use his or her cognitive and linguistic abilities to hypothesize about the information contained within the linguistic aspects of the text. These hypotheses operate at various linguistic levels (e.g., lexical, syntactic, semantic) and involve a number of skills (e.g., decoding, inferencing, memory, the use of background knowledge), which are largely influenced by cognitive and linguistic development (Athey, 1983; Baker & Brown, 1980; Freebody, 1980). Thus, schema-oriented reading theorists emphasize the importance of the development of cognitive structures for reading ability (Rumelhart, 1980) whereas cognitive theorists emphasize their importance for language development (Piaget, 1967; Schlesinger, 1982). Although cognitive growth may be a requisite for grammatical and lexical development and later for reading development, it is the interaction of linguistic and cognitive skills that is important for continual development of language (Schlesinger, 1982) as well as for reading (Athey, 1983; Goldsmith, 1981).

Reading difficulty can be attributed in part to inadequate language development causing a breakdown in the interactive process. This has been demonstrated for the deaf population (see the reviews of Quigley & King, 1982a, and Quigley & Paul, 1984a) and for the language-variant populations under study here: learning-disabled (Das, Mulcahy, & Wall, 1982; Gerber & Bryen, 1981), mentally-retarded (Kamhi & Johnston, 1982), and ESL students (Carrell, 1983; Gonzales, 1981). Research on other factors related to reading ability—for example, the use of prior knowledge, inferencing ability, and metacognitive skills—is in its infancy for the learning-disabled (Graybeal, 1981), the mentally-retarded (Kamhi & Johnston, 1982), and ESL students (Carrell, 1983).

QUANTITATIVE VERSUS QUALITATIVE DIFFERENCES

Developmental and difference theories revolve around the issue of whether quantitative or qualitative differences, or both, exist in the language acquisition process of language-variant populations (see the discussions in Kamhi, 1981, King, 1981, and Leonard, 1979). This issue has engendered intense debates in the literature. It is important since the outcome has pervasive implications for instructional practices as well as for the construction of special materials. Specifically, it is essential to know whether these endeavors should adhere to the growth patterns of the general population of children or follow some esoteric development uniquely attributed to the specific population in question.

The quantitative aspect refers to the degree of language acquisition whereas the qualitative aspect refers to the manner of acquisition. Briefly, if the linguistic development of a language-variant group is qualitatively similar to, but quantitatively different from, that of the general population, the language acquisition process of this group is said to be developmentally delayed. This means that this group proceeds through similar developmental stages within and across the linguistic structures, makes the same type and variety of errors, and employs learning strategies similar to ones the general population uses at a younger age (Brown, 1973; de Villiers & de Villiers, 1978; Menyuk, 1969). If, on the other hand, qualitative differences occur, the language acquisition process is claimed to be different from that of the general population. Essentially, this means that orders of difficulty within and across the linguistic components are different and that there are also marked differences in the types of errors and variety of error types. In addition, there may be differences in the learning strategies employed by the language-variant group. The position espoused here is that the English language acquisition process of most of the learning-disabled, mentally retarded, and ESL learners is qualitatively similar to—albeit quantitatively slower than—that of the general population. In general, the same has been argued for most deaf children and youth (Quigley & King, 1982a; Quigley & Paul, 1984a).

It should be borne in mind that demonstrating similarities within a qualitative framework does not obscure differences that may exist within these language-variant populations. Some researchers focus on establishing subgroups with their respective differences (Harber, 1981; Kaluger & Kolson, 1978), whereas others emphasize the similarities in development across the apparent groups (Gaskins, 1982; Vellutino, 1977, 1979). The establishment of subgroups is deemed important since reading disabilities result from a complex array of linguistic and cognitive deficiencies, and some groups may have more problems in one area than others. In addition, there is speculation that quantitative or qualitative differences, or both, may increase with age for some groups. Clarification of these issues is contingent on the establishment of subgroups and the delineation of their various linguistic and cognitive abilities (Keogh, 1982; Leonard, 1979; Lott, 1983; Torgesen, 1982).

ANALYSES OF LINGUISTIC PERFORMANCE

To evaluate whether quantitative or qualitative differences, or both, exist, data from spontaneous and elicited spoken language samples are presented here and discussed, as are those from the performances on standardized (norm-referenced) and criterion-referenced linguistic measurements. Most of the research studies examined development within the phonological and the morphological-syntactic components with a few studies concentrating on semantics and pragmatics. The phonological studies are of little value owing to the impracticality of comparing the results with those available for most deaf children. In general, the studies on morphology detail the use of derivational and inflectional markers similar to those reported for nonvariant children (Brown, 1973; de Villiers & de Villiers, 1973). The studies on syntax were concerned with the combination of words in a particular order within the major syntactic structures of English (e.g., wh-questions, negation, passive constructions), and within minor structures (e.g., the use of determiners and demonstratives). Research on semantics concentrates mainly on the acquisition of word meanings, logicogrammatical relationships, and relational categories. The very few studies on pragmatics focus on communicative competence. A more detailed description of these components can be found in Bloom and Lahey (1978), Dale (1976), and Lucas (1980). As stated in Quigley and Paul (1984a) and elsewhere (de Villiers & de Villiers, 1978), it is difficult—albeit possible—to discuss language development in each of these components separately. The division of linguistic growth into each of these areas for research purposes is defined arbitrarily, and occasionally shrouded with controversies. For example, there is disagreement as to whether morphology is part of the syntactic or semantic component or a part of both (Brown, 1973; de Villiers & de Villiers, 1978). There is agreement, however, that morphology and syntax constitute the grammar of a language.

Another aspect of linguistic assessment is error analyses. Discussions of these techniques have often concentrated on establishing categories that ensure a consistent and relevant assessment. These categories include areas such as the frequency of particular errors, the frequency and generality of structures involved in an error, and the linguistic classification of errors (Burt & Kiparsky, 1974; Lott, 1983). Analyses of errors have resulted in controversies owing to conflicting views and contradictory results, especially in the research on second language acquisition. Some problematic issues of this research relevant to ESL students are discussed later. In general, even for first language learners, it is extremely difficult to categorize the errors. For example, the production of similar errors by different language learners may be indicative of different learning strategies. In addition, the same language learner may produce the same error at different times for different reasons (Lott, 1983; Richards 1974a). In spite of these concerns, the limited data from error analyses of the language-variant groups tentatively reveal that, in general, most members employ learning strategies similar to those used by the general population at younger ages.

LEARNING DISABILITY

Prior to the emergence of a discipline termed learning disability (LD), children who experienced learning difficulties not related to sensory deprivation or mental retardation frequently were classified as lazy, stubborn, or unmotivated (Gerber, 1981; Smith, 1981). The term learning disability was introduced initially by S. Kirk at a conference in 1963 for parents of children who had perceptual handicaps (Gerber, 1981). At this conference,

Kirk attempted to focus on the behavioral or educational manifestations of the disability. As occurs in any emerging discipline, widely disparate views concerning the nature of learning disability were espoused. Subsequently, two general models emerged during this period: the medical model and the behavioral or educational model. The medical model attempted to explain learning disability from an organic etiological perspective and employed terms that included, but were not limited to, the following: organic brain disease or dysfunction, minimal brain damage or injury, minimal cerebral damage, and minimal brain dysfunction syndrome (the most widely used term). The behavioral or educational model employed one or more of the following labels: hyperkinetic syndrome, dyslexia, specific reading disability, perceptual handicaps, aphasoid syndrome, and (specific) learning disability (Gerber, 1981; Kirk & Kirk, 1971; Wong, 1979a, 1979b).

Early research on learning disability was dominated by theories of neurological impairment, particularly perceptual-motor theories. The learning-disabled child was seen as having average or near average intelligence but with perceptual and attentional behavioral deficits. The use of the term minimal brain dysfunction was considered appropriate since it differentiated the children with this disorder from those with severe brain disorders (e.g., cerebral palsy). Thus, learning-disabled children were said to have problems with eye-motor coordination, figure-ground relationship, form constancy, auditory processing, intersensory integration, and spatial relationship (Gerber, 1981; Wiig & Semel, 1976; Wong, 1979a, 1979b). Within this theoretical framework, most of the attention was on reading disability, and this problem was argued to be primarily the result of visual-perceptual and motor problems (Kephart, 1960).

The hypothesis that learning or reading disabilities, or both, were related to language disabilities also had proponents. Although these language theorists (Johnson & Myklebust, 1967; Orton, 1937) were heavily influenced by the neurological perspectives, there were some major differences. For example, Johnson and Myklebust (1967) adhered to theories of visual and auditory processing and argued that the factors related to dyslexia (i.e., specific reading disability) were different from or went beyond those associated with a general learning or language disability. Contrariwise, Orton (1937), one of the first researchers to introduce the term developmental delay considered dyslexia as part of an overall language delay. Specifically, he equated dyslexia with learning disability and maintained that both are the results of language problems.

The emergence of theories of specific learning disabilities resulted from the shift to the behavioral or educational framework. These theories were based generally on the current linguistic thinking relating to language acquisition and use. Within the educational view, the concept of learning disability has recently evolved to encompass a heterogeneous group composed of children who exhibit problems in the production and comprehension of spoken or written language or both (Das, Mulcahy, & Wall, 1982; Kirk

& Kirk, 1971). This definition includes children who have the following disorders: minimal brain dysfunction, dyslexia, and developmental aphasia. It excludes, however, those with learning problems due primarily to sensory or motor impairments, mental retardation, emotional disturbances, or cultural or environmental influences. Thus, in this view, learning disability implies a basic disorder in the language comprehension process, which, in turn, leads to problems in areas of later development (e.g., reading, writing, and mathematics).

With respect to reading, several researchers maintain that children with reading disabilities (e.g., dyslexia) do not form a homogeneous group, thus making it imperative to establish subgroups based on specific deficits uncovered (Fletcher & Satz, 1979; Harber, 1981; Johnson & Myklebust, 1967; Kaluger & Kolson, 1978). There are others, however, who consider reading disability synonymous with learning or language disability, and thus due to a general language comprehension problem (Gaskins, 1982; Idol-Maestas, 1980; McCaughrin & Idol-Maestas, 1983; Wiig & Semel, 1976). Vellutino (1977, 1979, 1980) reviewed much of the available data on correlates of early reading difficulties and concluded that these were due to deficits in verbal ability rather than deficiencies in visual or auditory processing. Specifically, he argued that certain behaviors of dyslexia (e.g., letter reversals) were mainly secondary or surface manifestations of a deeper deficit in verbal abilities. The evidence suggested that the difficulties of poor readers were related to problems in the various components of language. Those who argue for homogeneous subgroups within the reading disabled population disagree (Fletcher & Satz, 1979). At present, no acceptable operational definition exists for making the distinction between learning and reading disabilities or between language and reading disabilities, although research is currently being conducted to clarify these issues (e.g., see the discussion in Das, Mulcahy, & Wall, 1982). It is maintained, as initially suggested by Orton (1937), that most perceptual differences, although they are important enough to be considered, are essentially secondary manifestations of a deeper problem, namely that of the language comprehension process influenced by early cognitive structures and later by the interaction of linguistic and cognitive factors.

Research Considerations

It has been argued that most of the recent research on learning disability has been fraught with methodological problems, such as questionable designs, incorrect measurements, inadequate control of extraneous variables (e.g., intelligence), and incomplete descriptions of the population under study (Harber, 1981; Kavale & Nye, 1981; Torgesen & Dice, 1980). Similar problems have been observed in the literature on deaf children (Quigley & King, 1982a). There is concern, for example, with the manner in which learning-disabled children are equated with their nondisabled counterparts.

A number of criteria have been employed for various purposes: chronological age, mental age (determined by scores on nonverbal performance scales of standardized intelligence tests or by cognitive tasks or both), mean length of utterance (MLU) (Brown, 1973), and performance on standardized linguistic or reading measurements. Discussion of the merits of these comparisons is beyond the scope of this chapter.

With these caveats in mind, an attempt was made to include a representative sample of studies thought to be relatively free of major methodological problems. Generally, the learning-disabled subjects in these studies had normal intelligence as determined by the nonverbal performance scale of a standardized measurement. In addition, they possessed no other educationally significant disability except for corrected vision. Essentially, the problems of these subjects were not related to sensory impairments, emotional problems, cultural or environmental deprivation, or gross physical or perceptual deficits. The subjects also exhibited marked delays (i.e., one to two years) on standardized linguistic or reading measurements. These delays were not accompanied by physiological articulatory or other speech disorders (e.g., cleft palate). Finally, the subjects were between the ages of 2 years and 18 years 11 months. Since learning disability is an educational term, it is highly unlikely that a child would receive this label prior to the beginning of his or her formal education. Nevertheless, children as young as two or three years of age have been suspected to have language impairments by speech-language clinicians, and without early intervention, these children would eventually be classified as learning disabled in formal educational programs (see the discussions in Leonard, 1979, and Lubert, 1981). The data are presented and discussed in three sections: morphology and syntax, semantics, and pragmatics.

Morphology and Syntax

The developmental order of English morphemes has received considerable attention in the literature on deaf children (Crandall, 1978; Raffin, 1976; Raffin, Davis, & Gilman, 1978; Schlesinger & Meadow, 1972). Quigley and Paul (1984a) reviewed much of this research and concluded, as others have, that although deaf children have deficits in the knowledge and use of English morphology, their order of acquisition is generally similar to that reported for nondeaf (normally hearing) children (i.e., the grammatical morphemes were acquired in a consistent order and at specific language stages; Brown, 1973, de Villiers & de Villiers, 1973). Similar conclusions can be drawn from the data on learning-disabled children (Johnston & Schery, 1976; Vogel, 1975; Wiig, Semel & Crouse, 1973).

Wiig, Semel, and Crouse (1973) studied the comprehension of morphological structures by three groups of children: high-risk, learning-disabled, and non-disabled controls. Of interest here are the comparisons between the latter two groups. Twelve learning-disabled children between the ages of 8 years 4 months and 10 years 1 month were matched with 12 controls on the variables of sex, age, intelligence, and socioeconomic status. Neither group exhibited previously diagnosed speech disorders. The mean grade level of the learning-disabled (LD) group on the *Metropolitan Achievement Test* was reported to be 2.57, with a range from 0 to 3.3.

Wiig et al. (1973) adapted the experimental test of morphology designed by Berko (1958). As expected, the LD subjects made significantly fewer correct responses than their controls. Within the morphological categories, the progressive tense was found to be the easiest for both groups, whereas the derivational aspects were the most difficult. It also was reported that the greatest relative differences between the LD and the control groups occurred for third person singular verbs, possessives, and adjectival inflections. Wiig et al. concluded that the knowledge of morphology is related to the language processing ability of the learning-disabled child.

Johnston and Schery (1976) observed the use of grammatical morphemes in spoken language samples of 287 linguistically deficient children, from 3 years to 16 years 2 months of age and enrolled in special day classes. They had average intelligence; however, their performance on two auditory-verbal language scales was two standard deviations or more below expected mental age performance. The results were based on the analyses of a sample of 100 utterances from each subject. It was found that the degree and rate of acquisition differed across language levels. No significant differences were found between language levels for the number of children using a particular morpheme. It was noted, however, that improvement in the consistency of usage varied with the increase in MLU. Johnston and Schery concluded that the order of acquisition resembled that reported by Brown (1973) and de Villiers and de Villiers (1973). Specifically, the language-impaired children acquired these grammatical morphemes in a similar manner as the nonimpaired children, but at later developmental levels. In addition, they concluded that, similar to normal acquisition, the results demonstrated a developmental relationship between MLU and the use of morphemes.

Menyuk (1964) matched 10 children with infantile speech with 10 normal-speaking children on the variables of age, sex, intelligence, and socioeconomic status. The age range of the subjects was 3 years to 5 years 10 months. Analyses of the spontaneous speech samples of the subjects were conducted on three levels: phrase structure, transformational, and morphological. Errors (i.e., restricted or deviant forms) were categorized as either substitution, redundancy, or omission on the three levels. In general, the normal-speaking subjects produced more transformationally complex syntax than the language-impaired group, whereas the language-impaired group produced more restricted forms, particularly omissions. Some examples of the errors are given in Table 10.

A number of these errors, with similar terminologies, have also been found in the written language samples of deaf children (Quigley et al., 1976) and in students learning English as a second language (e.g., see the review in

Table 10. **Examples of Errors of 10 Children with Infantile Speech**

Restricted Forms	Examples
Verb Phrase Omission	This green
Article Omission	Daddy has new office
No Question	Who he is kissing
Verb Form Omission	She like that
Pronoun Subject Substitution	Me like that
	Him is a bad boy

King, 1981). Even more important, the phrase-structure and transformational forms used by some language-impaired subjects were also present in the grammar of the younger nonimpaired subjects in Menyuk's study and in other first language learners reported in the literature (Brown, 1973; de Villiers & de Villiers, 1973; Menyuk, 1963).

Similar findings were reported by Menyuk and Looney (1972). They studied the effects of sentence length and structure on the accuracy of sentence repetition. The sentences were from three to five words long and were primarily imperatives, active-declaratives, negatives, and question sentences. Thirteen language-disordered children, ranging in age from 4 years 5 months to 7 years 9 months, with a mean of 6 years 2 months, were compared with 13 nonimpaired children, with a mean age of 4 years 6 months. In general, the language-disordered children produced fewer errors in their repetitions of imperative and active-declarative sentences than with negative and question sentences. Within the more difficult structures, there were more repetition errors in the question sentences than in the negative sentences, and there were more errors in the negative subject and passive sentences than in the question sentences. Sentence length and structure had no significant effect on the accuracy of sentence repetition for the nonimpaired children. The order of difficulty and the type of errors produced by the language-impaired subjects were similar to those reported in the literature for younger nonimpaired children and for deaf children. Table 11 shows a sample of these errors.

In addition to the errors found in Table 11, the most frequent error observed for the negative subject construction was the omission of the auxiliary. For example, the sentence "Nobody is going downtown" was repeated as "Nobody going downtown." In the passive construction, the auxiliary or the passive marker was frequently omitted. Thus, "That boy is named Tommy" may appear as either "That boy named Tommy," "That boy name Tommy," or "That boy is name Tommy." Menyuk and Looney hypothesized that the language-impaired group's difficulty was not simply a matter of remembering the items but one of not understanding the transformation operations necessary for the generation of the particular sentence type.

Table 11. Samples of Errors Produced by Language-Disordered Children

NEGATIVE SENTENCES

Sentences	Repetition Error
They won't play with me	They no not play with me
I can't sing	I no can sing
He doesn't have money	He no have money
She isn't very old	She not very old
The children can't run fast	The children no can run fast

QUESTION SENTENCES

Sentences	Repetition Error
What is that?	What that?
How will he get there?	How he will get there?
Where is he going?	Where he going?
When will he come?	When he will come?

Leonard (1972) compared the morphological-syntactic development of nine language-impaired children from 4 years 10 months to 5 years 10 months of age with nine nonimpaired children of similar ages. Employing the methodologies developed by Menyuk (1964) and Lee and Canter (1971), he analyzed the children's spontaneous language behavior. He found, as others have, that the mature morphological-syntactic structures typical of adult usage appeared more frequently in the speech of nonimpaired children, whereas the restricted or underdeveloped forms (e.g., verb phrase omissions) appeared more frequently in the language-impaired children's speech. In sum, he argued for the developmental delay hypothesis.

Additional support for the slower but similar development of syntax can be found in a study by Morehead and Ingram (1973), who analyzed the spontaneous language samples of 15 linguistically impaired and 15 nonimpaired children involved in learning base syntax (i.e., two-word utterances). The two groups were matched according to the five linguistic levels developed by Brown (1973). Five aspects of syntactic development were investigated: phrase structure rules, transformation, construction or sentence type, inflectional morphology, and minor lexical categories (e.g., pronouns, demonstratives, prepositions, and modals). In general, the results indicated that, across the linguistic levels, few significant differences existed in the use of phrase structure rules, frequently occurring transformations, and inflectional morphology or in the development of minor lexical categories. Significant differences, however, were found in favor of the nonimpaired group for the structures that occur less frequently and require knowledge of more difficult transformations (e.g., tag questions ["I go, don't I?"] and verb particle shift ["I pick ball up" to "I pick up ball"]). Research has also demonstrated that deaf children experience difficulty in comprehending tag questions (e.g., see the review in Quigley et al., 1976) and verb particle constructions (Payne, 1982).

In general, Morehead and Ingram concluded that the older language-impaired group showed a marked delay in the onset and acquisition time for learning base syntax. In addition, they reported no differences between the two groups in their organization or use of the specific components of base syntactic structures; thus, their development was qualitatively similar. It is interesting to note, however, that the language-impaired subjects who had a developed linguistic system did not produce utterances that were as creative or as multifarious as those of the nonimpaired subjects.

The developmental delay hypothesis has received substantial support from a number of more recent studies and reviews of the literature by Wiig and her associates (Semel & Wiig, 1975, 1980; Wiig & Semel, 1973, 1974, 1976; Wiig, Semel, & Abele, 1981). The studies that focused on morphological-syntactic aspects are discussed here, whereas those that focused on both syntax and semantics or primarily on semantics are discussed later.

Semel and Wiig (1975) evaluated the performance of learning-disabled students ranging in age from 7 years to 11 years 6 months on the *Assessment of Children's Language Comprehension Test* (ACLC) and the *Northwestern Syntax Screening Test* (NSST). The data on the LD subjects were compared with those of a control group matched for age range, sex, and intelligence, and with existing norms for the tests. The study also compared the performance of the younger LD subjects (ages 7 years to 9 years) with that of the older group (ages 9 years 1 month to 11 years).

On the NSST, the LD subjects demonstrated significant quantitative reductions in both the comprehension and expression of syntactic structures. Performance on the receptive subtest was significantly inferior to that on the expressive subtest (i.e., a greater percentage of LD subjects scored below the 10th percentile on the receptive subtest). The performance of the LD subjects on the ACLC was similar to the norms available for nondisabled children from 6 years to 6 years 6 months of age (Foster, Giddan, & Stark, 1972). Thus, the LD subjects also demonstrated quantitative reductions in their ability to process and synthesize verbal elements (e.g., using prepositions in isolation and in a sequence, as in "Monkey sitting on fence").

It was also reported that no significant differences were observed between the younger and older LD groups on the subtests of both the NSST and the ACLC. Even the percentages of the two groups scoring below the 10th percentile on the subtests of the NSST were similar. Finally, the error patterns of the LD subjects on the NSST supported the earlier findings by Menyuk and Looney (1972); namely, that the LD subjects experienced greater difficulty with sentences deemed to be of higher grammatical complexity (e.g., question sentences, sentences with demonstratives [this, that], *wh* forms, possessive relationships, and relationship between direct and indirect objects).

Semel and Wiig interpreted these findings to mean that delays in the acquisition of syntactic rules were not significantly reduced with age. This was substantiated by Andolina (1980), who investigated the acquisition of syntactic structures across four age levels: 7 years 5 months to 8 years 11 months, 9 years to 10 years 5 months, 10 years 6 months to 11 years 11 months, and 12 years to 12 years 5 months of age. In addition, Wiig, Lapointe, and Semel (1977) reported that, similarly to deaf children (e.g., Quigley et al., 1976), learning-disabled adolescents reached a performance plateau in linguistic abilities. It appears that the notion of a plateau effect should be further investigated across language-impaired populations, as it may provide additional insights regarding the reading difficulties of these groups.

Wiig and Semel (1976) and Semel and Wiig (1980) reviewed most of the data available regarding the expressive and receptive abilities of learning-disabled children and youth. The data on morphological and syntactic abilities concur with those presented earlier. The intent here is to discuss briefly the performance of LD children on the passive construction. For example, it was reported that nonreversible passives were easier to comprehend than reversible passives. Thus, a sentence such as "The ball was thrown by the boy" was easier to process than "The boy was hit by the girl." In addition, analyses of error patterns of the LD subjects seemed to indicate that they employed a subject-verb-object strategy in interpreting the passive constructions. These findings concurred with those reported for deaf children (Power & Quigley, 1973) and for younger nonimpaired children (e.g., Hayhurst, 1967; Turner & Rommetveit, 1967).

Syntactic deficiencies have also been documented in the written language of learning-disabled children (Anderson, 1982). Systematic research in this area, however, is fairly recent. Nevertheless, it appears that—as suggested by Vogel (1975), who employed dyslexic children as subjects—it is important to assess oral syntax in the evaluation and diagnosis of children with language or reading deficits, or both.

Semantics

The work of Wiig and her associates is representative of much of the research on LD children on semantic or syntactic-semantic related tasks. Areas of investigation were the acquisition of lexical items, the comprehension of logicogrammatical and other semantic relations, and the interpretation of ambiguous sentences. Similar to earlier findings, the learning-disabled children's performance, as compared with nondisabled peers, was quantitatively reduced but qualitatively similar.

Wiig and Semel (1973, 1974) investigated learning-disabled children's comprehension of logicogrammatical sentences expressing comparative, familial, passive, spatial, and temporal relationships. Examples of sentences used are the following:

Passive: Mary was pushed by Jane. Who was pushed?
Temporal: Does spring come before winter?
Spatial: The elephant sat on the mouse? Who was on the bottom?
Familial: Give another name for your mother's father.

At the least, this task required the LD subjects to use both syntactic and semantic skills. In the 1973 study, the LD subjects ranged in age from 7 years 4 months to 11 years 4 months, with a mean of 9 years 1 month. Those in the 1974 study ranged in age from 12 years 4 months to 16 years 1 month, with a mean of 13 years 7 months. All subjects exhibited marked academic retardation (i.e., from one to two years) in one or more areas, and none possessed auditory or visual deficits. In addition, these subjects had normal articulation ability. Each LD group was compared with a group of nonimpaired peers.

As expected, the findings indicated that the LD groups exhibited quantitative reductions in the comprehension of logicogrammatical constructions. In general, most of the errors occurred on the structures depicting familial relationships, followed in decreasing order of difficulty by spatial, temporal, passive, and comparative relationships. Apparently these deficits do not decrease with age. With the exception of familial relationships, the order of difficulty of these relationships was in accordance with the developmental data reported for nondisabled children (e.g., Clark, 1973; see the review by Lucas, 1980).

Difficulty with the logicogrammatical constructions also accounts for LD children's problems with the temporal relationship expressed by the "before-after" construction (Wiig & Semel, 1976). These problems resembled those reported for *oral* deaf children and younger normally hearing children (Jarvella & Lubinsky, 1975). Essentially, the performance on sentences with the temporal order preserved (i.e., *after* clause first or *before* clause second) was superior to that with the order reversed.

Wiig and Semel (1976), Wiig et al. (1981), and Bryen (1981) have suggested that deficits in semantic relations may account, in part, for the difficulties LD children have in processing multimeaning words or sentences, idioms, metaphors, puns, and other aspects of figurative language. These problems have also been observed in deaf children (Giorcelli, 1982; Paul, 1984; Payne, 1982) and in the limited research on normally hearing children (e.g., Mason, Kniseley, & Kendall, 1979).

Wiig et al. (1981) studied the abilities of learning-disabled students ranging in age from 12 years to 12 years 4 months, and three nondisabled groups to perceive and interpret lexical and syntactic ambiguities in sentences. One nondisabled group was matched with the LD group, and the other two groups were younger: 7 years 5 months to 8 years 3 months and 5 years 4 months to 6 years 3 months. As expected, the results demonstrated that the performance of the LD group was significantly inferior to that of the matched control group. With respect to lexical ambiguities only, the LD group performed as well as the two younger nondisabled groups.

A study by Levi, Capozzi, Fabrizi, and Sechi (1982) demonstrated the relationship of reading difficulties to language disorders, particularly in the areas of syntax and semantics. Two groups of language-disordered children were studied. One group consisted of 16 children, from 6 years 7 months to 7 years 5 months of age, who exhibited a language delay mainly on a phonological level (i.e., at least a one and a half year delay with less than a year's delay for syntactic and semantic development). The second group also consisted of 16 children, from 6 years to 7 years 8 months of age, who exhibited delays of 18 months or more in all three components. A significant difference in reading achievement was found in favor of the group with a marked delay mainly in phonological development. Levi et al. concluded that reading achievement appeared to be associated mainly with syntactic and semantic competence.

While semantic deficits have been observed in most learning-disabled children, a qualitatively similar development has also been observed by Leonard et al. (1982), Chapman, Leonard, Rowan, and Weiss (1983), and Lorsbach (1982). Leonard et al. examined early lexical development in 14 language-impaired children, aged 2 years 8 months to 4 years 2 months, matched for linguistic level (i.e., single-word utterances) with younger, nonimpaired children, aged 1 year 5 months to 1 year 10 months. Delays of at least one year in language production and six months in language comprehension in language-impaired subjects were reported using the *Test for Auditory Comprehension of Language, Preschool Language Scale*, and *Developmental Sentence Types*. The results demonstrated that similar comprehension-production gaps were observed for the groups. In addition, for both groups, the comprehension and production of words representing objects was greater than that for words representing actions. The inappropriate word extensions (i.e., overextensions) of some of the language-impaired subjects were analyzed and reported by Chapman et al. (1983). Again, the findings indicated that the language-impaired subjects, aged 2 years 8 months to 3 years 4 months, and the control subjects matched for linguistic levels had similar percentages of inappropriate word extensions. For both groups, these errors were indicative of the varying levels of lexical knowledge.

Lorsbach (1982) studied the performance of LD and nondisabled subjects, equated for age (mean was 10 years 9 months) and intelligence, on semantic orienting tasks that measured the speed and accuracy of the categorization of individual words. As expected, the semantic encoding processes of LD children were generally slower than those of the nondisabled controls. More importantly, however, Lorsbach concluded that the LD children did not possess qualitative differences in the structure of their semantic memory.

Pragmatics

Research on the pragmatic abilities of learning-disabled children is limited (Prinz & Ferrier, 1983). The studies cited here are relevant with respect to the issue of quantitative versus qualitative differences. Several recent studies have shown that the linguistic problems of learning-disabled children are not restricted to linguistic structures; the problems extend to pragmatic competence since these children exhibit difficulty in acquiring rules that govern the function of language, especially in social contexts (see Bates, 1976, for a discussion of pragmatics). Deficits were observed in the ability of these children to provide adequate referent descriptions comparable to those of nonimpaired children (Spekman, 1981) and to request clarification of ambiguous messages produced by other speakers (Donahue, Pearl, & Bryan, 1982). Essentially, it appears that the quality of communication interactions is affected by the level of linguistic competence.

With reference to the developmental versus deviant issue, Gallagher and Darnton (1978) studied the use of revisions by 12 language-disordered children, four at each of Brown's first three developmental stages (Brown, 1973). These children exhibited a marked delay in their receptive and expressive abilities (i.e., they are at least one year below *chronological* age level). The subjects were evaluated in their ability to revise their utterances in response to a listener's misunderstanding. Examples of revisions are as follows (Gallagher, 1977):

> *Phonetic*
> Child: He kit ball.
> Experimenter: What?
> Child: He kick ball.
> *Substitution*
> Child: He kick ball.
> Experimenter: What?
> Child: He kick it.

It was reported that the revision strategies of the language-disordered subjects did not match their linguistic competence. In addition, Gallagher and Darnton concluded that qualitative differences exist in the response strategies used by these children compared with those of the nondisordered children.

Van Kleeck and Frankel (1981) reported findings to the contrary. They were interested in evaluating and comparing the use of discourse devices by language-disordered children with those observed for nondisordered children. Discourse devices, similar to referential and revision strategies, are part of communicative functions that speakers used to perpetuate communication (e.g., substitution operations in which the speakers provide descriptions, statements, requests for action, and requests for information).

Detailed descriptions of these functions can be found in Dore (1974, 1975) and Lucas (1980). Three language-disordered children, ages 3 years 1 month, 3 years 11 months, and 4 years 2 months, who showed delays in receptive and expressive language skills as assessed by the *Sequenced Inventory of Communication Development*, were employed as subjects. Adapting the methodology of Keenan (1974), a language sample of each subject was secured and analyzed.

The results indicated that the discourse devices employed by the young language-disordered subjects resembled those observed for nondisordered children. In addition, the language-disordered subjects proceeded through similar developmental stages in the use of these devices. Thus, Van Kleeck and Frankel concluded that no qualitative differences existed between the two groups compared. Finally, in defense of conclusions based on a small sample size, they argued that their sample was more homogeneous than those of other studies (notably Gallagher & Darnton, 1978). Therefore, they concluded that contradictory findings in other studies regarding quantitative versus qualitative differences may be due primarily to methodological problems.

Summary: Learning Disability

Research on learning disability has shifted from a medical model to an educational or behavioral model (Gerber, 1981). Within this theoretical framework, the data have been interpreted in light of current linguistic thinking. In addition, the concept of learning disability covers a heterogeneous group of children whose problems have been given various labels (Das, Mulcahy, & Wall, 1982; Kirk & Kirk, 1971). Although the importance of establishing subgroups is not denied, research has demonstrated, nevertheless, that most of these children possess a basic disorder in the language comprehension process which in turn affects the later development of secondary skills, notably reading comprehension (Gaskins, 1982; Vellutino, 1977, 1979). Essentially, it seems that the process of reading cannot be separated from the process of language comprehension, and it may be difficult, if not impossible, to separate reading disabilities from learning disabilities or language disabilities.

Another area of importance is the developmental versus difference issue. Similarly to most deaf children, most learning-disabled children exhibit quantitative reductions in the knowledge and use of the various linguistic structures compared with nondisabled peers. More importantly, however, the development within and across the linguistic components was generally found to be qualitatively similar, and the learning strategies appeared to be those employed by younger normal children (Leonard, 1979; Wiig & Semel, 1976). Some researchers have argued that contradictory findings regarding the quantitative versus qualitative issue were due to methodological problems (e.g., incomplete description of the population under study;

Leonard, 1979; Van Kleeck & Frankel, 1981). Consequently, as for most deaf children, it appears that instructional practices and the construction of special materials should adhere to the developmental patterns of nondisabled children for the purposes of teaching language or reading skills.

MENTAL RETARDATION

Controversies in the field of mental retardation are remarkably similar to those of learning disability and of deafness. For example, mentally-retarded children also constitute a heterogeneous group, and current research is attempting to establish homogeneous subgroups (see the discussion in Kamhi & Johnston, 1982). Such endeavors, however, are contingent on an understanding of what constitutes mental retardation. Debates have revolved around factors such as intelligence, adaptive behavior, etiology, and type of education or training program. Kirk (1962) has asserted that defining mental retardation is difficult since it is a condition, not a disease, that involves a number of criteria.

Traditionally, attempts to define mental retardation have been based on factors associated with one of three categories: intelligence quotient (IQ), index of social performance, and etiology. It has been stated that any definition of mental retardation should consider the level of intelligence and the impairment of adaptive behaviors that emerge during the developmental period (Herber, 1961; Ingalls, 1978; Schiefelbusch, Copeland, & Smith, 1967). The history of mental retardation is replete with debates on the interrelationships of factors associated with the nature-nurture and the developmental-difference theories (e.g., intelligence, cognition, language, etiology, education, and environmental influences; see the discussions in Kamhi, 1981, Scott, 1978, and Zigler, 1969). Thus, the understanding of this term is affected by recent thinking on the concepts of intelligence and learning theory. One researcher has argued that advances in knowledge in the field are limited until the interrelationships of learning, intelligence, and development are clearly understood (Scott, 1978). At present, the most widely accepted definition is that adopted by the American Association of Mental Deficiency:

> Mental retardation refers to significantly subaverage general intellectual functioning existing concurrently with deficits in adaptive behavior, and manifested during the developmental period.
>
> (Grossman, 1973, p. 11)

Mental retardation has generally been determined educationally by a child's performance on a standardized intelligence test, notably, the *Wechsler Intelligence Scale for Children* (WISC) or the *Stanford Binet*. Thus, subaverage intellectual functioning means that the individual scored at least two standard deviations below the norm for his or her age group. Essentially, this means that IQs below 68 on the *Stanford-Binet* or below 70 on one of the Wechsler

Table 12. Levels of Retardation

Level of Intelligence	IQ Range
Borderline (slow learner)	69–84
Mildly Retarded (educable)	52–68
Moderately Retarded (trainable)	36–51
Severely Retarded	20–35
Profoundly Retarded	19 and below

scales. In general, most classification systems adhere to the levels of retardation given in Table 12 (the numbers may vary somewhat according to the test employed) (Gillespie & Johnson, 1974; Ingalls, 1978).

It has been remarked that there is a need for the schools to consider assessment of adaptive behavior (e.g., using the *Vineland Social Maturity Scale* or the *Adaptive Behavior Scale* in conjunction with intelligence test scores [Chinn, Drew, & Logan, 1979; Ingalls, 1978]). With respect to this classification system, most of the retarded populace in schools and in general society has been reported to be in the mild or borderline range (Carney, 1979; Kamhi & Johnston, 1982). This is significant in considering the development of linguistic and reading skills (Carney, 1979; Welch, 1981).

As discussed previously, the development of language and subsequent reading skills are dependent on the development of cognitive functioning. Robinson and Robinson (1965) reported that the cognitive abilities of mentally-retarded individuals can be described in relation to the developmental stages of Piaget. In general, the level of cognitive skill increases as the degree of retardation (determined by IQ) decreases. For example, the profoundly retarded individual has been reported to be operating at the level of sensorimotor intelligence. The moderately retarded individual may function in one of the preoperational subperiods, whereas the mildly retarded individual may be at the level of concrete operations. Finally, the borderline individual is said to have the ability to perform some of the simpler formal operations. There is some recent research to support these assertions (Kahn, 1979). Piaget's stages, however, should be used as guidelines only, not as fixed systems. Reviews of the literature by several researchers have led to the conclusion that mentally-retarded children—namely, those in the educable or borderline range—are not reading on a level commensurate with their mental age capacity (Carney, 1979; Dunn, 1954; Welch, 1981).

Reading and Mental Retardation

One of the greatest challenges that still faces the nation and its school system is learning how to deal effectively with mentally-retarded children. In spite of our technology, no answer has been found for the treatment, education, and training of mental retardation.

(Gillespie & Johnson, 1974, p. 1)

This quotation describes the viewpoint of many current investigators (Carney, 1979; Kamhi & Johnston, 1982; Welch, 1981). In considering reading and mental retardation, two major problems appear to be the heterogeneity of retarded children (due to definitional issues) and the lack of emphasis on the teaching of reading—or, rather, whether reading is a desirable and realistic goal for most retarded children. These issues are similar to those discussed earlier in this book in relation to reading and deafness (see Chapter 3).

A number of researchers have argued that language and reading competency can be realistic goals for most retarded children who fall in the educable or borderline range (Carney, 1979; Dunn, 1954). Essentially, they argue that adequate instruction should help these children read at a level commensurate with their mental age. Dunn (1954) reviewed 14 studies in the literature from 1918 to 1952. The results showed that mentally retarded children in special classrooms tended to read at a level below expectancy. Dunn hypothesized, however, that if reading were given special emphasis, these students' reading levels should match their mental age. Similar conclusions were drawn by Carney (1979) in a more recent and extensive review of the literature. Carney cited two general weaknesses in most instructional practices: (1) overemphasis on word recognition strategies, and (2) inadequate emphasis on comprehension processes.

The complex relationship between language and reading has been discussed previously. Most of the data seem to suggest that reading difficulties are largely due to inadequate language competence (Idol-Maestas, 1980; Vellutino, 1977, 1979). If the acquisition of language is important for the later development of reading, the nature of this acquisition should be described with implications for instructional practices. As is the case with the learning-disabled and the deaf populations, one of the major issues in research on language and mental retardation is that of quantitative versus qualitative differences.

Quantitative Versus Qualitative Differences

There is agreement that the linguistic abilities of mentally retarded students are not commensurate with those of their nonretarded peers (Jordan, 1967; Lackner, 1968; Welch, 1981; Yoder & Miller, 1972). Whereas quantitative reductions are generally accepted, the issue of qualitative similarity has been intensely debated (Kamhi, 1981; Zigler, 1969). Research in this area was inspired by the work of Lenneberg (1967), who argued that the language development of retarded children differed quantitatively but was qualitatively similar with respect to mental age (MA).

In the literature on mental retardation, the most common procedure employed for comparing language competence with cognitive level has been to match retarded and nonretarded subjects for MA, which is determined by psychometric tests (e.g., IQ). There are problems with this procedure, as MA may not be an adequate index of a general cognitive level (Kamhi,

1981; Scott, 1978; Zigler, 1969). It is also possible to obtain a measure of cognitive level using Piagetian tasks. This procedure likewise is not without problems. Like MA, cognitive tasks may not be an adequate index of overall cognitive ability. In addition, some of these tasks may be influenced by linguistic abilities (Quigley & Kretschmer, 1982). Thus, at present, it is difficult to measure cognitive ability. From another perspective, there have been attempts to describe the interrelationships among IQ, chronological age (CA), and MA (Kappauf, 1973, 1976); however, more research is needed in this area. In essence, studies that reported that the linguistic competence of retarded subjects did not match their MAs should be interpreted with caution. It is possible that, theoretically, language development may be commensurate with cognitive ability but not with MA. The more important question here is whether the language development of mentally retarded students resembles that of the nonretarded population. The general conclusion that can be drawn from the representative sample of studies discussed is best illustrated by the following quotation (Ingalls, 1978):

> Mental retardation is on a continuum with normalcy, and where the line is drawn...is entirely arbitrary. Most retarded people do not differ qualitatively from nonretarded people. More importantly, there is a good deal of overlap in abilities. (p. 2)

Research Considerations

The relationship between language acquisition and mental retardation involves the consideration of a number of factors (e.g., etiology, the severity of the retardation, educational placement, and age). There has been little success, however, in finding consistent relationships among these variables (Kamhi & Johnston, 1982, Scott, 1978). For example, no evidence has been reported that suggests that instruction in a particular type of educational program (e.g., regular or self-contained classroom) is most conducive to academic achievement (Carney, 1979; Carter, 1975). Determining the cause of mental retardation may be important for research and educational purposes; however, it has been stated that 75% to 80% of retarded individuals suffer retardation of unknown causes, or rather, those attributed to the cultural or familial domain (Ingalls, 1978; Scott, 1978). In addition, debate is continuing as to whether certain retarded subjects afflicted with specific genetic defects (e.g., Down's syndrome) should be included with subjects with nongenetic-based retardation in the same study (Coggins, 1979; Kamhi & Johnston, 1982). There is some research suggesting that the language development of the former group may also be slower than—albeit similar to—that in the nonretarded population (Coggins, 1979).

As much as possible, the studies discussed here were investigations in which the subjects were classified as educable mentally-retarded or borderline, slow learners. Some of the studies, however, included students who were in the moderate range. In addition, an attempt was made to include studies involving subjects enrolled in educational programs in public schools. For the most part, these were students in regular or self-contained classes. A few of the earlier studies, however, contained students from special schools or training centers for retarded individuals. Finally, for illustrative purposes, one study was included that employed subjects afflicted with a specific genetic defect (i.e., Down's syndrome). This was reported owing to its relevant results and implications for further research. The data are presented and discussed in two sections: morphology and syntax, and semantics and pragmatics.

Morphology and Syntax

With respect to morphological development, a few studies employed an adaptation of Berko's (1958) test (Dever & Gardner, 1970; Lovell & Bradbury, 1967; Newfield & Schlanger, 1968). Similar to the findings for learning-disabled and deaf children, the acquisition of morphological structures in retarded children resembled that of younger, nonretarded children. The study by Newfield and Schlanger (1968) is illustrative.

Newfield and Schlanger selected 30 educable mentally-retarded (EMR) students from a residential school and 30 nonretarded students from an elementary school in the same district as the EMR subjects. The mental ages (based on IQ scores) of the EMR subjects ranged from 4 years 10 months to 8 years, with a mean of 6 years 2 months. No IQ scores were available for the nonretarded subjects; thus, MA was a covariate factor. The EMR subjects were older than the normal subjects. The mean CA of the EMR subjects was 10 years 4 months, whereas that of the nonretarded subjects was 6 years 10 months. Both groups had normal articulatory abilities.

The results indicated that the order of acquisition of the inflectional forms employed in morphological constructions was similar for both groups in nonsense word tasks and nearly similar in lexicon tasks. In general, the most regular and common forms were mastered initially with the more difficult forms mastered later. Statistically significant differences, however, were reported between the correct responses on the lexicon and nonsense word items for both groups. The differences between the scores on the two measures were greater for the retarded subjects. From this, it was hypothesized that there may be differences between the groups in the ability to generalize from familiar to new words. Newfield and Schlanger (1968) concluded that the retarded subjects learned the morphological forms in a manner comparable to the nonretarded subjects. Specifically, the retarded subjects proceeded at a slower rate, and their differences were quantitative not qualitative.

Lackner (1968) examined the development of grammatical structure in five mentally retarded children with mental ages ranging from 2 years 3 months to 8 years 10 months and in five nonretarded children with CAs ranging from 2 years 8 months to 5 years 9 months. He analyzed spontaneous language samples, which consisted of 1,000 utterances per subject. Lackner wrote transformational phrase-structure grammars describing the language of the retarded subjects. The development of grammar in each subject was investigated in relation to MA. In general, each retarded subject's grammar contained all structures delineated in an adult's grammar. Specifically, each subject's grammar could be considered a subset of the mature grammar. Thus, as MA increased, the phrase structure rules of the subjects became more differentiated, and the number of transformations increased. It was concluded that the language development of nonretarded and retarded children was not qualitatively different.

A number of investigations have examined retarded students' use of syntactic structures. Graham and Graham (1971) analyzed the language samples of nine subjects with CAs ranging from 10 years to 18 years and MAs from 3 years 3 months to 10 years. The IQ range was from 36 to 64. A total of 1,436 sentences were analyzed syntactically and the results were compared with those reported for nonretarded, normal children (Menyuk, 1969). Similar to Lackner's results, the findings showed that the use of transformations was related to the level of MA. The retarded subjects with lower MAs (i.e., lower half of the range) used primarily base structure rules and no application of transformational rules. The use of the more complex transformational rules was shown by subjects with high MAs (i.e., the upper half of the range). This development was noted to be similar to that of nonretarded children (Menyuk, 1969).

Analyses of errors revealed that the verbal aspect presented the greatest difficulties for most of the subjects. The following examples are illustrative:

> *Errors*
> I going
> They eating
> I been
> I got (for I've got)
> Cindy's go home Saturday
> She's eat

These errors have also been reported in the productions of LD, deaf, and some ESL students (see Table 9 in Chapter 7). Although the omission of the verbal aspect was the predominant type of error, the subjects did not generally experience problems with the auxiliary mode expansion. Modals were used appropriately even in question and negation constructions. In addition, it was found that the errors of the subjects decreased as MA increased. In sum, an increase of language competence with a concomitant decrease in errors was found to be related to the level of MA. From this, Graham and Graham concluded, as have others, that the syntactic development of retarded children proceeds at a different rate, but in a similar manner, as for nonretarded peers.

Naremore and Dever (1975) matched 30 EMR subjects with nonretarded subjects for MA levels from 6 years to 10 years. The IQs of the retarded subjects ranged from 74 to 84. Two five-minute speech samples were elicited from each subject and were analyzed in terms of syntactic and functional (e.g., fluency) variables. In general, for MAs 6 years to 9 years, the developmental trend of the syntactic variables was similar for both groups. At MA 10 years, however, the difference between the groups became apparent as the nonretarded group shifted toward the use of more complex sentences with clausal constructions. Naremore and Dever interpreted this to mean that substantial qualitative differences between the retarded and the nonretarded groups emerge at higher MA levels.

This interpretation should be treated with caution. As described by Leonard (1979) for language and learning-disabled children and by Quigley et al. (1976) for deaf children, it appears that some language-impaired populations rarely use certain complex syntactic structures (e.g., relative clauses) in either spoken or written productions. The absence of such constructions does not support the qualitative difference hypothesis. In fact, the paucity of data in this area precludes such an analysis. Quantitative reductions can be argued, and this is indicative of the difficulty of these syntactic structures, which may not be mastered even by the time a child finishes his or her formal education. In some instances, there seems to be a limit to the growth of specific structures (plateau effect) as shown by Quigley et al. (1976) for deaf children and by Wiig et al. (1977) for learning-disabled children.

A more recent study on syntactic development was conducted by McLeavey, Toomey, and Dempsey (1982). Two groups of nonretarded children and one group of retarded children served as subjects. One of the nonretarded groups was matched with the retarded group for MA (5 years) whereas the other group had a lower average MA (3 years). Nonverbal intelligence was assessed on the *Leiter International Performance Scale*. The mean IQ of the retarded group was 57.

An elicited imitation task was designed to evaluate syntactic ability. Eighteen structures were included with the selected transformations based on the work of several investigators, notably Menyuk (1969) and Lackner (1968). The subjects were instructed to repeat the sentences. On the total task, the results indicated that the nonretarded subjects of higher MA significantly outperformed the other two groups, whereas no significant difference was observed between the retarded and the lower MA nonretarded groups. In-depth analyses of the performances of the three groups on individual sentence types revealed a similar pattern. No significant differences were found between the retarded and the lower MA nonretarded groups, whereas the higher MA group outperformed the retarded group on the following sentence types: relative clause, conjunction *so*, preposition, auxiliary *have*, and *have got*.

The errors associated with the relative clause construction are illustrative of the performances of the retarded and lower MA subjects. For example, one test item was: "The baby who spilled the milk cried." The responses of these groups were indicative of an earlier form of this construction with no permutation reported for other young, normal children (e.g., "The baby spilled the milk who cried"). In addition, both groups produced responses in which the *who* element was omitted, the pronoun *he* was used redundantly, or the sentence was changed to a simpler version (e.g., "The baby spilled the milk and the baby cried"). Again, these errors have been observed in other young, normal children and in other language-impaired populations (e.g., deaf, learning-disabled, and ESL learners).

Several conclusions were stated by McLeavey et al. First, with respect to syntactic structures, the retarded children's performance was not commensurate with their MA level. The reader is reminded to interpret this assertion with caution since the interrelationships of IQ, MA, and cognitive ability are not clear. Second, and more importantly, the syntactic order of development was similar for the retarded and both normal groups. Finally, analyses of errors revealed that the strategies of the retarded children resembled those used by the lower MA group. McLeavey et al. concluded, as have others, that these findings support the hypothesis that the difference between nonretarded and retarded children in syntactic development is quantitative rather than qualitative in nature.

Semantics and Pragmatics

Duchan and Erickson (1976) examined nonretarded and retarded subjects' performances on a comprehension test in which four semantic relations were presented in three verbal contexts. The four semantic relations selected were those commonly reported to be present in the spoken language of young normal children (Bloom, 1970, 1973; Brown, 1973; Lucas, 1980): agent-action, action-object, possessive, and locative. The three verbal contexts were expanded, telegraphic, and nonsense (see the discussions in Bloom & Lahey, 1978, and Shipley, Smith, & Gleitman, 1969). Twelve nonretarded and 12 retarded children served as subjects. The IQs of the retarded subjects were not reported; however, they were selected from an educational program that served students with IQs from 50 to 80. In addition, the MLUs of this group ranged from 1.10 to 2.12 with a mean of 1.67, whereas those of the nonretarded group ranged from 1.05 to 2.15 with a mean of 1.56 (Brown, 1973). For this task, the subjects were required to manipulate various objects in response to verbal stimuli.

The results indicated that the performances of the groups from highest to lowest in the three verbal contexts were as follows: expanded, telegraphic, and nonsense. For the groups, no significant differences were found between the expanded and telegraphic contexts; however, a significant difference was observed between the expanded and nonsense contexts. In addition, the orders of difficulty of the semantic relations were reported to be similar for both groups. The order from easiest to most difficult was possessive, action-object, agent-action, and locative. It was noted that this order in comprehension was different from the order in production reported elsewhere: agent-action, action-object, possessive, and locative (Brown, 1973). Duchan and Erickson (1976) hypothesized that the discrepancy may be due to the task or to the abilities of the subjects. Finally, it is interesting to note that no significant, quantitative differences were found between the nonretarded and retarded subjects matched for MLUs.

Within a pragmatic framework, the functions of young, normal children's lexical usage have been investigated (Bates, 1976; Halliday, 1975). It seems that young children's single-word utterances are not solely aimed at labeling or informing the caregiver or listener of an object's name; rather, the goal is to attract or direct his or her attention. Greenfield and Smith (1976) have argued that the changing or informative element of a communicative situation is more likely to elicit a label than a redundant or unchanging aspect. The informative aspect is said to provide the most information. In addition, the ability to label this element is indicative of the level of presuppositional development in the child. Presuppositional awareness is the ability of the speaker to take into account the information level of his or her listener.

One of the first studies conducted on the informativeness of retarded children's lexical usage was that of Leonard, Cole, and Steckol (1979). Two experiments were performed. In the first, 12 preschool retarded children, aged 27 to 46 months, served as subjects, whereas 16 preschool retarded children, aged 27 to 42 months, were subjects for the second experiment. For both groups, the causes of retardation were unknown. The children's retardation was determined by their performance on the Mental Scale of the *Bayley Scales of Infant Development*, for which the scores ranged from the 14th to the 24th month level.

In the first experiment, three examples each of 18 objects (e.g., toy, telephone) were used. For the first condition, three examples of six objects were successively presented to each subject and the name of the object was requested on the third presentation. This naming represented an unchanging or redundant situation. The same procedure was followed for the second condition, except that the subjects were required to name the object on the first presentation. This represented the informative situation. For the third condition, the three examples were presented singly and randomly for a control situation. For all conditions, the results showed that, in general, the subjects' labels were appropriate and that they produced a significantly greater number of object labels in unfamiliar or informative situations than in familiar or redundant situations.

A similar pattern emerged from the second experiment. In an elicited imitation task with the same conditions as the first experiment, the subjects imitated a significantly greater number of lexical items in the informative situation than in the redundant one. Leonard et al. (1979) concluded that the labeling behavior of these retarded children reflected a level of presuppositional development that was essentially commensurate with that reported for younger normal children (Greenfield & Smith, 1976).

As discussed previously, the effects of etiology and degree of retardation on the learning of linguistic and subsequent reading skills are still open to debate (Kamhi & Johnston, 1982; Scott, 1978). It may be that an understanding of mental retardation is contingent on the establishment and investigation of homogeneous subgroups. It is obvious that generalizations of findings across dissimilar groups impedes the advancement of knowledge and, consequently, prevents the amelioration of academic problems. The following investigation serves as an example for future research. It is the only study discussed employing subjects whose retardation is genetically based.

Coggins (1979) examined development of early semantic functions in severely retarded children with Down's syndrome (i.e., mental retardation associated with chromosomal abnormality). The purpose was to determine if the relational meaning encoded in the two-word utterances (Stage I, Bowerman, 1975) of these children was similar to that of normal children in the early stages of their linguistic development. Four children with normal audition and vision and no evidence of maladaptive behavior served as subjects. In addition, these subjects had no prior institutionalization experience and were living at home. Language samples of 100 consecutive utterances from each subject were analyzed. Nine semantic categories, based on the work of Bloom (1970) and Brown (1973), were used to classify the subjects' utterances. The results indicated that these categories accounted for 88% of all two-word utterances. It was found that these retarded children expressed the same set of relational meanings as in normal children's early lexical development. Coggins's conclusion is obvious and has been expressed repeatedly in this chapter: Retarded children acquire language in a similar manner to nonretarded children but at a slower rate. More importantly, Coggins suggested that these data should be compared in children with different types and degrees of mental retardation to determine whether these findings are specific to this subgroup (i.e., those with Down's syndrome) or whether they can be generalized to other subgroups of retarded children.

The study by Kamhi and Johnston (1982) was one of the first to examine the syntactic and semantic abilities of normal, retarded, and language and learning-disabled children. It is discussed in depth here. Ten children of each group from the public school system, the preschool center, and the speech, language, and hearing centers served as subjects. The children in all three groups had normal hearing. The normal and retarded subjects were free from physiological speech and language defects. The normal and LD groups had average IQs. The LD (labeled language-impaired by the researchers) group was diagnosed by a speech-language pathologist as having a primary language disorder. This was supplemented by test scores indicating at least a 1 year delay on one or more standardized measures of expressive and receptive language (e.g., the *Carrow Elicited Language Inventory*, the *Northwestern Syntax Screening Test*, and the *Zimmerman Preschool Language Scale*). Subjects from the three groups were matched individually for MA based on their performances on the *Arthur Adaptation of the Leiter International Performance Scale*. The CAs of the LD and normal groups were the same, whereas the retarded subjects were older than the other two groups. Finally, the retarded subjects were enrolled in EMR classrooms, and their retardation was not genetically based.

One hundred language utterances of each subject were analyzed linguistically. The *Developmental Sentence Scoring* (DDS) procedure was employed to measure the use of syntactic and other grammatical markers. The assessment of semantics was based on the procedure established by Parisi and Antinucci (1976). Within this framework, the underlying propositional meaning of an utterance rather than its surface form is analyzed.

Comparing the normal and retarded groups, it was found that the retarded children produced significantly (1) fewer questions, (2) more sentences conjoined by *and*, and (3) more sentences in the progressive aspect. In addition, they used less complex structures than the normal group; however, the difference was not significant. On the contrary, the retarded and normal subjects produced constructions that were syntactically similar and expressed similar propositional relations. Neither group had difficulty with grammatical markers. Thus, in general, for MAs of five years, little difference existed between the retarded and normal groups.

The same was not true for the learning and language-impaired group. The performance of this group was inferior not only to that of the normal but also to that of the retarded group. The LD subjects had considerable difficulty with encoding grammatical markers in a correct manner. In addition, they produced sentences that were shorter in length and propositionally less complex than those produced by the other two groups. The performance of the LD group, however, was indicative of that of normal children at a younger mental age. Several conclusions were drawn by Kamhi and Johnston (1982). First, it was argued that the language of the LD group was quantitatively reduced but qualitatively similar to that of the other two groups. Unexpectedly, the development of language in this group was slower than that of the EMR group. It may be that either the LD or the EMR sample was not representative. No further explanation of this finding was proffered. Finally, Kamhi and Johnston argued that the few language differences that existed between the normal and EMR groups matched for MAs were probably due to deficient adaptive and motivational behaviors on the part of the latter group. In sum, they asserted that these deficient behaviors may account for the findings of previous studies demonstrating discrepancies between linguistic or reading achievement, or both, and MA levels of EMR children. Thus, as discussed previously, it appears that the levels of intelligence and adaptive behavior are important factors to consider in defining and understanding mental retardation.

Additional support for the developmental delay hypothesis can be found in a more recent study by Bilsky, Walker, and Sakales (1983). Twenty-four mildly retarded adolescents and 24 nonretarded fourth grade children served as subjects. The retarded children had a mean IQ of 62. Both samples were matched for MA. A list of 36 sentences was constructed, and the subjects were instructed to repeat each sentence after hearing it. Specific cues were given to prompt responses. As expected, the results indicated that the overall recall performance of the retarded adolescents was significantly inferior to that of the normal subjects. More importantly, based on the analyses of types of cues employed, additional results showed that both groups used similar inferential strategies during sentence comprehension.

Summary: Mental Retardation

Within the field of mental retardation, there is debate as to whether reading is a desirable and realistic goal for most retarded children (Carney, 1979; Gillespie & Johnson, 1974). Considering the abilities of these groups (Carney, 1979; Kamhi & Johnston, 1982; Robinson & Robinson, 1965), a number of investigators have argued that language and reading competency can be realistic goals. Reviews of the literature by several researchers revealed that most of these children are not reading on a level commensurate with their mental age capacity (Carney, 1979; Dunn, 1954; Welch, 1981). It has been argued that inadequate instructional practices (Carney, 1979) and deficient adaptive and motivational behaviors (Kamhi & Johnston, 1982) may account for these discrepancies.

Similar to the learning-disabled and the deaf student populations, the issue of quantitative versus qualitative differences has been debated intensely in the field of mental retardation (Kamhi, 1981; Zigler, 1969). Whether the performance of retarded subjects matched with nonretarded subjects for MAs is quantitatively similar is open to debate (McLeavey et al., 1982; Naremore & Dever, 1975). There is little disagreement, however, that the language development process of most retarded subjects is qualitatively similar to that of nonretarded children and proceeds at a slower rate (Kamhi, 1981; Kamhi & Johnston, 1982; Lackner, 1968); this has been found to be true for most of the retarded children who were in the borderline and mild ranges, with some in the moderate range. Whether these results can be generalized across the other ranges or whether they include students with specific genetic defects (e.g., Down's syndrome) should be clarified by further research (Coggins, 1979).

LEARNERS OF ENGLISH AS A SECOND LANGUAGE

Thus far, it has been argued that the development of language in two language-impaired populations is similar to but slower than that of the normal population. Data were presented demonstrating that these groups make errors and use learning strategies that, in general, resemble those of younger, normal children. The same has been reported also for deaf children and youth (Quigley & King, 1982a; Quigley et al., 1976). It can be hypothesized that the language acquisition process of most language-impaired populations proceeds through similar developmental stages as the normal population but at a delayed pace. The intent here is to discuss this issue with regard to the populations for whom English is a second language (ESL).

Any discussion of second language learning should consider the issues of bilingualism and other related concepts representing a set of complex phenomena that have only recently been investigated in an interdisciplinary manner (McLaughlin, 1982; Troike, 1981). One of the major goals of ESL and bilingual programs is to develop English literacy skills. There is still little agreement on the best instructional method for accomplishing this purpose. One of the most important issues in this field can be stated as a question: Is second language (L_2) learning similar to learning of the first language (L_1)? The development of instructional methodologies and materials is contingent on the response to this question. In addition, the answer should consider, at the least, the following issues: definition of second language learning and type of educational program.

Definitions

An acceptable operational definition of second language learning or bilingualism does not exist in the literature (Cordasco, 1978; Hornby, 1977; McLaughlin, 1982). This issue has been examined in numerous ways by psycholinguists and sociolinguists who generally argue that both linguistic and sociological criteria should be included. McLaughlin (1978, 1982) suggested that to differentiate bilingualism from second language learning requires a distinction between simultaneous and successive second language acquisition. In this view, simultaneous acquisition or bilingualism occurs if the child is exposed to two languages prior to the age of two years. After three years of age, the acquisition of the two languages is said to be successive (second language learning). McLaughlin cited research showing that children raised from birth with two languages did not differentiate them at age two years; however, differentiation was observed by the age of three years.

Lamendella (1977) distinguishes between bilingualism and second language (L_2) learning through the use of the following terminologies: primary language acquisition, secondary language acquisition, and foreign language learning. Primary language acquisition refers to the normal language learning process, which occurs between the ages of two and five years regardless of the number of languages involved and the manner in which they are introduced. Secondary language acquisition (i.e., two or more languages learned simultaneously or successively) occurs in a naturalistic setting after the primary period. Foreign language learning involves the learning of L_2 in a formal classroom environment and is considered to be cognitively different from secondary language acquisition. It should be borne in mind that the time period for primary language acquisition, as suggested by Lamendella, is open to question. This issue, known as the critical period hypothesis, has not been resolved (Krashen, 1973; Seliger, 1978).

A second aspect of the definitional issue is the degree of mastery or competence in each of the two languages. Essentially, this should be measured in both the comprehension and production modes. Second language learners are said to be competent in at least one language (L_1) prior to the learning of L_2 whereas bilinguals purportedly are competent in two languages. This distinction may be more apparent than real, especially for many elementary-age students in ESL and bilingual programs in the United States. Troike (1981) and McLaughlin (1982) argue that it is best to recognize that bilingualism or second language learning is not an all-or-nothing property, but an individual characteristic that may exist in varying degrees from minimal competency to complete mastery of more than one language.

Type of Educational Program

At present, the distinction between second language learners of English (ESL) and bilinguals (learning English) may not be important for placement in an ESL or bilingual educational program. It has been argued that both types of programs are (or should be) synonymous (Alatis, 1978). To be effective bilingual educational programs should include an ESL component that follows current linguistic thinking on the language acquisition process (Cordasco, 1978; Hornby, 1977; Troike, 1981). Similarly, ESL programs should employ instructional practices that consider the L_1 and culture of the students while promoting literacy in L_2 (Eddy, 1978; Gamez, 1979; Gonzales, 1981). Thus, the maintenance of the mother tongue and the development of literacy skills in the second language (e.g., English) are (or should be) common goals for both programs.

Similar to Lamendella's assertions (1977), Krashen (1978) contends that L_2 learning can occur in an environment that is conducive to either subconscious or conscious language acquisition. In subconcious language learning, the speakers are not concerned with the form and structure of their utterances but rather with the intent to communicate meaning. Rule learning and error correction are deemphasized and are not considered relevant to language acquisition. Contrariwise, the instruction in rules and the correction of errors are imperative in conscious language learning environments. These procedures aid the language learner in developing an appropriate mental model of linguistic generalizations of the target language. Approaches in the subconscious setting are analogous to the natural methods used in the education of deaf children (Groht, 1958; van Uden, 1977), whereas those of the conscious setting resemble the structural approaches (Anderson, Boren, Caniglia, Howard, & Krohn, 1980; Blackwell, Engen, Fischgrund, & Zarcadoolas, 1978). In general, L_2 acquisition in either approach is essentially similar to the L_1 acquisition of normal children. It is possible, however, that structural approaches are more likely to produce an order sequence different from the normal acquisition sequence owing to factors such as inappropriate teaching strategies or differences in motivation and attitude levels of the students (Fillmore, 1979; Krashen, 1978; Quigley & Paul, 1984a).

Does L_2 = L_1? Research on Adults

Using the *Bilingual Syntax Measure*, some researchers found that adolescents and adults acquired English morphemes in a similar manner regardless of linguistic background; however, this order did not resemble that observed in the L_1 acquisition of children (Bailey, Madden, & Krashen, 1974; Larsen-Freeman, 1975). Bailey et al. investigated the acquisitional sequence of eight English morphemes in 73 adult ESL subjects (ages 17 to 55 years) of varying language backgrounds and levels of ESL proficiency. The subjects were classified as Spanish or non-Spanish speaking. The non-Spanish group represented 11 different languages (Greek, Persian, Italian, Turkish, Japanese, Chinese, Thai, Afghan, Hebrew, Arabic, and Vietnamese). Correlational analyses were performed on the accurracy of use of the morphemes between the two groups and among eight instructional levels. The results revealed that the orders of acquisition of the English morphemes by the groups were similar regardless of language background or instructional level. In addition, it was found that the adult order was similar to the children's L_2 order reported by Dulay and Burt (1973, 1974a, 1974b). Thus, Bailey et al. concluded that the acquisition of morphemes was similar for L_2 learners regardless of language background or age. It should be noted that the L_2 morpheme order found by Bailey et al. and Dulay and Burt did not correspond to that reported by Brown (1973) or de Villiers and de Villiers (1973) for L_1 learners. Dulay and Burt argued that the differences were due to the cognitive and linguistic maturity of the subjects, who were older than the L_1 children in other studies. Thus, although English morphemic acquisition may be similar for most L_2 learners, it may not be similar to acquisition process in L_1 learners.

Similar results using different tests and different subsets of morphemes have been reported (e.g., for adults, Krashen, Sferlazza, Feldman, & Fathman, 1976; for children, Fathman, 1975). Contrariwise, several investigators have argued that the adult natural order is an artifact of the use of the test instrument (Hakuta & Cancino, 1977; Larsen-Freeman, 1975; Porter, 1977; Rosansky, 1976). Essentially, these researchers espoused the view that the order of acquisition is dependent on the nature of the first language. A response to this counterattack has been provided (e.g., see the discussions in Chun, 1980, and Krashen, 1978). Although the evidence favors a similar order of English morphemic acquisition for most L_2 learners, it is still possible, however, that the differences between adults' L_2 order and children's L_1 order may be due to the use of the test instrument. This issue is discussed later.

Research on the developmental sequence of certain syntactical constructions (e.g., negation, interrogation, complex types [eager to please, easy to please]) of L_2 learners generally support the contention that the developmental sequence is similar for most L_2 learners and that, in general, $L_2 = L_1$. Again the few studies that presented evidence to the contrary have argued that acquisition is heavily influenced by the characteristics of the individual, particularly the language background (Cancino, Rosansky, & Schumann, 1975; and the discussion in Fillmore, 1979). The more recent studies have lent support to the $L_2 = L_1$ hypothesis (Bongaerts, 1983; Cooper, Olshtain, Tucker, & Waterbury, 1979; d'Anglejan & Tucker, 1975); however, at least one study has shown that certain attributes of the native language of L_2 learners may have some effects on second language acquisition.

Bongaerts (1983), for example, investigated the comprehension of three complex English structures by Dutch subjects who were between 14 and 18 years of age. The complex structures were of the following types: (1) easy to see, eager to see, (2) promise, tell, and (3) ask, tell (Chomsky, 1969). In general, Dutch subjects performed similarly to the French Canadian subjects of d'Anglejan and Tucker (1975) and the Egyptian and Israeli subjects of Cooper et al. (1979). For instance, all groups had more difficulty interpreting sentences in which the surface subject and deep subject were not congruent. This is similar to the results of other language-impaired populations and to those of young children learning English as a first language (Chomsky, 1969). The only difference among the three groups was that the Dutch subjects experienced little difficulty with the "easy to see" construction. It was hypothesized that this structure was within the L_1 learning environment of Dutch speakers. Bongaerts favored the $L_2 = L_1$ hypothesis; however, he argued that L_2 learners do use their L_1 knowledge during the acquisition of the second language. The question of how much L_1 knowledge is used has yet to be answered.

Analyses of Errors

Additional support for the $L_2 = L_1$ in developmental sequence hypothesis has come from analyses of errors, particularly error or noncontrastive analyses (e.g., see the discussions in Richards, 1974c; Schachter & Celce-Murcia, 1977; Scott & Tucker, 1974). The other two systematic approaches to the problem of errors have been the use of contrastive analyses and the interlanguage concept. Sridhar (1980) briefly discussed the merits of all three approaches and concluded that each can and has contributed to the understanding of the process of second language learning and teaching. Other scholars agree (Altenberg & Vago, 1983; Schachter & Celce-Murcia, 1977).

In spite of the relative contributions of each approach, there are still contradictory results in the field of second language acquisition. These may be attributed to the complexity of the errors, to the limited knowledge of the processes involved in second language learning, and to variability in the following factors: type of teaching, age, attitude, and motivation of the student, and the influences of the first language on the target language (Lott, 1983). From another perspective, Richards (1974c) argues that contrastive analyses may be most predictive at the level of phonology and least predictive at the syntactic level. Furthermore, he argues that error analysis has been most predictive at the syntactic level. Although all approaches may be important, the following discussion is limited to contrastive and error analyses.

The finding that second language acquisition is different from that of the first has been explained, in part, by studies employing the contrastive analysis hypothesis. This hypothesis, consisting of weak and strong versions, was originally based on the notions of structural linguistics and behaviorism (Dulay & Burt, 1974c; Schachter & Celce-Murcia, 1977; Sridhar, 1980). Essentially, the assertion is that in learning a second language, the learner is inclined to use L_1 structures in his or her L_2 speech. Thus, when the structures of L_1 and L_2 differ, the learner produces errors. In general, this hypothesis assumes that deviations from the target language are mainly due to interference from the native language (i.e., interlingual errors). In this view, it should be possible to predict the occurrence of deviations by comparing the structures of the two languages. The influence of a native language (e.g., American Sign Language—ASL), or a communication system (e.g., Signing Exact English) on the development of English has often been considered one of the major causes of differences in the linguistic abilities of deaf children (Quigley & Kretschmer, 1982; Quigley & Paul, 1984a). It has generally been accepted, however, that the language development of most deaf children regardless of communication mode or age is qualitatively similar to that of normally hearing children. It is possible that research will focus on the influence of ASL on the later development of English literacy in bilingual and ESL settings (Quigley & Paul, 1984b).

The error analysis hypothesis states that the L_2 learners hypothesize about the target language in a manner similar to the L_1 learners. Although interlingual influences are considered, the emphasis is on intralingual errors and developmental strategies—e.g., overextensions (Richards, 1974a, 1974b, 1974c). It has been shown that the errors are similar for most L_2 learners regardless of language background. In addition, the L_2's errors resembled those produced by other language-impaired and normal populations acquiring the target language as a first language.

A recent study by Mukattash (1980) is illustrative for adult L_2 learners. Mukattash analyzed 6,000 yes-no question constructions by 600 first-year university, Arabic-speaking students. These students were instructed to transform 10 declarative sentences into yes-no questions. Results indicated that the largest percentage of errors involved the form of the verb (e.g., tense and aspect). For example:

Errors
Does he knew the answer?
Does he knows the answer?
Is Maha eating an apple when they came?

A number of errors were due to the substitution of *do* for *be* and vice versa. For example:

> BE *replacing* DO
> Is the girl know many languages?
> DO *replacing* BE
> Do(es)/did the house almost built?

Finally, there were redundant uses of either *do* or *be*. These are indicative of the phenomenon of overgeneralization or overextension.

> Redundant *be*: Is the house is almost built?
> Redundant *do*: Do(es)/did the house is almost built?

Based on these and other findings, Mukattash argued that none of the errors were due to interference of the native language. In essence, these were similar to those reported by others in Richards (1974b)—errors that appear regardless of the learner's language background. Finally, it was concluded that the errors were indicative of developmental strategies employed by young normal children learning English as a first language.

Does $L_2 = L_1$? Research on Children

Another major issue in the field of second language learning is whether there are differences between adults (or late adolescents) and children in second language acquisition. It has been argued that clarification of this issue varies with views on the critical period hypothesis (McLaughlin, 1982). Generally, the evidence has suggested that the differences between these groups are mainly in the rate and degree of language acquisition (see the discussions in Dulay & Burt, 1974c; Gaies, 1978; and McLaughlin, 1982). Furthermore, these differences are influenced largely by psychological and sociological factors (e.g., motivation, aptitude, interest, and attitude; Gardner & Lambert, 1972; McLaughlin, 1982). The bulk of the evidence favors the notions that L_2 learning is similar for both groups, and that it also resembles L_1 learning.

Like adolescent and adult L_2 learners, children's L_2 acquisitional sequence of certain syntactic structures corresponds to other children's L_1 syntactic development in the same language. Support for this assertion has come from cross-sectional and longitudinal studies. Ravem (1974a, 1974b) reported on the syntactic development of his son (age 6 years 6 months), and later of his daughter (about 4 years old) during the late 1960s. Norwegian was the native language for these children. For example, the *wh*-question acquisitional stages were similar to those reported by Brown (1973) for L_1 learners of English. Consider the following stages:

> *Base:* The boy will read the book tomorrow.
> *Sequence 1:* The boy will read the book when?

Sequence 2: When the boy will read the book?
Sequence 3: When will the boy read the book?

Prior to mastery (i.e., sequence 3), both children produced errors resembling those of Brown's subjects. For example:

What you eating?
What she is doing?
What that is?
What Jane give him?
What you want?

Briefly, these errors can be categorized into two areas: (1) absence of the auxiliary, and (2) failure to invert the auxiliary and subject. Ravem argued that these were developmental, not interference, errors since Norwegian requires inversion in the absence of modal auxiliaries (e.g., "What saying you?" for "What are you saying?").

Natalicio and Natalicio (1971) investigated the acquisition of English plurals by native Spanish children in grades 1, 2, 3, and 10. One hundred forty-four boys, half of whom were native Spanish speakers and half native English speakers, were selected as subjects. The researchers constructed a morphology test similar to that designed by Berko (1958). The results revealed that both groups acquired the /s/ and /z/ plural allomorphs prior to the /iz/. It was also found that the native Spanish speakers produced fewer correct responses than the native English speakers. More importantly, it was concluded that the similar orders of acquisition indicated that Spanish L_1 structures were not transferred to English L_2 speech.

Dulay and Burt (1973) performed two analyses on children's second language acquisition of morphological and syntactic structures. First, they analyzed the errors in elicited speech samples of 145 Spanish-speaking subjects, ages 5 years to 8 years, learning English as a second language. Using the *Bilingual Syntax Measure*, Dulay and Burt investigated the errors produced by these children in six syntactic structures that were different in Spanish and English. These errors were classified into one of three areas: (1) developmental (i.e., those similar to L_1 acquisition); (2) interference (i.e., those reflecting Spanish structure); and (3) unique (i.e., those that could not be classified into one of the two other areas). The results showed that most of the L_2 syntactic errors in English resembled those produced by children learning English as a first language. Similar findings were reported from another study in which Dulay and Burt (1974b) analyzed 513 elicited utterances from 179 Spanish-speaking children, ages 5 to 8 years. In this study, developmental strategies (L_1) accounted for 87.1% of the errors, whereas interference accounted for only 4.7%. Consequently, Dulay and Burt argued for a creative construction hypothesis, which states that L_2 learners are as creative as L_1 learners. In addition, they argued that L_2 errors are indicative of the use of universal language processing strategies described in the research on first language acquisition. For example, both L_1 and L_2 learners have been reported to rely on word order of the target language to express semantic relations.

For the second analysis of the 1973 study, Dulay and Burt examined the order and degree of acquisition of eight morphemes (Brown, 1973). Again, using the *Bilingual Syntax Measure*, speech samples of 151 Spanish-speaking subjects, ages 5 to 8 years, were elicited and analyzed. The subjects exhibited different levels of proficiency in English. The order and degree of English morphemic acquisition were found to be similar for the subjects. As indicated earlier, this order was different from that found in L_1 acquisition of children. Thus, again, on a morphemic level, it may be that L_2 is not similar to L_1.

These results were substantiated by a subsequent investigation. Dulay and Burt (1974a) studied the acquisitional sequence of 11 English morphemes in 55 Chinese and 60 Spanish children, ages 6 years to 8 years. An expanded version of the *Bilingual Syntax Measure* was employed in eliciting speech samples. Similar orders of acquisition were observed for both groups. These orders, however, were not compared with those of L_1 acquisition.

Strong evidence for the $L_2 = L_1$ hypothesis on a syntactic level may be found in more recent studies (Gillis & Weber, 1976; Milon, 1974). Milon (1974) examined the acquisition of negation structures in English by a seven year old Japanese boy. A marked similarity was found between the developmental stages reported and those described by Klima and Bellugi (1966). Gillis and Weber (1976) also studied the acquisition of certain syntactic structures (e.g., negation, interrogative, and imperatives) by two Japanese boys, ages 6 years 11 months and 7 years 6 months. The free speech of the subjects was analyzed for five months. Again, the results indicated similarities in developmental stages between these subjects and those observed for L_1 learners (Klima & Bellugi, 1966). Finally, in both studies, it was concluded that there was no substantial evidence of interference from the native language of the subjects.

A similar pattern of findings and conclusions has been reported in recent reviews by Chun (1980), Felix (1981), and Hatch (1978). Similar developmental stages for English morphological and syntactic constructions has been observed for most L_2 learners regardless of linguistic background, age, and amount of exposure to English. The evidence for $L_2 = L_1$ is strongest for the acquisition of specific syntactic structures, whereas that for the acquisition of morphemes is equivocal. It has been suggested previously that the discrepancy may be attributable to the nature of the test employed. For example, using Berko's test (1958), Natalicio and Natalicio (1971) found support for the $L_2 = L_1$ hypothesis. Similar findings have been obtained with this instrument for other language-impaired populations learning English as a first language (e.g., learning or language-disabled, mentally-retarded, and deaf students). Conflicting results were reported by Dulay and Burt (1973) for L_2 children and by Bailey et al. (1974) for L_2 adults using the

Bilingual Syntax Measure. Whether the differences are artifacts of these test instruments needs to be investigated further.

Reading and Second Language Learning

It is well accepted that instruction in English reading should not begin until the second language or bilingual student can comprehend the syntactic and semantic variables in English texts (Gonzales, 1981). Although the importance of initiating reading instruction in the child's strongest language may be generally agreed upon (Gamez, 1979; Modiano, 1968; Troike, 1981), it is not clear when the shift to English reading instruction should be made. This issue is of utmost importance in considering the establishment of bilingual or ESL programs for deaf students, for whom ASL may be a first or native language (Quigley & Paul, 1984b). The problem is even more complex for some deaf students since ASL does not, at present, have a widely accepted written component.

The research reported here demonstrated that, in general, the English language skills of most L_2 learners develop in a creative, sequential manner that resembles that of children learning English as a first language. It has been established that effective bilingual and ESL programs nurture the development of the culture and native language of the students. This, in turn, aids the acquisition of L_2 skills that are prerequisites for the development of L_2 reading. Thus, language improvement should be an integral aspect of reading instruction on all levels, particularly for ESL and bilingual students. As indicated throughout this chapter, instruction in language or reading should follow the developmental patterns of young, normal L_1 learners.

Summary: Second Language Learning

In describing second language learning, the issues of bilingualism and other related concepts were discussed. Within this perspective, definitions and types of educational programs were considered. It was stated that no widely accepted definitions of second language acquisition or bilingualism exist although several models have beem proposed (Hornby, 1977; Krashen, 1978; Lamendella, 1977; McLaughlin, 1982). Generally, it is best to recognize that such definitions are not all-or-nothing phenomena. Competence in one or two languages may range from minimal to complete mastery (McLaughlin, 1982; Troike, 1981).

Owing to definitional issues and wide ranges of abilities, it may be difficult or impractical to make a distinction between students in ESL and those in bilingual education programs. In addition, there may be little difference between these types of programs (Alatis, 1978). Specifically, the main goal of both should be to develop English literacy skills. This purpose cannot be accomplished without the consideration of the first language and culture of the students (Eddy, 1978; Gonzales, 1981; Troike, 1981). At present, there is no instructional methodology that has been generally accepted. As with other language-impaired and nonimpaired populations, both natural and structural approaches have been employed (Krashen, 1978).

One of the most important issues in the field of second language acquisition can be stated as a question: Is L_2 development similar to L_1? The major focus has been on the qualitative aspect of this question although the quantitative aspect is not dismissed as unimportant. Most of the research has concentrated on the morphological and syntactic development of adults and children as second language learners (Felix, 1981; Hatch, 1978). The data on analyses of errors were presented with reference to two perspectives: contrastive and error (noncontrastive) analyses.

The hypothesis that L_2 does not resemble L_1 received its strongest support from the data on morphemic acquisition assessed by the *Bilingual Syntax Measure*. Contradictory results have been reported when Berko's morphology test (1958) was employed (Natalicio & Natalicio, 1971). It has been suggested that this discrepancy may be related to the nature of the test instruments. Thus, although the acquisitional sequence of certain English morphemes has been reported to be similar *for* most L_2 learners regardless of language background, age, or level of proficiency in English, it is still not clear whether this sequence is similar *to* that of L_1 learners.

Additional support that L_2 does not resemble L_1 has come from data on contrastive analyses (e.g., see the discussions in Dulay & Burt, 1974c, and Richards, 1974c). This type of analysis has been claimed to be most predictive on the morphemic level. In this view, the errors of the language learners varies proportionately with the differences between the native and target language (Schachter & Celce-Murcia, 1977; Sridhar, 1980). Thus, the production of errors is due to the interference of the native language. The contrastive hypothesis asserts that by analyzing the differences between the two languages, it should be possible to predict errors.

The bulk of the evidence in second language learning supports the hypothesis that L_2 resembles L_1. Most of the data have come from studies reporting the acquisitional sequence of specific syntactic structures and from those employing error analyses (Chun, 1980; Felix, 1981; Hatch, 1978; McLaughlin, 1982). Similar orders of acquisition were found for most L_2 students, and these orders also resembled those observed in young L_1 children. In essence, most of the errors were labeled developmental, not interference, and were considered to be indicative of universal linguistic processing strategies.

With respect to reading and second language learning, one of the major issues has been the stage at which reading should be introduced in the second language, specifically of reading English (Gonzales, 1981). At the least, the bilingual or ESL student should not begin to read until he or she has a working knowledge of the syntactic and semantic factors in English usage. Since reading is considered a part of the overall language comprehension process, the continual development of language is indispensable to good reading development. For bilingual and L₂ students, this involves also the continual development of the first or native language (Alatis, 1978; Eddy, 1978; Troike, 1981).

In sum, the manner in which English literacy skills should be taught has been a major concern of educators in ESL and bilingual programs. As stated repeatedly, this has also been the case for educators of other language-impaired populations discussed in this chapter, namely, those with learning disability, mental retardation, and deafness. Most of the data support the contention that the language development of these groups is qualitatively similar to—albeit quantitatively slower than—that of the nonimpaired, normal population. From this, it is generally concluded that instructional practices and the construction of special materials for teaching language and reading skills should adhere to the developmental stages of the normal acquisitional process.

Appendix A

An Outline

SUGGESTED PROCEDURES FOR PREPARING READING MATERIALS

The topics addressed herein include (1) guiding principles for preparation of materials, (2) a diagram of steps in preparing materials (an overview), (3) an explanation of specific processes involved in the steps of writing, and (4) resources that provide detailed guidance on the writing process.

Guiding Principles

I: Adaptations and original texts are most successful when the writer functions as a conscientious author whose major goal is to produce text that is "considerate" of the readers' needs and interests. The writer must balance the need for appropriate levels of linguistic and conceptual complexity and the need for a meaningful, coherent, and cohesive message. He or she must consider (1) the goals for the lesson in which the text will be used, (2) the specific tasks that will be used to measure comprehension (e.g., questions, free recall), (3) the content to be covered, (4) the reading and language skills of the students for whom the text was prepared, and (5) the interests and backgrounds of these students.

II: Effective writing skills and an in-depth knowledge of reading and language are essential for writers of children's materials. Writers must also have a thorough understanding of the complexities of and interrelations of the various factors that contribute to text difficulty.

Steps in Preparing Reading Materials

An Overview

Writing is a complex process. In practice, the writing steps identified herein, and specific tasks within the steps, will interact and influence each other. Simplified, linear progressions are shown in the diagram and description of steps in this document. Remember, however, that the actual writing process will not follow a linear progression through the steps.

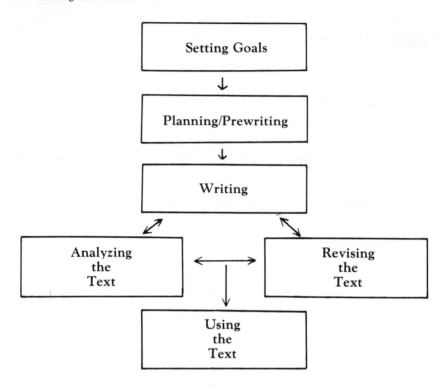

A Diagram: The Writing Process

The Process

Setting Goals

1. *Determine (a) the purpose for which you are preparing the materials, and (b) the specific tasks the reader will perform in using the materials.*

   Set realistic goals that are sufficiently narrow.

   Consider the following task-based and situation-based variables:

   - Instructional goals that focus on the development of: reading strategies; language; reading skills; thinking skills (e.g., synthesis or analysis); conceptual information; aesthetic, cultural, and moral values; socialization skills; reading as a life-long habit
   - Instructional goals that focus on different types of reading: "learning to read," pleasure reading, "reading to learn" (skimming, scanning, and studying)
   - The form in which reading will occur (oral or silent)
   - Tasks which the reader will perform (e.g., answering questions, free recall, exchanging "have I got a great book for you" experiences)
   - Level of comprehension required (e.g., getting the gist, understanding the details, analysis of content, evaluation of content)

2. *Identify the characteristics of the students for whom you are writing (i.e., your audience).*

   Consider the following reader-based variables:

   Language abilities, cognitive abilities, existing background experience, familiarity with content, cultural values, interest, motivation (self- and teacher-generated), learning styles.

Planning-Prewriting

The planning or prewriting step is the most important step in the writing process. Spend sufficient time with the following activities before starting to write.

3. *Determine the level of difficulty you wish the materials to have in relation to the students' current level of functioning (easy, on-level, challenging).*

   For original texts, consider the readers' characteristics and the characteristics of the reading task.

   For adapted texts, consider the reader, the reading task, and the current level of difficulty in the materials you wish to revise.

4. *Develop a conceptual outline for your text. Determine the relative importance of the ideas you want to present in the text. Make tentative decisions about organizational structure.*

   You may want to use a story grammar or discourse structure frame (e.g., comparison-contrast) in this process (see Table 3 and Figure 1 in this book).

   For adapted texts, rank order the concepts in the unadapted text in terms of importance.

5. *Identify the text-based variables which you want to control or sequence in your text to meet your instructional goals and the needs of your audience. Rank these in order of importance.*

   Consider the following:

   Vocabulary, figurative language, syntax, discourse structures, cohesion and redundancy, time sequencing (e.g., flashbacks), background experience required, inferential skills, format considerations

6. *Determine the criteria you will use in controlling or sequencing the text's difficulty (e.g., vocabulary word lists, levels of syntactic complexity, levels of inferential demand). Select resources to aid you in controlling the text aspects you've chosen.*

   Refer to Chapter 6 and the list at the end of this Appendix for suggested resources. During the writing phrase, *do not* use readability formulas or other quantitative measures designed to estimate text difficulty.

7. *For adapted texts (only), construct a list of all "difficult" aspects of the text that you think might negatively influence students' comprehension. Determine which of these you want to change and which you may leave in for exposure purposes.*

   Identification of difficult aspects of texts is usually dependent on the writer's knowledge of language and reading and his or her experiences with teaching reading. Refer to the linguistic analyses cited in Chapter 5 for help in developing skills in analyzing texts (also see the references listed at the end of this Appendix). You may also want to use the original text with a small group of students to obtain first-hand knowledge of aspects that cause difficulty.

8. *Tentatively identify any specific writing techniques you will use to make your text more comprehensible. Determine the format you will use for the materials.*

Examples of writing techniques include: textual aids such as pictures, headings, and tables; literary techniques (flashbacks, standard opening lines [Once upon a time, . . .]); directive contexts for learning words in context (see Chapter 5 and the resources cited there).

Questions to consider in relation to the format include: How will you present the text? Will you use book format? Chart paper? Regular paper? Non-print media?

How will the physical layout of the text be arranged? Where will you place any pictures or textual aids you choose to include? What type of orthography (e.g., print, handwriting, sign print) will you use? Do you want page breaks to occur at specific places within the text and will line breaks be important? (Consult the research base provided in Chapter 5)

9. *Make some tentative decisions about the balance you wish to achieve between form and meaning.*

Remember that the relative importance of form and meaning will fluctuate within various parts of a text. In revising a text, for example, the writer might decide to remove a passive sentence within one paragraph because the potential for student misinterpretation is high, yet leave one in a subsequent paragraph because the potential for misinterpretation was low.

Writing

Writing, analyzing, and revising are recursive processes that interact and influence one another. Each is treated here separately, but readers should remember that they are not separate processes.

10. *During the writing process, remember to balance attention to meaning and form. Keep the goal of "cohesive, comprehensible, and appropriate materials" firmly in mind. Attempt to provide situations in the text in which students will need to apply the reading strategies and skills you have identified as instructional goals.*

An example: One instructional goal might be to teach students to comprehend anaphoric devices in texts (see the example on page 90 in Chapter 4). An author might design a text in which specific anaphoric devices are used repeatedly.

11. *Prepare the first (or second, third, or later) draft of your text.*

In your writing, use the resources you prepared in the first two steps—e.g., lesson objectives, knowledge of readers' skills and needs, outline of conceptual development, guidelines for linguistic and format features, and the level of difficulty you are trying to achieve.

For adapted texts, you may select one of two general approaches to rewriting: (1) put away the original text and use only your list of propositions (concepts from the original) in reconstructing the text, or (2) use both the original text and the list of prioritized propositions to aid in the rewriting process. (*Note:* Although the second approach is useful in maintaining a strong relationship between the original and adapted text, use of the original text during the rewriting process may lead the adaptor to a word level or sentence level reconstruction.) Remember that the degree of relationship between an original and adapted text can vary–you do not need to include all concepts from the original in your text.

12. *Have other people read drafts of your text to see if anything is "fuzzy" or incomprehensible.*

    It may be useful to have both adults and children read the draft. (*Note:* The exposure your students get to adult models who write and revise their work is an added benefit of preparing your own texts.)

Analyzing the Text

During the writing process, an author is constantly analyzing and revising the text. Such analysis is an integral part of the writing process. More formal analysis, in which authors explicitly compare their writing goals with the actual text, is discussed here.

13. *Compare your text with the instructional goals you established during the first two steps. Also compare the text against the guidelines you selected for controlling text-based variables.*

    Examples of this process include (a) the comparison of the vocabulary in the text with the Dale List of 3000 Common Words, (b) the comparison of syntactic controls in the text with the three levels of syntactic complexity identified by the Captioning Center, and (c) comparison of the inferential demand of the text with the levels of inferences listed by Wilson in the captioning guide.

14. *(Optional) Apply one or more of the tools that provide quantified measures of text difficulty to your text.*

    See Chapter 6 for examples.

Revising the Text

Revision is an integral part of the writing phase. Detailed discussions of revision techniques can be found in many of the resources provided at the end of this Appendix. Such discussions require copious examples and explanations, and space limitations do not permit their inclusion here. The revision steps outlined here simply are the final steps in the writing-analyzing-revising process.

15. *Make revisions in the text as you receive feedback from the others who have read it and from the analyses you perform.*

16. *Determine the final format for your text and prepare a copy of the material as it will be presented to the students.*

Using the Text

17. *Prepare the final lesson plans for the text you have prepared (based on the instructional goals set in step one).*

18. *Use the text with students. Evaluate the text in terms of how well you provided a match between the students, the text, and the instructional goals.*

    For adapted texts, three strategies for using original and adapted materials can be identified: (1) use the adapted text only, (2) use both the original and adapted texts, and (3) allow students to self-monitor their use of the adapted text (i.e., working on the students' own comprehension-monitoring abilities). These uses are complementary; selection should be based on the specific goals of the lesson.

19. *After the initial use of the text, modify the text, your teaching strategies, and the reading tasks associated with text on the basis of student responses. You may also want to revise the text to use it for another purpose or for another group of students with different abilities and interests.*

Resources

The following types of resources are helpful in developing the knowledge base and skills needed to become an effective writer: (1) texts on writing for children, (2) texts on preparing materials for deaf children, (3) texts on adapting materials, (4) texts that critically review existing materials, (5) texts on general writing, (6) texts on linguistic features of language, and (7) texts on the development of reading and language.

Many references to such resources are provided elsewhere in this text (see Chapters 5 and 6 and Appendix B). Some additional resources are provided here. References cited in the text and Appendix B are not repeated here.

Applebee, A. (1978). *The child's concept of story: Ages two to seventeen.* Chicago: University of Chicago Press.

Bettelheim, B. (1976). *The uses of enchantment. The meaning and importance of fairy tales.* New York: Alfred A. Knopf.

Dintenfass, P., & Dintenfass, M. (1967). *How to adapt and use reading materials.* Nairobi: Oxford University Press.

Duffy, T., & Waller, R. (Eds.). (in press). *Designing usable texts.* New York: Academic Press.

Flesch, R. (1979). *How to write plain English.* New York: Barnes and Noble.

Green, G. (1984). On the appropriateness of adaptations in primary-level basal readers: Reaction to remarks by Bertram Bruce. In R. Anderson, J. Osborn, & R. Tierney (Eds.), *Learning to read in American schools: Basal readers and content texts* (pp. 175–191). Hillsdale, NJ: Lawrence Erlbaum Associates.

Halliday, M., & Hasan, R. (1976). *Cohesion in English*. London: Longman.

Karl, E. (Ed.) (1981). *Advances in content analysis*. Beverly Hills, CA: Sage Publications.

Kerr, S. (1981). How teachers design their materials: Implications for instructional design. *Instructional Science, 10*, 363–378.

Klare, G. (1975). *A manual for readable writing*. Glen Burnie, MD: REM Company.

Langer, J., & Smith-Burke, M. T. (1982). *Reader meets author/Bridging the gap*. Newark, DE: International Reading Association.

Leech, G., & Svartvik, J. (1975). *A communicative grammar of English*. London: Longman.

Madsen, H., & Bowen, J. (1978). *Adaptation in language learning*. Rowley, MA: Newbury House Publishers.

Omanson, R. (1982). An analysis of narratives: Identifying central, supportive, and distracting content. *Discourse Processes, 5*, 195–224.

Osborn, J. (1984). Purposes, uses, and contents of workbooks. In R. Anderson, J. Osborn, & R. Tierney (Eds.), *Learning to read in American schools: Basal readers and content texts* (pp. 45–111). Hillsdale, NJ: Lawrence Erlbaum Associates.

Quirk, R., Greenbaum, S., Leech, G., & Svartvik, J. (1972). *A grammar of contemporary English*. London: Longman.

Steinberg, C., & Bruce, B. (1980). *Higher-level features in children's stories; Rhetorical structures and conflict* (Reading Education Report No. 18). Urbana, IL: University of Illinois, Center for the Study of Reading.

Tannen, D. (Ed.) (1982). *Analyzing discourse: Text and task. Georgetown University Roundtable on Language and Linguistics*. Washington, DC: Georgetown University Press.

Willows, D., Borwick, D., & Hayvren, M. (1981). The content of school readers. In G. MacKinnon & T. Waller (Eds.), *Reading research: Advances in theory and practice* (pp. 97–175). New York: Academic Press.

Appendix B

Suggested Methods for Teaching Reading to Deaf Children
A Selected Bibliography

GENERAL REFERENCES

Alberta Department of Education. (1982). *The hearing-impaired student in the regular classroom*. Edmonton, Canada: Alberta Department of Education. (ERIC Document Reproduction Service No. ED 231 130)

Allabough, B. (1893). Reading as an aid to language-teaching. *American Annals of the Deaf, 38*, 118–124.

Anderson, N., & Laird, R. (1972). Teaching the deaf child to read. *Audiovisual Instruction, 17*, 19–20.

Athey, I. (1978). Language, reading, and the deaf. *Proceedings of the Gallaudet conference on reading in relation to deafness* (pp. 260–297). Washington, DC: Gallaudet College.

Bannon, J., Davis, S., Lobb, N., Graham, M., & Shetler, K. (1982). Four components in a reading project. *1980's schools . . . Portals to century 21: Selected papers: Convention of American Instructors of the Deaf 49th biennial meeting* (pp. 230–240). Silver Spring, MD: Convention of American Instructors of the Deaf.

Bateman, L., & LeRoy, R. (1980). Myths dissolved and mysteries solved: Hearing-impaired students in the college classroom. In L. Johnson (Ed.), *Reading and the adult learner* (pp. 69–76). Newark, DE: International Reading Association.

Bell, A. (1891). Reading before writing. *American Annals of the Deaf, 36*, 141–142.

Bell, A. (1929). On reading as a means of teaching language to the deaf. *Volta Review, 31*, 191–195.

Blackwell, P., Engen, E., Fischgrund, J., & Zarcadoolas, C. (1978). Chapters 3, 4, 5, 6, 7, and 8: The role of reading and literature in the curriculum. *Sentences and other systems: A language and learning curriculum for hearing-impaired children*. Washington, DC: Alexander Graham Bell Association for the Deaf.

Blanton, W. (1973). The management of reading instruction. *The report of the proceedings of the 46th Meeting of the Convention of American Instructors of the Deaf* (pp. 24–29, 53–54). Silver Spring, MD: Convention of American Instructors of the Deaf.

Bockmiller, P. (1981). Hearing-impaired children: Learning to read a second language. *American Annals of the Deaf, 126,* 810–813.

Brooks, P. (1978). Some speculations concerning deafness and learning to read. In L.S. Liben (Ed.), *Deaf children: Developmental perspectives* (pp. 87–101). New York: Academic Press.

Browns, F. (1979). Beginning reading instruction with hearing-impaired children. *Volta Review, 81,* 100–108.

Bryans, B. (1979). Breaking the sentence barrier in language and reading instruction. *Volta Review, 81,* 421–430.

Buell, E. (1915). Reading for the deaf. *American Annals of the Deaf, 60,* 1–5.

Caroll, D. (1875). Teaching deaf-mutes to read. *American Annals of the Deaf, 20,* 228–229.

Clark, R., & Sewell, D. (1979). Some comments on Gormley and Franzen. *American Annals of the Deaf, 124,* 847–848.

Clark, T. (1970). Language and reading in the educational process of the hard of hearing child (pp. 331–348). In F. Berg & S. Fletcher (Eds.), *The hard of hearing child.* New York: Grune and Stratton.

Clarke, B., Rogers, W., & Booth, J. (1982). How hearing-impaired children learn to read: Theoretical and practical issues, *Volta Review, 84,* 57–69.

Cole, N., Berliner, C., Hurry, S., & Seet, J. (1977). *Deaf children and readiness for beginning reading.* Indianapolis, IN: Project Literacy, Indiana School for the Deaf.

Cole, N., Berliner, C., Hurry, S., Seet, J., & Ursiny, K. (1977). Project literacy (on language development). *Teaching English to the Deaf, 4*(1), 15–17.

Conrad, R. (1979). Chapter 6: Deafness and reading. *The deaf school child* (pp. 140–174). London: Harper and Row.

Costello, M. (1971). The various aspects of growth in reading on a primary level. *The report of the proceedings of the 46th meeting of the Convention of American Instructors of the Deaf* (pp. 199–205). Washington, DC: Convention of American Instructors of the Deaf.

Crandall, K. (1978). Reading and writing skills and the deaf adolescent. *Volta Review, 80,* 319–332.

Daniels, M. (1983). Integrating reading, English grammar, and composition into the English curriculum. *Directions, 3*(4), 16–20.

Ewoldt, C. (1978). Reading for the hearing or hearing impaired, a single process. *American Annals of the Deaf, 123,* 945–948.

Ewoldt, C. (1981a). A descriptive analysis of reading behavior exhibited by one hearing-impaired child. *Directions, 2,* 55–56.

Ewoldt, C. (1981b). Factors which enable deaf readers to get meaning from print. In S. Hudelson (Ed.), *Learning to read in different languages* (pp. 45–132). Washington, DC: Center for applied Linguistics.

Ewoldt, C. (1982). New techniques for research and evaluation in the reading of the deaf. *1980's schools . . . Portals to century 21: Selected papers: Convention of American*

Instructors of the Deaf 49th biennial meeting (pp. 240–246). Silver Spring, MD: Convention of American Instructors of the Deaf.

Fitzgibbon, C. (1973). The young teen-age deaf and reading. *The report of the proceedings of the 46th meeting of the Convention of American Instructors of the Deaf*, (pp. 239–243). Silver Springs, MD: Convention of American Instructors of the Deaf.

Gates, A. (1926). Methods and theories of teaching reading tested by studies of deaf children. *Journal of Educational Research*, *14*, 21–32.

Gates, A., & Chase, E. (1976). Methods and theories of learning to spell tested by studies of deaf children. *Visible Language*, *10*, 339–350.

Geoffrion, L. (1980). Reading without sound: An instructional model for teaching reading to non-oral deaf children. *Proceedings of the Gallaudet conference on reading in relation to deafness* (pp. 245–259). Washington, DC: Gallaudet College.

Geoffrion, L., & Athey, I. (1980). Post-conference reflections. *Proceedings of the Gallaudet conference on reading in relation to deafness* (pp. 303–311). Washington, DC: Gallaudet College.

Geoffrion, L., & Schuster, K. (1980). *Auditory handicaps and reading: An annotated bibliography*. Newark, DE: International Reading Association.

Gibson, E., & Levine, H. (1975). How well do deaf children learn to read? *Psychology of reading* (pp. 501–504). Cambridge, MA: MIT Press.

Gonzales, B. (1971). *The introduction of reading to pre-school hearing-impaired children*. Unpublished doctoral dissertation, University of Tennessee, Knoxville.

Gormley, K., & Franzen, A. (1978). Why can't the deaf read? Comments on asking the wrong question. *American Annals of the Deaf*, *123*, 542–547.

Groht, M. (1955). Some thoughts on reading. *Volta Review*, *57*, 294–296.

Hammermeister, F., & Israelite, N. (1983). Reading instruction for the hearing-impaired: An integrated language arts approach. *Volta Review*, *85*, 136–148.

Hamp, N. (1972). Reading attainment and some assorted factors in deaf and partially hearing children. *Teacher of the Deaf*, *70*, 203–215.

Hargis, C. (1982). *Teaching reading to handicapped children*. Denver, CO: Love Publishing Company.

Harrison, T.A. (1979). Thoughts on teaching reading. *Teacher of the Deaf*, *3*, 74–75.

Hart, B. (1962). *Teaching reading to deaf children*. Washington, DC: Alexander Graham Bell Association for the Deaf.

Hart, B. (1967). Language and reading: Similar or identical twins? *Proceedings of the International Conference on Oral Education of the Deaf* (Vol. 2, pp. 1490–1503). Washington, DC: Alexander Graham Bell Association for the Deaf.

Hart, B. (1975). Learning to read begins at birth. *Volta Review*, *77*, 168–172.

Hart, B. (1978). *Teaching reading to deaf children*. Washington, DC: Alexander Graham Bell Association for the Deaf.

Hasenstab, M., & Laughton, J. (1982). *Reading, writing, and the exceptional child: A psycho-socio-linguistic approach*. Rockville, MD: Aspen Systems Corporation.

Henderson, J. (1976). Learning to read: A case study of a deaf child. *American Annals of the Deaf*, *121*, 502–506.

Hill, W. (1920). Reading and language development. *Volta Review*, *22*, 298–301.

Howes, E. (1928). Teaching young deaf children to read. *Volta Review, 30,* 19–20.

Jenson, P. (1967). Some applications of linguistics to teaching reading to the deaf. *The report of the proceedings of the 43rd meeting of Convention of American Instructors of the Deaf* (pp. 362–368). Washington, DC: Convention of American Instructors of the Deaf.

Kennedy, E. (1959). Teaching the deaf child to read. *American Annals of the Deaf, 104,* 372–382.

Kluwin, T. (1979). A path analytic model of the relationship of written production of English and reading abilities of hearing-impaired adolescents. *Teaching English to the Deaf, 6,* 15–21.

Knight, D. L. (1982). *Narrative schemata in hearing-impaired readers.* Unpublished doctoral dissertation, Catholic University of America.

Kopp, H. (1963). Silent reading for the deaf. *The report of the proceedings of the 41st meeting of the Convention of American Instructors of the Deaf* (pp. 527–535). Washington, DC: Convention of American Instructors of the Deaf.

Kretschmer, R.E. (1982). Reading and the hearing-impaired individual: Summation and application. *Volta Review, 84,* 107–122.

Kyle, J. (1980). Reading development of deaf children. *Journal of Research in Reading, 3,* 86–97.

Lenneberg, E. (1967). Prerequisites for language acquisition. *Proceedings of the International Conference on Oral Education of the Deaf* (pp. 1302–1362). Washington, DC: Alexander Graham Bell Association for the Deaf.

Lieding, R., & Gammel, C. (1982). Reading in the preschool. *Volta Review, 84,* 166–170.

Ling, D., & Ling, A. (1978). Chapter 12: Language and reading. *Aural habilitation: The foundations of verbal learning in hearing-impaired children* (pp. 242–265). Washington, DC: Alexander Graham Bell Association for the Deaf.

Luetke-Stahlman, B. (1982). An optimistic look at literacy and hearing impairment. *Teaching English to Deaf and Second-Language Students, 1,* 18–29.

Madachy, J. (1979). Reading possibilities. *Teaching English to the Deaf, 6,* 22–23.

Manson, M. (1982). Explorations in language arts for preschoolers (who happen to be deaf). *Language Arts, 59,* 33–39.

Mary, Sr. B. (1963). Reading—An evaluation of what it is and what part it can have in the education of the deaf. *The report of the proceedings of the 41st meeting of the Convention of American Instructors of the Deaf* (pp. 523–527). Washington, DC: Convention of American Instructors of the Deaf.

Maxwell, M. (1980). Language acquisition in a deaf child of deaf parents: Speech, sign variations, and print variations. In K. E. Nelson (Ed.), *Children's language* (Vol. 4) (pp. 283–311). Hillsdale, NJ: Lawrence Erlbaum Associates.

Metcalf, M. (1979). Helping hearing-impaired students. *School Library Journal, 26,* 27–29.

Morariu, J. (1982). A look at the processes of concept development and the application of decision-making strategies in hearing-impaired learners: Implications for instructional materials development and adaptation. *Focus on infusion: Volume One. Selected papers from the 50th biennial meeting of Convention of American Instructors of the Deaf* (pp. 154–163). Silver Spring, MD: Convention of American Instructors of the Deaf.

Naiman, D. (1965). A different emphasis in reading for deaf children. *Volta Review*, 67, 632–634.

Newby, R. (1974). Language and reading: A visual structure. *American Annals of the Deaf*, 119, 752–755.

Newlee, C. (1930). Reading as a means of teaching language to the deaf. *American Annals of the Deaf*, 75, 345–361.

Newton, M. (1964). Readers, not leaf-turners. *Volta Review*, 66, 67–69.

Pauls, M. (1958). Development of language through reading. *Volta Review*, 60, 105–107, 142.

Perman, B. (1978). Reading attainment in hearing-impaired children: A comparison of higher and lower achievers. *Journal of Communication Disorders*, 11, 227–235.

Pugh, B. (1962). Utilizing research in teaching reading. *Volta Review*, 64, 379–387.

Quigley, S. (1980). Effects of hearing impairment on reading development. *Proceedings of the Gallaudet conference on reading in relation to deafness* (pp. 9–37). Washington, DC: Gallaudet College.

Quigley, S. (1982). Reading achievement and special reading materials. *Volta Review*, 84, 95–106.

Quigley, S., & Paul, P. (1984). Chapter 4: Reading. *Language and deafness* (pp. 101–140). San Diego, CA: College Hill Press.

Redgate, G. (1973). *Research into the teaching of reading to deaf children. Annual report, 1973: University of Manchester, Department of Audiology and Education of the Deaf*. Manchester, England: University of Manchester.

Restaino, L. (1968). *Identification, assessment, and prediction of reading competency in deaf children. Final report*. New York: Lexington School for the Deaf. (ERIC Document Reproduction Service No. ED 030 254)

Reynolds, H. (1980a). Development of reading ability in relation to deafness (Conclusions), *Teaching English to the Deaf*, 6(3), 31–34.

Reynolds, H. (1980b). The postconference discussion: Some research needs in reading related to deafness. *Proceedings of the Gallaudet conference on reading in relation to deafness* (pp. 298–302). Washington, DC: Gallaudet College.

Rompf, S. (1981). Helping the deaf community college student improve his reading skills. *American Annals of the Deaf*, 126, 825–828.

Rudloff, J. (1966). The hearing handicapped retarded reader. *Volta Review*, 68, 567–571.

Schnepel, J. (1980). Experiences and an approach to teaching reading to hearing-impaired children. *Volta Review*, 82, 236–241.

Schwartz, J. (1980). Teaching reading to the hearing-impaired child. In D. Sawyer (Ed.), *Disabled readers: Insight, assessment, instruction* (pp. 117–124). Newark, DE: International Reading Association.

Smith, L. (1980). *The college student with a disability: A faculty handbook*. Washington, DC: President's Committee on Employment of the Handicapped. (ERIC Document Reproduction Service No. ED 198 766)

Stevens, R. (1976). Children's language should be learned and not taught. *Sign Language Studies, 11,* 97–108.

Stoker, R. (1982). Letter to the editor: A reply to Bockmiller. *American Annals of the Deaf, 127,* 316–317.

Stone, P. (1981). Reading and cognitive development. *Volta Review, 83,* 117–121.

Streng, A. (1964). *Reading for deaf children.* Philadelphia: Pennsylvania School for the Deaf.

Streng, A., Kretschmer, R., & Kretschmer, L. (1978). Chapter 7: Reading and writing in the curriculum. *Language, learning, and deafness: Theory, application, and classroom management* (pp. 129–166). New York: Grune and Stratton.

Strickland, R. (1958). The interrelationship between language and reading. *Volta Review, 60,* 334–336.

Suzuki, S., & Notoya, M. (1984). Teaching written language to deaf infants and preschoolers. *Topics in Early Childhood Special Education, 3*(4), 10–16.

Truax, R. (1979). Reading and language. In R. Kretschmer, & L. Kretschmer, *Language development and intervention with the hearing impaired* (pp. 279–310). Baltimore: University Park Press.

Truax, R., & Edwards, A. (1980). Learning to read: A developmental socio-psycholinguistic process. *Volta Review, 82,* 360–369.

van Uden, A. (1972). *A world of language for the deaf: A maternal reflective method.* Rotterdam, Netherlands: Rotterdam Publishing Company.

Walker, M. (1978). An approach to teaching language and reading at the primary level. *Teacher of the Deaf, 2,* 11–16.

Weintraub, S. (1972). *Auditory perception and deafness. Reading research profiles. A bibliography series of ERIC and IRA.* Bloomington, IN: ERIC Clearinghouse on Reading. (ERIC Document Reproduction Service No. ED 066 713)

White, H. (1879). Reading as a means of acquiring a good command of language. *American Annals of the Deaf, 24,* 100–104.

Williams, A. (1982). The relationship between two visual communication systems: Reading and lipreading. *Journal of Speech and Hearing Research, 25,* 500–503.

Wood, M. (1973). *Teaching reading to deaf children: A study in education.* Unpublished doctoral dissertation, University of Pennsylvania, Philadelphia.

Woodward, H. (1963). The structural component of linguistic meaning and the reading of normally hearing and deaf children. *The report of the proceedings of the 41st meeting of the Convention of American Instructors of the Deaf* (pp. 536–543). Washington, DC: Convention of American Instructors of the Deaf.

MODELS OF READING IN RELATION TO DEAFNESS

Andrews, J., & Mason, J. (1984). *How do young deaf children learn to read?* (Tech. Rep. No. 329). Urbana, IL: University of Illinois, Center for the Study of Reading.

Athey, I. (1979). Theoretical models of reading. *Directions, 1*(1), 29–42.

Cornett, R., Knight, D., Reynolds, H., & Williams, C. (1979). A theoretical model of the development of reading in hearing-impaired children. *Directions, 1*(1), 43–68.

Cornett, R., Knight, D., Reynolds, H., & Williams, C. (1980). A theoretical model of the development of reading in hearing-impaired children. *Proceedings of the Gallaudet conference on reading in relation to deafness* (pp. 38–101). Washington, DC: Gallaudet College.

INSTRUCTIONAL TECHNIQUES FOR TEACHING READING TO DEAF CHILREN*

Anderson, E. (1930). Reading in the advanced department. *Volta Review, 32,* 403–409.

Austin, G., & Kirby, C. (1974). Improved reading skills for hearing-impaired young adults. *Journal of Rehabilitation of the Deaf, 8,* 24–28.

Avondino, J. (1930). Silent reading. *Volta Review, 32,* 623–624.

Bennett, J. (1934). Reading in the primary grades. *Volta Review, 36,* 337–339, 378.

Bennett, J. (1938). Reading in the primary grades. *Volta Review, 40,* 5–9.

Benning, D. (1934). An outline of reading for the first year. *American Annals of the Deaf, 79,* 109–119.

Benning, D. (1937). A unit of reading for deaf children. *American Annals of the Deaf, 82,* 440–444.

Berg, L. (1932). Some oral reading problems in the education of the deaf. *American Annals of the Deaf, 77,* 257–260.

Bernadine, Sr. A. (1958). A developmental curriculum. *Volta Review, 60,* 337–340.

Browns, F. (1981). A storyreading program at the pre-reading level with language-deficient hearing-impaired children. *Reading-Canada-Lecture, 13,* 11–16.

Bruce, L. (1934). Creating an interest in reading. *Volta Review, 36,* 588–591.

Campbell, H. (1984). The effectiveness of cued text in teaching pronoun reference in written English to deaf students. In D. Martin (Ed.), *International symposium on cognition, education, and deafness: Trends in research and instruction* (Vol. 2) (pp. 404–418). Washington, DC: Gallaudet College.

Carlsen, J. (1985). Between the deaf child and reading: The language connection. *Reading Teacher, 38,* 424–427.

Casey, S. (1954). Teaching reading to the hearing handicapped child. *Volta Review, 56,* 251–254.

Church, L. (1931). Reading for the deaf adolescent. *Volta Review, 33,* 251–252, 279.

Coleman, L. (1971). Individual reading. *The report of the proceedings of the 46th meeting of the Convention of American Instructors of the Deaf* (pp. 186–194). Washington, DC: Convention of American Instructors of the Deaf.

Cory, P. (1957). Library work with the deaf. *Volta Review, 59,* 169–173.

Cory, P. (1964).Special library reading project for teenagers. *Volta Review, 66,* 63–66.

Crandall, M. (1946). Reading in the primary grades. *Volta Review, 48,* 669–671.

Davey, B., & LaSasso, C. (1982). The theoretical framework for a pilot clinical reading program for deaf students at Gallaudet College. *Focus on infusion:*

---

*See general reference list for additional resources.

Volume one. Selected papers presented at the 50th biennial meeting of the Convention of American Instructors of the Deaf (pp. 109–115). Washington, DC: Convention of American Instructors of the Deaf.

Davies, R. (1948). Silent reading but oral English. *Volta Review, 50*, 437–442.

Davis, M. (1929). A silent reading experiment in grade one. *Volta Review, 31*, 66–72.

De LaSalle, Sr. M. (1932). Supervised reading in the high school. *Volta Review, 34*, 111–113.

Dean, K. (1929). Our first experience with reading. *Volta Review, 31*, 787–788.

Doctor, P. (1953). Reading for the deaf. *Volta Review, 55*, 132–143.

Edge, L. (1957). Book week at Western Pennsylvania School for the Deaf. *Volta Review, 59*, 402–406.

Eickhoff, A. (1931). The library period. *Volta Review, 33*, 445–446.

Ervin, A. (1926). Reading—The open sesame to language. *Volta Review, 28*, 695–699.

Farquhar, G. (1927). Reading for intermediate pupils. *Volta Review, 29*, 194–196.

Fitzgerald, M. (1924). Silent reading. *American Annals of the Deaf, 69*, 448–454.

Fitzgerald, M. (1958). Improving the reading ability of deaf children. *Volta Review, 60*, 341–343.

Fosmark, L. (1931). Reading for pleasure. *Volta Review, 33*, 214, 233.

Fritz, K. (1912). First lessons in reading. *Volta Review, 14*, 602–604.

Gamble, H. (1983). An alternative strategy for teaching reading to hearing-impaired high school students. *Teaching English to Deaf and Second-Language Learners, 2*, 4–7.

Gawith, F. (1909). Reading in intermediate grades. *Volta Review, 11*, 397–403.

Gesner, E. (1930). Some points on reading comprehension and vocabulary building. *Volta Review, 32*, 24–36.

Goda, S. (1953). Early reading for the hard of hearing child. *Volta Review, 55*, 106–108.

Gregory, J. (1982). The underlining technique: Imparting a phrase sense in reading. *Teaching English to Deaf and Second-Language Students, 1*, 26–30.

Griffith, M. (1931). Comparing results in speech-reading and in silent reading. *Volta Review, 33*, 270–272.

Gulick, M. (1954). A reading program for first-year deaf school children. *Volta Review, 56*, 447–448.

Hagemeyer, A. (1975). *The public library talks to you.* Washington, DC: Gallaudet College, Center for Continuing Education. (ERIC Document Reproduction Service No. ED 125 221)

Hammer, H. (1929). The second step in a silent reading experiment. *Volta Review, 31*, 196–198.

Hammer, H. (1931). A nature study unit in reading. *Volta Review, 33*, 101–102.

Hasenstab, P. (1892). An instructor in reading. *American Annals of the Deaf, 37*, 183–188.

Hoover, R. (1972). Language for the deaf according to Henry. *American Annals of the Deaf, 117*, 590–594.

Hurst, F. (1932). On teaching reading. *American Annals of the Deaf, 77*, 161–180.

Hurst, F. (1938). A reading project. *American Annals of the Deaf, 83*, 338–342.

Kaufman, M. (1965). A reading consultant in a school for the deaf. *Volta Review*, 67, 197–200.

Kendall, E. (1934). A reading and language unit—The three bears. *American Annals of the Deaf*, 79, 214–222.

Kennard, M. (1947). Exercises in reading readiness. *Volta Review*, 49, 213–214.

Kennedy, E. (1959). Teaching the deaf child to read. *American Annals of the Deaf*, 104, 372–382.

Kidder, K. (1926). To each his own in reading. *Volta Review*, 28, 300–302.

Kirkley, J. (1938). What should be done about reading in our schools for the deaf. *American Annals of the Deaf*, 83, 197–208.

Kraft, D. (1945). Reading for the deaf. *American Annals of the Deaf*, 90, 164–173.

LaSasso, C. (1983). Using the *National Enquirer* with unmotivated or language-handicapped readers. *Journal of Reading*, 26, 546–548.

LaSasso, C. (1984). A modeling strategy for improving hearing-impaired students' comprehension and use of question forms. *Volta Review*, 86, 102–105.

Magner, M. (1964). Reading: Goals and achievements at Clarke School for the Deaf. *Volta Review*, 66, 464–468.

Martin, C. (1975). *Project F.A.S.T. Facilitating academic study techniques for handicapped children. Volume 1. Final report.* College Station, TX: Texas A & M Research Foundation. (ERIC Document Reproduction Service No. ED 117 866)

Martin, C. (1975). *Project F.A.S.T. Facilitating academic study techniques for handicapped children. Volume 2. Final report.* College Station, TX: Texas A & M Research Foundation. (ERIC Document Reproduction Service No. ED 081 037)

Mangan, K. (1962). An optimistic outlook toward teaching reading to deaf children. *Volta Review*, 64, 392–393.

Maxwell, M. (1974). Teaching reading as a problem-solving activity. *American Annals of the Deaf*, 119, 721–723.

McDermott, E. (1971). Storytelling: A relaxed and natural path to lipreading, language and reading. *Volta Review*, 73, 54–57.

McNeil, M. (1946). Group reading. *Volta Review*, 48, 671–673.

Monteith, M. (1980). ERIC/RCS: The older deaf student and the reading teacher. *Journal of Reading*, 24, 74–77.

Moog, J. (1981). Instructional program at Central Institute for the Deaf: Reading. *American Annals of the Deaf*, 126, 892–899.

Morrow, E. (1930). An introduction to interpretative reading. *Volta Review*, 32, 277–281, 294.

Moss, M. (1931). Reading. *Volta Review*, 33, 446–447.

Mothner, H. (1980). A technique for teaching the unmotivated reader. *American Annals of the Deaf*, 125, 551–553.

Naiman, D. (1965). A different emphasis in reading for deaf children. *Volta Review*, 67, 632–634, 651.

Newlee, C. (1928). A study in silent reading with deaf children of kindergarten age. *Volta Review*, 30, 523–526.

Nicoll, M. (1932). Reading. *Volta Review*, 34, 623–624, 649.

Northrop, H. (1924). Reading for the deaf. *American Annals of the Deaf*, 69, 401–425.

Ostern, B. (1960). Home help with reading. *Volta Review, 62,* 494–496.

Panara, R. (1979). On teaching poetry to the deaf (Or: Let the student be the poem!). *American Annals of the Deaf, 124,* 825–828.

Parks, R. (1937). Objectives and skills in teaching reading in schools for the deaf. *American Annals of the Deaf, 82,* 425–432.

Patten, H. (1930). Reading (Incidental uses of reading seat work activities). *American Annals of the Deaf, 75,* 196–200.

Pottshart, E. (1983). Literature on tape and the hearing-impaired: Listening while reading with *Winne-the-Pooh* and *Candide. Volta Review, 85,* 285–288.

Pugh, B. (1961). Teaching children to use the dictionary. *Volta Review, 63,* 178–185.

Pugh, G. (1945). Teaching reading to the deaf. *American Annals of the Deaf, 90,* 180–187.

Pugh, G. (1947). Recreational and study-type reading. *Volta Review, 49,* 547–548, 582–584.

Pugh, G. (1948a). Reading for deaf children. *Volta Review, 50,* 426–431.

Pugh, G. (1948b). Study-type reading. *Volta Review, 50,* 205–207, 242–244.

Pugh, G. (1949). Recreational reading for deaf children. *Volta Review, 51,* 437–440, 484–486.

Read, E. (1931). Cultivating the reading habit. *Volta Review, 33,* 125–126.

Renee, Sr. A. (1951). Reading for deaf children. *Volta Review, 53,* 104–107, 134.

Richards, E. (1930). Flash cards for silent reading. *American Annals of the Deaf, 75,* 201–203.

Richardson, P. (1957). A reading lesson using the Fitzgerald Key headings. *Volta Review, 59,* 255–256.

Rittenhouse, R., & Sterns, K. (1982). Teaching metaphor to deaf children. *American Annals of the Deaf, 127,* 12–17.

Roberts, L. (1914). Cultivation of the reading habit. *Volta Review, 16,* 82–85.

Rose, Sr. A. (1956). They can't help but read. *Volta Review, 58,* 381–385.

Ruthven, H. (1933). Early steps in reading. *Volta Review, 35,* 216–217.

Sanford, A. (1966). The learner and the printed page—The place of graphics in a learning system. *American Annals of the Deaf, 111,* 626–632.

Schwartz, J. (1978). Teaching reading to the hearing-impaired child. *Reading Horizons, 18,* 249–257.

Schwartz, J. (1979). Reading readiness for the hearing-impaired. *Academic Therapy, 15,* 65–75.

Serumgard, I. (1928). Teaching the love of reading. *Volta Review, 30,* 333–334.

Slemenda, J. (1982). The reading resource room. *Perspectives for Teachers of the Hearing-Impaired, 1*(1), 2–3.

Sinclair, M. (1960). Interesting the disinterested reader. *Volta Review, 62,* 488–492.

Smith, J. (1891). Reading for the little ones. *American Annals of the Deaf, 36,* 190–193.

Smith, J. (1915). Reading in the schoolroom. *American Annals of the Deaf, 60,* 242–253.

Staton, J. (1983). *Dialogue journals: A new tool for teaching communication.* (ERIC Document Reproduction Service No. ED 227 701)

Sterne, L. (1965). Using context clues in a reading program for the deaf. *Volta Review*, 67, 371–375.

Stoefen, J. (1980). Instructional alternatives for teaching content reading to mainstreamed hearing-impaired students. *Journal of Reading*, 24, 141–143.

Stoefen, J., Brunsen, J., Dam, L., Kelly, K., Kingsbury, M., LaGow, R., & Morariu, J. (1980). Focus on reading: Project update. *American Annals of the Deaf*, 125, 751–764.

Stone, E. (1914). Reading for the deaf. *American Annals of the Deaf*, 59, 131–134.

Streeter, H. (1956). A study of the dependent clause in primary reading of the deaf. *American Annals of the Deaf*, 101, 288–297.

Tate, M. (1979). A measure of readability for the classroom. *Teacher of the Deaf*, 3, 16–20.

Taylor, N. (1919). Teaching the deaf to read. *American Annals of the Deaf*, 64, 374–379.

Thompson, H. (1927). *An experimental study of the beginning reading of deaf-mutes. Columbia University Contributions to Education*, Teachers College Series No. 254. New York: Teachers College, Columbia University.

Thompson, H. (1964). An early attempt in profusely illustrated language instruction. *Exceptional Children*, 30, 349–353.

Tims, E., & Ives, L. (1980). An experiment in the teaching of temporal causal sequencing skills with a small group of severely subnormal hearing-impaired pupils. *Teacher of the Deaf*, 1, 21–28.

Topoe, D., Zarcadoolas, C., & Engen, E. (1979). *The role of teacher questioning in developing reading abilities*. Unpublished manuscript. Providence: Rhode Island School for the Deaf.

Vermillion, F. (1916). Visual reading. *Volta Review*, 18, 430–434.

Vermillion, F. (1947). Children's experiences in written form (chart stories). *Volta Review*, 49, 374, 382–384.

Walter, J. (1969). The reading of paragraphs. *American Annals of the Deaf*, 114, 71–75.

Whitman, M. (1929). Reading made interesting. *Volta Review*, 31, 199–200.

Wilman, M. (1946). Reading in the upper school. *Volta Review*, 48, 673–675.

Winters, L. (1946). Reading readiness and beginning reading in the pre-school. *Volta Review*, 48, 667–669.

Wood, M. (1944). A comparison of techniques for increasing the rate of comprehension in reading by deaf children. *American Annals of the Deaf*, 89, 111–131; 182–213.

Woodward, H. (1960). Read with your children. *Volta Review*, 62, 517–519.

READING ASSESSMENT

Brill, R. (1942). Measurement of progress in reading. *American Annals of the Deaf*, 87, 135–139.

Ewoldt, C. (1982). Diagnostic approaches and procedures and the reading process. *Volta Review*, 84, 83–94.

Fordyce, C. (1917). Testing the efficiency in reading. *Volta Review, 19*, 518–520.

Golladay, L. (1979). Suggestions for assessing reading levels and for preparing written materials. In M. Bishop (Ed.), *Mainstreaming: Practical ideas for educating hearing-impaired students* (pp. 120–134). Washington, DC: Alexander Graham Bell Association for the Deaf.

Kelly, L., & Ewoldt, C. (1984). Interpreting nonverbatim cloze responses to evalute program success and diagnose student needs for reading instruction. *American Annals of the Deaf, 129*, 45–51.

LaSasso, C., & Swaiko, N. (1983). Considerations in selecting and using commercially prepared informal reading inventories with deaf children. *American Annals of the Deaf, 124*, 449–452.

McCaughrin, W. (1981). Reading and writing tests for deaf students ages 6 through adult. In D. Johnson et al. (Eds.), *Communication performance evaluation with deaf students: A review* (pp. 113–150). Rochester, NY: National Technical Institute for the Deaf.

Zieziula, F., (Ed.) (1982). *Assessment of hearing-impaired people: A guide for selecting psychological, educational, and vocational tests.* Washington, DC: Gallaudet College Press.

TEACHING VOCABULARY TO DEAF CHILDREN

Barmeier, A. (1981). *A nonvocal method for teaching reading and spelling to the deaf.* Unpublished doctoral dissertation, Western Michigan University, Kalamazoo.

Bland, E. (1981). *The effect of three instructional modalities on reading and vocabulary comprehension of deaf children.* Unpublished doctoral dissertation, University of Maryland, College Park.

Bodner, B. (1973). *The effects of teaching sight vocabulary to preschool deaf children using student-produced and commercially-produced visual referents.* Unpublished doctoral dissertation, Syracuse University, Syracuse.

Braverman, B., Egelston-Dodd, J., Hertzog, M., Quinsland, L., & Austin, A. (1980). The effects of training in the use of diacritical markings on the learning of medical terminology by young hearing-impaired adults. *Volta Review, 82*, 468–475.

Devine, F. (1970). *An attempt to increase specific reading vocabulary by means of programmed instruction among children with impairment of hearing.* Unpublished doctoral dissertation, University of Nebraska, Lincoln.

Ewoldt, C. (1982). Teaching new vocabulary? Skip it! In J. Price (Ed.), *Teaching handicapped students in the English classroom* (pp. 26–27). Urbana, IL: National Council of Teachers of English.

Falconer, G. (1961). A mechanical device for teaching sight vocabulary to young deaf children. *American Annals of the Deaf, 106*, 251–257.

Geoffrion, L. (1981). Developing word-identification skills within a total communication program. *American Annals of the Deaf, 126*, 49–56.

Geoffrion, L. (1982). Developing word-identification skills within a total communication program. *1980's schools... Portals to century 21: Selected papers: Conven-*

tion of American Instructors of the Deaf 49th biennial meeting (pp. 212–219). Silver Spring, MD: Convention of American Instructors of the Deaf.

Johnston, W. (1978). Vocabulary learning in multiply handicapped hearing-impaired subjects. Teacher of the Deaf, 2, 54–57.

Marbut, M. (1941). A fundamental vocabulary suggested for deaf children for the first five years of school. American Annals of the Deaf, 88, 137–138.

Quinsland, L., Templeton, D., & Egelston-Dodd, J. (1980). Facilitating the learning of medical terminology through the use of effective mediation strategies: A model for the teaching of technical vocabulary. American Annals of the Deaf, 125, 780–785.

LISTS OF READING MATERIALS FOR DEAF CHILDREN*

Bockmiller, P. (1980). The child with impaired hearing in children's books. Education Unlimited, 2(2), 55–57.

Braertsoen, E. (1979). BRT's weekly news magazine for the deaf and for people with impaired hearing. EBU Review, 30, 20–24.

Browns, F., & Arnell, D. (1981). A guide to the selection and use of reading instructional materials. Washington, DC: Alexander Graham Bell Association for the Deaf.

Cory, P. (1955, 1956, 1957, 1958, 1959, 1960, 1961, 1962, 1963). Leisure reading for deaf children. Volta Review, 57, 449–451; 58, 33–34, 123–125, 169–171, 213–214, 267–269, 409–411, 447–448; 59, 27, 38, 72, 85, 217–219, 314–315, 365–366, 409–410; 60, 35–36, 178–179, 447–449, 503, 506, 547; 61, 36–36, 181–183, 187, 228–230, 239, 429; 62, 36–38, 521; 63, 244–245, 453, 464; 64, 45–46, 153, 570–571; 65, 245–246, 430–431.

Crosby, L. (1948). Books of high interest and low vocabulary level to meet the needs of deaf students in grades seven through twelve. American Annals of the Deaf, 93, 339–359.

Gilbert, L. (1981). Materials and program suggestions for hearing-impaired children. Directions, 2(1), 64–68.

Goda, S. (1946). Good books for children's reading. Volta Review, 48, 199–200, 252–254.

Guella, B. (1983). Short stories with deaf fictional characters. American Annals of the Deaf, 128, 25–33.

Instructional Materials Center for Special Education. (1973). Instructional materials appropriate for use in deaf education. Los Angeles: University of Southern California. (ERIC Document Reproduction Service No. ED 085 929)

Jones, C. (1981). English instruction materials: A bibliography of the Gallaudet Library holdings. Teaching English to the Deaf, 7, 24–26.

Jones, C. (1982). English instruction materials: A bibliography of the Gallaudet Library holdings (continued). Teaching English to Deaf and Second-Language Learners, 1, 31–33.

---

* See Chapter 6 for additional resources.

MacDonald, N. (1950). Books suitable for small deaf children. *Volta Review, 52*, 256, 292.

Magrath, D. (1984). Learner friendly readings for ESL. *Teaching English to Deaf and Second-Language Students, 2*, 10–13.

McCarr, D. (1974). *Teacher recommended materials for use with hearing-impaired students.* Las Cruces, NM: Southwest Regional Media Center for the Deaf. (ERIC Document Reproduction Service No. ED 143 195)

McCarr, D. (1976). *Curricular materials which are helpful for hearing-impaired students.* Beaverton, OR: Dormac.

McEntee, M. (1981). The right to heritage: The teaching of deaf history. *American Annals of the Deaf, 126*, 402–403.

Newton, M. (1943). Books for the hard of hearing child. *Volta Review, 45*, 455–458, 470–476.

Newton, M. (1962). *Books for deaf children.* Washington, DC: Alexander Graham Bell Association for the Deaf.

Peters, N., & Peters, J. (1973). Better reading materials for the content areas. *Volta Review, 75*, 375–387, 445–448, 509–513, 564–567.

Schimmel, R., & Monaghan, C. (1983). Deaf awareness through literature using deaf adults as role models. *American Annals of the Deaf, 128*, 890–893.

Western Pennsylvania School for the Deaf. (1978). *Simplified reading materials for language handicapped persons.* Pittsburgh: Western Pennsylvania School for the Deaf.

Woodward, H. (1953). Books for the deaf child. *Volta Review, 55*, 391–399.

SUGGESTIONS CONCERNING READING MATERIALS FOR DEAF CHILDREN*

Andrews, J., & Dexheimer, A. (1976). JAWS in the classroom. *Teaching Exceptional Children, 9*, 10–11.

Blinton, G., & Ash, P. (1979). *Time project report, 1979-1980. An aid in the selection of special education materials.* Indianapolis, IN: Indiana State Department of Public Instruction. (ERIC Document Reproduction Service No. ED 184 284)

Bockmiller, P., & DuBois, J. (1982). Developing thinking skills with preschool hearing-impaired children through picture books. *Focus on infusion: Volume one, Paper presented at the 50th Biennial Meeting of Convention of American Instructors of the Deaf* (pp. 100–102). Silver Spring, MD: Convention of American Instructors of the Deaf.

Bornstein, H. (1978). Signed English readers. *Proceedings of the Gallaudet conference on reading in relation to deafness* (pp. 235–244). Washington, DC: Gallaudet College.

---

* See Chapter 6 for additional references.

Bower, D. (1960). Comics—a meaningful teaching experience in the language arts. *American Annals of the Deaf, 105*, 230–231.

Carter, J., & LeNard, J. (1982). Easier reading? The opinions differ. *Perspectives for Teachers of the Hearing-Impaired, 1*(2), 10–11.

Cory, P. (1958). Recreational reading and library program. *Volta Review, 60*, 343–347.

Cory, P. (1959). A child's first books should be fun. *Volta Review, 61*, 411–412.

Ernest, M. (1982). Tapping literature's language growth potentials for the secondary school hearing-impaired student—the study guide. *Volta Review, 84*, 109–120.

Ewoldt, C. (1983). Text simplication: A solution with many problems. *Perspectives for Teachers of the Hearing-Impaired, 1*, 23–25.

Ewoldt, C. (1984). Problems with rewritten materials. *American Annals of the Deaf, 129*, 23–28.

Fuchs, V. (1978). The BEH marketing program: Resources to provide materials for the hearing impaired. *American Annals of the Deaf, 123*, 682–688.

Gillespie, P. (1983). Practical and theoretical concerns of using basal reading programmes with hearing-impaired children. *Association of Canadian Educators of the Hearing Impaired Journal, 9*, 94–103.

Golladay, L. (1979). Suggestions for assessing reading levels and for preparing written materials. In M. Bishop (Ed.), *Mainstreaming: Practical ideas for educating hearing-impaired students* (pp. 120–134). Washington, DC: Alexander Graham Bell Association for the Deaf.

Gormley, K. (1981). On the influence of familiarity on deaf students' text recall. *American Annals of the Deaf, 126*, 1024–1030.

Gormley, K. (1982). The importance of familiarity in hearing-impaired readers' comprehension of text. *Volta Review, 84*, 71–80.

Hargis, C. (1970). The relationship of available instructional reading materials to deficiency in reading achievement. *American Annals of the Deaf, 115*, 27–29.

Hargis, C. (1978). *Guidelines for the preparation of reading and language materials for hearing-impaired children.* Paper presented at the National Convention of the Alexander Graham Bell Association for the Deaf, St. Louis, June 25, 1978.

Hargis, C., Evans, C., & Masters, C. (1973). A criticism of the direct discourse form in primary level basal readers. *Volta Review, 77*, 557–563.

Heffernan, P., Loysen, G., & Parrish, R. (1980). The support services of library-media, curriculum, and reading at the Rochester School for the Deaf. *American Annals of the Deaf, 125*, 662–673.

Heinl, S. (1951a). A library project to determine suitability of recreational reading of primary grades in the Illinois School for the Deaf, Jacksonville, Illinois. *American Annals of the Deaf, 96*, 447–466.

Heinl, S. (1951b). A library project to determine the suitability of books for purchase on the third grade reading level in the Illinois School for the Deaf, Jacksonville, Illinois (1949–1950). *American Annals of the Deaf, 96*, 524–543.

Hendricks, P., Fleharty, J., & Northup, N. (1981). Television program + script

= High motivation in vocabulary and English. *American Annals of the Deaf*, *126*, 755–759.

Hiney, E. (1974). *World Traveler* in the classroom, 1969–1974. *Volta Review, 76*, 368–373.

Holmes, D. (1982). Adapting reading materials for hearing-impaired children with low reading achievement. In B. Baskin & K. Harris (Eds.), *The mainstreamed library: Issues, ideas, and innovations* (pp. 50–55). Chicago: American Library Association.

Krug, K., & Hawkins, F. (1970). *A project to develop and evaluate the effectiveness of instructional materials for the deaf, designed to emphasize the syntactical meaning of words: Final report.* Boulder: University of Colorado.

LaGow, R., Stoefen, J., Brunsen, J., Dam, L., Kelly, K., Kingsbury, M., & Morariu, J. (1979). Design and development of a basic reading program for the hearing impaired. *American Annals of the Deaf, 124*, 635–651.

LaSasso, C. (1982). Forum: An examination of assumptions underlying the rewriting of materials for hearing-impaired students. *Volta Review, 84*, 163–165.

Ling, D., & Phillips, A. (1977). *Basic vocabulary and language thesaurus for hearing-impaired children.* Washington, DC: Alexander Graham Bell Association for the Deaf.

McLean, B., & Menhusen, B. (1978). Status of year one: A media materials center for the severely handicapped. *American Annals of the Deaf, 123*, 689–693.

Quigley, S. (1982). Reading achievement and special reading materials. *Volta Review, 84*, 95–106.

Reiss, M. (1952). Can the comics help? *Volta Review, 54*, 155–157, 186.

Rush, M. (1972). Writing for children with language and reading deficiencies. *Volta Review, 74*, 493–501.

Schmitt, R., & Winters, E. (1981). Turned on poetry: Creating poetic mood with media. *American Annals of the Deaf, 126*, 646–653.

Schragle, P. (1982). Preparing captioned slides for classroom use. *Focus on infusion: Volume One. Selected papers from the 50th biennial meeting of the Convention of American Instructors of the Deaf* (pp. 177–179). Silver Spring, MD: Convention of American Instructors of the Deaf.

Searle, B., Lorton, P., & Suppes, P. (1974). Structural variables affecting computer assisted instruction performance on arithmetic word problems of disadvantaged and deaf students. *Educational Studies in Mathematics, 5*, 371–384.

Shulman, J., & Decker, N. (1979). Multi-level captioning: A system for preparing reading materials for the hearing-impaired. *American Annals of the Deaf, 124*, 559–567.

Stark, B. (1976). A look at comic books at the Illinois School for the Deaf. *American Annals of the Deaf, 121*, 471–477.

Stassen, R. (1973). I have one in my class who's wearing hearing aids. In W. Northcott (Ed.), *Hearing-impaired children in the regular classroom.* Washington, DC: Alexander Graham Bell Association for the Deaf.

Stoefen, J., Brunsen, J., Dam, L., Kelly, K., Kingsbury, M., LaGow, R., & Morariu,

J. (1980). Focus on reading: Project update. *American Annals of the Deaf, 125,* 751–764.

THE LANGUAGE-EXPERIENCE APPROACH IN TEACHING READING TO DEAF CHILDREN

Godsave, C. (1978). The use of experience charts in language development with deaf children. *Teaching English to the Deaf, 5,* 7–8.

Gormley, K., & Geoffrion, L. (1980). Another view of using language experience to teach reading to deaf and hearing-impaired children. *Reading Teacher, 33,* 519–525.

Hurst, F. (1932). Chart work in reading. *American Annals of the Deaf, 77,* 202–205.

Joiner, E. (1926). The personal experience story. *Volta Review, 28,* 581–582.

LaSasso, C. (1983). Using the language experience approach with language-handicapped readers. *Journal of Reading, 27,* 152–154.

LaSasso, C., & Heidinger, V. (1983). The language experience approach with deaf readers: Whose language? *Teaching English to Deaf and Second-Language Students, 21,* 8–11.

LeBuffe, J. (1979). Developing language, reading, and writing of deaf students, Part I. *Teaching English to the Deaf, 6,* 24–30.

LeBuffe, J. (1982). Developing language, reading, and writing of deaf students, Part II. *Teaching English to the Deaf, 7,* 26–31.

Reed, R. (1977). The language story method. *American Annals of the Deaf, 122,* 482–488.

Stauffer, R. (1979). The language experience approach to reading instruction for deaf and hearing-impaired children. *Reading Teacher, 33,* 21–24.

Vermillion, F. (1947). Children's experiences in written form (Chart stories). *Volta Review, 49,* 374, 382–384.

ORTHOGRAPHY—ALTERNATIVES AND ADDITIONS TO STANDARD ENGLISH PRINT

Andrews, J. (1983). *A study of the letter, word and story reading abilities of forty-five young deaf residential children: A longitudinal perspective.* Unpublished doctoral dissertation, University of Illinois, Urbana.

Bornstein, H. (1978). Signed English readers. *Proceedings of the Gallaudet conference on reading in relation to deafness* (pp. 235–244). Washington, DC: Gallaudet College Press.

Duffy, J. (1966). ITA and the hearing impaired child. *Volta Review, 68,* 150–153.

Duffy, J. (1971). Utilizing Pitman's Initial Teaching Alphabet (I.T.A.) with infant deaf children. In J. Block (Ed.), *I/T/A as a language arts medium: Proceedings of the fourth international I.T.A. conference* (pp. 214–216). Quebec, Canada: McGill University. (ERIC Document Reproduction Service No. ED 047 903)

Jackson, C. (1980). *Comprehension of sign print by hearing-impaired children.* Unpublished thesis. Pennsylvania State University, University Park.

Robbins, N. (1981). *The effects of signed text on the reading comprehension of hearing-impaired children.* Unpublished doctoral dissertation, University of Nebraska, Lincoln.

Robbins, N. (1983). The effects of signed text on the reading comprehension of hearing-impaired children. *American Annals of the Deaf, 128,* 40–44.

Schoolfield, L., & Timberlake, J. (1974). *The phonovisual method.* Washington, DC: Phonovisual Products.

Solano, Sr. F. (1971). Using the I.T.A. with a group of first grade deaf children and its implications in relation to reading, speech, and language. In J. Block (Ed.), *I/T/A as a language arts medium: Proceedings of the fourth international I.T.A. conference* (pp. 211–213). Quebec, Canada: McGill University. (ERIC Document Reproduction Service No. ED 047 903)

Withrow, M. (1964). The augmented Roman alphabet—can it be used for teaching the deaf? *Volta Review, 66,* 540–543.

THE USE OF SIGN LANGUAGE IN TEACHING READING

Adler, E. (1964). Reading out loud in the language of signs: An effective way to develop reading skills in the illiterate or functionally illiterate young deaf adult. *American Annals of the Deaf, 109,* 364–366.

Brooks, G. (1980). Deaf schoolchildren, reading, and sign language. *Journal of Research in Reading, 3,* 98–105.

Greenberg, J., Vernon, M., Dubois, J., & McKnight, J. (1982). *The language arts handbook: A total communication approach.* Baltimore: University Park Press.

Knell, S. (1981). *Reading and language performance in deaf children: A comparison between oral and manual communication approaches.* Unpublished doctoral dissertation, Case Western Reserve University, Cleveland.

Hovland, C. (1975). Literature can live through signs. *American Annals of the Deaf, 120,* 558–563.

Vernon, M., Coley, J., & Ottinger, P. (1979). The use of sign language in the reading-language development process. *Sign Language Studies, 22,* 89–94.

GENERAL USE OF MEDIA IN TEACHING READING TO DEAF CHILDREN

Anderson, N., & Laird, R. (1969). Use of multimedia at the Wyoming School for the Deaf. *Volta Review, 71,* 420–431.

Carter, W. (1983). Serving handicapped students in the school media center. Part II. *Technological Horizons in Education, 10*(4), 97–100.

Crain, S. (1980). Introducing a core basal series through simplified media. *American Annals of the Deaf, 125,* 814–816.

Evans, J. (1981). Creating instructional media to meet the needs of preschool hearing-impaired children with developmental disabilities. *American Annals of the Deaf, 126,* 689–702.

Stepp, R. (1981). Educational media and technology for the hearing-impaired learner: An historical overview. *Volta Review*, *83*, 328–335.

Schowe, B. (1962). Projecting books as an aid to teaching reading. *Volta Review*, *64*, 421–422.

Swartz, T. (1977). Absolute visual reading in the classroom. *Teaching English to the Deaf*, *4*, 4–7.

MEDIA USE IN TEACHING READING TO DEAF CHILDREN— PROJECT LIFE

National Educational Association. (1972). *Project LIFE — Language Improvement to Facilitate Education: A multimedia instructional system for the deaf child.* Washington, DC: Author. (ERIC Document Reproduction Service No. ED 073 609)

Pfau, G. (1969). Project LIFE PI analysis. *American Annals of the Deaf*, *114*, 829–840.

Pfau, G. (1974). Project LIFE a decade later: Some reflections and projections. *American Annals of the Deaf*, *119*, 549–553.

Spidal, D. (1972). *A comparison of the Project LIFE vocabulary with a functional basic word list for special pupils.* Washington, DC: National Education Association. (ERIC Document Reproduction Service No. ED 074 653)

Vockell, K., Vockell, E., & Mattick, P. (1973). Language for mentally-retarded deaf children: Project LIFE. *Volta Review*, *75*, 431–439.

Wooden, H., & Willard, L. (1965). Project LIFE: Language improvement to facilitate education of hearing impaired children. *American Annals of the Deaf*, *110*, 541–552.

MEDIA USE IN TEACHING READING TO DEAF CHILDREN—USE OF COMPUTERS

Beckmeyer, T. (1963). Application of programmed instruction to remedial reading for the deaf. *Volta Review*, *65*, 415–417.

Cerf, V. (1978). The electronic mailbox: A new communication tool for the hearing impaired. *American Annals of the Deaf*, *123*, 768–772.

Cline, C. (1974). Teaching deaf children to read and write through programmed instruction. *Teacher of the Deaf*, *72*, 91–98.

Geoffrion, L., & Bergeron, R. (1976). *Initial reading through computer animation.* Durham: University of New Hampshire. (ERIC Document Reproduction Service No. ED 138 929)

Geoffrion, L., & Geoffrion, O. (1983). *Computers and reading instruction.* Reading, MA: Addison-Wesley.

Geoffrion, L., & Goldenberg, E., (1981). Computer-based exploratory learning systems for communication-handicapped children. *Journal of Special Education*, *15*, 325–332.

Goldenberg, E. (1979). *Special technology for special children.* Baltimore: University Park Press.

Goldenberg, E., Russel, S., Carter, C., Stokes, S., Sylvester, M., & Kelman, P. (1984). *Computers, education and special needs*. Reading, MA: Addison-Wesley.

Karlsen, B. (1965). A research basis for reading instruction of deaf children. *American Annals of the Deaf, 110*, 535-540.

Karlsen, B. (1966). *Teaching beginning reading to hearing-impaired children using a visual method and teaching machines*. Washington, DC: U.S. Office of Education. (ERIC Document Reproduction Service No. ED 015 603)

Pollard, G., & Shaw, C. (1982). Microcomputer reading comprehension improvement program for the deaf. *American Annals of the Deaf, 127*, 483–494.

Prinz, P., Nelson, K., & Stedt, J. (1982). Early reading in young deaf children using microcomputer technology. *American Annals of the Deaf, 127*, 529–535.

Sewell, D., Rostron, A., Phillips, R., & Clark, R. (1979). Mini-computers as aids for assisting in the linguistic development of deaf children. *Teacher of the Deaf, 2*, 36–41.

Ward, R., & Rostron, A. (1983). Computer-assisted learning for the hearing impaired: An interactive written language environment. *American Annals of the Deaf, 128*, 346–352.

READING COMPONENTS IN THE USE OF CAPTIONED FILMS, CAPTIONED TELEVISION, AND TELECOMMUNICATION DEVICES FOR THE DEAF (TDDs)

Austin, B. (1979). *The deaf audience for television: A bibliographic essay on empirical research, 1950-1978*. Rochester, NY: Rochester Institute of Technology.

Berman, V., & Jorgensen, J. (1980). Evaluation of a multilevel linguistic approach to captioning television for hearing-impaired children. *American Annals of the Deaf, 125*, 1072–1081.

Braverman, B. (1977). Review of the literature in instructional television: Implications for deaf learners. *American Annals of the Deaf, 122*, 395–402.

Braverman, B., Heffernan, P., Montandan, E., & Posell, A. (1982). Toward effective utilization of captioned material in the classroom. *Focus on infusion: Volume one: Selected papers presented at the 50th biennial meeting of the Convention of American Instructors of the Deaf* (pp. 102–109). Silver Spring, MD: Convention of American Instructors of the Deaf.

Boatner, E. (1951). Captioned films for the deaf. *American Annals of the Deaf, 96*, 346–352.

Boatner, E. (1981). Captioned films for the deaf. *American Annals of the Deaf, 126*, 520–525.

Boyd, J., & Vader, E. Captioned television for the deaf. *American Annals of the Deaf, 117*, 34–37.

D.E.A.F. Media. (1978). *Rainbow's End, An educational television series for deaf children and their families. Final Report. October 1, 1977 through September 30, 1978*. Oakland, CA: San Mateo Community College District. (ERIC Document Reproduction Service No. ED 168 228)

Earley, S. (1978). Captioning at WGBH-TV. *American Annals of the Deaf, 123*, 655–662.

Fitzgerald, M., & Jensema, C. (1981). Closed-captioned television viewing preferences. *American Annals of the Deaf, 126,* 536–539.

Freebaurn, T. (1977). Television for deaf and hearing impaired children. *Promise and performance: Children with special needs.* Cambridge, MA: Ballinger Publishing Company.

Geoffrion, L. (1982a). An analysis of teletype conversations. *American Annals of the Deaf, 127,* 747–752.

Geoffrion, L. (1982b). The ability of hearing-impaired students to communicate using a teletype system. *Volta Review, 84,* 96–108.

Liss, M., & Price, D. (1981). What, when, and why deaf children watch television. *American Annals of the Deaf, 126,* 493–498.

Montandon, B. (1982). Multi-level captioning: Alternatives that match the viewers' abilities. *Perspectives for Teachers of the Hearing-Impaired, 1,* 8–12.

Sendelbaugh, J. (1978). Television viewing habits of hearing-impaired teenagers in the Chicago metropolitan area. *American Annals of the Deaf, 123,* 536–541.

Sendelbaugh, J., & Powell, J. (1978). Television for the deaf: A comparative study of eleven nations. *American Annals of the Deaf, 123,* 31–34.

Shulman, J., & Decker, N. (1979). Multi-level captioning: A system for preparing reading materials for the hearing impaired. *American Annals of the Deaf, 124,* 559–567.

Appendix C

Resources on Reading Materials Developed for Hearing Children
A Selected Bibliography

SUGGESTED RESOURCES ON AGE-RELATED LITERATURE

Bogart, G. (1981). *Short story index 1980: An index to stories in collections and periodicals.* New York: H. W. Wilson Company.

Cranney, A. (1983). The literature of adult reading: Selected references. *Journal of Reading, 26,* 323–331.

Egoff, S. (1981). *Thursday's child: Trends and patterns in contemporary children's literature.* Chicago: American Library Association.

Greenlaw, M., & Wielan, O. (1979). A cross-referenced index for choosing reading materials by reading level. *Reading Teacher, 33,* 179–197. [Note: Reading levels are based on the publisher's designation, difficulty of books at a given level may vary]

Madsen, J., & Wickersham, E. (1980). A look at young children's realistic fiction. *Reading Teacher, 34,* 273–279.

McCormick, S. (1977). Choosing books to read to preschool children. *Language Arts, 54,* 543–548.

Spiegel, D. (1981). *Reading for pleasure: Guidelines.* Urbana, IL: Clearinghouse on Reading and Communication Skills, and Newark, DE: International Reading Association.

White, J., & White, M. (1979). *Books about children's books: An annotated bibliography.* Newark, DE: International Reading Association.

SUGGESTED RESOURCES ON BOOKS
FOR SPECIAL POPULATIONS*

Harris, A., & Sipay, E. (1980). Series books for remedial reading. *How to increase reading ability: A guide to developmental and remedial methods* (pp. 694–699). London: Longman.

Spache, G. (1978). *Good reading for poor readers*. Champaign, IL: Garrard.

White, M. (Ed.) (1979). *High interest–easy reading for junior and senior high school students*. Urbana, IL: National Council of Teachers of English.

Wilton, S. (1981). Juvenile science fiction involves reluctant readers. *Journal of Reading, 24*, 608–611.

SUGGESTED RESOURCES ON PICTURE BOOKS

Abrahamson, R. (1980). An analysis of children's favorite picture storybooks. *Reading Teacher, 34*, 167–170.

Abrahamson, R. (1981). An update on wordless picture books with an annotated bibliography. *Reading Teacher, 34*, 417–420.

Burris, N., & Lentz, K. (1983). Caption books in the classroom. *Reading Teacher, 36*, 872–880.

Kendall Demonstration Elementary School. (1982). Bibliography of wordless picture books. *Language arts curriculum*. Washington, DC: Gallaudet College, Outreach Programs.

McGee, L., & Tompkins, G. (1983). Wordless picture books are for older readers, too. *Journal of Reading, 27*, 120–126.

SUGGESTED RESOURCES ON PREDICTABLE BOOKS

Kendall Demonstration Elementary School. (1982). Bibliography of predictable books. *Language arts curriculum*. Washington, DC: Gallaudet College, Outreach Programs.

Rhodes, L. (1981). Predictable books as resources for reading and writing instruction. *Reading Teacher, 34*, 511–513.

Noyce, R., & Christie, J. (1981). Using literature to develop children's grasp of syntax. *Reading Teacher, 35*, 298–301.

Tompkins, G., & Webeler, M. (1983). What will happen next? Using predictable books with young children. *Reading Teacher, 36*, 498–502.

SUGGESTED RESOURCES—
BOOKS CATEGORIZED BY PLOT STRUCTURES

Abrahamson, R., & Shannon, P. (1983). A plot structure analysis of favorite picture books. *Reading Teacher, 37*, 44–48.

Zarcadoolas, C. (1980). Children's bibliography according to story structure. *Between the margins*. Providence: Rhode Island School for the Deaf.

---

* Also see pages 296 and 297 in Appendix A.

SUGGESTED RESOURCES ON THE INTEGRATION OF READING AND WRITING

Baghban, M. (1984). *Our daughter learns to read and write: A case study from birth to three*. Newark, DE: International Reading Association.

Bissex, G. (1980). *Gyns at wrk: A child learns to write and read*. Cambridge, MA: Harvard University Press.

Bridge, C., Hiebert, E., & Chesky, J. (1983). Classroom writing practices. In J. Niles & L. Harris (Eds.), *Searches for meaning in reading/language processing and instruction* (pp. 238–324). Rochester, NY: National Reading Conference.

Evans, M., Taylor, N., & Blum, I. (1979). Children's written language awareness and its relation to reading acquisition. *Journal of Reading Behavior, 11*, 7–19.

Frederiksen, C., Whiteman, M., & Dominic, J. (Eds.) (1981). *Writing: The nature, development, and teaching of written communication*. Hillsdale, NJ: Lawrence Erlbaum Associates.

Graves, D. (1982). *Writing: Teacher and children at work*. Exeter, NH: Heinemann Educational Books.

Hardt, U. (Ed.) (1983). *Teaching reading with the other language arts*. Newark, DE: International Reading Association.

Levin, J., Boruta, M., & Vasconcelios, M. (1983). Microcomputer-based environments for writing: A writer's assistant. In A. Wilkinson (Ed.), *Classroom computers and cognitive science*. New York: Academic Press.

Moffett, J., & Wagner, B. (1976). *Student-centered language arts and reading, K-13: A handbook for teachers*. Boston: Houghton Mifflin.

Parker, R., & Davis, F. (Eds.) (1983). *Developing literacy: Young children's use of language*. Newark, DE: International Reading Association.

Rubin, A., & Bruce, B. (1984). *QUILL: Reading and writing with a microcomputer* (Educ. Rep. 48). Urbana, IL: University of Illinois, Center for the Study of Reading.

Rubin, A., & Hansen, J. (1984). *Reading and writing: How are the first two "R's" related?* (Educ. Rep. No. 51). Urbana, IL: University of Illinois, Center for the Study of Reading.

Zacchei, D. (1982). The adventures and exploits of the dynamic Story Maker and Textman. *Classroom Computer News, 2*, 28–30, 76, 77.

Appendix D

Reading Skills Taxonomies and Comprehension Question Hierarchies

A Selected Bibliography

Barbe, W., & Abbott, J. (1975). Barbe reading skills check list. *Personalized reading instruction: New techniques that increase reading skill and comprehension* (pp. 154–167). West Nyack, NY: Parker Publishing Company.

Barrett, T. (1976). Taxonomy of reading comprehension. In R. Smith & T. Barrett, *Teaching reading in the middle grades*. Reading, MA: Addison-Wesley.

Beatty, R. (1975). Reading comprehension skills and Bloom's taxonomy. *Reading World*, 15, 101-108.

Graham, K., & Robinson, H.A. (1984). *Study skills handbook: A guide for all teachers.* Newark, DE: International Reading Association.

Grellet, F. (1981). *Developing reading skills: A practical guide to reading comprehension exercises.* Cambridge: Cambridge University Press.

Hunkins, F. (1972). *Questioning strategies and techniques.* Boston: Allyn and Bacon.

Hunkins, F. (1976). *Involving students in questioning.* Boston: Allyn and Bacon.

Johnson, D., & Pearson, P.D. (1978). *Teaching vocabulary.* New York: Holt, Rinehart and Winston.

Keith, J. (1978). *Comprehension joy.* Naperville, IL: Reading Joy.

Mason, J., Osborn, J., & Rosenshine, B. (1977). *A consideration of skill hierarchy approaches to the teaching of reading* (Tech. Rep. No. 42). Urbana, IL: University of Illinois, Center for the Study of Reading.

Otto, W., & Askov, E. (1974). *Rationale and guidelines: The Wisconsin design for reading skill development.* Minneapolis, MN: National Computer Systems.

Pearson, P.D., & Johnson, D. (1978). *Teaching reading comprehension.* New York: Holt, Rinehart and Winston.

Rosenshine, B. (1980). Skill hierarchies in reading comprehension. In R. Spiro, B. Bruce, & W. Brewer (Eds.), *Theoretical issues in reading comprehension: Perspectives from cognitive psychology, linguistics, artificial intelligence, and education* (pp. 534–554). Hillsdale, NJ: Lawrence Erlbaum Associates.

Appendix E

Resources on How to Prepare Informal Reading Tests
A Selected Bibliography

Allen, P., & Watson, D. (1976). *Findings of research in miscue analysis: Classroom implications*. Urbana, IL: Clearinghouse on Reading and Communication Skills and the National Council of Teachers of English.

Burns, P., & Roe, B. (1980). *Informal reading assessment*. Chicago: Rand McNally.

Cohen, D., & Stern, V. (1978). *Observing and recording the behavior of young children*. New York: Teachers College Press.

Goodman, K., & Goodman, Y. (1983). *Reading miscue analysis*. New York: Macmillan.

Johns, J., Garton, S., Schoenfelder, P., & Skriba, P. (1977). *Assessing reading behavior: Informal reading inventories (an annotated bibliography)*. Newark, DE: International Reading Association.

Kingore, B., & Kurth, R. (1981). A workshop for teachers in teaching reading comprehension. *The Reading Teacher, 35*, 173-179.

Keith, J. (1978). *Comprehension joy*. Naperville, IL: Reading Joy.

LaSasso, C., & Swaiko, N. (1983). Considerations in selecting and using commercially prepared informal reading inventories with deaf students. *American Annals of the Deaf, 128*, 449-452.

Miller, W. (1978). *Reading diagnosis kit*. West Nyack, NY: Center for Applied Research in Education.

Rubin, D. (1982). *Diagnosis and correction in reading instruction*. New York: Holt, Rinehart and Winston.

Rae, G., & Thomas, C. (1981). *Informal reading diagnosis: A practical guide for the classroom teacher*. Englewood Cliffs, NJ: Prentice-Hall.

Schreiner, R. (Ed.) (1979). *Reading tests and teachers: A practical guide*. Newark, DE: International Reading Association.

References

Adams, M. (1979a). Models of word recognition. *Cognitive Psychology, 112,* 133–176.

Adams, M. (1979b). Some differences between good and poor readers. In M. Kamel & A. Moe (Eds.), *Reading research: Studies and applications* (pp. 140–144). Clemson, SC: National Reading Conference.

Adams, M. (1980). Failures to comprehend and levels of processing in reading. In R. Spiro, B. Bruce, & W. Brewer (Eds.), *Theoretical issues in reading comprehension* (pp. 11–32). Hillsdale, NJ: Lawrence Erlbaum Associates.

Adams, M., & Bruce, B. (1980). *Background knowledge and reading comprehension* (Reading Ed. Rep. No. 13). Urbana, IL: University of Illinois, Center for the Study of Reading. (ERIC Document Reproduction Service No. ED 181 431)

Alatis, J. (1978). Linguistics, TESOL, and bilingual education: An overview. In R. Light & A. Osman (Eds.), *Collected papers in teaching English as a second language and bilingual education: Themes, practices, viewpoints* (pp. 4–15). New York: New York State English to Speakers of Other Languages and Bilingual Educators Association.

Alessi, S., Anderson, T., & Goetz, E. (1979). *An investigation of lookbacks during studying* (Tech. Rep. No. 140). Urbana, IL: University of Illinois, Center for the Study of Reading. (ERIC Document Reproduction Service No. ED 177 494)

Allen, T., White, C., & Karchmer, M. (1983). Issues in the development of a special edition for hearing-impaired students of the 7th edition of the SAT. *American Annals of the Deaf, 128,* 34–39.

Alexander, F., & Gannon, J. (1984). *Deaf heritage* (Student text and workbook). Silver Spring, MD: National Association of the Deaf.

Allington, R. (1977). If they don't read much, how they ever gonna get good? *Journal of Reading, 21,* 57–61.

Allington, R. (1980). Teacher interruption behaviors during primary-grade oral reading. *Journal of Educational Psychology, 72,* 371–374.

Allington, R. (1984). Content coverage and contextual reading in reading groups. *Journal of Reading Behavior, 16,* 85–96.

Altenberg, E., & Vago, R. (1983). Theoretical implications of an error analysis of second language phonology production. *Language Learning, 33,* 427–447.

Alvermann, D., & Boothby, P. (1982). Text differences: Children's perceptions at the transition stage in reading. *Reading Teacher, 36,* 298–302.

Amble, R., & Kelly, F. (1979). Phrase reading development training with fourth grade students. *Journal of Reading Behavior, 2,* 85–96.

Amidon, A. (1976). Children's understanding of sentences with contingent relations: Why are temporal and conditional connectives so difficult. *Journal of Experimental Child Psychology, 22,* 423–437.

Anastasi, A. (1976). *Psychological testing.* New York: Macmillan.

Anderson, M., Boren, N., Caniglia, J., Howard, W., & Krohn, E. (1980). *Apple tree.* Beaverton, OR: Dormac.

Anderson, P. (1982). A preliminary study of syntax in the written expression of learning disabled children. *Journal of Learning Disabilities, 15,* 359–362.

Anderson, R. (1972). How to construct achievement tests to assess comprehension. *Review of Educational Research, 42,* 145–170.

Anderson, R. (1981). *A proposal to continue a center for the study of reading* (Tech. Proposal, 4 vols.). Urbana, IL: University of Illinois, Center for the Study of Reading.

Anderson, R. (1982). Reading specialists respond. Boring primers? The great debate continues. *Principal, 61,* 10–43.

Anderson, R., & Biddle, W. (1975). On asking people questions about what they are reading. In G. Bower, (Ed.) *Psychology of learning and motivation* (Vol. 9) (pp. 89–133). New York: Academic Press.

Anderson, R., & Freebody, P. (1979). *Vocabulary knowledge* (Tech. Rep. No. 136). Urbana, IL: University of Illinois, Center for the Study of Reading. (ERIC Document Reproduction Service No. ED 177 480)

Anderson, R., Osborn, J., & Tierney, R. (1984). *Learning to read in American schools: Basal readers and content texts.* Hillsdale, NJ: Lawrence Erlbaum Associates.

Anderson, R., Reynolds, R., Schallert, D., & Goetz, E. (1976). *Frameworks for comprehending discourse* (Tech. Rep. No. 12). Urbana, IL: University of Illinois, Center for the Study of Reading. (ERIC Document Reproduction Service No. ED 134 935)

Anderson, R. J., & Sisco, F. (1977). *Standardization of the WISC-R performance scale for deaf children* (Series T, No. 1). Washington, DC: Gallaudet College, Office of Demographic Studies.

Anderson, S. (1978). *An investigation of the effect of syntactic modification of reading material on the comprehension of hearing-impaired students.* Unpublished doctoral dissertation, University of Maryland, College Park.

Anderson, T. (1978). *Study skills and learning strategies* (Tech. Rep. No. 104). Urbana, IL: University of Illinois, Center for the Study of Reading. (ERIC Document Reproduction Service No. ED 161 000)

Anderson, T., & Armbruster, B. (1984). Studying. In P.D. Pearson (Ed.), *Handbook of reading research* (pp. 657–679). London: Longman.

Anderson, T., Armbruster, B., & Kantor, R. (1980). *How clearly written are children's textbooks? Or, of Bladderworts and Alfa* (Ed. Rep. No. 16). Urbana, IL: University of Illinois, Center for the Study of Reading. (ERIC Document Reproduction Service No. ED 192 275)

Anderson, T., Wardrop, J., Hively, W., Muller, K., Anderson, R., Hastings, C., & Fredericksen, J. (1978). *Development and trial of a model for developing domain referenced tests of reading comprehension* (Tech. Rep. No. 86). Urbana, IL: University of Illinois, Center for the Study of Reading. (ERIC Document Reproduction Service No. ED 157 036)

Andolina, C. (1980). Syntactic maturity and vocabulary richness of learning disabled children at four age levels. *Journal of Learning Disabilities, 13*, 372–377.

Andre, T. (1979). Does answering higher-level questions while reading facilitate productive learning? *Review of Educational Research, 49*, 280–318.

Andrews, J. (1978a). What do deaf adults read? *Journal of Rehabilitation of the Deaf, 11*(3), 9–22.

Andrews, J. (1978b). *Ed's day off*. Silver Spring, MD: National Association of the Deaf.

Andrews, J. (1983). *A study of the letter, word, and story reading abilities of forty-five young deaf residential children: A longitudinal study*. Unpublished doctoral dissertation, University of Illinois at Urbana-Champaign.

Andrews, J., & Mason, J. (1984). *How do young deaf children learn to read?* (Tech. Rep. No. 329). Urbana, IL: University of Illinois, Center for the Study of Reading.

Anken, J., & Holmes, D. (1977). Use of adapted "classics" in a reading program for deaf students. *American Annals of the Deaf, 122*, 8–14.

Annis, L. (1979). Effect of cognitive style and learning passage organization on study technique effectiveness. *Journal of Educational Psychology, 71*, 620–626.

Applebee, A. (1978). *The child's concept of story*. Chicago: University of Chicago Press.

Aquino, M., Mosberg, L., & Sharron, M. (1969). Reading comprehension difficulty as a function of content area and linguistic complexity. *Journal of Experimental Education, 32*, 1–4.

Arlin, P. (1977). *The function of Piagetian operational levels in the preference and production of metaphors*. Paper presented to the Society for Research in Child Development, New Orleans.

Armbruster, B., & Anderson, T. (1981). Research synthesis on study skills. *Educational Leadership, 37*, 154–156.

Armbruster, B., & Anderson, T. (1984). *Producing "considerate" expository text: Or easy reading is damned hard writing* (Ed. Rep. No. 46). Urbana, IL: University of Illinois, Center for the Study of Reading.

Armbruster, B., Echols, C., & Brown, A. (1982). The role of metacognition in reading to learn: A developmental perspective. *Volta Review, 84*, 45–56.

Arter, J., & Jenkins, J. (1978). *Differential diagnosis-prescriptive teaching: A critical appraisal* (Tech. Rep. No. 80). Urbana, IL: University of Illinois, Center for the Study of Reading. (ERIC Document Reproduction Service No. ED 150 578)

Aspen Software Company. (1981). *Grammatik*. Tijeras, NM: Aspen Software Company.

Athey, I. (1983). Language development factors related to reading development. *Journal of Educational Research, 76*, 197–203.

Austin, J. (1962). *How to do things with words*. London: Oxford University Press.

Babb, R. (1979). *A study of the academic achievement and language acquisition levels of deaf children of hearing parents in an educational environment using Signing Exact English as the primary mode of manual communication.* Unpublished doctoral dissertation, University of Illinois at Urbana-Champaign.

Baddeley, A. (1979). Working memory and reading. In H. Bouma (Ed.), *Processing of visible language* (Vol. 1) (pp. 355–370). New York: Plenum Press.

Baddeley, A., Eldridge, M., & Lewis, V. (1981). The role of subvocalization in reading. *Quarterly Journal of Experimental Psychology, 33,* 439–454.

Baddeley, A., & Hitch, G. (1974). Working memory. In G. Bower (Ed.), *The psychology of learning and motivation. Advances in research and theory* (Vol. 8) (pp. 47–89). New York: Academic Press.

Bailey, N., Madden, C., & Krashen, S. (1974). Is there a "natural sequence" in adult second language learning? *Language Learning, 24,* 235–243.

Baker, L., & Brown, A. (1980). *Metacognitive skills and reading* (Tech. Rep. No. 188). Urbana, IL: University of Illinois, Center for the Study of Reading.

Baker, L., & Stein, N. (1978). *The development of prose comprehension skills* (Tech. Rep. No. 102). Urbana, IL: University of Illinois, Center for the Study of Reading. (ERIC Document Reproduction Service No. ED 159 663)

Bakker, D. (1972). *Temporal order in disturbed reading.* Rotterdam, Netherlands: Rotterdam University.

Baratz, S., & Baratz, J. (1970). Early childhood intervention: The social science base of institutional racism. *Harvard Educational Review, 40,* 29–50.

Barnes, B., & Clawson, E. (1975). Do advance organizers facilitate learning? Recommendations for further research based on an analysis of 32 studies. *Review of Educational Research, 45,* 637–659.

Barnitz, J. (1979). Developing sentence comprehension in reading. *Language Arts, 56,* 902–908.

Barnitz, J. (1980). Syntactic effects on the reading comprehension of pronoun-referent structures by children in grades two, four, and six. *Reading Research Quarterly, 15,* 268–289.

Baron, T. (1973). Phonemic stage not necessary for reading. *Quarterly Journal of Experimental Psychology, 25,* 241–246.

Barr, R. (1984). Beginning reading instruction: From debate to reformation. In P.D. Pearson (Ed.), *Handbook of reading research* (pp. 545–582). London: Longman.

Bartlett, F. (1932). *Remembering.* Cambridge: Cambridge University Press.

Bartley, D., & Politzer, R. (1972). *Practice-centered teacher training: Standard English for speakers of nonstandard dialects.* Philadelphia: The Center for Curriculum Development.

Bates, E. (1976). *Language and context: The acquisition of pragmatics.* New York: Academic Press.

Baumann, J., & Stevenson, J. (1982). Understanding standardized reading achievement test scores. *Reading Teacher, 35,* 648–654.

Beck, I., & McCaslin, E. (1978). *An analysis of dimensions that affect the development of code-breaking ability in eight beginning reading programs.* Pittsburgh: University of Pittsburgh, Learning Research and Development Center.

Beck, I., McKeown, M., McCaslin, E., & Burkes, A. (1979). *Instructional dimensions that may affect reading comprehension: Examples from two commercial reading programs*. Pittsburgh: University of Pittsburgh, Learning Research and Development Center.

Beck, I., McKeown, M., Omanson, R., & Pople, M. (1984). Improving the comprehensibility of stories: The effects of revisions that improve coherence. *Reading Research Quarterly, 19*, 263–277.

Beck, I., Omanson, R., & McKeown, M. (1982). An instructional redesign of reading lessons: Effects of comprehension. *Reading Research Quarterly, 17*, 462–480.

Bell, A. (1929). On reading as a means of teaching language to the deaf. *Volta Review, 31*, 191–195.

Bell, H., Bird, A., & Burroughs-Keith, J. (1977). *Relative clause development in school-age children*. Paper presented at the American Speech and Hearing Association Convention, Chicago.

Bellugi, U. (1967). *The acquisition of the system of negation in children's speech*. Unpublished doctoral dissertation, Harvard University, Cambridge, MA.

Bellugi, U., & Fischer, S. (1972). A comparison of sign language and spoken language. *Cognition, 1*, 173–200.

Bellugi, U., Klima, E., & Siple, P. (1974). Remembering in signs. *Cognition, 3*, 93–125.

Belmont, J., & Karchmer, M. (1978). Deaf people's memory: There are problems testing special populations. In M. Gruneberg, P. Morris, & R. Sykes (Eds.), *Practical aspects of memory* (pp. 581–588). New York: Academic Press.

Belmont, J., Karchmer, M., & Pilkonis, P. (1976). Instructed rehearsal strategies' influence on deaf memory processing. *Journal of Speech and Hearing Research, 19*, 36–47.

Belmore, S., Matthews, P., Bridge, C., Moskow, S., & Cohen, S. (1982). Effects of initial mention and orienting task on readers' comprehension of main idea. In J. Niles & L. Harris (Eds.), *New inquiries in reading: Research and instruction. Thirty-first yearbook of the National Reading Conference* (pp. 29–36). Rochester, NY: National Reading Conference.

Bender, R. (1960). *The conquest of deafness*. Cleveland: The Press of Western Reserve University.

Berger, A., & Peebles, J. (1976). *Rates of comprehension: An annotated bibliography*. Newark, DE: International Reading Association.

Berko, J. (1958). The child's learning of English morphology. *Word, 14*, 150–177.

Bever, T. (1970). The cognitive basis for linguistic structures. In J. Hayes (Ed.), *Cognition and the development of language* (pp. 279–362). New York: John Wiley and Sons.

Best, B., & Roberts, G. (1976). Early cognitive development in hearing-impaired children. *American Annals of the Deaf, 121*, 560–564.

Bettelheim, B., & Zelan, K. (1981). *On learning to read: The child's fascination with meaning*. New York: Alfred A. Knopf.

Betts, E. (1946). *Foundations of reading instruction*. New York: American Book Company.

Biemiller, A. (1977–1978). Relationship between oral reading rates for letters, words, and simple text in the development of reading achievement. *Reading Research Quarterly, 13*, 223–253.

Billow, R. (1975). A cognitive developmental study of metaphor comprehension. *Developmental Psychology, 11*, 415–423.

Bilsky, L., Walker, N., & Sakales, S. (1983). Comprehension and recall of sentences by mentally retarded and nonretarded individuals. *American Journal of Mental Deficiency, 87*, 558-565.

Black, J., & Bower, G. (1980). Story understanding as problem-solving. *Poetics, 9*, 223–250.

Blackwell, P., Engen, E., Fischgrund, J., & Zarcadoolas, C. (1978). *Sentences and other systems: A language and learning curriculum for hearing-impaired children*. Washington, DC: Alexander Graham Bell Association for the Deaf.

Blair, F. (1957). A study of the visual memory of deaf and hearing children. *American Annals of the Deaf, 102*, 254–263.

Blanton, R., & Nunnally, J. (1964). Semantic habits and cognitive style processes in the deaf. *Journal of Abnormal and Social Psychology, 68*, 397–402.

Blatt, J., & Sulzer, J. (1981). Captioned television and hearing-impaired viewers: The report of a national survey. *American Annals of the Deaf, 126*, 1017–1023.

Blohm, P. (1982). Computer-aided glossing and facilitated learning in prose recall. In J. Niles & L. Harris (Eds.), *New inquiries in reading: Research and instruction. Thirty-first yearbook of the National Reading Conference* (pp. 24–28). Rochester, NY: National Reading Conference.

Blom, G., Waite, R., & Zimet, S. (1970). A motivational content analysis of children's primers. In H. Levin & J. Williams (Eds.), *Basic studies on reading* (pp. 188–221). New York: Basic Books.

Bloom, L. (1970). *Language development: Form and function in emerging grammars*. Cambridge, MA: MIT Press.

Bloom, L. (1973). *One word at a time: The use of single-word utterances before syntax*. The Hague, The Netherlands: Mouton.

Bloom, L., & Lahey, M. (1978). *Language development and language disorders*. New York: John Wiley and Sons.

Bloom, L., Lightbown, P., & Hood, L. (1975). Structure and variation in child language. *Monographs of the Society for Research in Child Development, 40* (2), Serial No. 160.

Boatner, M., & Gates, J. (1975). *A dictionary of American idioms*. Woodbury, NY: Barron's Educational Series.

Bobrow, D., & Norman, D. (1975). Some principles of memory schemata. In D. Bobrow & A. Collins (Eds.), *Representation and understanding: Studies in cognitive science* (pp. 131–149). New York: Academic Press.

Bockmiller, P., & Coley, J. (1981). A survey of methods, materials, and teacher preparation among teachers of reading to the hearing impaired. *Reading Teacher, 34*, 526–529.

Bode, L. (1974). Communication of agent, object, and indirect object in signed and spoken languages. *Perceptual and Motor Skills, 39*, 1151–1158.

Bond, G., & Dykstra, R. (1967). The cooperative research program in first-grade reading instruction. *Reading Research Quarterly, 2*, 5–142.

Bongaerts, T. (1983). The comprehension of three complex English structures by Dutch learners. *Language Learning, 33*, 159–182.

Borg, W., & Gall, M. (1979). *Educational research: An introduction.* New York: David McKay Company.

Bormuth, J. (1966). Readability: A new approach. *Reading Research Quarterly, 1*, 79–132.

Bormuth, J. (1968). The cloze readability procedure. *Elementary English, 45*, 429–436.

Bormuth, J. (1970). *On the theory of achievement test items.* Chicago: University of Chicago Press.

Bormuth, J., Manning, J., Carr, J., & Pearson, P. D. (1970). Children's comprehension of between-and within-sentence syntactic structures. *Journal of Educational Psychology, 61*, 349–357.

Bornstein, H. (1971). Some effects of verbal load on achievement tests. *American Annals of the Deaf, 116*, 44–48.

Bornstein, H. (1978). The design of Signed English Readers. In H. Reynolds & C. Williams (Eds.), *Proceedings of the Gallaudet conference on reading in relation to deafness* (pp. 235–244). Washington, DC: Gallaudet College.

Bornstein, H., & Kannapell, B. (1971). More on the effects of verbal load on achievement tests. *American Annals of the Deaf, 116*, 575–579.

Bornstein, H., Saulnier, K., & Hamilton, L. (1980). *Little Red Riding Hood* (3rd ed.). The Signed English series. Washington, DC: Gallaudet College Press.

Bornstein, H., Saulnier, K., & Hamilton, L. (1973–1984). *The Signed English series.* Washington, DC: Gallaudet College Press.

Botel, M., & Granowsky, A. (1972). A formula for measuring syntactic complexity: A directional effort. *Elementary English, 49*, 513–516.

Bowe, F., & Steinberg, M. (1973). *I'm deaf too, twelve deaf Americans.* Silver Spring, MD: National Association of the Deaf.

Bowerman, M. (1975). Cross-linguistic similarities at two stages of syntactic development. In E.H. Lenneberg & E. Lenneberg (Eds.), *Foundation of language development: A multidisciplinary approach* (Vol. 1) (pp. 267–282). New York: Academic Press.

Boyd, W. (1982). *Industrial America.* Washington, DC: Gallaudet College, Outreach Programs.

Braden, J. (1984). LPAD applications to deaf populations. In D. Martin (Ed.), *International symposium on cognition, education, and deafness: Trends in research and instruction* (Vol. 1) (pp. 221–238). Washington, DC: Gallaudet College.

Bradley, J. (1976). Using readability to improve the content validity of informal placement tests. *Reading Improvement, 13*, 182–192.

Bradley, J., & Ames, W. (1976). The influence of intrabook readability variation on oral reading performance. *Journal of Educational Research, 70*, 101–105.

Bragman, R. (1982a). Review of research on test instructions for deaf children. *American Annals of the Deaf, 127*, 337–346.

Bragman, R. (1982b). Effects of different methods of conveying test directions on deaf children's performance on pattern recognition tasks. *Journal of Rehabilitation of the Deaf, 16,* 17–26.

Brannon, J. (1968). Linguistic word classes in the spoken language of normal, hard-of-hearing, and deaf children. *Journal of Speech and Hearing Research, 11,* 279–287.

Bransford, J., & Johnson, M. (1972). Contextual prerequisites for understanding: Some investigations of comprehension and recall. *Journal of Verbal Learning and Verbal Behavior, 11,* 717–726.

Brasel, K., & Quigley, S. (1977). The influence of certain language and communication environments in early childhood on the development of language in deaf individuals. *Journal of Speech and Hearing Research, 20,* 95–107.

Braverman, B. (1981). Television captioning strategies: A systematic research and development approach. *American Annals of the Deaf, 126,* 1031–1036.

Braverman, B., Egelston-Dodd, J., Hertzog, M., Quinsland, L., & Austin, A. (1980). The effects of training in the use of diacritical markings on the learning of medical terminology by young hearing impaired adults. *Volta Review, 82,* 468–475.

Braverman, B., Harrison, M., Bowker, D., & Hertzog, M. (1981). Effects of language level and visual display on learning from captioned instruction. *Educational Communication and Technology, 29,* 147–154.

Braverman, B., & Hertzog, M. (1980). The effects of caption rate and language level on comprehension of a captioned video presentation. *American Annals of the Deaf, 125,* 943–948.

Brecht, R. (1977). Testing format and instructional level with the informal reading inventory. *Reading Teacher, 31,* 57–59.

Brewer, W. (1975). Memory for ideas: Synonym substitution. *Memory and Cognition, 3,* 458–464.

Brewer, W. (1980). Literary theory, rhetoric, stylistics: Implications for psychology. In R. Spiro, B. Bruce, & W. Brewer (Eds.), *Theoretical issues in reading comprehension* (pp. 221–239). Hillsdale, NJ: Lawrence Erlbaum Associates.

Brewer, W., & Lichtenstein, E. (1980). *Event schemas, story schemas, and story grammars* (Tech. Rep. No. 197). Urbana, IL: University of Illinois, Center for the Study of Reading. (ERIC Document Reproduction Service No. ED 199 668)

Bridge, C., Winograd, P., & Haley, D. (1983). Using predictable materials vs. preprimers to teach beginning sight words. *Reading Teacher, 36,* 884–891.

Brill, R. (1974). *The education of the deaf: Adminstrative and professional developments.* Washington, DC: Gallaudet College Press.

Brown, A. (1980). Metacognitive development and reading. In R. Spiro, B. Bruce, & W. Brewer (Eds.), *Theoretical issues in reading comprehension* (pp. 453–481). Hillsdale, NJ: Lawrence Erlbaum Associates.

Brown, A., Campione, J., & Day, J. (1981). Learning to learn: On training students to learn from texts. *Educational Research, 10,* 14–21.

Brown, A., & Day, J. (1980). *Strategies and knowledge for summarizing texts: The development of expertise.* Unpublished manuscript, University of Illinois, Center for the Study of Reading, Urbana, IL.

Brown, A., & French, L. (1979). *The zone of potential development: Implications for intelligence testing in the year 2000* (Tech. Rep. No. 128). Urbana, IL: University of Illinois, Center for the Study of Reading. (ERIC Document Reproduction Service No. ED 170 737).

Brown, A., & Palincsar, A. (1982). *Inducing strategic learning from texts by means of informed, self-control training* (Tech. Rep. No. 262). Urbana, IL: University of Illinois, Center for the Study of Reading.

Brown, R., (1973). *A first language: The early stages.* Cambridge, MA: Harvard University Press.

Browns, F. (1979). Beginning reading instruction with hearing-impaired children. *Volta Review, 81*, 100–108.

Browns, F., & Arnell, D. (1981). *A guide to the selection and use of reading instructional materials.* Washington, DC: Alexander Graham Bell Association for the Deaf.

Brozo, W., Schmelzer, R., & Spires, H. (1983). The beneficial effect of chunking on good readers' comprehension of expository prose. *Journal of Reading, 26,* 442-445.

Bruce, B. (1981). *A new point of view on children's stories* (Ed. Rep. No. 25). Urbana, IL: University of Illinois, Center for the Study of Reading. (ERIC Document Reproduction Service No. ED 205 913)

Bruce, B., & Rubin, A. (1984). Strategies for controlling hypothesis formation in reading. In J. Flood (Ed.), *Promoting reading comprehension* (pp. 97–112). Newark, DE: International Reading Association.

Bruce, B., Rubin, A., & Starr, K. (1981). *Why readability formulas fail* (Ed. Rep. No. 28). Urbana, IL: University of Illinois, Center for the Study of Reading. (ERIC Document Reproduction Service No. ED 205 915)

Bruce, D. (1964). The analysis of word sounds by young children. *British Journal of Educational Psychology, 31,* 158–169.

Bryen, D. (1981). Language and language problems. In *Language and learning disabilities* (pp. 27–60). Baltimore: University Park Press.

Buchanan, C. (1973). The discriminative validity of selected subtests of the *Stanford Achievement Test, Intermediate I Battery,* for hearing-impaired students: Spring 1971. *Studies in achievement testing, hearing-impaired students. United States: Spring, 1971* (Series D, No. 11). Washington, DC: Gallaudet College, Office of Demographic Studies.

Buell, E. (1915). Reading for the deaf. *American Annals of the Deaf, 60,* 1–5.

Burt, M., & Kiparsky, C. (1974). Global and local mistakes. In J. Schumann & N. Stenson (Eds.), *New frontiers in second language learning* (pp. 71–80). Rowley, MA: Newbury House.

Caccamise, F., & Norris, C. (1973–1974a). *Community in signs.* Eureka, CA: Alinda Press.

Caccamise, F., & Norris, C. (1973–1974b). *Animals in signs.* Eureka, CA: Alinda Press.

Caccamise, F., & Norris, C. (1973–1974c). *Home in signs.* Eureka, CA: Alinda Press.

Caccamise, F., & Norris, C. (1973–1974d). *Food in signs.* Eureka, CA: Alinda Press.

Caldwell, D. (1973). Use of graded captions with instruction television for deaf learners. *American Annals of the Deaf, 118,* 500–507.

Calfee, R. (1982). Application of experimental design principles to research on reading instruction. In J. Niles & L. Harris (Eds.), *New inquiries in reading: Research and instruction. Thirty-first yearbook of the National Reading Conference* (pp. 1–28). Rochester, NY: National Reading Conference.

Campbell, D., & Stanley, J. (1963). Experimental and quasi-experimental designs for research on teaching. In N. Gage (Ed.), *Handbook of research on teaching* (pp. 171–246). Chicago: Rand McNally.

Campbell, H. (1984). The effectiveness of cued text in teaching pronoun reference in written English to deaf students. In D. Martin (Ed.), *International symposium on cognition, education, and deafness: Trends in research and instruction* (Vol. 2) (pp. 404–418). Washington, DC: Gallaudet College.

Cancino, H., Rosansky, E., & Schumann, J. (1975). The acquisition of the English auxiliary by native Spanish speakers. *TESOL Quarterly, 9,* 421–430.

Carlson, J., & Dillon, R. (1978). Measuring intellectual capabilities of hearing-impaired children: Effects of testing-the-limits procedures. *Volta Review, 80,* 216–224.

Carlson, P., & Anisfeld, M. (1969). Some observations on the linguistic competence of a two-year old child. *Child Development, 40,* 565–575.

Carney, J. (1979). *What research says about reading for the mentally retarded child.* Paper presented at the annual meeting of the International Reading Association. (ERIC Document Reproduction Service No. ED 176 458)

Carrell, P. (1983). Three components of background knowledge in reading comprehension. *Language Learning, 33,* 183–207.

Carroll, C. (1980–present). *World around you: A magazine for deaf and hard of hearing youths.* Washington, DC: Gallaudet College, Outreach Programs.

Carroll, J., Davies, P., & Richman, B. (1971). *The American Heritage word frequency book.* Boston: Houghton Mifflin.

Carter, J. (1975). Intelligence and reading achievement of EMR children in three educational settings. *Mental Retardation, 13,* 26–27.

Carter, J. (1981a). *Interaction: Made-up stories.* Washington, DC: Gallaudet College, Outreach Programs.

Carter, J. (1981b). *Interaction: True stories and directions.* Washington, DC: Gallaudet College, Outreach Programs.

Carter, J. (1981c). *Reading sampler* (Book Two). Washington, DC: Gallaudet College, Outreach Programs.

Carter, J. (1983a). *Interaction: Information.* Washington, DC: Gallaudet College, Outreach Programs.

Carter, J. (1983b). *Interaction: Word play.* Washington, DC: Gallaudet College, Outreach Programs.

Carter, J., & LeNard, J. (1982). Easier reading? The opinions differ. *Perspectives for teachers of the hearing impaired, 1* (2), 10–11.

Carter, J., & Kearney, J. (1982). *Young American adventurers* (Syntactic structures series). Washington, DC: Gallaudet College, Outreach Programs.

Carter, J., & Kearney, J. (1983a). *Folk tales from around the world* (Syntactic structures series). Washington, DC: Gallaudet College, Outreach Programs.

Carter, J., & Kearney, J. (1983b). *Great escapes* (Syntactic structures series). Washington, DC: Gallaudet College, Outreach Programs.

Carver, R. (1970). Effects of a chunked typography on reading rate and comprehension. *Journal of Applied Psychology, 54*, 288–296.

Cattell, J. (1886). The time it takes to see and name objects. *Mind, 11*, 63–65.

Center for Assessment and Demographic Studies. (1983). *Administering the 1982 Stanford Achievement Test to hearing-impaired students* (seventh edition). Washington, DC: Gallaudet College, Center for Assessment and Demographic Studies.

Center for Sutton Movement Writing. (1983). *The sign writer: The newspaper written in sign language and spoken language.* (The Movement Shorthand Society, Inc., PO Box 7344, Newport Beach, CA 92660.)

Chafe, W. (1970). *Meaning and the structure of language.* Chicago: University of Chicago Press.

Chafe, W. (1976). Giveness, contrastiveness, definiteness, subjects, topics, and point of view. In C. Li (Ed.), *Subject and topic* (pp. 25–55). New York: Academic Press.

Chall, J. (1967). *Learning to read: The great debate.* New York: McGraw-Hill.

Chall, J. (1977). *Reading 1967–1977: A decade of change and promise.* Bloomington, IN: Phi Delta Kappan Educational Foundation.

Chall, J. (1984). Readability and prose comprehension: Continuities and discontinuities. In J. Flood (Ed.), *Understanding reading comprehension* (pp. 233–246). Newark, DE: International Reading Association.

Chapman, K., Leonard, L., Rowan, L., & Weiss, A. (1983). Inappropriate word extensions in the speech of young language disordered children. *Journal of Speech and Hearing Disorders, 48*, 55–62.

Charrow, R., & Charrow, V. (1979). Making legal language understandable: A psycholinguistic study of jury instructions. *Columbia Law Review, 79*, 1306–1374.

Charrow, V. (1981). Lowering the difficulty of texts intended for adults: Implications for "plain language" in legal documents. In A. Davison, R. Lutz, & A. Roalef (Eds.), *Text readability: Proceedings of the March 1980 conference* (Tech. Rep. No. 213). Urbana, IL: University of Illinois, Center for the Study of Reading. (ERIC Document Reproduction Service No. ED 207 021)

Charrow, V., & Fletcher, J. (1973). *English as a second language of deaf students* (Tech. Rep. No. 208). Stanford, CA: Stanford University, Institute for Research in the Social Sciences.

Chen, K. (1976). Acoustic image in visual detection for deaf and hearing college students. *Journal of General Psychology, 94*, 243–246.

Chinn, P., Drew, C., & Logan, D. (1979). *Mental retardation* (2nd ed.). St. Louis: C.V. Mosby.

Chomsky, C. (1969). *The acquisition of syntax in children from 5 to 10.* Cambridge, MA: MIT Press.

Chomsky, N. (1957). *Syntactic structures*. The Hague, Netherlands: Mouton.

Chomsky, N. (1965). *Aspects of the theory of syntax*. Cambridge, MA: MIT Press.

Chomsky, N. (1968). *Language and mind*. New York: Harcourt, Brace, and World.

Christensen, F. (1965). A generative rhetoric of the paragraph. *College Composition and Communication, 16,* 144–156.

Christopherson, S., Schultz, C., & Waern, Y. (1981). The effect of two contextual conditions on recall of a reading passage and on thought processes in reading. *Journal of Reading, 24,* 573–578.

Chun, J. (1980). A survey of research in second language acquisition. *The Modern Language Journal, 64,* 287–296.

Cioffi, G., & Carney, J. (1982). Dynamic assessment of reading disabilities. *Reading Teacher, 36,* 764–768.

Clark, E. (1973). What's in a word? On the child's acquisition of semantics in his first language. In T. Moore (Ed.), *Cognitive development and the acquisition of language* (pp. 66–110). New York: Academic Press..

Clark, R., & Sewell, D. (1979). Some comments on Gormley and Frazen. *American Annals of the Deaf, 124,* 847–848.

Clarke, B., Rogers, W., & Booth, J. (1982). How hearing-impaired children learn to read: Theoretical and practical issues. *Volta Review, 84,* 57–69.

Clarke School Faculty. (1978). *Trips and treats*. Northampton, MA: Clarke School for the Deaf.

Clay, M. (1979). *Reading: The patterning of complex behaviour* (2nd ed.). Exeter, NH: Heinemann Educational Books.

Coggins, T. (1979). Relational meaning encoded in the two-word utterances of stage 1 Down's syndrome children. *Journal of Speech and Hearing Research, 22,* 166–178.

Cohen, A. (1975). *A sociolinguistic approach to bilingual education*. Rowley, MA: Newbury House.

Cohen, S., & Stover, G. (1981). Effects of teaching sixth-grade students to modify format variables of math word problems. *Reading Research Quarterly, 16,* 175–200.

Colby, J. (1967). *Writing, illustrating, and editing children's books*. New York: Hastings House.

Cole, N. (1979). *Apple tree story books*. Beaverton, OR: Dormac.

Coleman, E. (1962). Improving comprehensibility by shortening sentences. *Journal of Applied Psychology, 46,* 131–134.

Coleman, E. (1964). The comprehensibility of several grammatical transformations. *Journal of Applied Psychology, 48,* 186–190.

Coleman, E. (1971). Developing a technology of written instruction: Some determiners of the complexity of prose. In E. Rothkopf & P. Johnson (Eds.), *Verbal learning research and the technology of written instruction* (pp. 155–204). New York: Columbia University, Teachers College Press.

Coley, J., & Bockmiller, P. (1980). Teaching reading to the deaf: An examination of teacher preparedness and practices. *American Annals of the Deaf, 125,* 909–915.

Collins, A., Brown, A., Morgan, J., & Brewer, W. (1977). *The analysis of reading tasks and texts* (Tech. Rep. No. 43). Urbana, IL: University of Illinois, Center for the Study of Reading. (ERIC Document Reproduction Service No. ED 145 404)

Collins-Ahlgren, M. (1975). Language development of two deaf children. *American Annals of the Deaf, 120,* 524–539.

Cometa, M., & Eson, M. (1978). Logical operations and metaphor interpretations: A Piagetian model. *Child Development, 49,* 649–659.

Conley, J. (1976). Role of idiomatic expressions in the reading of deaf children. *American Annals of the Deaf, 121,* 381–385.

Conrad, R. (1964). Acoustic confusion in immediate memory. *British Journal of Psychology, 55,* 75–84

Conrad, R. (1970). Short-term memory processes in the deaf. *British Journal of Psychology, 61,* 179–195.

Conrad, R. (1971a). The effect of vocalizing on comprehension in the profoundly deaf. *British Journal of Psychology, 62,* 147–150.

Conrad, R. (1971b). The chronology of the development of covert speech in children. *Developmental Psychology, 5,* 398–405.

Conrad, R. (1972). Short-term memory in the deaf: A test for speech coding. *British Journal of Psychology, 63,* 173–180.

Conrad, R. (1973). Internal speech in profoundly deaf children. *The Teacher of the Deaf, 71,* 384–389.

Conrad, R. (1979). *The deaf school child.* London: Harper & Row.

Conrad, R., Freeman, P., & Hull, A. (1965). Acoustic factors versus language factors in short-term memory. *Psychonomic Science, 3,* 57–58.

Conrad, R., & Rush, M. (1965). On the nature of short-term memory encoding by the deaf. *Journal of Speech and Hearing Disorders, 30,* 336–343.

Cooper, R., Olshtain, E., Tucker, G., & Waterbury, M. (1979). The acquisition of complex English structures by adult native speakers of Arabic and Hebrew. *Language Learning, 29,* 255–275.

Cordasco, F. (Ed.). (1978). *Bilingualism and the bilingual child: Challenges and problems.* New York: Arno Press.

Cowie, A., & Mackin, R. (1976). *Oxford dictionary of current idiomatic English.* London: Longman.

Craig, W., & Collins, J. (1970). Communication patterns in classes for deaf children. *Exceptional Children, 37,* 283–289.

Crandall, K. (1978). Inflectional morphemes in the manual English of young hearing impaired children and their mothers. *Journal of Speech and Hearing Research, 21,* 372–386.

Crandall, K. (1979). *Adapting written English for NTID students.* Rochester, NY: National Technical Institute for the Deaf.

Crandall, K., & Albertini, J. (1980). An investigation of variables of instruction and their relation to rate of English language learning. *American Annals of the Deaf, 125,* 427–434.

Crismore, A. (1981). *Readability and the black box.* Paper presented at the Indiana

State Council of the International Reading Association annual meeting. Indianapolis, IN. (ERIC Document Reproduction Service No. ED 203 295)

Crittenden, J. (1975). Categorization of cheremic errors in sign language reception. *Sign Language Studies, 5*, 64–71.

Crocker, G., Jones, M., & Pratt, M. (1966). *Language stories and drills* (Books I, II, III, and IV). Brattleboro, VT: The Vermont Publishing Company.

Cromer, R. (1976). The cognitive hypothesis of language acquisition and its implications for child language deficiency. In D. Morehead & A. Morehead (Eds.), *Normal and deficient child language* (pp. 283–333). Baltimore: University Park Press.

Cromer, W. (1970). The difference model: A new explanation for some reading difficulties. *Journal of Educational Psychology, 61*, 471–488.

Cronbach, L. (1950). Further evidence of response sets and test design. *Educational and Psychological Measurement, 10*, 3–31.

Crosby, L. (1948). Books of high interest and low vocabulary level to meet the needs of deaf students in grades seven through twelve. *American Annals of the Deaf, 93*, 339–359.

Cummins, J. (1979). Linguistic interdependence and the educational development of bilingual children. *Review of Educational Research, 49*, 222–251.

Cunningham, J., & Cunningham, P. (1978). Validating a limited-cloze procedure. *Journal of Reading Behavior, 10*, 211–213.

Cunningham, J., & Tierney, R. (1984). Research on teaching reading comprehension. In P. D. Pearson (Ed.), *Handbook on reading research* (pp. 609–655). New York: Longman.

Cunningham, P. (1982). Diagnosis by observation. In J. Pikulski & T. Shanahan (Eds.), *Approaches to the informal evaluation of reading* (pp. 12–22). Newark, DE: International Reading Association.

Cunningham, P. (1983). When is reading? *Reading Teacher, 36*, 928-931.

Dale, E., & O'Rourke, J. (1976). *The living word vocabulary: A national vocabulary inventory*. Elgin, IL: Field Enterprises.

Dale, P. (1976). *Language development: Structure and function*. New York: Holt, Rinehart and Winston.

Dalgleish, B. (1975). Communication preference and the social conditions of language learning in the deaf. *American Annals of the Deaf, 120*, 70–77.

Daneman, M., & Carpenter, P. (1980). Individual differences in working memory and reading. *Journal of Verbal Learning and Verbal Behavior, 19*, 450–466.

d'Anglejan, A., & Tucker, G. (1975). The acquisition of complex English structures by adult learners. *Language Learning, 25*, 281–296.

Danner, F. (1976). Children's understanding of intersentence organization in the recall of short descriptive passages. *Journal of Educational Psychology, 68*, 174–183.

Dansereau, D., Collins, K., McDonald, B., Holley, C., Garland, J., Diekhoff, G., & Evans, S. (1979). Development and evaluation of a learning strategy training program. *Journal of Educational Psychology, 71*, 64–73.

Das, J., Mulcahy, R., & Wall, A. (Eds.). (1982). *Theory and research in learning disabilities*. New York: Plenum Press.

Davey, B., & LaSasso, C. (1983). An examination of hearing-impaired readers' test-taking abilities on reinspection tasks. *Volta Review, 85,* 279–284.

Davey, B., & LaSasso, C. (1985). Relations of cognitive style to assessment components of reading comprehension for hearing-impaired adolescents. *Volta Review, 87,* 17–27.

Davey, B., & LaSasso, C. (in press). The interaction of reader and task factors in the assessment of reading comprehension. *Journal of Experimental Education.*

Davey, B., LaSasso, C., & Macready, G. (1983). Comparison of reading comprehension task performance for deaf and hearing readers. *Journal of Speech and Hearing Research, 26,* 622–628.

Davis, F. (1944). Fundamental factors of comprehension of reading. *Psychometrika, 9,* 185–197.

Davis, F. (1968). Research in comprehension in reading. *Reading Research Quarterly, 4,* 499–545.

Davis, F. (1972). Psychometric research on comprehension in reading. *Reading Research Quarterly, 7,* 628–678.

Davison, A. (1981). *Readability: Appraising text difficulty* (Ed. Rep. No. 24). Urbana, IL: University of Illinois, Center for the Study of Reading. (ERIC Document Reproduction Service No. ED 208 340)

Davison, A., Kantor, R., Hannah, J., Hermon, G., Lutz, R., & Salzillo, R. (1980). *Limitations of readability formulas in guiding adaptation of texts* (Tech. Rep. No. 162). Urbana, IL: University of Illinois, Center for the Study of Reading. (ERIC Document Reproduction Service No. ED 184 090)

Davison, A., Lutz, R., & Roalef, A. (Eds.). (1981). *Text readability: Proceedings of the March 1980 conference* (Tech. Rep. No. 213). Urbana, IL: University of Illinois, Center for the Study of Reading. (ERIC Document Reproduction Service No. ED 207 021)

Dawkins, J. (1975). *Syntax and readability*. Newark, DE: International Reading Association.

Day, J. (1980). *Training summarization skills: A comparison of teaching methods*. Unpublished doctoral dissertation, University of Illinois at Urbana–Champaign.

Decker, N. (1981). Application of the guidelines. In J. Shulman & N. Decker (Eds.), *Readable English for hearing-impaired students. Multi-level guidelines for linguistically controlled reading materials*. Boston: The Caption Center, WGBH-TV.

Denbow, C. (1973). *An experimental study of the effects of a repetition factor on the relationship between readability and listenability*. Unpublished doctoral dissertation, Ohio University.

Dever, R., & Gardner, W. (1970). Performance of retardates and normals on Berko's test of morphology. *Language and Speech, 13,* 162–177.

de Villiers, J., & de Villiers, P. (1973). A cross-sectional study of the acquisition of grammatical morphemes in child speech. *Journal of Psycholinguistic Research, 2,* 267–278.

de Villiers, J., & de Villiers, P. (1978). *Language acquisition*. Cambridge, MA: Harvard University Press.

DiFrancesca, S. (1972). *Academic achievement test results of a national testing program for hearing-impaired students—United States, Spring* (Series D, No. 9). Washington, DC: Gallaudet College, Office of Demographic Studies.

DiFrancesca, S., & Carey, S. (1972). *Item analysis of an achievement testing program for hearing-impaired students—United States: Spring, 1971.* Washington, DC: Gallaudet College, Office of Demographic Studies.

DiSomma, E., & McTiernan, M. (1985a). *Black Beauty* (Simple English classics series). Beaverton, OR: Dormac.

DiSomma, E., & McTiernan, M. (1985b). *Little women* (Simple English classics series). Beaverton, OR: Dormac.

DiSomma, E., & McTiernan, M. (1985c). *The prince and the pauper* (Simple English classics series). Beaverton, OR: Dormac.

DiStefano, P., & Valencia, S. (1980). The effects of syntactic maturity on comprehension of graded reading passages. *Journal of Educational Research, 73,* 247–251.

Distad, L., & Paradis, E. (1983). The effects of the temporal conjunctions *before* and *after* on reading comprehension by primary grade children. In J. Niles & L. Harry (Eds.), *Searches for meaning in reading/language processing and instruction: Thirty-second yearbook of the National Reading Conference* (pp. 95–100). Rochester, NY: National Reading Conference.

Dixon, K., Pearson, P., & Ortony, A. (1980). *Some reflections on the use of figurative language in children's textbooks.* Paper presented at the annual meeting of the National Reading Conference, San Diego.

Doblmeier, J. (1981). *Environmental science.* Washington, DC: Gallaudet College, Outreach Programs.

Donahue, M., Pearl, R., & Bryan, T. (1982). Learning disabled children's syntactic proficiency on a communicative task. *Journal of Speech and Hearing Disorders, 47,* 397–403.

Dore, J. (1974). A pragmatic description of early language development. *Journal of Psycholinguistic Research, 3,* 343–350.

Dore, J. (1975). Holophrases, speech acts, and language universals. *Journal of Child Language, 2,* 21–40.

Doyle, W. (1981). Research on classroom contexts. *Journal of Teacher Education, 32,* 3–6.

Drahozal, E., & Hanna, G. (1978). Reading comprehension subscores: Pretty bottles for ordinary wine. *Journal of Reading, 21,* 416–420.

Dreher, J., & Singer, H. (1980). Story grammar instruction unnecessary for intermediate grade students. *Reading Teacher, 34,* 261–268.

Drury, A., & Walter, G. (1979). The effects of syntactic complexity on readability for deaf college students. *Directions, 1* (2), 38–45.

Duchan, J., & Erickson, J. (1976). Normal and retarded children's understanding of semantic relations in different verbal contexts. *Journal of Speech and Hearing Research, 19,* 767–776.

Duffelmeyer, F. (1979). The effect of rewriting prose material on reading comprehension. *Reading World, 19,* 1–11.

Duffelmeyer, F. (1980). A comparison of reading test results in grades nine and twelve. *Journal of Reading, 23,* 606–608.

Duffy, G. (1983). Context variables in reading teacher effectiveness. In J. Niles & L. Harry (Eds.), *Searches for meaning in reading/language processing and instruction: Thirty-second yearbook of the National Reading Conference* (pp. 289–295). Rochester, NY: National Reading Conference.

Dulay, H., & Burt, M. (1972). Goofing: An indication of child second language learning strategies. *Language Learning, 22,* 235–252.

Dulay, H., & Burt, M. (1973). Should we teach children syntax? *Language Learning, 23,* 245–258.

Dulay, H., & Burt, M. (1974a). Natural sequences in child second language acquisition. *Language Learning, 24,* 37–53.

Dulay, H., & Burt, M. (1974b). Errors and strategies in child second language acquisition. *TESOL Quarterly, 8,* 129–136.

Dulay, H., & Burt, M. (1974c). You can't learn without goofing: An analysis of children's second language 'errors.' In J. Richards (Ed.), *Error analysis: Perspectives on second language acquisition* (pp. 95–123). London: Longman.

Duncan, N. (1975). *Samson, The strongest.* Springfield, MO: Gospel Publishing House.

Dunn, F. (1921). Interest factors in primary reading material. *Teachers College, Columbia University Contributions to Education, 113,* 1–70.

Dunn, L. (1954). A comparison of the reading processes of mentally retarded and normal boys of the same mental age. In L. Dunn, & R. Capobianco, Studies of reading and arithmetic in mentally retarded boys. *Monograph of the Society for Research in Child Development, 19,* 7–99.

Dunn, L., & Markwardt, F. (1970). *Peabody individual achievement test.* Circle Pines, MN: American Guidance Service.

Durkin, D. (1966). *Children who read early.* New York: Columbia Unversity, Teachers College Press.

Durkin, D. (1978-1979). What classroom observations reveal about reading comprehension instruction. *Reading Research Quarterly, 14,* 481–533.

Durkin, D. (1980). *What is the value of the new interest in reading comprehension?* (Ed. Rep. No. 19). Urbana, IL: University of Illinois, Center for the Study of Reading. (ERIC Document Reproduction Service No. ED 198 499)

Durkin, D. (1981). Reading comprehension instruction in five basal reader series. *Reading Research Quarterly, 16,* 515–544.

Durkin, D. (1984). Is there a match between what elementary teachers do and what basal reader manuals recommend? *Reading Teacher, 37,* 734–745.

Eddy, P. (1978). Does foreign language study aid native language development? *ERIC/CLL News Bulletin, 1,* 1–2.

Edelman, J. (1981). The impact of the mandated testing program on classroom practices: Teacher perspectives. *Education, 102,* 56–59.

Edwards, P. (1974). Idioms and reading comprehension. *Journal of Reading Behavior, 46,* 287–293.

Elkonin, D. (1963). The psychology of mastering the elements of reading. In B. Simon & J. Simon (Eds.), *Educational psychology in the U.S.S.R.* (pp. 165–179). London: Routledge and Kegan Paul.

Ellenberger, R., & Steyaert, M. (1978). A child's representation of action in American Sign Language. In P. Siple (Ed.), *Understanding language through sign language research* (pp. 261–269). New York: Academic Press.

Endicott, A. (1973). A proposed scale for syntactic complexity. *Research and the Teaching of English, 7,* 5–12.

Ernest, M. (1982). Tapping literature's language growth potential for the secondary school hearing-impaired student—The study guide. *Volta Review, 84,* 109–120.

Ervin-Tripp, S. (1974). Is second language learning like the first? *TESOL Quarterly, 8,* 111–128.

Evans, R. (1972-1973). The effect of transformational simplification on the reading comprehension of selected high school students. *Journal of Reading Behavior, 73,* 273–281.

Ewoldt, C. (1977). *A psycholinguistic description of selected deaf children reading in sign language.* Unpublished doctoral dissertation, Wayne State University.

Ewoldt, C. (1981a). Factors which enable deaf readers to get meaning from print. In S. Hudelson (Ed.), *Learning to read in different languages* (pp. 45–53). Washington, DC: Center for Applied Linguistics.

Ewoldt, C. (1981b). A psycholinguistic description of selected deaf children reading in sign language. *Reading Research Quarterly, 17,* 58–89.

Ewoldt, C. (1982a). Diagnostic approaches and procedures and the reading process. In R. E. Kretschmer (Ed.), Reading and the hearing-impaired individual. *Volta Review, 84,* 83–94.

Ewoldt, C. (1982b). Teaching new vocabulary? Skip it! In J. Price (Ed.), *Teaching handicapped students in the English classroom* (pp. 26–27). Urbana, IL: National Council of Teachers of English.

Ewoldt, C. (1983). Research reports—text simplification: A solution with many problems. *Perspectives for Teachers of the Hearing Impaired, 1,* 23–25.

Ewoldt, C. (1984). Problems with rewritten materials as exemplified by "To build a fire." *American Annals of the Deaf, 129,* 23–28.

Farhady, H. (1979). The disjunctive fallacy between discrete-point and integrative tests. *TESOL Quarterly, 13,* 347–357.

Farr, R., & Tuinman, J. (1972). The dependent variable: Measurement issues in reading research. *Reading Research Quarterly, 7,* 413–423.

Fathman, A. (1975). Language background, age, and the order of acquisition of English structures. In M. Burt & H. Dulay (Eds.), *On TESOL 1975: New directions in second language learning, teaching, and bilingual education* (pp. 33–43). Washington, DC: TESOL.

Federal Register. (August 23, 1977). *Public Law 94-142.* (p. 42494.)

Felix, S. (1981). The effect of formal instruction on second language acquisition. *Language Learning, 31,* 87–112.

Felker, D. (Ed). (1980). *Document design: A review of the relevant research.* Washington, DC: American Institutes for Research.

Felker, D., Pickering, F., Charrow, V., Holland, V., & Redish, J. (1981). *Guidelines for document designers.* Washington, DC: American Institutes for Research.

Feuerstein, R., Rand, Y., & Hoffman, M. (1979). *The dynamic assessment of retarded performers: The learning potential assessment device, theory, instruments, and techniques.* Baltimore: University Park Press.

Fillmore, C. (1968). The case for case. In E. Bach & R. Harms (Eds.), *Universals in linguistic theory* (pp. 1–88). New York: Holt, Rinehart and Winston.

Fillmore, L. (1979). Individual differences in second language acquisition. In C. Fillmore, D. Kempler, & W. Wang (Eds.), *Individual differences in language ability and language behavior* (pp. 203–228). New York: Academic Press.

Fischer, S., & Gough, B. (1978). Verbs in American Sign Language. *Sign Language Studies, 18,* 17–48.

Fischler, I. (1983). Contextual constraint and comprehension of written sentences by deaf college students. *American Annals of the Deaf, 128,* 418–424.

Fishman, A. (1978). The effects of anaphoric references and noun phrase organizers in paragraph comprehension. *Journal of Reading Behavior, 10,* 159–70.

Fitzgerald, G. (1981). How many samples give a good readability estimate?–The Fry graph. *Journal of Reading, 24,* 404–410.

Flesch, R. (1955). *Why Johnny can't read and what you can do about it.* New York: Harper.

Flesch, R. (1979). *How to write plain English: A book for lawyers and consumers.* New York: Harper and Row.

Fletcher, J., & Satz, P. (1979). Unitary deficit hypotheses of reading disabilities: Has Vellutino led us astray? *Journal of Learning Disabilities, 12,* 155–159.

Flood, J. (1984a). *Promoting reading comprehension.* Newark, DE: International Reading Association.

Flood, J. (1984b). *Understanding reading comprehension.* Newark, DE: International Reading Association.

Fleury, P. (1979, 1982). *Controlled language science series.* Beaverton, OR: Dormac.

Foster, R., Giddan, J., & Stark, J. (1972). *Assessment of children's language comprehension.* Palo Alto, CA: Consulting Psychologists Press.

Frase, L. (1967). Learning from prose material: Length of passage, knowledge of results, and position of questions. *Journal of Educational Psychology, 58,* 266–272.

Frase, L. (1968). Effect of question location, pacing, and mode upon retention of prose material. *Journal of Educational Psychology, 59,* 244–249.

Frederiksen, C. (1975). Acquisition of semantic information from discourse: Effects of repeated exposures. *Journal of Verbal Learning and Verbal Behavior, 14,* 158–169.

Freebody, P. (1980). *Effects of vocabulary difficulty and text characteristics on children's reading comprehension.* Unpublished doctoral dissertation, University of Illinois at Urbana–Champaign.

Freebody, P., & Anderson, R. (1981). *Effects of differing proportions and locations of difficult vocabulary on text comprehension* (Tech. Rep. No. 202). Urbana, IL: University of Illinois, Center for the Study of Reading. (ERIC Document Reproduction Service No. ED 201 992)

Freebody, P., & Anderson, R. (1983). Effects of vocabulary difficulty, text cohesion, and schema availability on reading comprehension. *Reading Research Quarterly, 18,* 277–294.

Freedle, R., & Fine, J. (1982). Prose comprehension in natural and experimental settings: The theory and its practical implications. In S. Rosenberg (Ed.), *Handbook of applied psycholinguistics* (pp. 257–294). Hillsdale, NJ: Lawrence Erlbaum Associates.

Frostig, M. (1973). *Selection and adaptation of reading materials.* San Rafael, CA: Academic Therapy Publications.

Fry, E. (1968). A readability formula that saves time. *Journal of Reading, 11,* 513–516.

Fry, E. (1972). *Reading instruction for classroom and clinic.* New York: McGraw-Hill.

Fry, E. (1977). Fry's readability graph: Clarification, valdity, and extension to level 17. *Journal of Reading, 21,* 242–252.

Funkhouser, G., & Maccoby, N. (1971). *Study on communicating science information to a lay audience, Phase II.* Stanford, CA: Stanford University, Institute for Communication Research.

Furth, H. (1964). Conservation of weight in deaf and hearing children. *Child Development, 35,* 143–150.

Furth, H. (1966a). A comparison of reading test norms of deaf and hearing children. *American Annals of the Deaf, 111,* 461–462.

Furth, H. (1966b). *Thinking without language: Psychological implications of deafness.* New York: Free Press.

Furth, H. (1970). A review and perspective on the thinking of deaf people. In J. Hellmuth (Ed.), *Cognitive Studies* (Vol. 1) (pp. 291–338). New York: Brunner/Mazel.

Furth, H., & Youniss, J. (1965). The influence of language and experience on discovery and use of logical symbols. *British Journal of Psychology, 56,* 381–390.

Fusaro, J., & Slike, S. (1979). The effect of imagery on the ability of hearing-impaired children to identify words. *American Annals of the Deaf, 124,* 829–832.

Fusfeld, I. (1955). The academic program of schools for the deaf. *Volta Review, 57,* 63–70.

Gadzuk, N., & Rosenbloom, B. (1981). *Reading sampler* (Book One). Washington, DC: Gallaudet College, Outreach Programs.

Gaies, S. (1978). ESL teachers' classroom speech: Support for the $L_1 = L_2$ hypothesis. In R. Light & A. Osman (Eds.), *Collected papers in teaching English as a second language and bilingual education: Themes, practices, viewpoints* (pp. 167–179). New York: New York State English to Speakers of Other Languages and Bilingual Educators Association.

Gaines, R., Mandler, J., & Bryant, P. (1981). Immediate and delayed story recall by hearing and deaf children. *Journal of Speech and Hearing Research, 24,* 463–469.

Gallagher, T. (1977). Revision behaviors in the speech of normal children developing language. *Journal of Speech and Hearing Research, 20,* 303–318.

Gallagher, T., & Darnton, B. (1978). Conversational aspects of the speech and language disordered children: Revision behaviors. *Journal of Speech and Hearing Research, 21,* 118–135.

Gamby, G. (1983). Talking books and taped books: Materials for instruction. *Reading Teacher, 36,* 366–369.

Gamez, G. (1979). Reading in a second language: Native language approach vs. direct method. *Reading Teacher, 32,* 665–670.

Gardner, R., & Lambert, W. (1972). *Attitudes and motivation in second-language learning.* Rowley, MA: Newbury House.

Garrison, W., & Coggiola, D. (1980). *Time limits in standardized testing: Effects on ability estimation* (Paper Series No. 37). Rochester, NY: National Technical Institute for the Deaf.

Garrison, W., Covill-Servo, J., & McKee, B. (1981). Item response formats and their relationship to test validity. *Volta Review, 83,* 14–21.

Garrity, R. (1981). *Partners in reading.* Pittsburgh: Western Pennsylvania School for the Deaf.

Gaskins, I. (1982). Let's end the reading disabilities/learning disabilities debate. *Journal of Learning Disabilities, 15,* 81–83.

Gates, A., & MacGinitie, W. (1965). *Gates-MacGinitie reading tests.* Boston: Houghton Mifflin.

Gelman, R. (1978). Cognitive development. *Annual Review of Psychology, 29,* 297–332.

Gentner, D. (1977). Playing with words (review of *Speech play: Research and sources for the study of linguistic creativity,* by B. Kirshenblatt-Gimblett, Ed.). *Contemporary Psychology, 22,* 762–763.

Gentner, D. (1978). On relational meaning: The acquisition of verb meaning. *Child Development, 49,* 988–998.

Geoffrion, L., & Geoffrion, O. (1983). *Computers and reading instruction.* Reading, MA: Addison-Wesley Publishing Company.

Geoffrion, L., & Goldenberg, E. (1976). *Initial reading through animation.* Durham, NH: University of New Hampshire. (ERIC Document Reproduction Service No. ED 138 929)

Gerber, A. (1981). Historical trends in the field of learning disabilities: An overview. In A. Gerber & D. Bryen (Eds.), *Language and learning disabilities* (pp. 1–23). Baltimore: University Park Press.

Gerber, A., & Bryen, D. (1981). *Language and learning disabilities.* Baltimore: University Park Press.

Gerrell, H., & Mason, G. (1983). Computer-chunked and traditional text. *Reading World, 22,* 241–245.

Gerweck, S., & Ysseldyke, J. (1975). Limitations of current psychological practices for the intellectual assessment of the hearing impaired: A response to the Levine study. *Volta Review, 77,* 243–248.

Getson, P. (1979). Captioning methodologies for enhanced reading level and vocabulary development. *Directions, 1*(3), 23–25.

Geva, E. (1983). Facilitating reading comprehension through flowcharting. *Reading Research Quarterly, 18*, 384-405.

Gibson, J. (1984). Field dependence of deaf students: Implications for education. In D. Martin (Ed.), *International symposium on cognition, education, and deafness: Trends in research and instruction* (Vol. 1) (pp. 47-66). Washington, DC: Gallaudet College.

Gillespie, P., & Johnson, L. (1974). *Teaching reading to the mildly retarded child.* Columbus, OH: Charles E. Merrill.

Gillis, M., & Weber, R. M. (1976). The emergence of sentence modalities in the English of Japanese-speaking children. *Language Learning, 26*, 77-94.

Giorcelli, L. (1982). *The comprehension of some aspects of figurative language by deaf and hearing subjects.* Unpublished doctoral dissertation, University of Illinois at Urbana-Champaign.

Glaser, R. (1979). Observations on research and practice in beginning reading. In L. Resnick & P. Weaver (Eds.), *Theory and practice of early reading* (Vol. 3) (pp. 307-316). Hillsdale, NJ: Lawrence Erlbaum Associates.

Gochnour, E., & Smith, T. (1977). *The language of life.* Danville, IL: Interstate Printers (rev. 1981).

Goetz, E. (1975). *Sentences in lists and connected discourse* (Tech. Rep. No. 3). Urbana, IL: University of Illinois, Center for the Study of Reading. (ERIC Document Reproduction Service No. ED 134 927)

Goetzinger, C., & Rousey, C. (1959). Educational achievement of deaf children. *American Annals of the Deaf, 104*, 221-231.

Goldenberg, E. (1979). *Special technology for special children.* Baltimore: University Park Press.

Goldfield, B., & Snow, C. (1984). Reading books with children: The mechanics of parental influence on children's reading achievement. In J. Flood (Ed.), *Promoting reading comprehension* (pp. 204-215). Newark, DE: International Reading Association.

Goldsmith, J. (1981). Decoding reexamined. *Elementary School Journal, 82*, 152-159.

Golladay, L. (1979). Suggestions for assessing reading levels and for preparing written materials. In M. Bishop (Ed.), *Mainstreaming: Practical ideas for educating hearing-impaired students* (pp. 120-134). Washington, DC: Alexander Graham Bell Association for the Deaf.

Gonzales, P. (1981). Beginning English reading for ESL students. *Reading Teacher, 35*, 154-162.

Gonzalez, P., & Elijah, D. (1975). Rereading: Effect on error patterns and performance levels on the IRI. *Reading Teacher, 28*, 647-652.

Goodman, K. (1967). Reading: A psycholinguistic guessing game. *Journal of the Reading Specialist, 4*, 126-135.

Goodman, K. (1970). Reading: A psycholinguistic guessing game. In H. Singer & R. Ruddell (Eds.), *Theoretical models and processes of reading* (pp. 259-272). Newark, DE: International Reading Association.

Goodman, K. (1976). Appendix A: The Goodman taxonomy of reading miscues. In P. Allen & D. Watson (Eds.), *Findings of research in miscue analysis: Classroom implications* (pp. 157–244). Urbana, IL: National Council of Teachers of English.

Goodman, K., & Gollasch, F. (1980). Word omissions: Deliberate and non-deliberate. *Reading Research Quarterly, 16,* 6–31.

Goodman, K., & Goodman, Y. (1978). *Reading of American children whose language is a stable rural dialect of English or a language other than English* (Final Report, Project NIE-D-00-3-0087). Washington, DC: United States Department of Health, Education, and Welfare, National Institute of Education.

Goodman, K., Olsen, H., Colvin, C., & VanderLinde, L. (1966). *Choosing materials to teach reading.* Detroit: Wayne State University Press.

Goodman, L. (1978). Meeting children's needs through materials modification. *Teaching Exceptional Children, 11,* 92–94.

Goodman, Y., & Burke, C. (1976). *The reading miscue inventory.* New York: Macmillan.

Goodman, Y., & Burke, C. (1983). *Reading miscue inventory manual.* Chicago: Richard C. Owen Publishers.

Gordon, R. (1980). The readability of unreadable texts. *English Journal, 69,* 60–61.

Gormley, K. (1981). On the influence of familiarity on deaf students' text recall. *American Annals of the Deaf, 126,* 1024–1030.

Gormley, K. (1982). The importance of familiarity in hearing-impaired readers' comprehension of text. *Volta Review, 84,* 71–80.

Gormley, K., & Franzen, A. (1978). Why can't the deaf read? Comments on asking the wrong question. *American Annals of the Deaf, 123,* 524–547.

Gough, P. (1972). One second of reading. In J. Kavanagh & I. Mattingly (Eds.), *Language by ear and by eye: The relationships between speech and reading* (pp. 331–358). Cambridge, MA: MIT Press.

Gourlay, J., & Catlin, J. (1978). Children's comprehension of grammatical structures in context. *Journal of Psycholinguistic Research, 7,* 419–434.

Gove, M. (1983). Clarifying teachers' beliefs about reading. *Reading Teacher, 37,* 261–268.

Graesser, A., Hoffman, N., & Clark, L. (1980). Structural components of reading time. *Journal of Verbal Learning and Verbal Behavior, 19,* 135–151.

Graham, J., & Graham, L. (1971). Language behavior of the mentally retarded: Syntactic characteristics. *American Journal of Mental Deficiency, 75,* 623–629.

Graves, M. (1978). Types of vocabulary to teach. *Minnesota English Journal, 9,* 2–17.

Graves, M. (1984). Selecting vocabulary to teach in the intermediate and secondary grades. In J. Flood (Ed.), *Promoting reading comprehension* (pp. 245–260). Newark, DE: International Reading Association.

Graves, M., Cooke, C., & LaBerge, M. (1983). Effects of previewing difficult short stories on low ability junior high school students' comprehension, recall, and attitudes. *Reading Research Quarterly, 18,* 262–276.

Graybeal, C. (1981). Memory for stories in language-impaired children. *Applied Psycholinguistics, 2,* 269–283.

Green, G. (1984). On the appropriateness of adaptations in primary-level basal readers: Reaction to remarks by Bertram Bruce. In R. Anderson, J. Osborn,

& R. Tierney (Eds.), *Learning to read in American schools: Basal readers and content texts* (pp. 175–191). Hillsdale, NJ: Lawrence Erlbaum Associates.

Green, G., Kantor, R., Morgan, J., Stein, N., Hermon, G., Salzillo, T., Sellner, M., Bruce, B., Gentner, D., & Webber, B. (1980). *Problems and techniques of text analysis* (Tech. Rep. No. 168). Urbana, IL: University of Illinois, Center for the Study of Reading. (ERIC Document Reproduction Service No. ED 185 513)

Green, J., & Bloome, D. (1983). Ethnography and reading: Issues, approaches, criteria, and findings. In J. Niles & L. Harry (Eds.), *Searches for meaning in reading/language processing and instruction: Thirty-second yearbook of the National Reading Conference* (pp. 6–30). Rochester, NY: National Reading Conference.

Greenfield, P., & Smith, J. (1976). *The structure of communication in early language development*. New York: Academic Press.

Gregory, J. (1981). *An investigation of word grouping in the speech and reading of the deaf*. Unpublished doctoral dissertation, Harvard University, Cambridge, MA.

Gregory, J. (1982). The underlining technique: Imparting a phrase sense in reading. *Teaching English to Deaf and Second-Language Students, 1*(1), 26–30.

Grice, H. (1975). Logic and conversations. In P. Cole & J. Morgan (Eds.), *Syntax and semantics: Speech acts* (Vol. 3) (pp. 41–58). New York: Academic Press.

Grinnell, P. (1984). *How can I prepare my young child for reading?* (A Micromonograph). Newark, DE: International Reading Association.

Griswold, E., & Cummings, J. (1974). The expressive vocabulary of preschool deaf children. *American Annals of the Deaf, 119*, 16–28.

Groht, M. (1955). Some thoughts on reading. *Volta Review, 57*, 294–296.

Groht, M. (1958). *Natural language for deaf children*. Washington, DC: Alexander Graham Bell Association for the Deaf.

Grossman, H. (1973). *Manual on terminology and classification in mental retardation, 1973 revision*. Washington, DC: American Association on Mental Deficiency.

Guralnik, D. (Ed.). (1970). *Webster's new world dictionary of the American language*. Nashville, TN: The Southwestern Company.

Guszak, F. (1967). Teacher questioning and reading. *Reading Teacher, 21*, 227–234.

Haber, L. (1977). *A linguistic definition of language delay: Evidence from AUX*. Paper presented at the Linguistic Society of America Summer Meeting, Champaign, IL.

Hakuta, K., & Cancino, H. (1977). Trends in second-language acquisition research. *Harvard Educational Review, 47*, 294–316.

Hall, W., & Tirre, W. (1979). *The communicative environment of young children: Social class, ethnic, and situational differences* (Tech. Rep. No. 125). Urbana, IL: University of Illinois, Center for the Study of Reading. (ERIC Document Reproduction Service No. ED 170 788)

Halle, J., Stoker, R., & Schloss, P. (1984). Facilitating teacher-conducted research: A tutorial on single-subject design—The multiple baseline. *Volta Review, 86*, 89–101.

Halliday, M. (1975). *Learning how to mean: Explorations in the development of language*. New York: Elsevier/North Holland.

Halliday, M., & Hasan, R. (1976). *Cohesion in English.* London: Longman.

Hamilton, E. (1961). Prefatory notes to the *Parmenides.* In E. Hamilton & C. Huntington (Eds.), *Plato's collected dialogues* (p. 920). Princeton, NJ: Princeton University Press.

Hammermeister, F. (1971). Reading achievement in deaf adults. *American Annals of the Deaf, 116,* 25–28.

Hammill, D., & Larsen, S. (1978). The effectiveness of psycholinguistic training: Reaffirmation of position. *Exceptional Children, 44,* 402–414.

Hanna, G., & Oaster, T. (1978). Toward a unified theory of context dependence. *Reading Research Quarterly, 14,* 226–243.

Hansche, L., & Gordon, G. (1983). An investigation of the relationship of story schema to reading ability and grade level. In J. Niles & L. Harris (Eds.), *Searches for meaning in reading/language processing and instruction. Thirty-second yearbook of the National Reading Conference* (pp. 255–259). Rochester, NY: National Reading Conference.

Hansen, J., & Pearson, P. D. (1980). *The effects of inference training and practice on young children's comprehension* (Tech. Rep. No. 166). Urbana, IL: University of Illinois, Center for the Study of Reading. (ERIC Document Reproduction Service No. ED 186 839)

Hanson, V. (1982). Short-term recall by deaf signers of American Sign Language: Implications of encoding strategy for order recall. *Journal of Experimental Psychology: Learning, Memory, and Cognition, 8,* 572–583.

Harber, J. (1981). Learning disability research: How far have we progressed? *Learning Disability Quarterly, 4,* 372–381.

Hardyck, C., & Petrinovich, L. (1970). Subvocal speech and comprehension level as a function of the difficulty level of reading material. *Journal of Verbal Learning and Verbal Behavior, 9,* 647–652.

Hargis, C. (1970). The relationship of available instructional reading materials to deficiency in reading achievement. *American Annals of the Deaf, 115,* 27–29.

Hargis, C. (1977). *English syntax: An outline for clinicians and teachers of language handicapped children.* Springfield, IL: Charles C Thomas.

Hargis, C. (1978). *Guidelines for the preparation of reading and language materials for hearing-impaired children.* Paper presented at the Alexander Graham Bell Association for the Deaf, St. Louis.

Harris, A., & Sipay, E. (1979). *How to teach reading: A competency-based program.* New York: Longman.

Harris, A., & Sipay, E. (1980). *How to increase reading ability* (7th ed.). New York: Longman.

Harrison, C. (1980). *Readability in the classroom.* Cambridge: Cambridge University Press.

Harrison, M., Keener, A., & O'Brien, D. (1981). *Controlled syntax biography series.* Beaverton, OR: Dormac.

Harste, J., & Burke, C. (1977). A new hypothesis for reading teacher research: Both teaching and learning of reading are theoretically based. *Reading theory, research, and practice. Twenty-sixth yearbook of the National Reading Conference* (pp. 27–39). Clemson, SC: National Reading Conference.

Harste, J., & Burke, C. (1979). *Reexamining retellings as comprehension devices.* Paper presented at the National Reading Conference, San Antonio.

Hasenstab, M., & Bevilacqua, T. (1980). Semantics: The forgotten component in teaching language to hearing-impaired children. *American Annals of the Deaf, 125,* 488–490.

Hasenstab, M., & McKenzie, C. (1981). A survey of reading programs used with hearing-impaired students. *Volta Review, 83,* 383–388.

Hatch, E. (1969). *Four experimental studies in syntax of young children* (Tech. Rep. No. 11). Inglewood, CA: Southwest Regional Laboratory for Educational Research and Development.

Hatch, E. (1978). *Second language acquisition.* Rowley, MA: Newbury House.

Hatcher, C., & Robbins, N. (1978). *The development of reading skills in hearing-impaired children.* Cedar Falls: University of Northern Iowa. (ERIC Document Reproduction Service No ED 167 960)

Hawes, M., & Danhauer, J. (1978). Perceptual features of the manual alphabet. *American Annals of the Deaf, 123,* 464–474.

Hayes, D., & Readence, J. (1982). Effects of cued attention to illustrations in text. In J. Niles & L. Harris (Eds.), *New inquiries in reading research and instruction: Thirty-first yearbook of the National Reading Conference* (pp. 60–63). Rochester, NY: National Reading Conference.

Hayes, D., & Tierney, R. (1980). *Increasing background knowledge through analogy: Its effects upon comprehension and learning* (Tech. Rep. No. 186). Urbana, IL: University of Illinois, Center for the Study of Reading. (ERIC Document Reproduction Service No. ED 195 953)

Hayhurst, H. (1967). Some errors of young children in producing passive sentences. *Journal of Verbal Learning and Verbal Behavior, 6,* 634–639.

Head, H. (1920). *Studies of neurology.* Oxford: Oxford University Press.

Heine, M. (1981). *Comprehension of high and low level information in expository passages: A comparison of deaf and hearing readers.* Unpublished doctoral dissertation, University of Pittsburgh.

Henderson, J. (1976). Learning to read: A case study of a deaf child. *American Annals of the Deaf, 121,* 502–506.

Henk, W. (1982). A response to Shanahan, Kamil, and Tobin: The case is not yet clozed. *Reading Research Quarterly, 17,* 591–595.

Hersen, M., & Barlow, D. (1976). *Single case experimental designs: Strategies for studying behavior change.* New York: Pergamon Press.

Hess, R., & Shipman, V. (1965). Early experience and the socialization of cognitive modes in children. *Child Development, 36,* 869–886.

Herber, R. (1961). *Manual on terminology and classification in mental retardation* (2nd ed.). Washington, DC: American Association on Mental Deficiency.

Hernandez, E. (1972). *Early code separation in the acquisition of English by Spanish speaking children.* Paper presented at the Stanford Child Language Research Forum, Stanford, CA.

Hiebert, E. (1983). An examination of ability grouping for reading instruction. *Reading Research Quarterly, 17,* 231–255.

Higgins, E. (1973). An analysis of the comprehensibility of three communication methods used with hearing impaired students. *American Annals of the Deaf, 118*, 46–49.

Hirsh-Pasek, K., & Treiman, R. (1982). Recoding in silent reading: Can the deaf child translate print into a more manageable form? *Volta Review, 84*, 71–82.

Hittleman, D., & Robinson, H. (1975). Readability of high school text passages before and after revision. *Journal of Reading Behavior, 7*, 369–382.

Hoffman, J., Kastler, L., Nash, M., & Daly, J. (1982). Students' beliefs and attitudes about oral reading instruction. In J. Niles & L. Harris (Eds.), *New inquiries in reading: Research and instruction. Thirty-first yearbook of the National Reading Conference* (pp. 140–144). Rochester, NY: National Reading Conference.

Hoffman, J., O'Neal, S., & Clements, R. (1982). The effects of differentiated patterns of verbal feedback to miscues on word identification strategies and success. In J. Niles & L. Harris (Eds.), *New inquiries in reading: Research and instruction. Thirty-first yearbook of the National Reading Conference* (pp. 145–151). Rochester, NY: National Reading Conference.

Hoffmeister, R. (1978). *The influential point.* Philadelphia: Temple University.

Holmes, D. (1982). Adapting reading materials for hearing-impaired children with low reading achievement. In B. Baskin & K. Harris (Eds.), *The mainstreamed library: Issues, ideas, and innovations* (pp. 50–55). Chicago: American Library Association.

Honeyfield, J. (1977). Simplification. *TESOL Quarterly, 11*, 431–440.

Hook, C., & Rosenshine, B. (1979). Accuracy of teacher reports of their classroom behavior. *Review of Educational Research, 49*, 1–12.

Horn, E. (1937). *Methods of instruction in the social sciences.* New York: Charles Scribner's Sons.

Hornby, P. (Ed.). (1977). *Bilingualism: Psychological, social, and educational implications.* New York: Academic Press.

Houck, J. (1982). *The effects of idioms on reading comprehension of hearing impaired students.* Unpublished doctoral dissertation, University of Northern Colorado (Abstract).

Howarth, S., Wood, D., Griffiths, A., & Howarth, C. (1981). A comparative study of the reading lessons of deaf and hearing primary school children. *British Journal of Educational Psychology, 51*, 156–162.

Huck, C. (1976). *Children's literature in the elementary school* (3rd ed.). New York: Holt, Rinehart and Winston.

Huey, E. (1910). *The psychology and pedagogy of reading.* New York: Macmillan.

Huntington, A., & Watton, F. (1981). Language and interaction in the classroom. Part I: Teacher talk. *Journal of the British Association of Teachers of the Deaf, 5*, 162–173.

Huntington, A., & Watton, F. (1982). Language and interaction in the classroom. Part II: Pupil talk. *Journal of the British Association of Teachers of the Deaf, 6*, 18–21.

Husak, G., Pahre, P., & Stewart, J. (1976a). *The health series.* Sewickley, PA: Hopewell Books.

Husak, G., Pahre, P., & Stewart, J. (1976b). *The money series.* Sewickley, PA: Hopewell Books.

Husak, G., Pahre, P., & Stewart, J. (1976c). *The work series.* Sewickley, PA: Hopewell Books.

Idol-Maestas, L. (1980). Oral language responses of children with reading difficulties. *Journal of Special Education, 14,* 385–404.

Ingalls, R. (1978). *Mental retardation: The changing outlook.* New York: Wiley.

Ingram, R. (1978). Theme, rheme, topic, and comment in the syntax of American Sign Language. *Sign Language Studies, 20,* 193–218.

Inhelder, B., & Piaget, J. (1958). *The growth of logical thinking from childhood to adolescence.* New York: Basic Books.

International Reading Association. (April, 1981). *Resolution: Misuse of grade equivalents.* Newark, DE: International Reading Association.

Iran-Nejad, A., Ortony, A., & Rittenhouse, R. (1981). The comprehension of metaphorical uses of English by deaf children. *Journal of Speech and Hearing Research, 24,* 551–556.

Irwin, J. (1980). The effects of explicitness and clause order on the comprehension of reversible causal relationships. *Reading Research Quarterly 15,* 477–488.

Irwin, J.,& Davis, C. (1980). Assessing readability: The checklist approach. *Journal of Reading, 24,* 124–130.

Israelite, N. (1981). *Direct antecedent context and comprehension of reversible passive voice sentences by deaf readers.* Unpublished doctoral dissertation, University of Pittsburgh.

Jackson, C. (1980). *Comprehension of sign print by hearing-impaired children.* Unpublished thesis, Pennsylvania State University.

Jarvella, R. (1971). Syntactic processing of connected speech. *Journal of Verbal Learning and Verbal Behavior, 10,* 409–416.

Jarvella, R. (1979). Immediate memory and discourse processing. In G. Bower (Ed.), *The psychology of learning and motivation* (Vol. 13) (pp. 379–421). New York: Academic Press.

Jarvella, R., & Lubinsky, J. (1975). Deaf and hearing children's use of language describing temporal order among events. *Journal of Speech and Hearing Research, 18,* 58–73.

Jenkins, J., & Pany, D. (1976). *Curriculum biases in reading achievement tests* (Tech. Rep. No. 16). Urbana, IL: University of Illinois, Center for the Study of Reading. (ERIC Document Reproduction Service No. ED 134 938)

Jenkins, J., Pany, D., & Schreck, J. (1978). *Vocabulary and reading comprehension: Instructional effects* (Tech. Rep. No. 100). Urbana, IL: University of Illinois, Center for the Study of Reading. (ERIC Document Reproduction Service No. ED 160 999)

Jensema, C. (1975). *The relationship between academic achievement and the demographic characteristics of hearing-impaired children and youth.* Washington, DC: Gallaudet College, Office of Demographic Studies.

Jensema, C. (1978). A comment on measurement error in achievement tests for the hearing impaired. *American Annals of the Deaf, 123,* 496–499.

Johns, J. (1982). The dimensions and uses of informal reading assessment. In J. Piluski & T. Shanahan (Eds), *Approaches to the informal evaluation of reading* (pp. 1–11). Newark, DE: International Reading Association.

Johnson, D., & Myklebust, H. (1967). *Learning disabilities: Educational principles and practices*. New York: Grune and Stratton.

Johnson, D., Toms-Gronowski, S., & Pittelman, S. (1982). Vocabulary development. *Volta Review, 84*, 11–24.

Johnson, J., McLaughlin, T., & Hunsaker, D. (1982). The effects of free reading time in the regular classroom as a consequence for increased performance in programmed reading for a hearing-impaired child in a resource classroom. *Journal of Special Education, 18*(3), 6–11.

Johnson, L., & Otto, W. (1982). Effects of alternations in prose style on the readability of college texts. *Journal of Educational Research, 75*(4), 19–25.

Johnson, M., & Kress, R. (1965). *Informal reading inventories*. Newark, DE: International Reading Association.

Johnson, N. (1977). A pattern-unit model of word identification. In D. LaBerge & S. Samuels (Eds.), *Basic processes in reading: Perception and comprehension* (pp. 91–125). Hillsdale, NJ: Lawrence Erlbaum Associates.

Johnson, P. (1981). Effects of reading comprehension of language complexity and cultural background of a text. *TESOL Quarterly, 15*, 169–181.

Johnston, J., & Schery, T. (1976). The use of grammatical morphemes by children with communication disorders. In D. Morehead & A. Morehead (Eds.), *Normal and deficient child language* (pp. 239–258). Baltimore: University Park Press.

Johnston, K. (1984). *Popsicles are cold*. Los Amitos, CA: Modern Signs Press.

Johnston, P. (1983). *Reading comprehension assessment: A cognitive base*. Newark, DE: International Reading Association.

Johnston, P., & Pearson, P. D. (1982). *Prior knowledge, connectivity, and the assessment of reading comprehension* (Tech. Rep. No. 245). Urbana, IL: University of Illinois, Center for the Study of Reading.

Jones, B. (1984). Assessment and language instruction. In S. Quigley & P. Paul, *Language and deafness* (pp. 199–227). San Diego: College-Hill Press.

Jones, M., & Quigley, S. (1979). The acquisition of question formation in English and American Sign Language by two hearing children of deaf parents. *Journal of Speech and Hearing Disorders, 44*, 196–208.

Jones, P., & Kaufman, G. (1975). The differential formation of response sets by specific determiner. *Educational and Psychological Measurement, 35*, 821–833.

Jones, R., Murphy, H., & Perrin, D. (1979). Adding sign language inserts on videotape. *American Annals of the Deaf, 124*, 627–634.

Jordan, K. (1975). A referential communication study of signers and speakers using realistic referents. *Sign Language Studies, 6*, 65–103.

Jordan, T. (1967). Language and mental retardation: A review of the literature. In R. Schiefelbusch, R. Copeland, & J. Smith (Eds.), *Language and mental retardation: Empirical and conceptual considerations* (pp. 20–38). New York: Holt, Rinehart and Winston.

Juel, C. (1980). Comparison of word identification strategies with varying context, word type, and reader skill. *Reading Research Quarterly, 3*, 358–376.

Just, M., & Carpenter, P. (1980). A theory of reading: From eye fixations to comprehension. *Psychological Review, 4*, 329–354.

Kachuck, B. (1981). Relative clauses may cause confusion for young readers. *Reading Teacher, 34*, 372–377.

Kahn, J. (1979). Applications of the Piagetian literature to severely and profoundly mentally retarded persons. *Mental Retardation, 17*, 273–280.

Kaluger, G., & Kolson, C. (1978). *Reading and learning disabilities* (2nd ed.). Columbus, OH: Charles E. Merrill.

Kameenui, E., & Carnine, D. (1982). An investigation of fourth-graders' comprehension of pronoun constructions in ecologically valid texts. *Reading Research Quarterly, 17*, 556–580.

Kameenui, E., Carnine, D., & Freschi, R. (1982). Effects of text construction and instructional procedures for teaching word meanings on comprehension and recall. *Reading Research Quarterly, 17*, 367–388.

Kamhi, A. (1981). Developmental vs. difference theories of mental retardation: A new look. *American Journal of Mental Deficiency, 86*, 1–7.

Kamhi, A., & Johnston, J. (1982). Towards an understanding of retarded children's linguistic deficiencies. *Journal of Speech and Hearing Research, 25*, 435–445.

Kane, M. (1980). Response to "How clearly written are children's textbooks?" In Anderson, T., Armbruster, B., & Kantor, R. *How clearly written are children's textbooks? Or, of Bladderworts and Alfa* (Ed. Rep. No. 16) (pp. 50–56). Urbana, IL: University of Illinois, Center for the Study of Reading. (ERIC Document Reproduction Service No. ED 192 275)

Kant, E. (1787/1963). *Critique of pure reason* (2nd ed.; N. Kemp Smith, trans.). London: Macmillan. (Original work published 1787)

Kappauf, W. (1973). Studying the relationship of task performance to the variables of chronological age, mental age, and IQ. In N. Ellis (Ed.), *International review of research in mental retardation* (Vol. 6) (pp. 257–317). New York: Academic Press.

Kappauf, W. (1976). Critique of the use of covariance adjustments for CA and MA in comparative studies of retarded and nonretarded persons. *American Journal of Mental Deficiency, 81*, 240–247.

Karchmer, M., & Belmont, J. (1976). *On assessing and improving deaf performance in the cognitive laboratory.* Paper presented at the American Speech and Hearing Association, Houston.

Karlin, R. (1973). Evaluation for diagnostic teaching. In W. MacGinitie (Ed.), *Assessment problems in reading* (pp. 8–13). Newark, DE: International Reading Association.

Karlsen, B. (1981). Foreword. In L. Schell (Ed.), *Diagnostic and criterion-referenced reading tests: Review and evaluation* (pp. v–vii). Newark, DE: International Reading Association.

Kavale, K., & Nye, C. (1981). Identification criteria for learning disabilities: A survey of the research literature. *Learning Disability Quarterly, 4*, 383–388.

Kavanagh, J., & Mattingly, I. (Eds.). (1972). *Language by ear and by eye: The relationship between speech and reading.* Cambridge, MA: MIT Press.

Kazdin, E. (1982). *Single-case research designs: Methods for clinical and applied settings.* New York: Oxford University Press.

Keane, K. (1984). Application of Feuerstein's mediated learning construct to deaf persons. In D. Martin (Ed.), *International symposium on cognition, education, and deafness: Trends in research and instruction* (Vol. 1) (pp. 207–220). Washington, DC: Gallaudet College.

Kearney, J. (1981). *Loans and credits.* Washington, DC: Gallaudet College, Outreach Programs.

Keenan, E. (1974). Conversational competence in children. *Journal of Child Language, 1,* 163–183.

Kelly, J., & Steer, M. (1949). Revised concept of rate. *Journal of Speech and Hearing Disorders, 14,* 222–226.

Kelly, L., & Ewoldt, C. (1984). Interpreting nonverbatim cloze responses. *American Annals of the Deaf, 129,* 45–51.

Kendall Demonstration Elementary School. (1981). *Language arts curriculum.* Washington, DC: Gallaudet College, Outreach Programs.

Kendall Demonstration Elementary School Faculty. (1981). *Coloring book classics.* Washington, DC: Gallaudet College, Outreach Programs.

Kender, J., & Rubenstein, H. (1977). Recall versus reinspection in IRI comprehension tests. *Reading Teacher, 30,* 776–779.

Keogh, B. (1982). Research in learning disabilities: A view of status and need. In J. Das, R. Mulcahy, & A. Wall (Eds.), *Theory and research in learning disabilities* (pp. 27–44). New York: Plenum Press.

Kephart, N. (1960). *The slow learner in the classroom.* Columbus, OH: Charles E. Merrill.

Kibby, M. (1979). Passage readability affects the oral reading strategies of disabled readers. *Reading Teacher, 32,* 390–396.

Kieras, D. (1978). Good and bad structure in simple paragraphs: Effects on apparent theme, reading time, and recall. *Journal of Verbal Learning and Verbal Behavior, 17,* 13–28.

Kieras, D. (1980). Problems of reference in text comprehension. In P. Carpenter & M. Just (Eds.), *Cognitive processes in comprehension* (pp. 249–269). Hillsdale, NJ: Lawrence Erlbaum Associates.

King, C. (1981). *An investigation of similarities and differences in the syntactic abilities of deaf and hearing children learning English as a first or second language.* Unpublished doctoral dissertation, University of Illinois at Urbana–Champaign.

King, C. (1983). *Survey of language methods and materials used with hearing-impaired students in the United States.* Paper presented at the Entre Amis '83 Convention of the Association of Canadian Educators of the Hearing Impaired, Convention of American Instructors of the Deaf, and the Convention of Executives for American Schools for the Deaf, Winnipeg, Canada.

King, C., & Quigley, S. (1984). *Reading milestones placement test battery.* Beaverton, OR: Dormac.

Kintsch, W. (1974). *The representation of meaning in memory.* Hillsdale, NJ: Lawrence Erlbaum Associates.

Kintsch, W., Kozminsky, E., Streby, W., McKoon, D., & Keenan, J. (1975). Comprehension and recall of text as a function of content variables. *Journal of Verbal Learning and Verbal Behavior, 14*, 196–214.

Kintsch, W., & Miller, J. (1984). Readability: A view from cognitive psychology. In J. Flood (Ed.), *Understanding reading comprehension* (pp. 220–232). Newark, DE: International Reading Association.

Kintsch, W., & van Dijk, T. (1978). Toward a model of text comprehension and production. *Psychological Review, 85*, 363–394.

Kintsch, W., & Vipond, D. (1979). Reading comprehension and readability in educational practice and psychological theory. In L. Nillson (Ed.), *Perspectives on memory research* (pp. 329–365). Hillsdale, NJ: Lawrence Erlbaum Associates.

Kirk, S. (1962). *Educating exceptional children.* Boston: Houghton Mifflin.

Kirk, S., & Kirk, W. (1971). *Psycholinguistic learning disabilities: diagnosis and remediation.* Chicago: University of Illinois Press.

Kirk, S., McCarthy, J., & Kirk, W. (1968). *Illinois test of psycholinguistic abilities* (rev. ed.). Urbana, IL: University of Illinois Press.

Klare, G. (1974–1975). Assessing readability. *Reading Research Quarterly, 1*, 62–102.

Klare, G. (1976). A second look at the validity of readability formulas. *Journal of Reading Behavior, 8*, 129–152.

Klare, G. (1984). Readability. In P. D. Pearson (Ed.), *Handbook of reading research* (pp. 681–744). London: Longman.

Klare, G., Mabry, J., & Gustafson, L. (1955). The relationship of style difficulty to immediate retention and to acceptability of technical material. *Journal of Educational Psychology, 46*, 287–295.

Kleiman, G. (1975). Speech recoding in reading. *Journal of Verbal Learning and Verbal Behavior, 14*, 323–339.

Klima, E., & Bellugi, U. (1966). Syntactic regularities in the speech of children. In J. Lyons & R. Wales (Eds.), *Psycholinguistic papers: The proceedings of the 1966 Edinburgh conference* (pp. 183–219). Edinburgh, Scotland: Edinburgh University Press.

Klima, E., & Bellugi, U. (1979). *The signs of language.* Cambridge, MA: Harvard University Press.

Kluwin, T. (1983). Discourse in deaf classrooms: The structure of teaching episodes. *Discourse Processes, 6*, 275–293.

Kluwin, T., Getson, P., & Kluwin, B. (1980). The effects of experience on the discourse comprehension of deaf and hearing adolescents. *Directions, 1*(3), 49.

Kogan, N. (1975). *Metaphoric thinking in children: Developmental and individual-difference aspects.* Paper presented at the meeting of the Society for Research in Child Development, Denver.

Krashen, S. (1973). Lateralization, language learning, and the critical period: Some new evidence. *Language Learning, 23*, 63–74.

Krashen, S. (1978). The monitor model for second-language acquisition. In R. Gingras (Ed.), *Second-language acquisition and foreign language teaching* (pp. 1–26). Arlington, VA: Center for Applied Linguistics.

Krashen, S., Sferlazza, L., & Fathman, A. (1976). Adult performance on the SLOPE test: More evidence for a natural sequence in adult second language acquisition. *Language Learning, 26,* 145–152.

Kretschmer, R. E. (1976). *Judgments of grammaticality by 11, 14, and 17 year old hearing and hearing impaired youngsters.* Unpublished doctoral dissertation. University of Kansas.

Kretschmer, R. E. (1982). Reading and the hearing-impaired individual: Summation and application. *Volta Review, 84,* 107–122.

Kurchak, B. (1977). *The effects of using an advance organizer on various levels of comprehension in fifth grade social studies.* Unpublished doctoral dissertation, University of Colorado.

Kyle, J. (1980). Reading development of deaf children. *Journal of Research in Reading, 3,* 86–97.

LaBerge, D., & Samuels, S. (1974). Toward a theory of automatic information processing in reading. *Cognitive Psychology, 6,* 293–323.

Labov, W. (1970). The logic of non-standard English. In F. Williams (Ed.), *Language and poverty* (pp. 153–189). Chicago: Markham.

Labov, W. (1972). *Language in the inner city: Studies in the black English vernacular.* Philadelphia: University of Pennsylvania Press.

Lackner, J. (1968). A developmental study of language behavior in retarded children. *Neuropsychologia, 6,* 301–320.

LaGow, R., Stoefen, J., Brunsen, J., Dam, L., Kelly, K., Kingsbury, M., & Morariu, J. (1979). Design and development of a basic reading program for the hearing impaired. *American Annals of the Deaf, 124,* 635–651.

Lake, D. (1980). Syntax and sequential memory in hearing-impaired children. In H. Reynolds & C. Williams (Eds.), *Proceedings of the Gallaudet conference on reading in relation to deafness* (pp. 193–212). Washington, DC: Gallaudet College.

Lamendella, J., (1977). General principles of neurofunctional organization and their manifestation in primary and nonprimary language acquisition. *Language Learning, 27,* 155–196.

Lance, D. (1970). The codes of the English-Spanish bilingual. *TESOL Quarterly, 4,* 343–351.

Lane, H., & Baker, D. (1974). Reading achievement of the deaf: Another look. *Volta Review, 76,* 489–499.

Lane, H., Boyes-Braem, P., & Bellugi, U. (1976). Preliminaries to a distinctive feature analysis of handshapes in American Sign Language. *Cognitive Psychology, 8,* 263–289.

Lanfrey, J. (1975). *Instructional reading materials for deaf children: Opinions and beliefs of educators of the deaf.* Unpublished doctoral dissertation, University of Georgia.

Larsen-Freeman, D. (1975). The acquisition of grammatical morphemes by adult ESL students. *TESOL Quarterly, 9,* 409–419.

LaSasso, C. (1978a). National survey of materials and procedures used to teach reading to hearing impaired children. *American Annals of the Deaf, 123,* 22–30.

LaSasso, C. (1978b). A report on preliminary findings of an investigation of the validity and reliability of the cloze procedure as a measure of readability and comprehension for prelingually, profoundly deaf subjects. In H. Reynolds & C. Williams (Eds.), *Proceedings of the Gallaudet conference on reading in relation to deafness* (pp. 222–234). Washington, DC: Gallaudet College.

LaSasso, C. (1979). The effects of WH question format versus incomplete statement format on deaf students' demonstration of comprehension of text-explicit information. *American Annals of the Deaf, 124,* 833–837.

LaSasso, C. (1980a). The validity and reliability of the cloze procedure as a measure of readability for prelingually, profoundly deaf students. *American Annals of the Deaf, 125,* 559–563.

LaSasso, C. (1980b). The validity of the Fry and Dale-Chall readability formulas for predicting relative passage difficulty for deaf students. *Teaching English to the Deaf, 7*(1), 25–28.

LaSasso, C. (1982a). The effectiveness of teacher judgment in determining relative text difficulty for prelingually, profoundly deaf students. *Teaching English to Deaf and Second Language Students, 1*(1), 13–17.

LaSasso, C. (1982b). Forum: An examination of assumptions underlying the rewriting of materials for hearing-impaired students. *Volta Review, 84,* 163–165.

LaSasso, C. (1983a). Using the language experience approach with language-handicapped readers. *Journal of Reading, 27,* 152–154.

LaSasso, C. (1983b). Using the *National Enquirer* with unmotivated or language-handicapped readers. *Journal of Reading, 26,* 546–548.

LaSasso, C. (1984). *A comparison of test-taking strategies of comparably-aged deaf and hearing readers with comparable reading levels.* Paper presented at the International Reading Association Conference, Special Interest Group on Reading and Hearing Impairment Session, Atlanta.

LaSasso, C. (1985). Visual matching test-taking strategies used by deaf readers. *Journal of Speech and Hearing Research, 28,* 2–7.

LaSasso, C., & Davey, B. (1983a). An examination of hearing-impaired readers' test-taking abilities on reinspection tasks. *Volta Review, 85,* 279–284.

LaSasso, C., & Davey, B. (1983b). An investigation of the criterion-related validity of the SAT-HI reading comprehension subtest for deaf students. *Directions, 3*(3), 66–69.

LaSasso, C., & Heidinger, V. (1983). The language experience approach with deaf readers: Whose language? *Teaching English to Deaf and Second-Language Students, 2*(1), 8–11.

LaSasso, C., & Swaiko, N. (1983). Considerations in selecting and using commercially-prepared informal reading inventories with deaf students. *American Annals of the Deaf, 128,* 449–452.

Lawson, R. (1978). Patterns of communication in intermediate level classrooms of the deaf. *Audiology and Hearing Education, 4,* 19–36.

Layton, T., & Holmes, D. (in press). *Carolina picture vocabulary test.* Tulsa, OK: Modern Education Corporation.

Layton, T., Schmucker, K., & Holmes, D. (1979). Vocabulary and syntactic structures in adapted "classics" readers for deaf children. *American Annals of the Deaf, 124,* 433–442.

LeBuffe, C. (1981). *Roots* (Teacher guide and student workbook). Washington, DC: Gallaudet College, Outreach Programs.

LeBuffe, J. (1979). Developing language, reading, and writing of deaf students. Part I. *Teaching English to the Deaf, 6,* 24–30.

LeBuffe, J. (1982). Developing language, reading, and writing of deaf students. Part II. *Teaching English to the Deaf, 7,* 26–31.

Lee, L., & Canter, S. (1971). Developmental sentence scoring: A clinical procedure for estimating syntactic development in children's spontaneous speech. *Journal of Speech and Hearing Disorders, 36,* 315–340.

Lenneberg, E. (1967). *Biological foundations of language.* New York: John Wiley and Sons.

Leonard, L. (1972). What is deviant language? *Journal of Speech and Hearing Disorders, 37,* 427–446.

Leonard, L. (1979). Language impairment in children. *Merrill-Palmer Quarterly, 25,* 205–232.

Leonard, L., Cole, B., & Steckol, K. (1979). Lexical usage of retarded children: An examination of informativeness. *American Journal of Mental Deficiency, 84,* 49–54.

Leonard, L., Schwartz, R., Chapman, K., Rowan, L., Prelock, P., Terrell, B., Weiss, A., & Messick, C. (1982). Early lexical acquisition in children with specific language impairment. *Journal of Speech and Hearing Research, 25,* 554–563.

Leslie, L., & Osol, P. (1978). Changes in oral reading strategies as a function of quantity of miscues. *Journal of Reading Behavior, 10,* 442–445.

Leu, D. (1982). Oral reading error analysis: A critical review of research and application. *Reading Research Quarterly, 17,* 420–437.

Levi, G., Capozzi, F., Fabrizi, A., & Sechi, E. (1982). Language disorders and prognosis for reading disabilities in developmental age. *Perceptual and Motor Skills, 54,* 1119–1122.

Levine, E. (1974). Psychological tests and practices with the deaf: A survey of the state of the art. *Volta Review, 76,* 298–319.

LeVine, R. (1970). Cross-cultural study in child psychology. In P. Mussen (Ed.), *Carmichael's manual of child psychology* (Vol. 2) (3rd ed.) (pp. 559–612). New York: John Wiley and Sons.

Levitt, H., & Newcomb, W. (1978). Computer-assisted analysis of written language: Assessing the written language of deaf children. *Journal of Communication Disorders, 11,* 257–277.

Levy, B. (1977). Reading: Speech and meaning processes. *Journal of Verbal Learning and Verbal Behavior, 16,* 623–638.

Liberman, I., Shankweiler, D., Liberman, A., Fowler, C., & Fischer, F. (1977). Phonetic segmentation and recoding in the beginning reader. In A. Reber & D. Scarborough (Eds.), *Towards a psychology of reading: The proceedings of the C.U.N.Y. conferences* (pp. 207–225). Hillsdale, NJ: Lawrence Erlbaum Associates.

Lichtenstein, E. (1983). *The relationships between reading processes and English skills of deaf students.* Rochester, NY: National Technical Institute for the Deaf.

Lichtenstein, E. (1984). Deaf working memory processes and English language skills. In D. Martin (Ed.), *International symposium on cognition, education, and deafness: Working papers* (Vol. 2) (pp. 331–360). Washington, DC: Gallaudet College.

Liddell, S. (1975). *Restrictive relative clauses in American Sign Language.* San Diego, CA: Salk Institute and University of California.

Lieding, R., & Gammel, C. (1982). Reading in the preschool. *Volta Review, 84,* 166–170.

Ling, D. (1976). *Speech and the hearing impaired child: Theory and practice.* Washington, DC: Alexander Graham Bell Association for the Deaf.

Ling, D., & Ling, A. (1978). *Aural habilitation: The foundations of verbal learning in hearing-impaired children.* Washington, DC: Alexander Graham Bell Association for the Deaf.

Linn, R., Levine, M., Hastings, C. & Wardrop, J. (1980). *An investigation of item bias in a test of reading comprehension* (Tech. Rep. No. 163). Urbana, IL: University of Illinois, Center for the Study of Reading. (ERIC Document Reproduction Service No. ED 184 091)

Livingston, S. (1981). *The acquisition and development of sign language in deaf children of hearing parents.* Unpublished doctoral dissertation, New York University.

Locke, J. (1978). Phonemic effects in the silent reading of hearing and deaf children. *Cognition, 6,* 175–187.

Locke, J., & Fehr, F. (1970). Subvocal rehearsal as a form of speech. *Journal of Verbal Learning and Verbal Behavior, 9,* 495–498.

Locke, J., & Locke, V. (1971). Deaf children's phonetic, visual, and dactylic coding in a grapheme recall task. *Journal of Experimental Psychology, 89,* 142–146.

Logan, J. (1982). Classroom observation systems: An historical perspective. In J. Niles & L. Harris (Eds.), *New inquiries in reading: Research and instruction. Thirty-first yearbook of the National Reading Conference* (pp. 191–195). Rochester, NY: National Reading Conference.

Long, G., & Aldersley, G. (1982). Evaluation of a technique to enhance reading comprehension. *American Annals of the Deaf, 127,* 816–820.

Long, G., & Conklin, D. (1979). The implementation and evaluation of a technique for improving the prose comprehension of deaf college students. In G. Propp (Ed.), *1980's schools... Portals to century 21. Selected papers* (pp. 158–170). Silver Spring, MD: Convention of American Instructors of the Deaf.

Long, J., Schaffran, J., & Kellogg, T. (1977). Effects of out-of-level survey testing on reading achievement scores of Title I, ESEA students. *Journal of Educational Measurement, 14,* 203–213.

Lorsbach, T. (1982). Individual differences in semantic encoding processes. *Journal of Learning Disabilities, 15,* 476–480.

Lott, D. (1983). Analyzing and counteracting interference errors. *English Language Teaching Journal, 37,* 256–261.

Lovell, K., & Bradbury, B. (1967). The learning of English morphology in educationally subnormal special school children. *American Journal of Mental Deficiency, 71,* 609–615.

Lovitt, T., & Fantasia, K. (1980). Two approaches to reading program evaluation: A standardization text and direct assessment. *Learning Disabilities Quarterly, 3*(4), 77–82.

Lubert, N. (1981). Auditory perceptual impairments in children with specific language disorders: A review of the literature. *Journal of Speech and Hearing Disorders, 46*, 3–9.

Lucas, E. (1980). *Semantic and pragmatic language disorders: Assessment and remediation.* Rockville, MD: Aspen Systems.

Luetke-Stahlman, B. (1982). A philosophy for assessing the language proficiency of hearing-impaired students to promote English literacy. *American Annals of the Deaf, 127*, 844–851.

Luetke-Stahlman, B. (1984). Determining first language composition using cognitively demanding/context-reduced tasks. In D. Martin (Ed.), *International symposium on cognition, education, and deafness: Trends in research and instruction* (Vol. 1) (pp. 186–206). Washington, DC: Gallaudet College.

Lumsden, J. (1976). Test theory. *Annual review of Psychology, 27*, 251–280.

MacGinitie, W. (1969). Flexibility in dealing with alternative meanings of words. In J. Rosenstein & W. MacGinitie (Eds.), *Verbal behavior of the deaf child: Studies of word meanings and associations* (pp. 45–55). New York: Columbia University, Teachers College Press.

MacGinitie, W., Kamons, J., Kowalski, R., MacGinitie, R., & MacKay, T. (1978). *Teacher manual: Gates-MacGinitie Reading Tests* (2nd ed). Boston: Houghton Mifflin.

Madaus, G. (1981). Reactions to the Pittsburgh papers. *Phi Delta Kappan, 62*, 634–636.

Madsen, H., & Bowen, J. (1978). *Adaptation in language teaching.* Rowley, MA: Newbury House Publishers.

Maeder, J. (1979). *Comparative effectiveness of inserted postquestions in prose learning on the reading comprehension of hearing-impaired children.* Washington, DC: Model Secondary School for the Deaf.

Maeder, J. (1981). *Career exploration* (Teacher guide and student reading book). Washington, DC: Gallaudet College, Outreach Programs.

Maeder, J. (1982). *Career awareness* (Teacher guide and student workbook). Washington, DC: Gallaudet College, Outreach Programs.

Malcolm, A. (1983). *A workbook in library science for NTID students.* Rochester, NY: National Technical Institute for the Deaf.

Mandler, J. (1978). A code in the node: The use of a story schema in retrieval. *Discourse Processes, 1*, 14–35.

Mandler, J., & Johnson, N. (1977). Remembrance of things parsed: Story structure and recall. *Cognitive Psychology, 9*, 111–151.

Marks, C., Doctorow, M., & Wittrock, M. (1974). Word frequency and reading comprehension. *Journal of Educational Research, 67*, 254–262.

Marr, M. (1983). An analysis of text variables in three current reading diagnostic tests. In J. Niles & L. Harry (Eds.), *Searches for meaning in reading/language processing and instruction: Thirty-second yearbook of the National Reading Conference* (pp. 115–122). Rochester, NY: National Reading Conference.

Marshman, K. (1974). *A descriptive study of reading instruction for the deaf in residential public schools in the United States.* Unpublished doctoral dissertation, University of Georgia.

Martuza, V. (1977). *Applying norm-referenced and criterion-referenced measurement in education.* Boston: Allyn and Bacon.

Mason, J. (1977). *Reading readiness: A definition and skills hierarchy from preschoolers' developing conceptions of print* (Tech. Rep. No. 59). Urbana, IL: University of Illinois, Center for the Study of Reading. (ERIC Document Reproduction Service No. ED 145 403)

Mason, J. (1984). Early reading from a developmental perspective. In P. D. Pearson (Ed.), *Handbook of reading research* (pp. 505–543). London: Longman.

Mason, J., & Kendall, J. (1978). *Facilitating reading comprehension through text structure manipulation* (Tech. Rep. No. 92). Urbana, IL: University of Illinois, Center for the Study of Reading. (ERIC Document Reproduction Service No. ED 157 041)

Mason, J., & Kendall, J. (1979). Facilitating reading comprehension through text structure manipulation. *Alberta Journal of Educational Psychology, 24,* 68–76.

Mason, J., Kniseley, E., & Kendall, J. (1979). Effects of polysemous words on sentence comprehension. *Reading Research Quarterly, 15,* 49–65.

Mason, J., & Osborn, J. (1982). *When do children begin "reading to learn"?: A survey of classroom reading instruction practices in grades two through five* (Tech. Rep. No. 261). Urbana, IL: University of Illinois, Center for the Study of Reading.

Mason, J., Osborn, J., & Rosenshine, B. (1977). *A consideration of skill hierarchy approaches to the teaching of reading* (Tech. Rep. No. 42). Urbana, IL: Center for the Study of Reading, University of Illinois. (ERIC Document Reproduction Service No. ED 150 549)

Maupin, D. (1981). *Deaf Eagle and the bank robber.* Washington, DC: Gallaudet College, Outreach Programs.

Max, L. (1935). An experimental study of the motor theory of consciousness: Action-current responses in deaf-mutes during sleep, sensory stimulation, and dreams. *Journal of Comparative Psychology, 19,* 469–486.

Maxwell, M. (1980). Language acquisition in a deaf child of deaf parents: Speech, sign variations, and print variations. In K. E. Nelson (Ed.), *Children's language* (Vol. 4) (pp. 283–311). Hillsdale, NJ: Lawrence Erlbaum Associates.

McCarr, D. (1973). Individualized reading for junior and senior high school students. *American Annals of the Deaf, 118,* 488–495.

McCarthy, D. (1954). Language development in children. In L. Carmichael (Ed.), *Manual of child psychology* (2nd ed.) (pp. 492–630). New York: John Wiley and Sons.

McCaughrin, W. (1981). Reading and writing tests for deaf students ages 6 through adult. In D. Johnson, G. Walter, K. Crandall, D. McPherson, J. Subtelny, H. Levitt, F. Caccamise, & M. Davis (Eds.), *Communication performance evaluation with deaf students: A review* (pp. 113–150). Rochester, NY: National Technical Institute for the Deaf.

McCaughrin, W., & Idol-Maestas, L. (1983). *Oral language performance of normal and poor readers.* Unpublished manuscript, University of Illinois, Department of Special Education, Champaign–Urbana.

McCawley, J. (1968). The role of semantics in a grammar. In E. Bach & R. Harms (Eds.), *Universals in linguistic theory* (pp. 125–169). New York: Holt, Rinehart and Winston.

McConkie, G. (1982). Some perceptual aspects of reading. In R. E. Kretschmer (Ed.), Reading and the hearing-impaired individual. *Volta Review, 84,* 35–43.

McConkie, G. (1984). *Computer-aided reading: A new environment for learning to read.* (Exhibit at the International Reading Association Convention, Atlanta). Savoy, IL: Reading Technology, Inc.

McConkie, G., & Rayner, K. (1976). Asymmetry of the perceptual span in reading. *Bulletin of the Psychonomic Society, 8,* 365–368.

McConkie, G., & Zola, D. (1979). Is visual information integrated across successive fixations in reading? *Perception and Psychophysics, 25,* 221–224.

McConkie, G., & Zola, D. (1981). Language constraints and the functional stimulus in reading. In A. Lesgold & C. Perfetti (Eds.), *Interactive processes in reading* (pp. 155–175). Hillsdale, NJ: Lawrence Erlbaum Associates.

McGee, L. (1982). The influence of metacognitive knowledge of expository text structure on discourse recall. In J. Niles & L. Harris (Eds.), *New inquiries in reading: Research and instruction. Thirty-first yearbook of the National Reading Conference* (pp. 64–70). Rochester, NY: National Reading Conference.

McGill-Franzen, A., & Gormley, K. (1980). The influence of context on deaf readers' understanding of passive sentences. *American Annals of the Deaf, 125,* 937–942.

McKee, B., & Bondi-Wolcott, J. (1982). Three studies of the relation of item format and estimates of achievement for hearing-impaired postsecondary students. In F. Solano, J. Egelston-Dodd, & E. Costello (Eds.), *Focus on infusion* (Vol. 1) (pp. 146–154). Silver Spring, MD: Convention of American Instructors of the Deaf.

McKee, B., & Hausknecht, M. (1980). Classroom assessment techniques for hearing impaired students: A literature review, *Directions, 1*(4), 9–15.

McKee, B., & Lang, H. (1982). A comparison of deaf students' performance on true-false and multiple-choice items. *American Annals of the Deaf, 127,* 49–54.

McKee, P., Harrison, M., McCowen, A., Lehr, E., & Durr, W. (1966). *Reading for meaning* (4th ed.). Boston: Houghton Mifflin.

McKenna, M. (1976). Synonymic versus verbatim scoring of the cloze procedure. *Journal of Reading, 20,* 141–143.

McLaughlin, B. (1978). *Second-language acquisition in childhood.* Hillsdale, NJ: Lawrence Erlbaum Associates.

McLaughlin, B. (1982). Second-language learning and bilingualism in children and adults. In S. Rosenberg (Ed.), *Handbook of applied psycholinguistics* (pp. 217–256). Hillsdale, NJ: Lawrence Erlbaum Associates.

McLaughlin, G. (1966). Comparing styles of presenting technical information. *Ergonomics, 9,* 257–259.

McLaughlin, J., & Andrews, J. (1975). The reading habits of deaf adults in Baltimore. *American Annals of the Deaf, 120,* 497–501.

McLeavey, B., Toomey, J., & Dempsey, P. (1982). Nonretarded and mentally retarded children's control over syntactic structures. *American Journal of Mental Deficiency, 86,* 485–494.

McNamara, W., & Weizman, J. (1945). The effect of choice placement on the difficulty of multiple-choice. *Journal of Educational Psychology, 36,* 103–113.

McNeil, J. (1984). *Reading comprehension: New directions for classroom practice.* Glenview, IL: Scott, Foresman, and Company.

McNeill, D. (1978). Speech and thought. In I. Markova (Ed.), *The social context of language* (pp. 177–197). New York: John Wiley and Sons.

Memory, D. (1982). Written questions as reading aids in the middle grades: A review of research. In J. Niles & L. Harris (Eds.), *New inquiries in reading: Research and instruction: Thirty-first yearbook of the National Reading Conference* (pp. 71–76). Rochester, NY: National Reading Conference.

Memory, D. (1983). Main idea prequestions as adjunct aids with good and low-average middle grade readers. *Journal of Reading Behavior, 15,* 37–48.

Menyuk, P. (1963a). A preliminary evaluation of grammatical capacity in children. *Journal of Verbal Learning and Verbal Behavior, 2,* 429–439.

Menyuk, P. (1963b). Syntactic structures in the language of children. *Child Development, 34,* 407–422.

Menyuk, P. (1964). Comparison of grammar of children with functionally deviant and normal speech. *Journal of Speech and Hearing Research, 7,* 109–121.

Menyuk, P. (1969). *Sentences children use.* Cambridge, MA: MIT Press.

Menyuk P., & Looney, P. (1972). A problem of language disorder: Length versus structure. *Journal of Speech and Hearing Research, 15,* 264–279.

Meyer, B. (1975). *The organization of prose and its effects on memory.* Amsterdam, Holland: North-Holland Publishing Co.

Meyer, B., Brandt, D., & Bluth, G. (1980). Use of top-level structures in text: Key for reading comprehension of ninth-grade students. *Reading Research Quarterly, 16,* 72–103.

Meyer, B., & Rice, G. (1984). The structure of text. In P. D. Pearson (Ed.), *Handbook of reading research* (pp. 319–351). London: Longman.

Meyer, L. (1982). The relative effects of word-analysis and word-supply correction procedures with poor readers during word-attack training. *Reading Research Quarterly, 17,* 544–555.

Milon, J. (1974). The development of negation in English by a second language learner. *TESOL Quarterly, 8,* 137–143.

Miller, J., & Chapman, R. (1982). *Systematic analysis of language transcripts* (computer program). Madison, WI: Language Analysis Laboratory, Waisman Center on Mental Retardation and Human Development.

Miller, R., & Paul, F. (1984). *Educational coloring books.* Berkeley, CA: Dawn Sign Press.

Miller, W. (1978). *Reading diagnosis kit.* Normal, IL: The Center for Applied Research in Education.

Mitchell, J., Bradley, J., & Ames, W. (1982). Original versus adapted short stories: The perceptions of adolescent readers. In J. Niles & L. Harris (Eds.), *New inquiries in reading: Research and instruction. Thirty-first yearbook of the National Reading Conference* (pp. 77–80). Rochester, NY: National Reading Conference.

Modiano, N. (1968). National or mother language in beginning reading: A comparative study. *Research in the Teaching of English, 2,* 32–43.

Mogford, K., Gregory, S., & Keay, S. (1978). Picture book reading with mother: A comparison between hearing-impaired and hearing children at 18 and 20 months. *Journal of British Association of Teachers of the Deaf, 3,* 43–45.

Monsen, R. (1979). The production of labial occlusives in young hearing-impaired children. *Language and Speech, 22,* 311–318.

Montandon, B. (1982). Multi-level captioning: Alternatives that match the viewers' abilities. *Perspectives for Teachers of the Hearing Impaired, 1(2),* 8–12.

Moog, J., & Geers, A. (1980). *Grammatical analysis of elicited language.* St. Louis: Central Institute for the Deaf.

Moores, D. (1967). *Applications of "cloze" procedures to the assessment of psycholinguitic abilities of the deaf.* Unpublished doctoral dissertation, University of Illinois at Urbana-Champaign.

Moores, D. (1978). *Educating the deaf: Psychology, principles, and practices.* Boston: Houghton Mifflin.

Mordecai, D., Palin, M., & Palmer, C. (1982). *Lingquest 1. Language sample analysis.* Napa, CA: Lingquest Software.

Morehead, D., & Ingram, D. (1973). The development of base syntax in normal and linguistically deviant children. *Journal of Speech and Hearing Research, 16,* 330–352.

Morgan, J., & Sellner, M. (1980). Discourse and linguistic theory. In R. Spiro, B. Bruce, & W. Brewer (Eds.), *Theoretical issues in reading comprehension* (pp. 165–200). New York: Lawrence Erlbaum Associates.

Mosenthal, P. (1984). Reading comprehension research from a classroom perspective. In J. Flood (Ed.), *Promoting reading comprehension* (pp. 16–29). Newark, DE: International Reading Association.

Mosenthal, P., & Na, T. (1980). Quality of children's recall under two classroom testing tasks: Towards a socio-psycholinguistic model of reading comprehension. *Reading Research Quarterly, 15,* 504–528.

Mothner, H. (1980). A technique for teaching the unmotivated reader. *American Annals of the Deaf, 125,* 551–553.

Moulton, R., & Beasley, D. (1975). Verbal coding strategies used by hearing-impaired individuals. *Journal of Speech and Hearing Research, 18,* 559–570.

Mukattash, L. (1980). Yes/no questions and the contrastive analysis hypothesis. *English Language Teaching Journal, 34,* 133–145.

Murphy, L. (1957). Tests of ability and attainments: Pupils in schools for the deaf aged six to ten. In A. Ewing (Ed.), *Educational guidance and the deaf child.* Manchester, England: Manchester University Press.

Murphy-Berman, V., & Jorgensen, J. (1980). Evaluation of a multilevel linguistic approach to captioning television for hearing-impaired children. *American Annals of the Deaf, 125,* 1072–1081.

Myborg, M. (1981a). *The fir tree* (Reading classics series). Washington, DC: Gallaudet College, Outreach Programs.

Myborg, M. (1981b). *Hans Brinker* (Reading classics series). Washington, DC: Gallaudet College, Outreach Programs.

Myborg, M. (1981c). *The legend of Sleepy Hollow* (Reading classics series). Washington, DC: Gallaudet College, Outreach Programs.

Myklebust, H. (1960). *The psychology of deafness*. New York: Grune & Stratton.

Nagy, W., & Herman, P. (1984). *Limitations of vocabulary instruction* (Tech. Rep. No. 326). Urbana, IL: University of Illinois, Center for the Study of Reading.

Naremore, R., & Dever, R. (1975). Language performance of educable mentally retarded and normal children at five age levels. *Journal of Speech and Hearing Research*, *18*, 82–95.

Nash-Webber, B. (1977). *Anaphora: A cross-disciplinary survey* (Tech. Rep. No. 31). Urbana, IL: University of Illinois, Center for the Study of Reading. (ERIC Document Reproduction Service No. ED 144 039)

Nash-Webber, B. (1978). *Inferences in an approach to discourse anaphora*. (Tech. Rep. No. 77). Urbana, IL: University of Illinois, Center for the Study of Reading. (ERIC Document Reproduction Service No. ED 150 552)

Natalicio, D., & Natalicio, L. (1971). A comparative study of English pluralization by native and non-native English speakers. *Child Development*, *42*, 1302–1306.

National Education Research. (1978). Teacher opinion poll: Group standardized tests. *Today's Education*, *67*, 20.

Nelson, K. (1974). Concept, word, and sentence: Interrelationships in acquisition and development. *Psychological Review*, *81*, 267–285.

Nelson, K. E. (1977). Cognitive development and the acquisition of concepts. In R. C. Anderson, R. J. Spiro, & W. E. Montague (Eds.), *Schooling and the acquisition of knowledge* (pp. 215–239). Hillsdale, NJ: Lawrence Erlbaum Associates.

Nelson, M. (1949). The evolutionary process of teaching language to the deaf. *American Annals of the Deaf*, *95*, 230–295, 354–396, 491–511.

Neuhaus, M. (1967). Modifications in the administration of the WISC performance subtest for children with profound hearing losses. *Exceptional Children*, *33*, 573–574.

Newby, R. (1984a). *Hansel and Gretel* (Simple language fairy tales series). Beaverton, OR: Dormac.

Newby, R. (1984b). *Jack and the beanstalk* (Simple language fairy tales series). Beaverton, OR: Dormac.

Newby, R. (1984c). *Little Red Riding Hood* (Simple language fairy tales series). Beaverton, OR: Dormac.

Newby, R. (1984d). *The three bears* (Simple language fairy tales series). Beaverton, OR: Dormac.

Newby, R. (1984e). *The three little pigs* (Simple language fairy tales series). Beaverton, OR: Dormac.

Newfield, M., & Schlanger, B. (1968). The acquisition of English morphology by normal and educable mentally retarded children. *Journal of Speech and Hearing Research*, *11*, 693–706.

Newport, E., & Ashbrook, E. (1977). The emergence of semantic relations in

American Sign Language. *Papers and Reports on Child Language Development*, *13*, 16–21.

Nolen, S., & Wilbur, R. (1984). Context and comprehension: Another look. In D. Martin (Ed.), *International symposium on cognition, education, and deafness: Trends in research and instruction* (Vol. 2) (pp. 389–403). Washington, DC: Gallaudet College.

Noretsky, M. (1981). *The effects of syntactic modifications of reading materials on reading comprehension for severely or profoundly deaf college-age students.* Unpublished doctoral dissertation, University of Maryland, College Park.

Norman, D. (1972). The role of memory in the understanding of language. In J. Kavanagh & I. Mattingly (Eds.), *Language by ear and by eye: The relationships between speech and reading* (pp. 277–288). Cambridge, MA: MIT Press.

Norman, D., & Bobrow, G. (1975). On data-limited and resource-limited processes. *Cognitive Psychology*, *7*, 44–64.

Norris, C. (1982). *Jean's Christmas stocking.* Los Amitos, CA: Modern Signs Press.

Norris, C. (1984). *In our house.* Los Amitos, CA: Modern Signs Press.

O'Neill, M. (1973). *The receptive language competence of deaf children in the use of the base structure rules of transformational generative grammar.* Unpublished doctoral dissertation, University of Pittsburgh, PA.

O'Shea, L., & Sindelar, P. (1983). The effects of segmenting written discourse on the reading comprehension of low- and high-performance readers. *Reading Research Quarterly*, *18*, 458–465.

Oaken, R., Weiner, M., & Cromer, W. (1971). Identification, organization, and reading comprehension for good and poor readers. *Journal of Educational Psychology*, *62*, 71–78.

Odom, P., Blanton, R., & McIntyre, C. (1970). Coding medium and word recall by deaf and hearing subjects. *Journal of Speech and Hearing Research*, *13*, 54–58.

Office of Demographic Studies (1973). *Stanford Achievement Test–Version for hearing-impaired students.* Washington, DC: Gallaudet College, Office of Demographic Studies. [Adapted from *Stanford Achievement Test*, 1972, New York: Harcourt Brace Jovanovich].

Office of Demographic Studies. (n.d.). *Normative tables. SAT-HI, Spring, 1974.* Washington, DC: Gallaudet College, Office of Demographic Studies.

Ogden, P. (1979). *Experiences and attitudes of oral deaf adults regarding oralism.* Unpublished doctoral dissertation, University of Illinois at Urbana-Champaign.

Oliver, L. (1977). The reading interests of children in the primary grades. *Elementary School Journal*, *77*, 401–406.

Olsen, H. (1984). *Skills for living.* Washington, DC: Gallaudet College, Outreach Programs.

Olson, J. (1974). *Song of Roland.* Silver Spring, MD: National Association of the Deaf.

Omanson, R., Warren, W., & Trabasso, T. (1978). Goals, inferential comprehension, and recall of stories by children. *Discourse Processes*, *1*, 337–354.

Orton, S. (1937). *Reading, writing, and speech problems in children.* New York: Norton.

Ortony, A. (Ed.) (1979). *Metaphor and thought.* Cambridge: Cambridge University Press.

Ortony, A., Schallert, D., Reynolds, R., & Antos, S. (1978). *Interpreting metaphors and idioms: Some effects of context on comprehension* (Tech. Rep. No. 93). Urbana, IL: University of Illinois, Center for the Study of Reading. (ERIC Document Reproduction Service No. ED 157 042)

Osborn, J. (1981). *The purposes, uses, and contents of workbooks and some guidelines for teachers and publishers* (Ed. Rep. No. 27). Urbana, IL: University of Illinois, Center for the Study of Reading. (ERIC Document Reproduction Service No. ED 207 020)

Osborn, J. (1984). The purposes, uses, and contents of workbooks and some guidelines for publishers. In R. Anderson, J. Osborn, & R. Tierney (Eds.), *Learning to read in American schools. Basal readers and content area texts* (pp. 45–111). Hillsdale, NJ: Lawrence Erlbaum Associates.

Osgood, J. (1977). *The influence of structural mode of written material on the comprehension scores of deaf and hearing children at the second and fourth-grade reading level.* Unpublished doctoral dissertation. University of Illinois at Urbana-Champaign.

Osguthorpe, R., Long, G., & Ellsworth, R. (1977). *The effect of reviewing class notes for deaf and hearing students.* Rochester, NY: National Technical Institute for the Deaf.

Ottem, E. (1980). An analysis of cognitive studies with deaf subjects. *American Annals of the Deaf, 125,* 564–575.

Otto, W., Barrett, J., & Koenke, K. (1969). Assessment of children's statements of the main idea in reading. *Proceedings of the International Reading Association, 13,* 692–697.

Otto, W., White, S., & Camperell, K. (1980). Text comprehension research to classroom application: Developing an instructional technique. *Reading Psychology, 1,* 184–191.

Page, S. (1981). *The effect of idiomatic language in passages on the reading comprehension of deaf and hearing students.* Unpublished doctoral dissertation, Ball State University (Abstract).

Palincsar, A. (1981). *A corrective feedback and strategy training program to improve the comprehension of poor readers.* Unpublished doctoral dissertation, University of Illinois at Urbana–Champaign.

Parasnis, I. (1983). The effects of parental deafness and early exposure to manual communication on the cognitive skills, English language skill, and field independence of young deaf adults. *Journal of Speech and Hearing Research, 26,* 588–594.

Parasnis, I., & Long, G. (1979). Relationships among spatial skills, communication skills, and field independence in deaf students. *Perceptual and Motor Skills, 49,* 887–897.

Paris, J., & Tracy, S. (1982). *Fables/Myths.* Beaverton, OR: Dormac.

Paris, S., & Lindauer, B. (1976). The role of inference in children's comprehension and memory. *Cognitive Psychology, 8,* 217–227.

Parisi, D., & Antinucci, F. (1976). *Essentials of grammar.* New York: Academic Press.

Paul, P. (1984). *The comprehension of multimeaning words from selected frequency levels by deaf and hearing subjects.* Unpublished doctoral dissertation, University of Illinois at Urbana–Champaign.

Payne, J.-A. (1982). *A study of the comprehension of verb-particle combinations among deaf and hearing subjects.* Unpublished doctoral dissertation, University of Illinois at Urbana–Champaign.

Pearson, P. D. (1974–1975). The effects of grammatical complexity on children's comprehension: Recall and conception of certain semantic relations. *Reading Research Quarterly, 10,* 155–92.

Pearson, P. D. (1978). *The text and the task in reading comprehension.* Paper presented at the International Reading Association Convention, Houston.

Pearson, P. D. (1984a). A context for instructional research on reading comprehension. In J. Flood (Ed.), *Promoting reading comprehension* (pp. 1–15). Newark, DE: International Reading Association.

Pearson, P. D. (Ed). (1984b). *Handbook of reading research.* London: Longman.

Pearson, P. D., Hansen, J., & Gordon, C. (1979). The effect of background knowledge on young children's comprehension of explicit and implicit information. *Journal of Reading Behavior, 11,* 201–210.

Pearson, P. D., & Johnson, D. (1978). *Teaching reading comprehension.* New York: Holt, Rinehart and Winston.

Peeck, J. (1974). Retention of pictorial and verbal content of a text with illustration. *Journal of Educational Psychology, 66,* 880–888.

Perfetti, C., & Hogaboam, T. (1975). The relationship between single word decoding and reading comprehension skill. *Journal of Educational Psychology, 67,* 461–469.

Perfetti, C., & Lesgold, A. (1977). Discourse comprehension and sources of individual differences. In M. Just & P. Carpenter (Eds.), *Cognitive processes*

Peter, Sr. M. (1973, 1974, 1978). *The Jack and Julie series.* Milwaukee, MI: St. Johns School for the Deaf.

Peterson, J., Greenlaw, M., & Tierney, R. (1978). Assessing instructional placement with the IRI: The effectiveness of comprehension questions. *Journal of Educational Research, 71,* 247–250.

Petrie, H. (1979). Metaphor and learning. In A. Ortony (Ed.), *Metaphor and thought* (pp. 438–461). Cambridge: Cambridge University Press.

Pfau, G. (1963–1974a). *Science series* (Project LIFE). Albany, NY: Instructional Industries.

Pfau, G. (1963–1974b). *Social studies series* (Project LIFE). Albany, NY: Instructional Industries.

Pfau, G. (1963–1974c). *Prereading series* (Project LIFE). Albany, NY: Instructional Industries.

Pfau, G. (1963–1974d). *Reading-Language series* (Project LIFE). Albany, NY: Instructional Industries.

Piaget, J. (1955). *The language and thought of the child*. New York: Meridian Books.

Piaget, J. (1967). *Six psychological studies*. (A. Tenzer, Trans.). New York: Random House. (Original work published 1964)

Pickert, S. (1978). Repetitive sentence patterns in children's books. *Language Arts, 55*, 800–806.

Pikulski, J., & Shanahan, T. (1982). Informal reading inventories: A critical analysis. In J. Piluski & T. Shanahan (Eds). *Approaches to the informal evaluation of reading* (pp. 94–116). Newark, DE: International Reading Association.

Pikulski, J., & Tobin, A. (1982). The cloze procedure as an informal assessment technique. In J. Piluski & T. Shanahan (Eds). *Approaches to the informal evaluation of reading* (pp. 42–62). Newark, DE: International Reading Association.

Pintner, R., Eisenson, J., & Stanton, M. (1941). *The psychology of the physically handicapped*. New York: Crofts.

Pintner, R., & Patterson, D. (1916). A measurement of the language ability of deaf children. *Psychological Review, 23*, 413–436.

Pintner, R., & Reamer, J. (1920). A mental and educational survey of schools for the deaf. *American Annals of the Deaf, 65*, 451–472.

Pollio, M., & Pollio, H. (1979). A test of metaphoric comprehension and some preliminary developmental data. *Journal of Child Language, 6*, 111–120.

Politzer, R., & Ramirez, A. (1973). An error analysis of the spoken English of Mexican-American pupils in bilingual and monolingual schooling. *Language Learning, 23*, 39–62.

Porter, R. (1977). A cross-sectional study of morpheme acquisition in first language learners. *Language Learning, 27*, 47–62.

Power, D., & Quigley, S. (1973). Deaf children's acquisition of the passive voice. *Journal of Speech and Hearing Research, 16*, 5–11.

Prickett, H., & Hunt, J. (1977). Education of the deaf—the next ten years. *American Annals of the Deaf, 122*, 365–381.

Prinz, P., & Ferrier, L. (1983). "Can you give me that one?": The comprehension, production, and judgment of directives in language impaired children. *Journal of Speech and Hearing Disorders, 48*, 44–54.

Prinz, P., & Nelson, K. E. (1984). A child-computer-teacher interactive method for teaching reading to young deaf children. In D. Martin (Ed.), *International symposium on cognition, education, and deafness: Trends in research and instruction* (Vol. 2) (pp. 419–444). Washington, DC: Gallaudet College.

Prinz, P., Nelson, K. E., & Stedt, J. (1982). Early reading in young deaf children using microcomputer technology. *American Annals of the Deaf, 127*, 529–535.

Pugh, G. (1946). Summaries from appraisal of the silent reading abilities of acoustically handicapped children. *American Annals of the Deaf, 91*, 331–349.

Pugh, R., & Brunza, J. (1975). Effects of a confidence weighted scoring system on measures of test reliability and validity. *Educational and Psychological Measurement, 35*, 73–78.

Pyrczak, F. (1975–1976). A responsive note on measures of the passage dependence of reading comprehension test items. *Reading Research Quarterly, 11*, 112–117.

Quigley, S. (1978). Effect of reading impairment on reading development. In H. Reynolds & C. Williams (Eds.), *Proceedings of the Gallaudet conference on reading in relation to deafness* (pp. 9–37). Washington, DC: Gallaudet College.

Quigley, S., & Frisina, R. (1961). *Institutionalization and psychoeducational development of deaf children, CEC Research Monograph.* Washington, DC: Council on Exceptional Children.

Quigley, S., & King, C. (Eds.). (1981, 1982, 1983, 1984). *Reading milestones.* Beaverton, OR: Dormac.

Quigley, S., & King, C. (1982a). The language development of deaf children and youth. In S. Rosenberg (Ed.), *Handbook of applied psycholinguistics: Major thrusts of research and theory* (pp. 429–475). Hillsdale, NJ: Lawrence Erlbaum Associates.

Quigley, S., & King, C. (Eds.). (1982b). *Reading milestones. Level 5.* Beaverton, OR: Dormac.

Quigley, S., & King, C. (Eds.). (1984). *Reading milestones. Level 8.* Beaverton, OR: Dormac.

Quigley, S., & Kretschmer, R. E. (1982). *The education of deaf children: Issues, theory, and practice.* Baltimore: University Park Press.

Quigley, S., & Paul, P. (1984a). *Language and deafness.* San Diego, CA: College-Hill Press.

Quigley, S., & Paul, P. (1984b). ASL and ESL? *Topics in Early Childhood Special Education, 3*(4), 17–26.

Quigley, S., Power, D., & Steinkamp, M. (1977). The language structure of deaf children. *Volta Review, 79,* 73–84.

Quigley, S., Smith, N., & Wilbur, R. (1974). Comprehension of relativized sentences by deaf students. *Journal of Speech and Hearing Research, 17,* 325–341.

Quigley, S., Steinkamp, M., Power, D., & Jones, B. (1978). *Test of syntactic abilities.* Beaverton, OR: Dormac.

Quigley, S., Wilbur, R., & Montanelli, D. (1974). Question formation in the language of deaf students. *Journal of Speech and Hearing Research, 17,* 699–713.

Quigley, S., Wilbur, R., Power, D., Montanelli, D., & Steinkamp, M. (1976). *Syntactic structure in the language of deaf children.* Urbana, IL: University of Illinois, Institute for Child Behavior and Development.

Quinn, L. (1981). Reading skills of hearing and congenitally deaf children. *Journal of Experimental Child Psychology, 32*(1), 139–161.

Raban, B. (1982). Text display effects on the fluency of young readers. *Journal of Research in Reading, 5,* 7–28.

Raffin, M. (1976). *The acquisition of inflectional morphemes by deaf children using Seeing Essential English.* Unpublished doctoral dissertation, University of Iowa, Iowa City.

Raffin, M., Davis, J., & Gilman, L. (1978). Comprehension of inflectional morphemes by deaf children exposed to a visual English sign system. *Journal of Speech and Hearing Research, 21,* 387–400.

Rankin, E. (1974). *The measurement of reading flexibility.* Newark, DE: International Reading Association.

Raphael, T. (1981). *The effect of metacognitive awareness training on students' question-answering strategies.* Unpublished doctoral dissertation. University of Illinois at Urbana-Champaign.

Raphael, T. (1982). Question-answering strategies for children. *Reading Teacher, 36,* 186–190.

Raphael, T. (1984). Teaching learners about sources of information for answering comprehension questions. *Journal of Reading, 27,* 303–311.

Raphael, T., & McKinney, J. (1983). An examination of fifth- and eighth-grade children's question-answering behavior: An instructional study in metacognition. *Journal of Reading Behavior, 15,* 67–86.

Raphael, T., & Pearson, P. D. (1982). *The effects of metacognitive training on children's question-answering behavior* (Tech. Rep. No. 238). Urbana, IL: University of Illinois, Center for the Study of Reading.

Raphael, T., Winograd, P., & Pearson, P.D. (1980). Strategies children use when answering questions. In M. Kamil & A. Moe (Eds.), *Perspectives on reading research and instruction. Twenty-ninth yearbook of the National Reading Conference* (pp. 56–63). Washington, DC: National Reading Conference.

Raphael, T., & Wonnacott, C. (1981). *The effect of type of response and type of post-test on understanding of and memory for text.* Paper presented at the National Reading Conference, Dallas, TX. (ERIC Document Reproduction Service No. ED 212 998)

Ravem, R. (1974a). Language acquisition in a second-language environment. In J. Richards (Ed.), *Error analysis: Perspectives on second language acquisition* (pp. 124–133). London: Longman.

Ravem, R. (1974b). The development of wh- questions in first and second language learners. In J. Richards (Ed.), *Error analysis: Perspectives on second language acquisition* (pp. 134–155). London: Longman.

Rawlings, B., & Allen, T. (1980). *1980 final report to the Texas Education Agency of the Texas statewide survey of hearing-impaired children and youth.* Washington, DC: Gallaudet College, Office of Demographic Studies.

Rayner, K., McConkie, G., & Zola, D. (1980). Integrating information across eye movements. *Cognitive Psychology, 12,* 206–226.

Redgate, G. (1973). *Reading into the teaching of reading to deaf children.* Annual Report: Department of Audiology and Education of the Deaf. University of Manchester, Manchester, England. (ERIC Document Reproduction Service No. ED 088 068)

Reed, M. (1973). Deaf and partially hearing children. In P. Mittler (Ed.), *The psychological assessment of mental and physical handicaps.* London: Tavistock Publications.

Resnick, D. (1981). Testing in America: A supportive environment. *Phi Delta Kappan, 62,* 625–628.

Resnick, L., & Weaver, P. (1979). *Theory and practice of early reading* (Vols. 1, 2, and 3). Hillsdale, NJ: Lawrence Erlbaum Associates.

Reynolds, H., & Booher, H. (1980). The effects of pictorial and verbal instructional materials on the operational performance of deaf subjects. *Journal of Special*

Education, 14, 175–187.

Reynolds, R., & Ortony, A. (1980). Some issues in the measurement of children's comprehension of metaphorical language. *Child Development, 51,* 1110–1119.

Richards, J. (1973). Error analysis and second language strategies. In J. Oller & J. Richards (Eds.), *Focus on the learner: Pragmatic perspectives for the language teacher* (pp. 114–135). Rowley, MA: Newbury House.

Richards, J., (1974a). Error analysis and second language strategies. In J. Schumann & N. Stenson (Eds.), *New frontiers in second language learning* (pp. 32–53). Rowley, MA: Newbury House.

Richards, J., (1974b). *Error analysis: Perspectives on second language acquisition.* London: Longman.

Richards, J., (1974c). A non-contrastive approach to error analysis. In J. Richards (Ed.), *Error analysis: Perspectives on second language acquisition* (pp. 172–188). London: Longman.

Richaudeau, F. (1981). Some French work on prose readability and syntax (translated by D. Staats). *Journal of Reading, 24,* 503–508.

Richek, M. (1976). Effects of sentence complexity on the reading comprehension of syntactic structures. *Journal of Educational Psychology, 68,* 800–806.

Richgels, D., & Hansen, R. (1984). Gloss I: Helping students apply both skills and strategies in reading content texts. *Journal of Reading, 27,* 312–317.

Richgels, D., & Mateja, J. (1984). Gloss II: Integrating content and process for independence. *Journal of Reading, 27,* 424–431.

Rittenhouse, R. (1977). *Horizontal decalage: The development of conservation in deaf students and the effect of the task instructions on their performance.* Unpublished doctoral dissertation, University of Illinois at Urbana–Champaign.

Rittenhouse, R., & Spiro, R. (1979). Conservation performance in day and residential school deaf children. *Volta Review, 81,* 501–509.

Robbins, N. (1983). The effects of signed text on the reading comprehension of hearing-impaired children. *American Annals of the Deaf, 128,* 40–44.

Robbins, N., & Hatcher, C. (1981). The effects of syntax on the reading comprehension of hearing-impaired children. *Volta Review, 83,* 105–115.

Robinson, H., & Robinson, N. (1965). *The mentally retarded child: A psychological approach.* New York: McGraw-Hill.

Rogers, W. (1983). Use of separate answer sheets with hearing impaired and deaf school age students. *British Columbia Journal of Special Education, 7*(1), 63–72.

Rogers, W., Leslie, P., Clarke, B., Booth, J., & Horvath, A. (1978). Academic achievement of hearing impaired students: Comparison among selected subpopulations. *British Columbia Journal of Special Education, 2,* 183–213.

Rosansky, E. (1976). Methods and morphemes in second language acquisition. *Language Learning, 26,* 409–425.

Roppelt, D., & Mowl, M. (1982). *Tomorrow, we're taking a test.* Silver Spring, MD: TJ Publishing Company.

Rosenbaum, J. (1980). Social implications of educational grouping. In D. Berliner (Ed.), *Review of research in education* (Vol. 8) (pp. 361–401). Chicago: Rand-McNally (American Educational Research Association).

Rosenberg, S. (1982). Applied psycholinguistics: Introduction, foundations and overview. In S. Rosenberg (Ed.), *Handbook of applied psycholinguistics: Major thrusts of research and theory* (pp. 1–31). Hillsdale, NJ: Lawrence Erlbaum Associates.

Rosenbloom, B. (1981). *Guidelines to writing or rewriting materials for deaf students with special emphasis on syntax.* Washington, DC: Gallaudet College, Outreach Programs.

Rosenstein, J. (1961). Perception, cognition, and language in deaf children. *Exceptional Children, 27,* 276–284.

Roser, N., & Frith, M. (1983). *Children's choices: Teaching with books children like.* Newark, DE: International Reading Association.

Roser, N., & Juel, C. (1982). Effects of vocabulary instruction on reading comprehension. In J. Niles & L. Harris (Eds.), *New inquiries in reading: Research and instruction. Thirty-first yearbook of the National Reading Conference* (pp. 110–118). Rochester, NY: National Reading Conference.

Royer, J., & Cunningham, J. (1978). *On the theory and measurement of reading comprehension* (Tech. Rep. No. 91). Urbana, IL: University of Illinois, Center for the Study of Reading. (ERIC Document Reproduction Service No. ED 157 040)

Rubin, A. (1981). *Conceptual readability: New ways to look at text* (Ed. Rep. No. 31). Urbana, IL: University of Illinois, Center for the Study of Reading. (ERIC Document Reproduction Service No. ED 208 370)

Ruddell, R., & Haggard, M. (1982). Influential teachers: Characteristics and classroom performance. In J. Niles & L. Harris (Eds.), *New inquiries in reading: Research and instruction. Thirty-first yearbook of the National Reading Conference* (pp. 227–231). Rochester, NY: National Reading Conference.

Rudner, L. (1978). Using standard tests with the hearing impaired: The problem of item bias. *Volta Review, 80,* 31–40.

Rumelhart, D. (1977). Toward an interactive model of reading. In S. Dornic (Ed.), *Attention and performance VI* (pp. 573–603). New York: Academic Press.

Rumelhart, D. (1980). Schemata: The building blocks of cognition. In R. Spiro, B. Bruce, & W. Brewer (Eds.), *Theoretical issues in reading comprehension* (pp. 33–58). Hillsdale, NJ: Lawrence Erlbaum Associates.

Rumelhart, D., & Norman, D. (1978). Accretion, tuning and restructuring: Three modes of learning. In J. Cotton & R. Klatzky (Eds.), *Semantic factors in cognition* (pp. 37–53). Hillsdale, NJ: Lawrence Erlbaum Associates.

Rumelhart, D., & Ortony, A. (1977). The representation of knowledge in memory. In R. Anderson, R. Spiro, & W. Montague (Eds.), *Schooling and the acquisition of knowledge* (pp. 99–135). Hillsdale, NJ: Lawrence Erlbaum Associates.

Rupley, W., Blair, T., & Wise, B. (1982). Specification of promising teacher effectiveness variables for reading instruction. In J. Niles & L. Harris (Eds.), *New inquiries in reading: Research and instruction. Thirty-first yearbook of the National Reading Conference* (pp. 232–236). Rochester, NY: National Reading Conference.

Rush, M. (1977). *The language of directions*. Washington, DC: Alexander Graham Bell Association for the Deaf.

Russo, A. (1980). *Made by hand: A catechesis for the deaf*. New Haven, CT: Knights of Columbus.

Sachs, J. (1974). Memory in reading and listening to discourse. *Memory and Cognition, 2*, 95–100.

Sapir, E. (1958). Language and environment. In D. Mandelbaum (Ed.), *Selected writings of Edward Sapir in language, culture, and personality* (pp. 89–121). Berkeley: University of California.

Sarnacki, R. (1979). Examination of test wiseness in the cognitive test domain. *Review of Educational Research, 49*, 252–279.

Schachter, J. (1974). An error in error analysis. *Language Learning, 24*, 205–214.

Schachter, J., & Celce-Murcia, M. (1977). Some reservations concerning error analysis. *TESOL Quarterly, 11*, 441–451.

Sattler, J. (1974). *Assessment of children's intelligence*. Philadelphia: W.B. Saunders Company.

Schallert, D. (1980). The role of illustrations in reading comprehension. In R. Spiro, B. Bruce, & W. Brewer (Eds.), *Theoretical issues in reading comprehension* (pp. 503–524). Hillsdale, NJ: Lawrence Erlbaum Associates.

Schallert, D., & Kleiman, G. (1979). *Some reasons why the teacher is easier to understand than the textbook* (Ed. Rep. No. 9). Urbana, IL: University of Illinois, Center for the Study of Reading. (ERIC Document Reproduction Service No. ED 172 189)

Schallert, D., Kleiman, G., & Rubin, A. (1977). *Analyses of differences between written and oral language* (Tech. Rep. No. 29). Urbana, IL: University of Illinois, Center for the Study of Reading. (ERIC Document Reproduction Service No. ED 144 038)

Schell, L. (Ed.). (1981). *Diagnostic and criterion-referenced reading tests: Review and evaluation*. Newark, DE: International Reading Association.

Schell, L. (1982). How accurate are oral reading test? *Reading World, 22*, 91–97.

Scherer, P., & Hayward, S. (1975). *Transitional reading series for hearing-impaired children*. Glenview, IL: Center on Deafness.

Schiefelbusch, R., Copeland, R., & Smith, J. (Eds.). (1967). *Language and mental retardation: Empirical and conceptual considerations*. New York: Holt, Rinehart and Winston.

Schlesinger, H., & Meadow, K. (1972). *Sound and sign: Childhood deafness and mental health*. Berkeley: University of California Press.

Schlesinger, I. (1977). The role of cognitive development and linguistic input in language acquisition. *Journal of Child Language, 4*, 153–169.

Schlesinger, I., (1982). *Steps to language: Toward a theory of native language acquisition*. Hillsdale, NJ: Lawrence Erlbaum Associates.

Schmidt, E. (1978). What makes reading difficult: The complexity of structures. In P. D. Pearson & J. Hansen (Eds.), *Reading: Disciplined inquiry in process and practice. Twenty-seventh yearbook of the National Reading Conference* (pp.

106–110). Clemson, SC: National Reading Conference.

Schoolfield, L. (1974). *Phonovisual launch—the phonics program.* Rockville, MD: Phonovisual Products.

Schulze, B. (1965). An evaluation of vocabulary development by thirty-two deaf children over a three year period. *American Annals of the Deaf, 110,* 424–435.

Schwartz, J. (1977). Standardizing a reading test. *Reading Teacher, 30,* 364–368.

Scott, K., (1978). Learning theory, intelligence, and mental development. *American Journal of Mental Deficiency, 82,* 325–336.

Scott, M., & Tucker, G. (1974). Error analysis and English-language strategies of Arab students. *Language Learning, 24,* 69–97.

Scouten, E. (1980). An instructional strategy to combat the word-matching tendencies in prelingually deaf students. *American Annals of the Deaf, 125,* 1057–1059.

Searle, J. (1969). *Speech acts.* Cambridge: Cambridge University Press.

Sebesta, S., Calder, J., & Cleland, L. (1982). A story grammar for the classroom. *Reading Teacher, 36,* 180–184.

Seidenberg, M. (1981). Comprehension of captioned television. In A. Davison, R. Lutz, & A. Roalef (Eds). *Text readability: Proceedings of the March 1980 conference* (Tech. Rep. No. 213) (pp. 98–118). Urbana, IL: University of Illinois, Center for the Study of Reading.

Seliger, H. (1978). Implications of a multiple critical periods hypothesis for second language learning. In W. Ritchie (Ed.), *Second language acquisition research: Issues and implications* (pp. 11–19). New York: Academic Press.

Semel, E., & Wiig, E. (1975). Comprehension of syntactic structures and critical verbal elements by children with learning disabilities. *Journal of Learning Disabilities, 8,* 46–51.

Semel, E., & Wiig, E. (1980). *Clinical evaluation of language functions.* Columbus, OH: Charles E. Merrill.

Serwatka, T., Hesson, D., & Graham, M. (1984). The effect of indirect intervention on the improvement of hearing-impaired students' reading scores. *Volta Review, 86,* 81–88.

Shanahan, T., & Kamil, M. (1982). The sensitivity of cloze and recall to passage organization. In J. Niles & L. Harry (Eds.), *New Inquiries in reading: Research and instruction. Thirty-first yearbook of the National Reading Conference* (pp. 204–208). Rochester, NY: National Reading Conference.

Shanahan, T., & Kamil, M. (1983). A further comparison of sensitivity of cloze and recall to passage organization. In J. Niles & L. Harry (Eds.), *Searches for meaning in reading/language processing and instruction: Thirty-second yearbook of the National Reading Conference* (pp. 123–128). Rochester, NY: National Reading Conference.

Shanahan, T., Kamil, M., & Tobin, A. (1982). Cloze as a measure of intersentential comprehension. *Reading Research Quarterly, 17,* 229–255.

Shankweiler, D., Liberman, I., Mark, L., Fowler, C., & Fischer, F. (1979). The speech code and learning to read. *Journal of Experimental Psychology: Human Learning and Memory, 5,* 531–545.

Shannon, P. (1980). Effects of methods of standardized reading-achievement test administration on attitude toward reading. *Journal of Reading, 23,* 684–686.

Shannon, P. (1983). The use of commercial reading materials in American elementary schools. *Reading Research Quarterly, 19,* 68–85.

Sheehan, D., & Marcus, M. (1977). Validating criterion-referenced reading tests. *Journal of Reading Behavior, 9,* 129–135.

Shipley, E., Smith, C., & Gleitman, L. (1969). A study in the acquisition of language: Free responses to commands. *Language, 45,* 322–342.

Shroyer, E., & Birch, J. (1980). Captions and reading rates of hearing impaired students. *American Annals of the Deaf, 125,* 916–922.

Shulman, J. (Ed.). (1979). *Captioning reference manual.* Boston: The Caption Center, WGBH-TV.

Shulman, J., & Decker, N. (Eds.). (1981). *Readable English for hearing-impaired students.* Boston: WGBH-TV.

Shuy, R. (1979). The mismatch of child language and school language: Implications of beginning reading instruction. In L. Resnick & P. Weaver (Eds.), *Theory and practice of early reading* (Vol. 1) (pp. 187–208). Hillsdale, NJ: Lawrence Erlbaum Associates.

Siegel, F. (1979). Adapted miscue analysis. *Reading World, 19,* 36–43.

Silverman, B. (1979). Test bias and ability testing. *Journal of School Psychology, 17,* 255–259.

Silverman-Dresner, T., & Guilfoyle, G. (1972). *Vocabulary norms for deaf children.* Washington, DC: Alexander Graham Bell Association for the Deaf.

Singer, H., & Dreher, J. (1983). Attitudes towards testing and test results of reading achievement. *Journal of Reading Behavior, 15,* 19–32.

Siple, P., Fischer, S., & Bellugi, U. (1977). Memory for nonsemantic attributes of American Sign Language signs and English words. *Journal of Verbal Learning and Verbal Behavior, 16,* 561–574.

Slater, B. (1981). *History—economics—political science.* Beaverton, OR: Dormac.

Slobin, D. (1979). *Psycholinguistics* (2nd ed.). Glenview, IL: Scott, Foresman.

Slowiaczek, M., & Clifton, C. (1980). Subvocalization and reading for meaning. *Journal of Verbal Learning and Verbal Behavior, 19,* 573–582.

Smith, D. (1981). *Teaching the learning disabled.* Englewood Cliffs, NJ: Prentice-Hall.

Smith, F. (1971). *Understanding reading.* New York: Holt, Rinehart and Winston.

Smith, F. (1973). *Psycholinguistics and reading.* New York: Holt, Rinehart and Winston.

Smith, F. (1975). The role of prediction in reading. *Elementary English, 52,* 305–311.

Smith, F. (1978). *Understanding reading* (rev. ed.). New York: Holt, Rinehart and Winston.

Snow, R. (1974). Representative and quasi-representative designs for research on teaching. *Review of Educational Research, 44,* 265–291.

Sokolov, A. (1972). *Inner speech and thought.* New York: Plenum Press.

Spache, G. (1976). *Investigating the issues of reading disabilities.* Boston: Allyn and Bacon.

Spearitt, D. (1972). Identification of subskills of reading comprehension by maximum likelihood factor analysis. *Reading Research Quarterly, 8,* 92–111.

Spekman, N. (1981). A study of the dyadic verbal communication abilities of learning disabled and normally achieving 4th and 5th grade boys. *Learning Disability Quarterly, 4,* 139–151.

Spiro, R. (1977). Remembering information from text: Theoretical and empirical issues concerning the "State of Schema" reconstruction hypothesis. In R. Anderson, R. Spiro, & W. Montague (Eds.), *Schooling and the acquisition of knowledge* (pp. 137–165). Hillsdale, NJ: Lawrence Erlbaum Associates.

Spiro, R. (1980). *Schema theory and reading comprehension: New directions* (Tech. Rep. No. 191). Urbana, IL: University of Illinois, Center for the Study of Reading. (ERIC Document Reproduction Service No. ED 199 662)

Spiro, R., Bruce, B., & Brewer, W. (Eds.) (1980). *Theoretical issues in reading comprehension.* Hillsdale, NJ: Lawrence Erlbaum Associates.

Spiro, R., & Tirre, W. (1980). Individual differences in schema utilization during discourse processing. *Journal of Educational Psychology, 72,* 204–208.

Sridhar, S. (1980). Contrastive analysis, error analysis, and interlanguage. In K. Croft (Ed.), *Readings on English as a second language: For teachers and teacher trainees* (2nd ed.) (pp. 91–119). Boston: Little, Brown.

Stanovich, K. (1980). Toward an interactive-compensatory model of individual differences in the development of reading fluency. *Reading Research Quarterly, 16,* 32–71.

Stanovich, K., & West, R. (1979). Mechanisms of sentence context effects in reading: Automatic activation and conscious attention. *Memory and Cognition, 7,* 77–85.

Stansell, J., Moss, R., & Robeck, C. (1982). The development of theoretical orientation to reading among preservice teachers: Effects of a professional training program. In J. Niles & L. Harris (Eds.), *New inquiries in reading: Research and instruction. Thirty-first yearbook of the National Reading Conference* (pp. 242–250). Rochester, NY: National Reading Conference.

Star, R. (1980). *We can!* (Vols. 1 and 2). Washington, DC: Alexander Graham Bell Association for the Deaf.

Stauffer, R. (1970). *The language-experience approach to the teaching of reading.* New York: Harper and Row.

Stein, N. (1978). *How children understand stories: A development analysis* (Tech. Rep. No. 69). Urbana, IL: University of Illinois, Center for the Study of Reading. (ERIC Document Reproduction Service No. ED 153 205)

Stein, N., & Glenn, C. (1979). An analysis of story comprehension in elementary school children. In R. Freedle (Ed.), *New directions in discourse processing: Advances in discourse processes* (Vol. 2) (pp. 53–120). Norwood, NJ: Ablex.

Stein, N., & Trabasso, T. (1981). *What's in a story: An approach to comprehension and instruction* (Tech. Rep. No. 200). Urbana, IL: University of Illinois, Center for the Study of Reading. (ERIC Document Reproduction Service No. ED 201 990)

Steinberg, C. & Bruce, B. (1980). Higher-level features in children's stories:

Rhetorical structure and conflict. In M. Kamil & A. Moe (Eds.). *Perspectives in reading research and instruction* (pp. 117–125). Washington, DC: National Reading Conference.

Stenning, P. C. (1979). *The relationship of testwiseness, achievement and degree of hearing loss for hearing impaired adolescents.* Unpublished doctoral dissertation, Texas A & M University.

Stetz, F., & Beck, M. (1980). Teachers oppose halting all standardized testing. *Phi Delta Kappan, 61,* 648.

Stevens, K. (1981). Chunking material as an aid to reading comprehension. *Journal of Reading, 25,* 126–129.

Stoefen, J., & Holmze, A. (1979). Content interests and media preferences of hearing-impaired students. In G. Propp (Ed.), *1980's schools . . . Portals to century 21. Selected papers* (pp. 136–148). Silver Spring, MD: Convention of American Instructors of the Deaf.

Stoodt, B. (1972). The relationship between understanding grammatical conjunctions and reading comprehension. *Elementary English, 49,* 502–504.

Stowitscheck, J., Gable, R. & Hendrickson, J. (1980). *Instructional materials for exceptional children: Selection, management, and adaptation.* Germantown, MD: Aspen Systems Corporation.

Streng, A. (1965). *Reading for deaf children.* Washington, DC: Alexander Graham Bell Association for the Deaf.

Streng, A., Kretschmer, R. R., & Kretschmer, L. (1978). *Language, learning, and deafness: Theory, application, and classroom management.* New York: Grune and Stratton.

Strickland, R. (1962). *The language of elementary school children: Its relationship to the language of reading textbooks and the quality of reading of selected children* (Bulletin of the School of Education). Bloomington, IN: Indiana University, School of Education.

Stuckless, E. R., & Hurwitz, A. (1982). Recording speech in real-time print: Dream or reality? *The Deaf American, 34,* 10–15.

Stuckless, E. R., & Matter, J. (1982). *Word accuracy and error in steno/computer transliteration of spoken lectures into real-time graphic display* (RTGD Working Paper No. 1). Rochester NY: National Technical Institute for the Deaf.

Stuckless, E. R., & Pollard, G. (1977). Processing of fingerspelling and print by deaf students. *American Annals of the Deaf, 122,* 475–479.

Sullivan, J. (1978). Comparing strategies of good and poor comprehenders. *Journal of Reading, 21,* 710–715.

Summers, E. (1977). Instruments for assessing reading attitudes: A review of research and bibliography. *Journal of Reading Behavior, 9,* 137–165.

Takemori, W., & Snyder, J. (1972). Materials and techniques used in teaching language to deaf children. *American Annals of the Deaf, 117,* 455–458.

Takeuchi, R. (1978). Attitudes of elementary teachers toward testing: Use and abuse of standardized tests in California, 1976–1977. *Dissertation Abstracts, 388-A,* 4500.

Talcove, A. (1981). *Resource guide for hearing-impaired students.* Washington, DC:

Gallaudet College, Outreach Programs.

Tamor, L. (1981). Subjective text difficulty: An alternative approach to defining the difficulty level of written text. *Journal of Reading Behavior, 13*, 165–172.

Tatham, S. (1970). Reading comprehension of materials written with select oral language patterns: A study at grades two and four. *Reading Research Quarterly, 5*, 402–426.

Taylor, N., & Connor, U. (1982). Silent vs. oral reading: The rational instructional use of both processes. *Reading Teacher, 35*, 440–443.

Templeton, S., Cain, C., & Miller, J. (1981). Reconceptualizing reading: The relationship between surface and underlying structure analyses in predicting the difficulty of basal reader stories. *Journal of Educational Research, 74*, 382–387.

Tennessee School for the Deaf. (1980). *Language-based reading curriculum.* Knoxville, TN: Tennessee School for the Deaf.

Terwilliger, J. (1972). *Some problems associated with the concept of mastery.* Unpublished manuscript, University of Minnesota.

Thompson, H. (1927). *An experimental study of the beginning reading of deaf-mutes* (Contributions to Education, Series No. 254). New York: Teachers College, Columbia University.

Thompson, H. (1964). An early attempt in profusely illustrated language instruction. *Exceptional Children, 30*, 349–353.

Thorndike, R. (1973). *Reading comprehension education in fifteen countries.* New York: John Wiley and Sons.

Thorndike, R. (1974). Reading as reasoning. *Reading Research Quarterly, 9*, 137–147.

Thorndike, R., & Hagen, E. (1977). *Measurement and evaluation in psychology and education.* New York: John Wiley and Sons.

Thorndyke, P. (1977). Cognitive structures in comprehension and memory of narrative discourse. *Cognitive Psychology, 9*, 77–110.

Tierney, R., & Cunningham, J. (1980). *Research on teaching reading comprehension* (Tech. Rep. No. 187). Urbana, IL: University of Illinois, Center for the Study of Reading. (ERIC Document Reproduction Service No. ED 195 946)

Tierney, R., & Cunningham, J. (1984). Research on teaching reading comprehension. In P. D. Pearson (Ed.), *Handbook of reading research* (pp. 609–655). London: Longman.

Tierney, R., & Mosenthal, J. (1982). Discourse comprehension and production: Analyzing text structure and cohesion. In J. Langer & M. Smith-Burke (Eds.), *Reader meets author/Bridging the gap* (pp. 55–104). Newark, DE: International Reading Association.

Tierney, R., Mosenthal, J., & Kantor, R. (1984). Classroom applications of text analysis: Toward improving text selection and use. In J. Flood (Ed.), *Promoting reading comprehension* (pp. 139–160). Newark, DE: International Reading Association.

Toole, D. (1981a). *Successful deaf Americans.* Beaverton, OR: Dormac.

Toole, D. (1981b). *Courageous deaf Americans.* Beaverton, OR: Dormac.

Torgesen, J. (1982). The use of rationally defined subgroups in research on learning disabilities. In J. Das, R. Mulcahy, & A. Wall (Eds.), *Theory and research in learning disabilities* (pp. 111-131). New York: Plenum Press.

Torgesen, J., & Dice, C. (1980). Characteristics of research on learning disabilities. *Journal of Learning Disabilities, 13,* 531-535.

Tortelli, J. (1976). Simplified psycholinguistic diagnosis. *Reading Teacher, 30,* 637-639.

Trabasso, T. (1980). *On the making of inferences during reading and their assessment* (Tech. Rep. No. 157). Urbana, IL: University of Illinois, Center for the Study of Reading. (ERIC Document Reproduction Service No. ED 181 429)

Trapini, F., & Walmsley, S. (1981). Five readability estimates: Differential effects of simplifying a document. *Journal of Reading, 24,* 398-403.

Trelease, J. (1982). *Read-aloud handbook.* New York: Penguin Books.

Troike, R. (1978). Research evidence for the effectiveness of bilingual education. *NABE Journal, 3,* 13-24.

Troike, R. (1981). Synthesis of research on bilingual education. *Educational Leadership, 38,* 498-504.

Truax, R. (1978). Reading and language. In R. R. Kretschmer & L. Kretschmer, *Language development and intervention with the hearing impaired* (pp. 279-310). Baltimore, MD: University Park Press.

Trybus, R. (1978). What the *Stanford Achievement Test* has to say about the reading abilities of deaf children. In H. Reynolds & C. Williams (Eds.), *Proceedings of the Gallaudet conference on reading in relation to deafness* (pp. 213-221). Washington, DC: Gallaudet College.

Trybus, R., & Buchanan, G. (1973). Patterns of achievement test performance. *Studies in achievement testing, hearing-impaired students. United States, 1971* (Series D, No. 11). Washington, DC: Gallaudet College, Office of Demographic Studies.

Trybus, R., & Karchmer, M. (1977). School achievement scores of hearing impaired children: National data on achievement status and growth patterns. *American Annals of the Deaf Directory of Programs and Services, 122,* 62-69.

Tuinman, J. (1974). Determining the passage dependence of comprehension questions in five major tests. *Reading Research Quarterly, 9,* 206-223.

Tuinman, J. (1979). Reading is recognition–When reading is not reasoning. In J. Harste & R. Carey (Eds.), *New perspectives on comprehension* (Monograph in Language and Research Studies No. 3) (pp. 38-48). Bloomington, IN: Indiana University.

Turner, E., & Rommetveit, R. (1967). The acquisition of sentence voice and reversibility. *Child Development, 38,* 649-660.

Tweeney, R., Hoeman, H., & Andrews, C. (1975). Semantic organization in deaf and hearing subjects. *Journal of Psycholinguistic Research, 4,* 61-73.

Tyler, R., & White, S. (1979). *Testing, teaching, and learning* (Chairman's report of a conference on research on testing). Washington, DC: National Institute of Education.

Tzeng, O., Hung, D., & Wang, W. (1977). Speech recoding in reading Chinese characters. *Journal of Experimental Psychology: Human Learning and Memory, 3,* 621-630.

Valmont, W. (1972). Creating questions for informal reading inventories. *Reading*

Teacher, 25, 509–512.

Vande Kopple, W. (1980). Readability of a rhetorically linked expository paragraph. *Perceptual and Motor Skills, 51,* 245–246.

Van Kleeck, A., & Frankel, T. (1981). Discourse devices used by language disordered children: A preliminary investigation. *Journal of Speech and Hearing Disorders, 46,* 250–257.

van Uden, A. (1972). *A world of language for the deaf: A maternal reflective method.* Rotterdam, Netherlands: Rotterdam Publishing Company.

Vaughan, J., Castle, G., Gilbert, K., & Love, M. (1982). Varied approaches to preteaching vocabulary. In J. Niles & L. Harris (Eds.), *New inquiries in reading: Research and instruction: Thirty-first yearbook of the National Reading Conference* (pp. 94–98). Rochester, NY: National Reading Conference.

Veatch, D. (1982). *How to get the job you really want.* Silver Spring, MD: National Association of the Deaf.

Vellutino, F. (1977). Alternative conceptualizations of dyslexia: Evidence in support of a verbal-deficit hypothesis. *Harvard Educational Review, 47,* 334–354.

Vellutino, F. (1979). *Dyslexia: Theory and research.* Cambridge, MA: MIT Press.

Vellutino, F. (1980). Dyslexia: Perceptual deficiency or perceptual inefficiency. In J. Kavanagh & R. Venezky (Eds.), *Orthography, reading, and dyslexia* (pp. 251–270). Baltimore: University Park Press.

Vellutino, F. (1982). Theoretical issues in the study of word recognition: The unit of perception controversy reexamined. In S. Rosenberg (Ed.), *Handbook of applied psycholinguistics* (pp. 33–197). NJ: Lawrence Erlbaum Associates.

Venezky, R. (1974). *Testing in reading: Assessment and instructional decision making.* Urbana, IL: National Council of Teachers of English.

Venezky, R. (1976). *Theoretical and experimental base for teaching reading.* The Hague, Netherlands: Mouton.

Venezky, R. (1979). Harmony and cacophony from a theory-practice relationship. In L. Resnick & P. Weaver (Eds.), *Theory and practice of early reading* (Vol. 2) (pp. 271–284). Hillsdale, NJ: Lawrence Erlbaum Associates.

Venezky, R., & Winfield, L. (1979). *Schools that succeed beyond expectations in teaching reading* (Tech. Rep. No. 1). Newark, DE: University of Delaware, Studies on Education.

Ventry, I., & Schiavetti, N. (1980). *Evaluating research in speech pathology and audiology: A guide for clinicians and students.* Menlo Park, CA: Addison-Wesley.

Vernon, M. (1967). Relationship of language to the thinking process. *Archives of General Psychiatry, 16,* 325–333.

Vernon, M. (1968). Fifty years of research on the intelligence of deaf and hard-of-hearing children: A review of literature and discussion of implications. *Journal on Rehabilitation of the Deaf, 1,* 4–7.

Villaume, J., & Haney, W. (1977). *The follow-through planned variation experiment* (Vol. 5). Cambridge, MA: Huron Institute.

Vinsonhaler, J., Weinshank, A., Wagner, C., & Polin, R. (1983). Diagnosing children with educational problems: Characteristics of reading and learning disabilities specialists, and classroom teachers. *Reading Research Quarterly, 18,* 134–164.

Vogel, S. (1975). *Syntactic abilities in normal and dyslexic children*. Baltimore: University Park Press.

Volta Bureau. (1910). *The raindrop*. Washington, DC: Alexander Graham Bell Association for the Deaf.

Volta Bureau. (1974). *World traveler*. Washington, DC: Alexander Graham Bell Association for the Deaf.

Voss, J., Vesonder, G., & Spilich, G. (1980). Text generation and recall by high knowledge and low knowledge individuals. *Journal of Verbal Learning and Verbal Behavior, 19*, 651–667.

Vygotsky, L. (1962). *Thought and language*. Cambridge, MA: MIT Press.

Vygotsky, L. (1978). *Mind in society: The development of higher psychological processes*. In M. Cole, V. John-Steiner, S. Scribner, & E. Souberman (Eds. & Trans.). Cambridge, MA: Harvard University Press.

Walker, B. (1981). *Getting a job*. Washington, DC: Gallaudet College, Outreach Programs.

Walter, G. (1978a). Lexical abilities of hearing and hearing-impaired children. *American Annals of the Deaf, 123*, 976–982.

Walter, G. (1978b). *Frequency-based test of vocabulary* (Form A, Form B). Rochester, NY: National Technical Institute for the Deaf.

Walter, Sr. M. (1971). *The Jack and Julie series*. Milwaukee, WI: St. Johns School for the Deaf.

Wardrop, J., Anderson, T., Hively, W., Hastings, C., Anderson, R., & Muller, K. (1982). A framework for analyzing the inference structure of educational achievement tests. *Journal of Educational Measurement, 19*, 1–18.

Warren, W., Nicholas, D., & Trabasso, T. (1979). Event chains and inferences in understanding narratives. In R. Freedle (Ed.), *New directions in discourse processing* (pp. 23–52). Norwood, NJ: Ablex.

Watts, L., & Nisbet, J. (1974). *Legibility in children's books: A review of research*. Windsor, Ontario: National Foundation for Educational Research.

Weber, G. (1976). *Inner-city children can be taught to read: Four successful schools* (Occasional Paper No. 18). Washington, DC: Council for Basic Education.

Webster, A., Wood, D., & Griffiths, A. (1981). Reading retardation or linguistic deficit? I: Interpreting reading test performance of hearing impaired adolescents. *Journal of Research in Reading, 4*(2), 136–147.

Weinstein, R. (1976). Reading group membership in first grade: Behaviors and pupil experience over time. *Journal of Educational Psychology, 68*, 103–116.

Weiss, M. (1982). Children's preferences for format factors in books. *Reading Teacher, 35*, 400–406.

Welch, S. (1981). Teaching generative grammar to mentally retarded children: A review and analysis of a decade of behavioral research. *Mental Retardation, 19*, 277–284.

Wheeler, D. (1970). Processes in word recognition. *Cognitive Psychology, 1*, 59–85.

White, A., & Stevenson, V. (1975). The effects of total communication, manual communication, oral communication and reading on the learning of factual information in residential school deaf children. *American Annals of the Deaf, 120*, 48–57.

Wiig, E., Lapointe, C., & Semel, E. (1977). Relationships among language processing and production abilities of learning disabled adolescents. *Journal of Learning Disabilities*, *10*, 292–299.

Wiig, E., & Semel, E. (1973). Comprehension of linguistic concepts requiring logical operations by learning disabled children. *Journal of Speech and Hearing Research*, *16*, 627–637.

Wiig, E. & Semel, E. (1974). Logico-grammatical sentence comprehension by adolescents with learning disabilities. *Perceptual and Motor Skills*, *38*, 1331–1334.

Wiig, E. & Semel, E. (1976). *Language disabilities in children and adolescents.* Columbus, OH: Charles E. Merrill.

Wiig, E., Semel, E., & Abele, E. (1981). Perception and interpretation of ambiguous sentences by learning disabled twelve-year-olds. *Learning Disability Quarterly*, *4*, 3–12.

Wiig, E., Semel, E., & Crouse, M. (1973). The use of English morphology by high-risk and learning disabled children. *Journal of Learning Disabilities*, *6*, 457–465.

Wilbur, R. (1979a). *American Sign Language and sign systems.* Baltimore: University Park Press.

Wilbur, R. (1979b). Syntax. In J. Shulman (Ed.), *Captioning reference manual* (pp. 3.1–3.46). Boston: The Caption Center, WGBH-TV.

Wilbur, R. (1981). Syntax. In J. Shulman & N. Decker (Eds.), *Readable English for hearing-impaired students* (pp. 9–58). Boston: The Caption Center, WGBH-TV.

Wilbur, R., Fraser, J., & Fruchter, A. (1981). *Comprehension of idioms by hearing impaired students.* Paper presented at the American Speech-Language-Hearing Association Convention, Los Angeles.

Wilbur, R., Goodhart, W., & Montandon, E. (n.d.) *Syntactic research toward the development of linguistically controlled materials for deaf children* (final report). Boston, MA: The Caption Center, WGBH-TV.

Wilbur, R., Montanelli, D., & Quigley, S. (1976). Pronominalization in the language of deaf students. *Journal of Speech and Hearing Research*, *19*, 120–140.

Williamson, L., & Young, F. (1974). The IRI and RMI diagnostic concepts should be synthesized. *Journal of Reading Behavior*, *6*, 183–194.

Wilson, K. (1979a). *Inference and language processing in hearing and deaf children.* Unpublished doctoral dissertation, Boston University.

Wilson, K. (1979b). Inference. In J. Shulman (Ed.), *Captioning reference manual* (pp. 4.1–4.15). Boston: The Caption Center, WGBH-TV.

Wilson, K. (1981). Inference. In J. Shulman & N. Decker (Eds.), *Readable English for hearing-impaired students* (pp. 59–66). Boston: The Caption Center, WGBH-TV.

Wilson, K., Karchmer, M., & Jensema, C. (1978). Literal vs. inferential item analysis of reading achievement in hearing-impaired students. In H. Reynolds & C. Williams (Eds.), *Proceedings of the Gallaudet conference on reading in relation to deafness* (pp. 154–170). Washington, DC: Gallaudet College.

Wilson, L. (1974). *Noah and the rainbow.* Springfield, MO: Gospel Publishing House.

Wilson, P., & Dixon, K. (1980). *The use of pictures in basal reading materials.* Unpublished paper. Urbana, IL: University of Illinois, Center for the Study of Reading, Annual Teachers' Conference.

Winner, E., Engel, M., & Gardner, H. (1980). Misunderstanding metaphor: What's the problem? *Journal of Experimental Child Psychology, 30,* 22–32.

Withrow, F. (1968). Immediate memory span of deaf and normally hearing children. *Exceptional Children, 35,* 33–41.

Wittrock, M., Marks, C., & Doctorow, M. (1975). Reading as a generative process. *Journal of Educational Psychology, 67,* 484–489.

Wixson, K. (1983). Questions about a text: What you can ask about is what children learn. *Reading Teacher, 37,* 287–294.

Wixson, K., Bosky, A., Yochum, M., & Alvermann, D. (1984). An interview for assessing students' perceptions of classroom reading tasks. *Reading Teacher, 37,* 346–352.

Wolk, S., & Schildroth, A. (1984). Consistency of an associational strategy used on reading comprehension tests by hearing-impaired students. *Journal of Research in Reading, 7,* 135–142.

Wood, D., Griffiths, D., Howarth, S., & Howarth, C. (1982). The structure of conversation with 6- to 10-year old deaf children. *Journal of Child Psychology and Psychiatry and Allied Disciplines, 23,* 295–308.

Wood, D., Griffiths, D., & Webster, A. (1981). Reading retardation or linguistic deficit? II: Test-answering strategies in hearing and hearing-impaired school children. *Journal of Research in Reading, 4*(2), 148–156.

Wood, H., & Wood, D. (1984). An experimental evaluation of the effects of teacher conversation on the language of hearing-impaired children. *Journal of Child Psychology and Psychiatry and Allied Disciplines, 25,* 45–62.

Wong, B. (1979a). The role of theory in learning disabilities research: Part I. An analysis of problems. *Journal of Learning Disabilities, 12,* 585–595.

Wong, B. (1979b). The role of theory in learning disabilities research: Part II. A selection review of current theories of learning and reading disabilities. *Journal of Learning Disabilities, 12,* 649–658.

Worden, M. (1973). *Beowulf.* Silver Spring, MD: National Association of the Deaf.

World Bible Translation Center. (1975). *New Testament. English version for the deaf.* Grand Rapids, MI: Bakers House.

Wrightstone, J., Aronow, M., & Moskowitz, S. (1963). Developing reading test norms for deaf children. *American Annals of the Deaf, 108,* 311–316.

Yoder, D., & Miller, J. (1972). What we may know and what we can do: Input towards a system. In J. McClean, D. Yoder, & R. Schiefelbusch (Eds.), *Language intervention with the retarded: Developing strategies* (pp. 89–107). Baltimore: University Park Press.

Youniss, J., & Furth, H. (1966). Prediction of causal events as a function of transitivity and perceptual congruency in hearing and deaf children. *Child Development, 37,* 73–81.

Yussen, S., & Santrock, J. (1978). *Child development.* Dubuque, IA: W. C. Brown.

Zarcadoolas, C. (1981). *Rewriting the Oscar Wilde stories.* Unpublished manuscript. Corliss Park, RI: Rhode Island School for the Deaf.

Zhurova, L. (1963). The development of analysis of words into sounds by preschool children. *Soviet Psychology and Psychiatry, 2,* 17–27.

Zigler, E. (1969). Developmental versus difference theories of mental retardation and the problem of motivation. *American Journal of Mental Deficiency, 73,* 536–556.

Zola, D. (1981). *The effect of redundancy on the perception of words in reading* (Tech. Rep. No. 216). Urbana, IL: University of Illinois, Center for the Study of Reading. (ERIC Document Reproduction Service No. ED 208 367)

Author Index

H

Subject Index

F

G

W

Z